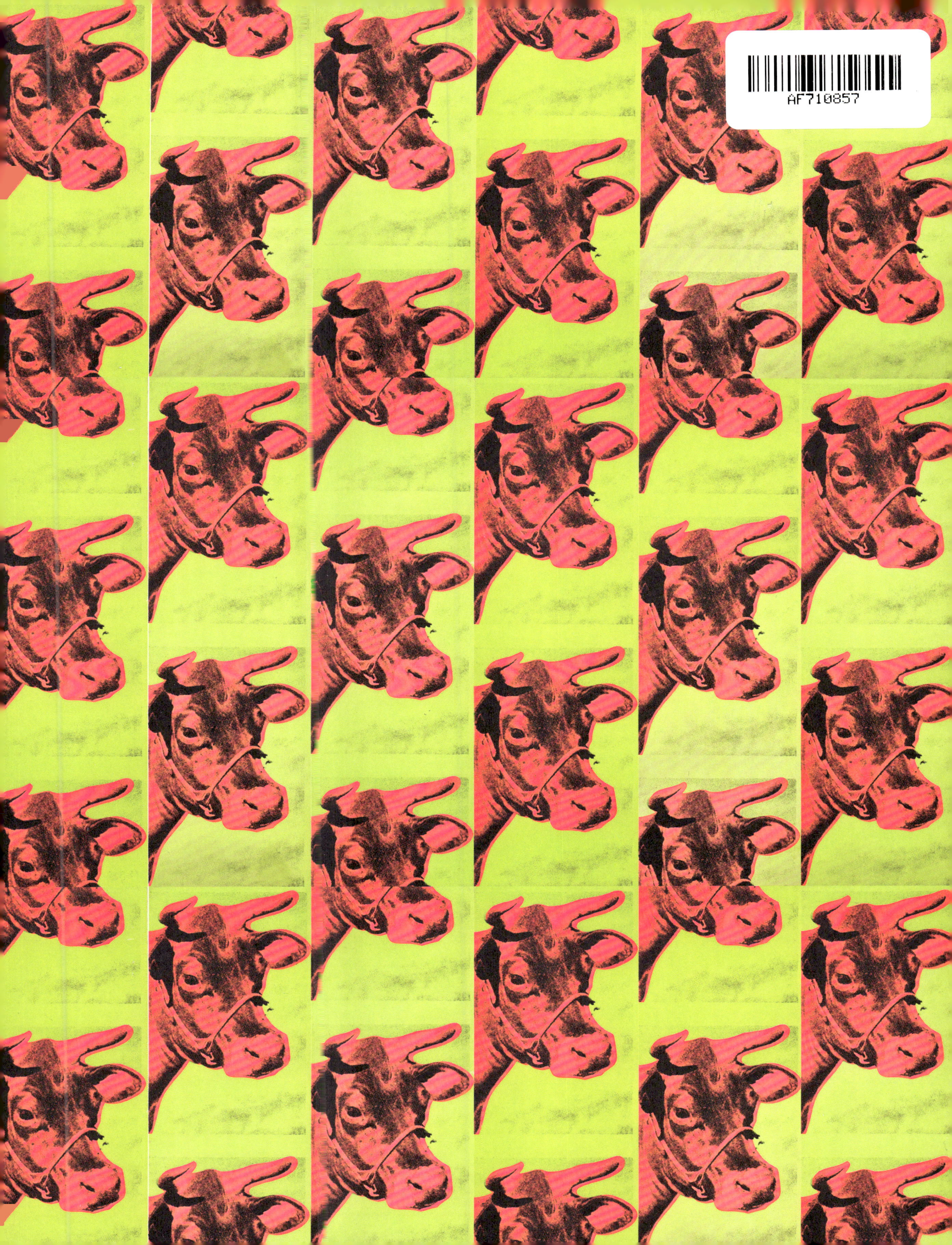

# Andy Warhol PRINTS

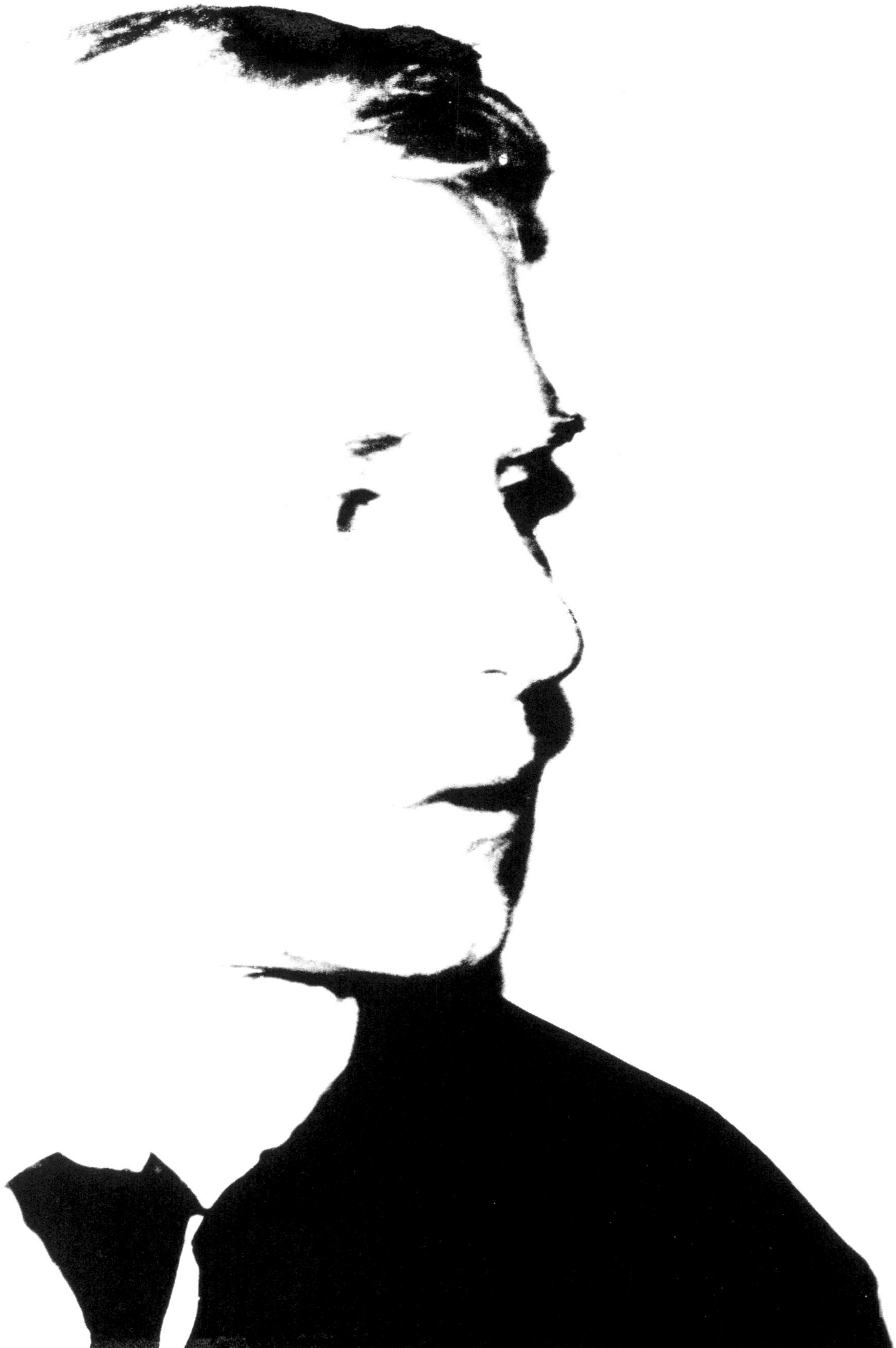

# Andy Warhol PRINTS

## FROM THE COLLECTIONS OF JORDAN D. SCHNITZER AND HIS FAMILY FOUNDATION

SARA KRAJEWSKI
WITH AN ESSAY BY RICHARD H. AXSOM

JORDAN SCHNITZER FAMILY FOUNDATION
IN ASSOCIATION WITH PORTLAND ART MUSEUM
PORTLAND, OREGON

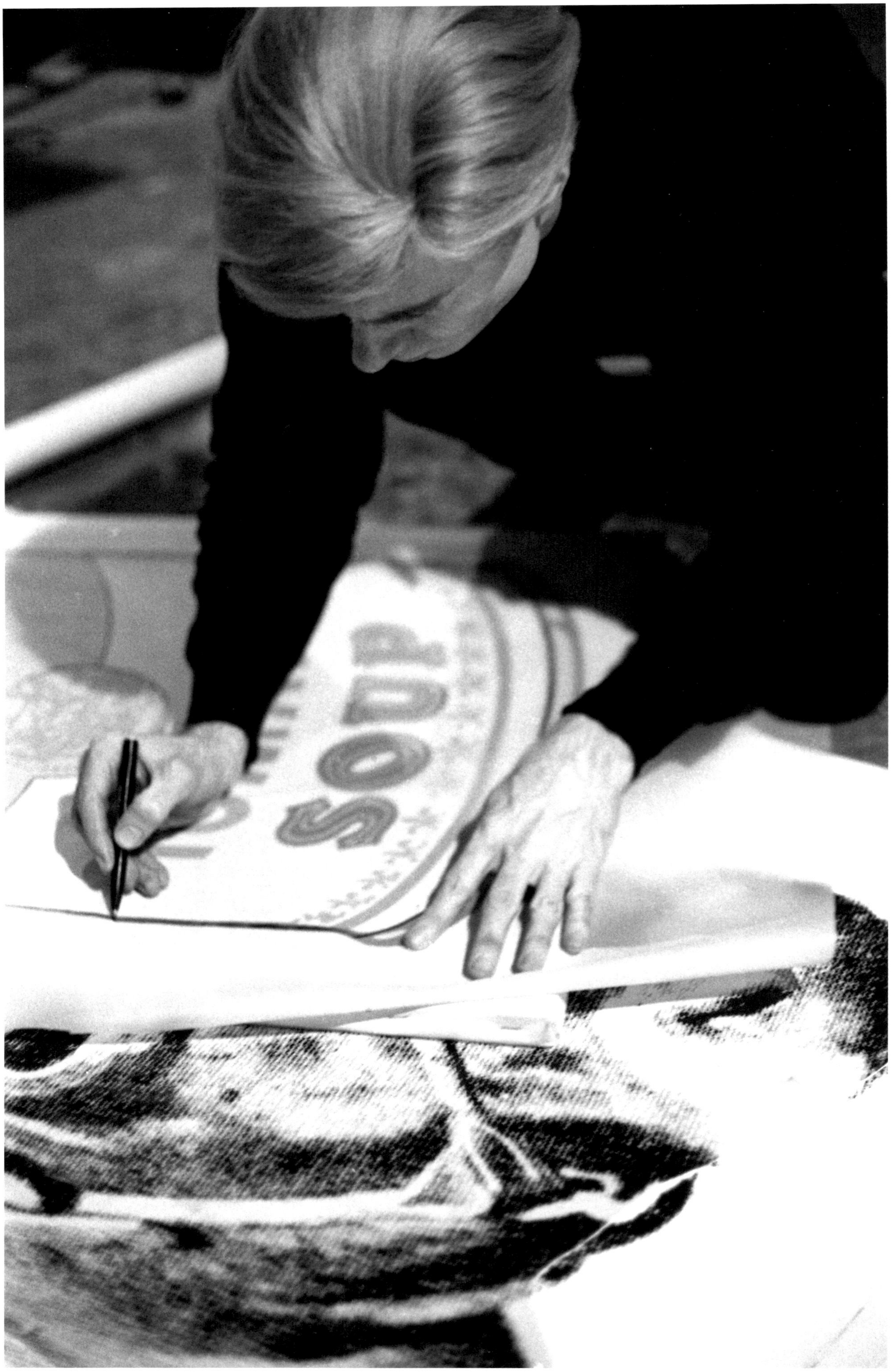
Soup

# Contents

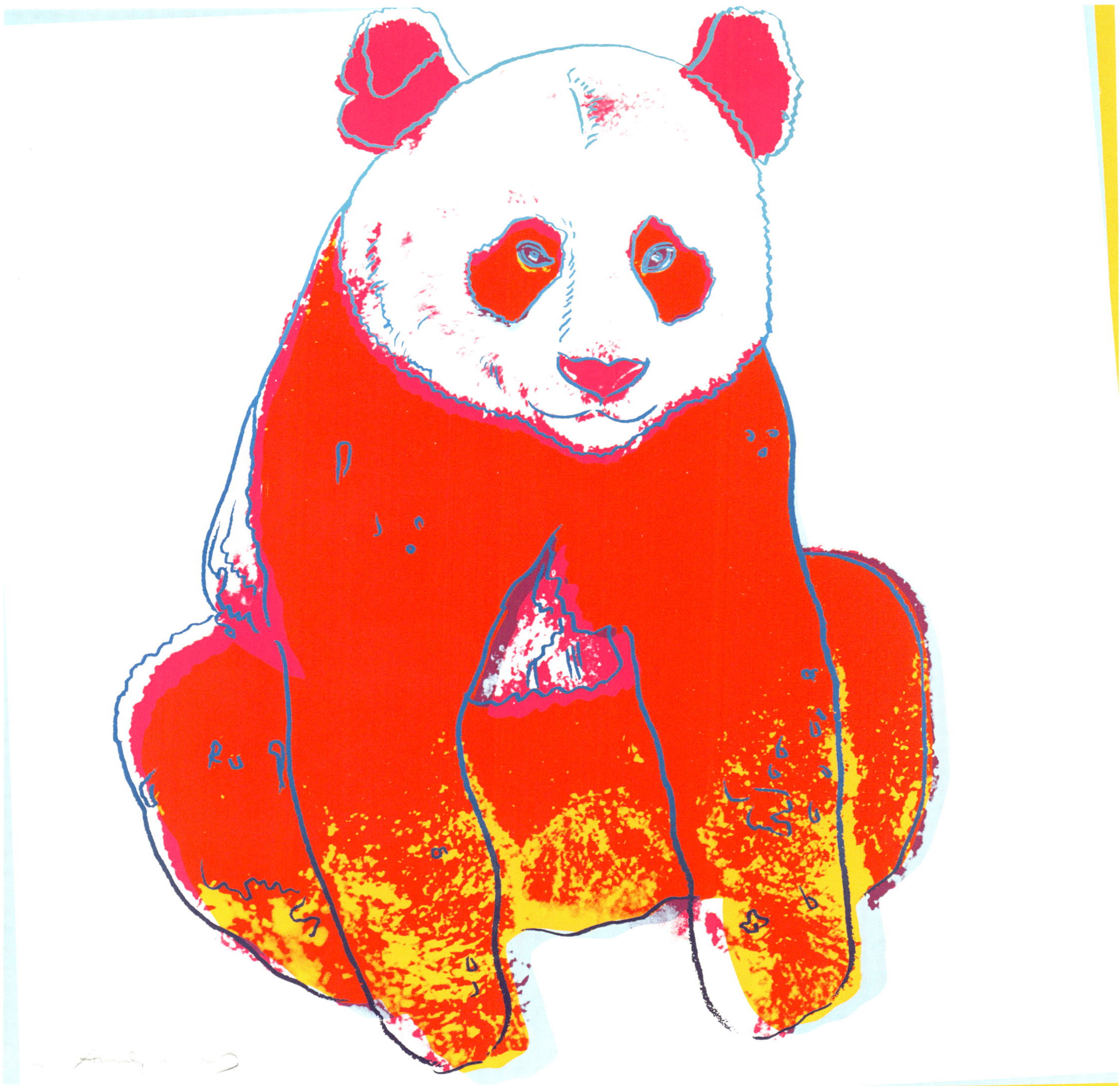

# Collector's Statement

Having *Andy Warhol: Prints from the Collections of Jordan D. Schnitzer and His Family Foundation* at the Portland Art Museum, in my hometown of Portland, Oregon, is like going back in time for me, back to the time when Andy Warhol started making his prints in the early 1960s.

When I was six years old and started grade school, my mother, Arlene Schnitzer, began taking art classes at the Portland Art Museum Art School, now known as the Pacific Northwest College of Art, beginning for me and our family a magical art journey that has led to this exhibition in 2016.

Three years later at the urging of some of her art teachers at the school, my mother and her mother, my grandmother Helen Director, opened the Fountain Gallery of Art. So named because one of the cheapest rentals in Portland at that time, $50 a month, was located in the New Market Theater building in Portland's Old Town; that 1889 building also happened to be next to a famous Portland landmark: the Skidmore Fountain.

Over the twenty-five years, from 1961 to 1986, that my mother operated the Fountain Gallery, I learned from her and from my father, who was building up the real estate company that I now run, the importance of not only living with art but also supporting the arts in our community.

In addition to receiving art for my birthdays and other holidays, I made my first purchase of a work of art when I was fourteen years old. A study by the renowned Portland artist Louis Bunce, it cost $60 and I paid $5 a month. As I have often said, if I missed a payment, my mother knew she could foreclose at any time since my bedroom was next to my parents'!

**Endangered Species: Giant Panda**, 1983. Screenprint, 38 x 38 in.

After my mother decided to pass on her gallery to a coworker, Laura Russo, I continued to buy art of our region. I wanted to do so not only because I love the work of our local artists but because of my steadfast commitment to support them.

While the regional art collection continued to grow, I also began to purchase prints and multiples by post–World War II American modern masters: Roy Lichtenstein, Jasper Johns, Ellsworth Kelly, Robert Rauschenberg, and more than 250 other artists, including Andy Warhol. Each time I bought a print, I saw a few more I wanted, and so the collection grew. Then, when I was asked by the director of what is now the Jordan Schnitzer Museum of Art at the University of Oregon to loan a few prints for an exhibition, a lifelong pursuit became clear to me: to create a significant collection of prints and multiples of post–World War II American artists that I could share with the public.

As of the date of this publication, we have had more than one hundred exhibitions at more than seventy-five museums throughout the country and a few internationally. I am able to offer these exhibitions at no cost to the museums, and in addition I support outreach programs, especially to help bring grade- and high-school students to see these exhibitions.

Of the 9,500 prints now in the collection, the largest number are by Andy Warhol. That is not surprising to me, because I believe that artists are chroniclers of our time and in my opinion there is no artist who chronicles the time of the late 1950s until his death in 1987 better than Andy Warhol.

To say he was brilliant is an understatement. His work is as meaningful today as when it was completed. A master colorist, his art is breathtaking visually and gripping thematically. I wish Warhol were alive and making art today to help us understand these complicated times we live in!

The exhibition and book are the result of the vision, work, and commitment of so many. To Brian Ferriso and all the staff at the Portland Art Museum, a hearty congratulations. Catherine Malone, Phil Kovacevich, Sara Krajewski, and Richard H. Axsom, thank you for helping make this book nationally significant. For everyone who helped financially, I hope you feel pride in what your contributions helped support.

Finally, my mother, Arlene, has been widely recognized for being instrumental in helping so many in Portland and the Pacific Northwest recognize the importance of owning and living with art. It is with deep appreciation, respect, and love that I thank my mother—who not only gave me life but also gave me the passion for art that enriches my life—and to her I dedicate this book and all that I do in the art world.

**JORDAN D. SCHNITZER**

# Director's Statement

The Portland Art Museum is honored to present *Andy Warhol: Prints from the Collections of Jordan D. Schnitzer and His Family Foundation* and to partner with the foundation to publish this impressive exhibition catalogue.

Andy Warhol (1928–1987) has always held a special place in the art world—from the early prints of shoes to his iconic Campbell's soup cans, Brillo boxes, and numerous celebrity portraits, Warhol treated his subjects with visual clarity and a sense of detachment. Consumer products, portraits of the famous, and horrific scenes all received a similar graphic treatment, redefining the world of contemporary art in the 1960s. With the breadth of his artistic output, Warhol also foresaw the image-saturated culture that was emerging and which would ultimately consume our lives. His is a powerful legacy that never ceases to amaze by forcing us to deal with the issues of his time.

This exhibition of Warhol's prints from the collections of Jordan D. Schnitzer is an exciting venture for the Portland Art Museum. With more than six hundred works to choose from, the Museum was able to assemble a body of work that captures the artist's vast range of subject matter over three decades of production. Although Warhol exhibitions abound, this one, entirely from the Portland-based collector Jordan D. Schnitzer, and its accompanying publication are unique. Looking at the artist's early watercolors and lithographs of bugs, shoes, and cats from the 1950s, the screenprint of the Birmingham race riots in the 1960s, the sunsets of the 1970s, and the camouflage prints of the 1980s, visitors and readers will gain a deeper appreciation of Warhol's work well beyond his ubiquitous Mao and Marilyn portraits. It is a visual journey that should leave all those who view the exhibition with a deep appreciation of this leading figure in twentieth-century art.

Portland is fortunate to be the home of Jordan D. Schnitzer, one of the country's most significant collectors of contemporary prints and one of the region's most generous philanthropists. Jordan lends work from his collections with the mission of inspiring and educating thousands about the importance of contemporary art and the collaborative and inventive nature of printmaking. All of us at the Portland Art Museum and in the Pacific Northwest region are indebted to Jordan for sharing his collections with us and for being such a strong advocate for art's ability to change lives. This Warhol exhibition has benefited not only from his generous loans, but also from his knowledge and insights, as well as his underwriting of this publication.

Jordan has followed the family commitment of giving back to the community begun by his late father, Harold, and his mother, Arlene, who continues to be one of our museum's most important patrons. The Museum is proud that both Arlene and Harold have been recognized as life trustees, and their unprecedented benevolence is reflected in their funding of the Arlene and Harold Schnitzer Center for Northwest Art, as well as for the named curatorial positions of the Arlene and Harold Schnitzer Curator of Asian Art and the Arlene and Harold Schnitzer Curator of Northwest Art. Their impressive legacy of giving back continues from one generation to another, as Jordan leads the family today into new and exciting areas of collecting and philanthropy.

As director of the Museum, and on behalf of our staff, many of whom are recognized in the acknowledgments in this book, I am confident that everyone who sees the exhibition or reads the book will be inspired by the visual voyage of this remarkable artist.

**BRIAN FERRISO**
The Marilyn H. and Dr. Robert B. Pamplin Director
Portland Art Museum
Portland, Oregon

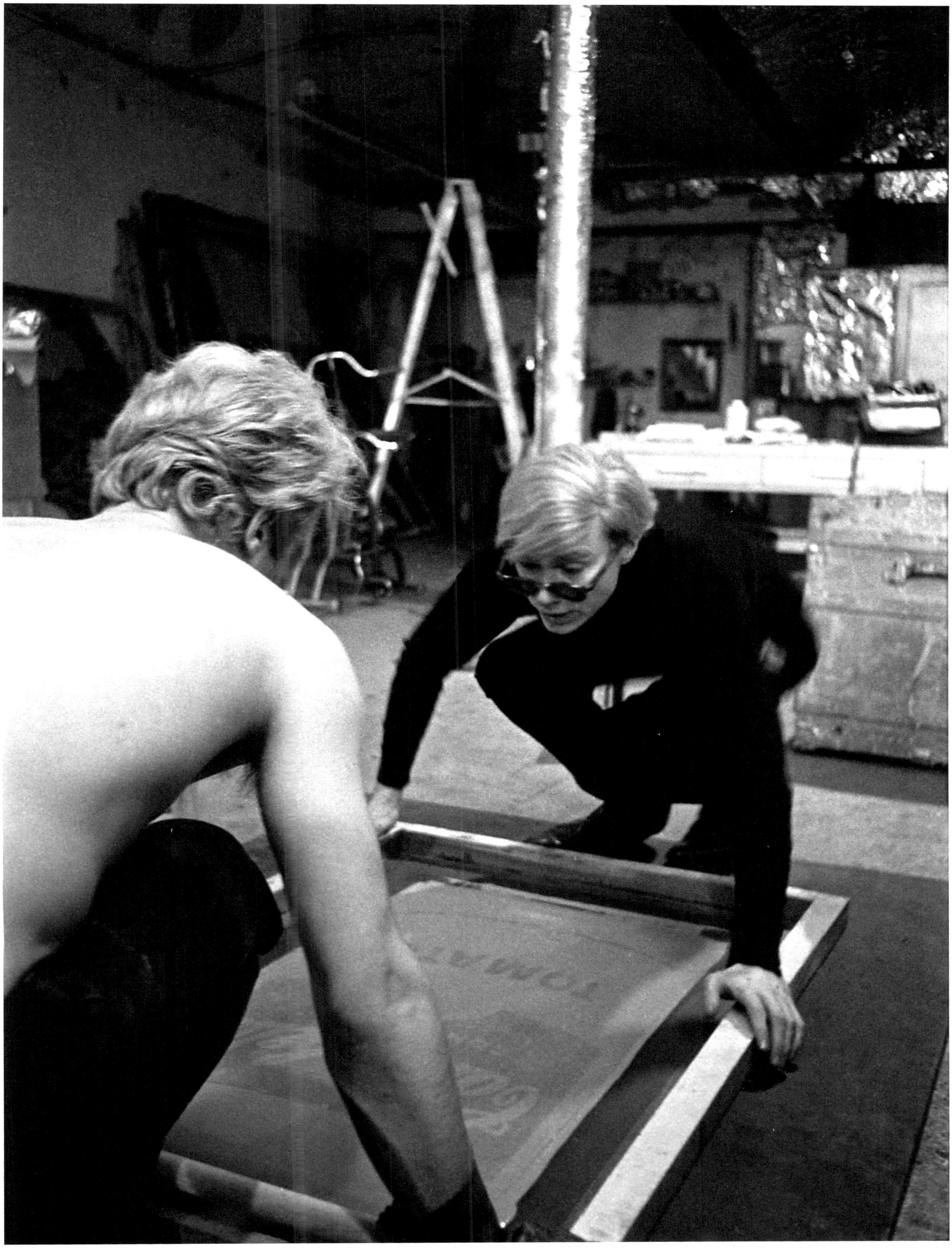

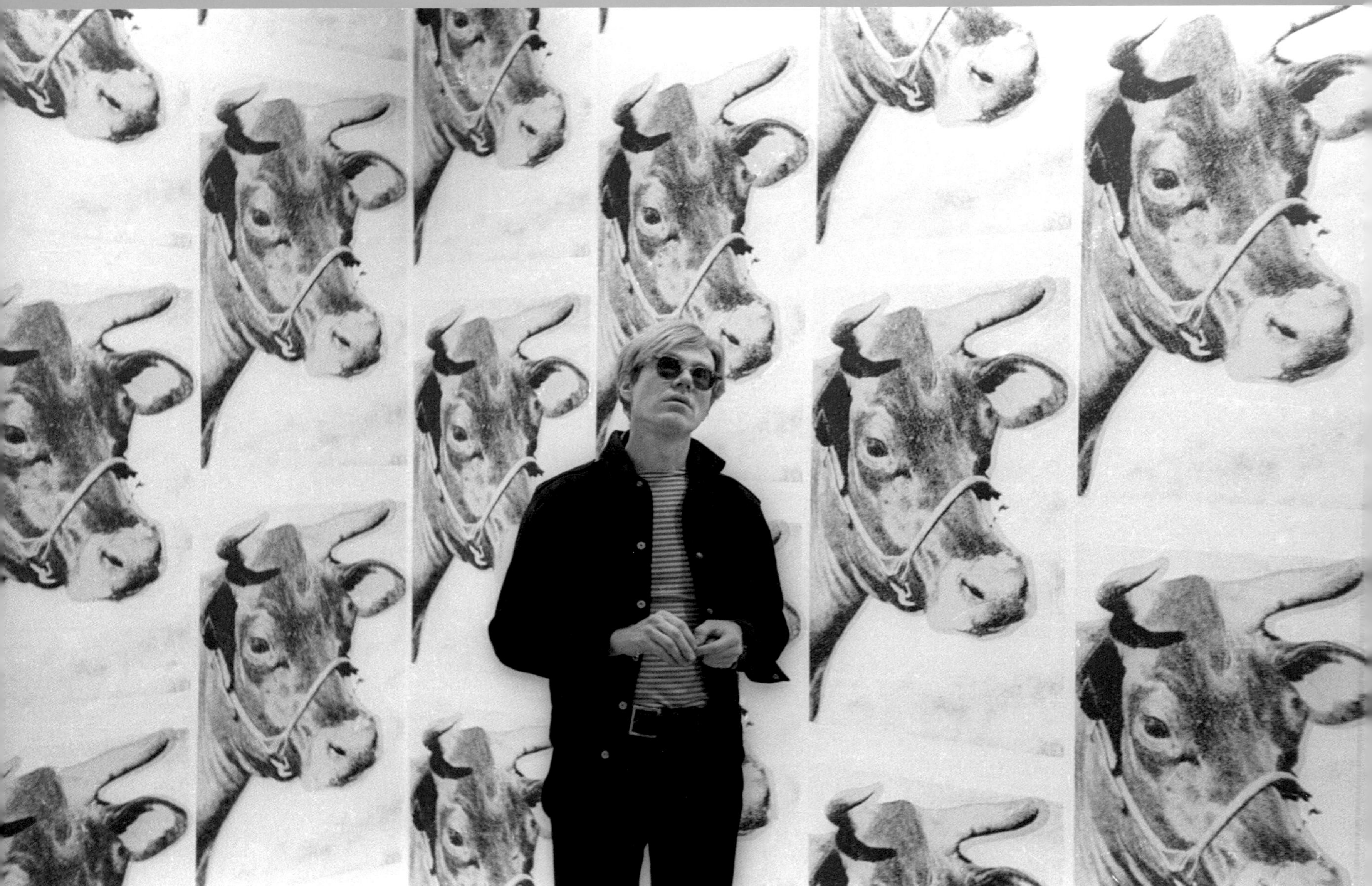

# Media and Medium: Andy Warhol's Prints and the Manufacture of Images

To create his iconic pop art—paintings and films, Polaroids and publishing enterprises—Andy Warhol harnessed the allure of media images of celebrity, consumer goods, sex, death, and disaster. The foundation of this career-spanning investigation lies in printmaking. From Warhol's earliest work as a commercial illustrator in the 1950s, through the collaborative silkscreens made at the Factory during the sixties, to the commissioned portfolios of his final years, Warhol manufactured prints whose images resonate with the seductive power of the photographic and the televisual. The accessible nature of the printed multiple enabled him to distribute his images widely, just as newspapers circulated or broadcasts transmitted to a mass audience.

*Andy Warhol: Prints from the Collections of Jordan D. Schnitzer and His Family Foundation* provides a comprehensive look at the artist's engagement with the late twentieth-century American mediascape. Organized as a chronological retrospective, the exhibition presents more than 250 works, offering a deep look into Warhol's conceptual and technical tussle with media images and the mechanisms that generate and circulate them. Warhol was drawn to the impact of mechanical applications that created, reproduced, and distributed photographic imagery. Such processes led celebrity portraits, news photographs, and other powerful pictures to take a firm grip on the popular imagination; they were designed to spur visual, physical, and emotional responses. Surveying Warhol's vast print production demonstrates his attempts to capitalize on the effects of technological image-making to enthrall the eye, incite action, and elicit desire.

Over his lifetime, Warhol witnessed the rapid evolution of imaging technology and its growing influence in pulp fanzines, the Madison Avenue advertising boom, and the consumer marketplace. During these decades, television, instant cameras, portable video recorders, and the first personal computers all emerged to exert great influence on popular culture.[1] While each of these platforms had a significant effect on Warhol's work, he specifically investigated photographs and the photographic process through his printmaking. He obsessively collected photos of all kinds, and this archive of images formed the basis of his artistic process. His assistant Gerard Malanga described the trove:

> I scrutinized Andy's photograph collection. . . . The photos were an odd assortment of car crashes, people being tortured, candid and posed movie stars, and nature lovers. I realized that the photos were the actual subject matter Andy reproduced in his silkscreens. From these photos, Andy was taking what he wanted stylistically from the media and from commercial art, elaborating and commenting on a technique and vision that was to begin with second-hand. He was a Social Realist in reverse; he was satirizing the methods of commercial art as well as the American scene. But instead of satirizing the products themselves, he had satirized the "artful" way they were presented.[2]

Malanga points to Warhol's grasp of the ways images are cropped, manipulated, staged, or taken out of context—techniques used by art directors and photo editors to guide the viewer's perception. Adopting such tactics, Warhol brought to his printmaking practice the strategies of designing media images, eschewing authorship, and promoting repetition and multiplicity in order to influence the viewer. In an interview with Malanga, Warhol explained: "I don't choose images randomly, but make a careful selection through elimination. . . . The images I've used have all been seen before via the media. I guess they're media images. Always from reportage photographs or from old books, or from four for a quarter photo machines." When Malanga asked if he changed the media images, Warhol responded: "No. I don't change the media, nor do I distinguish between my art and the media. I just repeat the media by utilizing the media for my work. I believe media *is* art."[3]

Warhol found the ideal fit for this pursuit in the mechanized processes of commercial printing. In the 1950s, he utilized offset lithography—a process typically used for high-volume publication—for self-published books and promotional materials to market his work as a commercial artist. By 1962, he turned to silkscreen printing, which he would employ until the end of his career. At this pivotal moment, Warhol morphed his experience working on advertising campaigns into a new approach that trafficked in the icons of popular culture. He transported logo-filled labels, celebrity headshots, and news photos of disasters from material for commonplace consumption to the rarefied space of fine art. Warhol and his pop art peers—Robert Rauschenberg, Jasper Johns, Roy Lichtenstein, and others—employed these recognizable images at a moment when artists and theorists began to think critically about the media and its role in shaping our understanding of social, cultural, and political events. Silkscreen printing, as a means of photomechanical reproduction, enabled artists like Warhol and Rauschenberg to lift images directly from newspapers and magazines and place them in an artistic context that encouraged heightened scrutiny of form and content.[4]

In 1963, Warhol discussed his process of silkscreen-printing images onto canvas: "The reason I'm painting this way is that I want to be a machine, and I feel that whatever I do and do machine-like is what I want to do."[5] This oft-quoted statement is a bald determination to challenge the prized status of the authentic and unique expression of the artist's hand. A machine executes the same action, making the same product, over and over. With his declaration, Warhol rejected an artist's typical relationship to subject matter and materials based on personal choice, preference, or intuition. When he shifted from printing on canvases to printing on paper, Warhol employed commercial printers rather than fine-art presses. His decision to link the prints to a publishing system distanced the artworks even further from his authorial oversight.

Warhol's 1960s studio, the Factory, emphasized art production through mechanical means, especially filmmaking and silkscreen printing. He oversaw assistants working in an assembly line–like fashion, making his Brillo boxes and canvases of Campbell's soup cans, Marilyns, and Elvises. Silkscreen printing enabled him to distinguish the aesthetic and mass cultural associations of the term "media," while he blurred the traditional boundaries separating painting, photography, and printmaking.[6] His actions called into question just what makes a print—the technical process, the paper substrate, the application of ink, the possibility of reproducing the image, the flatness of surface.

Silkscreen and its photomechanical process allowed Warhol to "more fully exploit the preconceived image."[7] From this point of view, the photographic media image is the everyday object to be appropriated and recontextualized as art. This strategy echoes Marcel Duchamp's concept of the readymade, which declared banal objects, such as a urinal, a bottle drying rack, or a shovel, to be art. The anti-art ideas of Duchamp and other Dada artists also embraced the objective appeal of the machine and the reproducible copy, recognizing that as the world becomes more mechanized, the role of art becomes destabilized. Better to embrace the machines and their aesthetic than have the machines wipe out art and artists.[8]

Duchamp recognized Warhol's 1962 serial silkscreening of Campbell's soup cans as a conceptual challenge to the notion of art as a "retinal image."[9] The retinal image for Duchamp indicated a traditional aesthetic experience of visual pleasure. When placed all together, Warhol's serial images of the late 60s and early 70s complicate the delight of experiencing the wholeness of a framed two-dimensional work, the experience that yields the pleasurable retinal image. Hanging the sets of *Marilyn*, *Mao*, *Electric Chairs,* or *Flowers* densely together, and sometimes on top of wallpaper bearing a grid of cow heads or Mao portraits, Warhol immersed the viewer in eye-popping color and pattern. His use of wallpaper as a backdrop and an overall visual field filled spaces with flat compositions expanding ad infinitum. While Warhol understood that media had trained viewers to absorb multiple and sequential images,[10] he exploited repetition to drive impact and defy a narrative resolution. His excessive repetition brings dissonance and disorientation. A reflection of visual culture inundated with media images, Warhol's installations seduce and exhaust simultaneously.

By the mid 1970s, Warhol embraced an unabashedly commercial approach to portrait and portfolio commissions, a practice he called "Business Art." This endeavor was an explicit capitalization of his fame in order to support more experimental projects like films and *Interview* magazine. Warhol's Business Art seamlessly melded with media images as he returned to advertising campaigns, magazine and album work, and other commercial projects. At this time, Warhol switched from found or appropriated imagery to his own Polaroid photography as the basis for his prints. The instant, point-and-shoot imaging system did not require the photographer to have much in the way of technical skills. Warhol favored the starkly flattened space and the way the Polaroid film washed out color into harsh contrasts. The results were easily translated to silkscreens for printing. Celebrities flocked to Warhol for portrait sittings. The sessions were like fashion shoots with specific makeup and dress and Warhol shooting many images. Occasionally, a series of photographs would be translated into a portfolio of prints: Mick Jagger seducing the camera frame after frame reads like a filmstrip frozen in time.

Warhol's exploration of the media image finds a philosophical echo in Vilém Flusser's notion of the technical image. For the Czech-born philosopher Flusser, technical images are made by machines, for example cameras and computers, and have a basis in science and mathematics. Operated by humans but working mechanistically apart from us, these apparatuses translate information about the world into visual form and transmit it through a program or directive controlled by powerful institutions, like governments, corporations, or the media. This program of technical images prohibits criticality and creativity, instead establishing conformity. However, Flusser claims that artists can reject this system: "The experimental photographer is consciously attempting to create unpredictable information, i.e. to release themselves from the camera and to place within the image something that is not in its program. They know they are playing against the camera."[11]

Warhol, as he claimed, wanted to be a machine and simulated the processes of a machine through the intake, manufacture, and reproduction of images. His conceptual agenda involved inhabiting this system, exploiting its operative logic and language and appropriating its powerful visual effects. He worked against the camera: for example, Warhol's prints are never exact duplicates of the source material. They introduce variations in color, line, and form that reveal moments of individuation within the media's larger program aimed at producing a more easily controlled sameness. What seems like a simple gesture transforms the image and replaces a repeatable icon with a new, divergent one of equal or greater impact.

Thirty years after his death in 1987, Warhol's pictures of celebrity, consumer goods, sex, disaster, and death continue to resonate within a culture beholden to the photograph and its digital descendants. His prints seem to prefigure the volume of images that saturate our screen-mediated visual field today. What once was working against the program—appropriation and reproduction, flat colors and off-register printing, and so on—has been absorbed by contemporary media. "The Warhol effect," a tool found in Photoshop and other imaging applications, allows us to create our own Warhol-like portrait. But to reduce Warhol to a style diminishes the significant exploration of media images and imaging technology he undertook. His example is a precursor to artists of this generation who probe further into the digital realm and the Internet, the most complete expression of Flusser's technical image program yet. With that in mind, it is vital to "play against the camera," as Warhol did, to circumvent technology's controlling force in our visual culture.

## Notes

1. Joseph D. Ketner II, *Image Machine: Andy Warhol & Photography* (Nuremburg: Verlag für moderne Kunst, 2012), 42.

2. Gerard Malanga, "A Conversation with Andy Warhol," *Print Collector's Newsletter* 1, no. 6 (1971): 125.

3. Malanga, "A Conversation," 127.

4. Richard Field, "Silkscreen, the Media Medium," *ARTnews* 71 (January 1972): 43.

5. G. R. Swenson, "What Is Pop Art? Answers from 8 Painters, Part 1" *ARTnews* 62 (November 1963): 15.

6. Donna De Salvo, "God Is in the Details: The Prints of Andy Warhol," in *Andy Warhol Prints: A Catalogue Raisonné 1962–1987* (New York: Distributed Art Publishers in conjunction with Ronald Feldman Fine Arts, Edition Schellman, and the Andy Warhol Foundation for the Visual Arts, 2003), 18.

7. Malanga, "A Conversation," 126.

8. Thierry de Duve, "Andy Warhol, or the Machine Perfected," trans. Rosalind Krauss, *October* 48 (Spring 1989): 10.

9. Samuel Adams Green, "Andy Warhol," in *The New Art*, ed. Gregory Battcock (New York: E. P. Dutton, 1966), 230.

10. Malanga, "A Conversation," 126.

11. Vilém Flusser, *Towards a Philosophy of Photography* (London: Reaktion, 2000), 81.

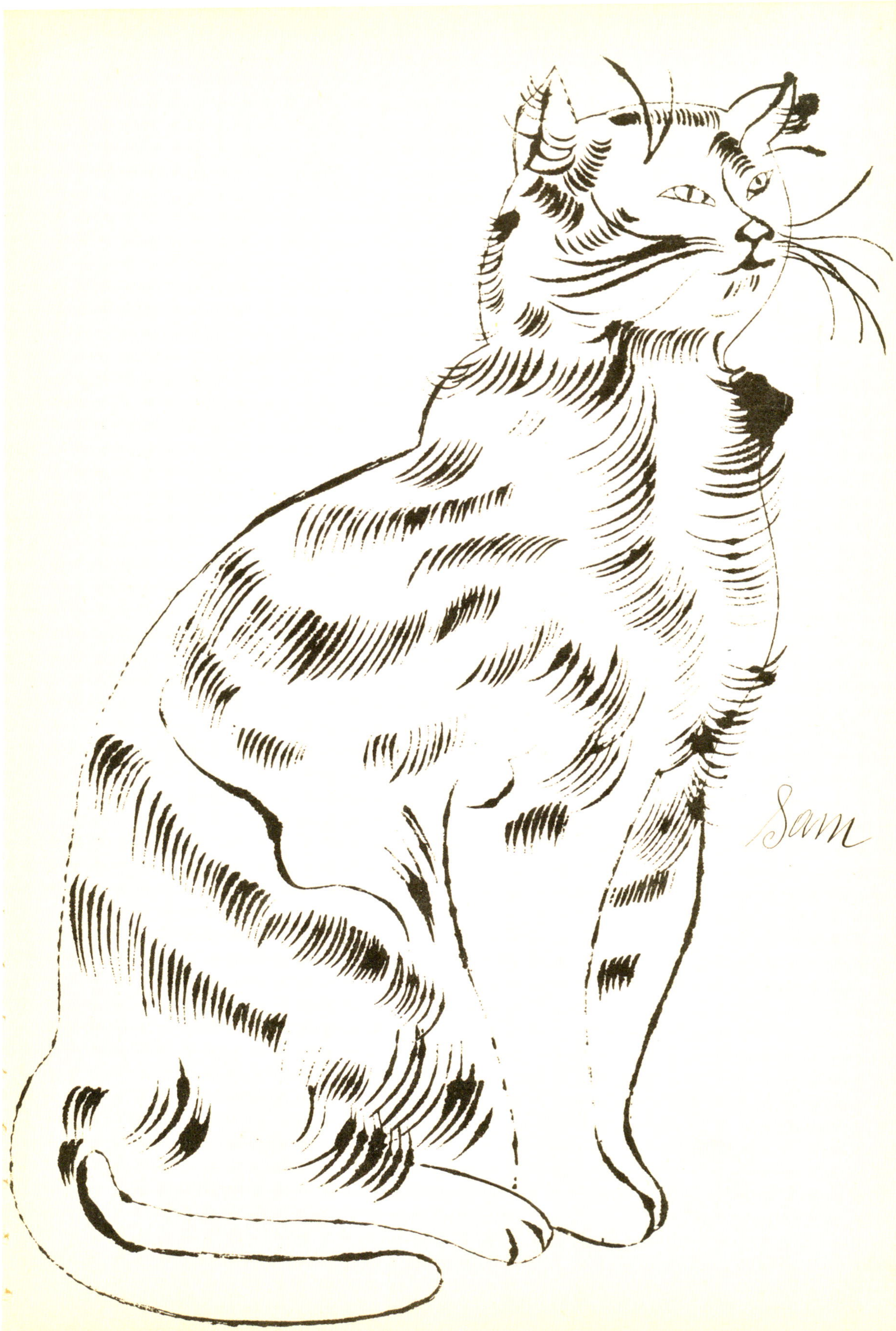
Sam

# Printed Books and Ephemera: 1953–1960

The techniques, economies, and visual language of printmaking took root in the earliest stage of Warhol's career. In 1945, at the age of sixteen, Warhol entered the Carnegie Institute of Technology in Pittsburgh. Primarily an engineering school, Carnegie Tech's art curriculum combined fine-art training with principles of the German Bauhaus movement that emphasized design fundamentals and interdisciplinary approaches. Students were also taught various commercial printing methods, such as screenprinting and lithography. When Warhol graduated in 1949 with a degree in pictorial design, he emerged with a practical aptitude in manufacturing images, an aptitude that became integral to his artistic identity when he moved to New York and began work as a freelance commercial artist. In many respects, Warhol was trained to be an art director, and he went on to apply a technical, collaborative, and idea-driven approach to his conceptual engagement with popular visual culture.[1]

As a student, Warhol experimented with a distinctive style that mimicked hand-drawn line art, a prevalent mode of illustration often done in black and white to create an image that could be easily reproduced by mechanical processes. In commercial publishing terms of the time, it was camera-ready art. With his commercial work, however, Warhol adopted a mechanical process a step ahead of most other illustrators. As he related in an interview, "Since I never thought I could draw, I was doing tracings, you know ink blots you drew on one side and then you could transfer it so it had a mechanical look."[2]

From **25 Cats Name(d) Sam and One Blue Pussy**, 1954. Lithograph, 8 15/16 x 5 7/8 in.

These "ink blots," known as the blotted-line technique, started with Warhol tracing a photograph or other graphic image and heavily inking it as a contour drawing onto a non-absorbent surface. He then pressed the traced image onto another piece of paper. He would sometimes ink and reink the same drawing in a simple monotype process, with the results varying from print to print.

As photography began to replace illustration in magazines and printed advertising, using traced photographs as source material became more widely used in the field, perhaps as a convenient means to speed up production while still keeping a conventional, representational style. The process hinged on the initial selection of a photograph, likely a stock or file photo; Warhol was a keen user of the visual resources section of the New York Public Library where he could easily access this material. Given the shifting industry standards and his obsessive consumption and collecting of images, Warhol was predisposed to manufacture an image based on another image, rather than create a new one to express a subject that had already been expressed. The mechanistic language of the copy was instilled here at the start of his career, as was the distancing effect from the subject of the original image. Warhol's work was twice removed from the original: first through tracing and then through blotting/printing, the latter a process that further obscured the source by reversing its orientation.[3] The transformation of the image becomes the subject matter, as the technique of transfer abstracts the verisimilitude of details and gives an aura of the handmade to the judiciously copied.

Moving to New York in 1949, Warhol sought out freelance graphic design assignments and found frequent work with fashion magazines. In this milieu, success depended on high volume: easily reproducible and widely distributed designs that turned the mundane into the desirable.[4] His idiosyncratic blotted-line drawing style carried a distinctive graphic power and became highly sought after for ad campaigns, book and album covers, and popular fashion magazines. Working alongside art directors, Warhol further observed and participated in the manipulation of images in layout preparation and the printing process to achieve the desired high degree of visual impact.

Warhol gained financial success and great renown as a commercial artist during these years; nevertheless he longed to establish himself as a fine artist. Working with his assistants, Warhol made books, cards, prints, and flyers as promotional materials to send to prospective clients or as gifts to friends. Themes of love, longing, and sex, and depictions of shoes, cats, and society characterize this output. Significantly, Warhol self-published this work, which gave him a degree of artistic license and self-determination early on vis-à-vis a print medium.[5]

Early publishing projects like *Love Is a Pink Cake* (opposite), a 1953 portfolio of twenty-five unbound sheets "by corkie & andy," point to the collaborative and interdisciplinary world Warhol thrived in, particularly the queer subculture of artists, writers, and fashion professionals who made up his circle. With witty poems by Ralph Thomas Ward ("corkie"), the portfolio features an array of star-crossed lovers from history and myth. Source materials ranged widely, including illustrations by the well-known middlebrow graphic artists Currier & Ives and J. J. Grandville, appropriated and transformed for this quirky and extended love poem.[6]

A short time later while in charge of a campaign for I. Miller shoes, Warhol conceived of the portfolio of prints *À la recherche du shoe perdu* (opposite and pp. 26, 28–29), a pun on Marcel Proust's *À la*

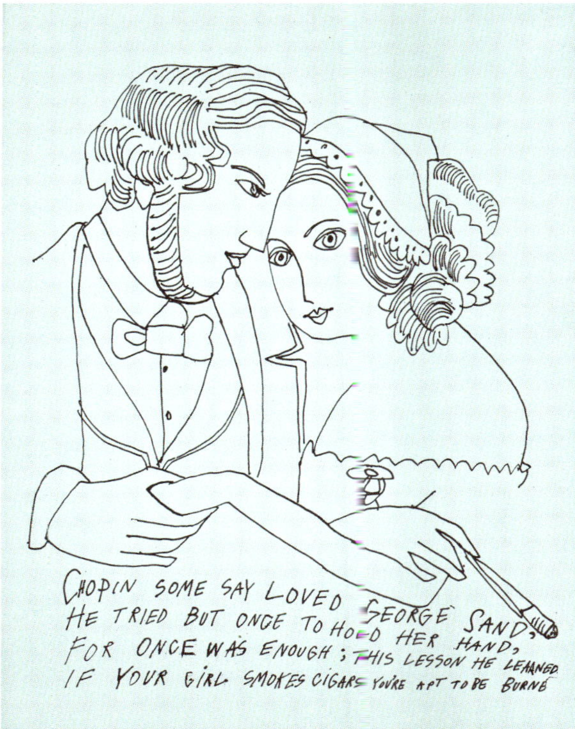


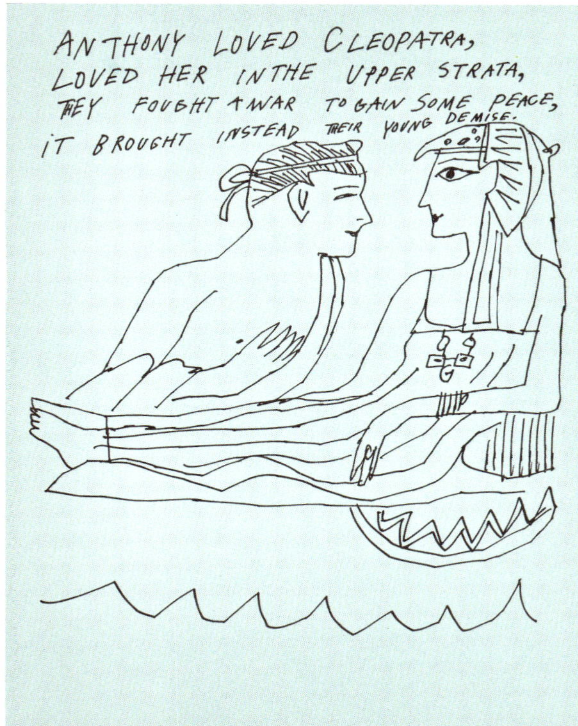


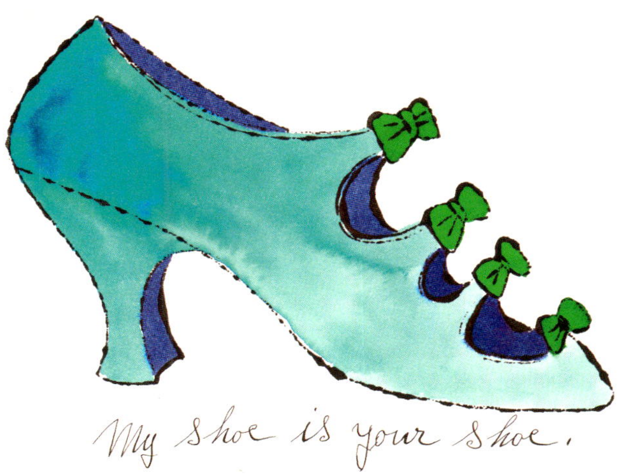


**Love Is a Pink Cake**, 1953. Offset lithographs on loose blue bond paper, 11 x 8 ½ in.

**À la recherche du shoe perdu**, 1955. Offset lithograph and watercolor on paper, 9 ¾ x 13 ¾ in.

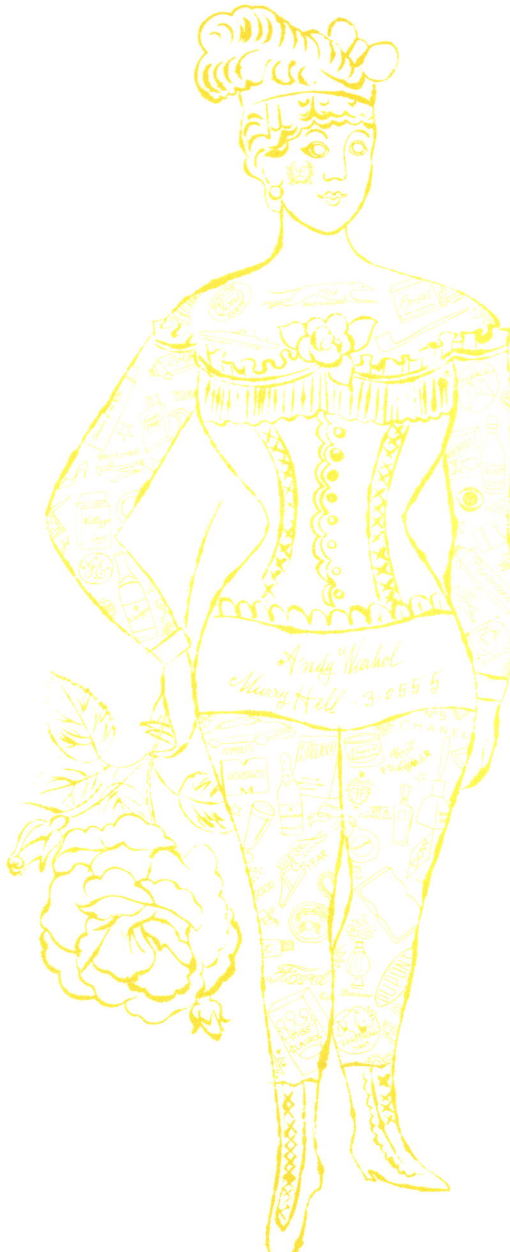

**Tattoed Woman Holding a Rose**, c. 1955. Offset lithograph, 29 7/8 x 11 3/8 in.

*recherche du temps perdu* (*In Search of Lost Time*, or *Remembrance of Things Past*). The collection of prints pairs shoe designs with witticisms derived from popular phrases: “Uncle Sam wants shoe!” or “See a shoe and pick it up, then all day long you’ll have good luck.” By 1955, Warhol had established a studio, and he delegated work to various people, from his mother whose script he employed for lettering, to assistants who executed the blotted-line works, to the offset lithographer Seymour Berlin who turned the blotted-line prints into editions of books or postcards. By 1957, the studio was incorporated as Andy Warhol Enterprises, Inc. Warhol also hosted coloring parties, precursors to the activities at the Factory in the 1960s, where friends and assistants finished each print by hand coloring, turning a mechanically reproduced image into a one-of-a-kind.

*Tattooed Woman Holding a Rose*, a lithograph from about 1955 (opposite), boldly depicts logos and brand names of products from Monsanto to Chanel No. 5 as tattoos covering a female body. The traced imagery naming consumer goods and services reads like a virtuosic sales pitch to potential corporate clients, complete with Warhol's phone number listed for easy contact. The woman as a walking billboard forms an eerie foreshadowing of the aggressive corporate branding our bodies host today, most commonly found in apparel and to a lesser extent in tattoos. The giant rose in the woman's hand anticipates the many flowers that appear in Warhol's prints throughout his career as decorative symbols and memento mori.

Warhol was astutely aware of image culture and its many manifestations in mid-twentieth century America, not just ads, logos, and fashion, but also the work of other artists. His blotted-line drawings recall the work of Ben Shahn, the illustrator, photographer, and social-realist artist from the preceding generation whose work conveyed political content. Warhol also mimicked the drawing styles of Henri Matisse, Pablo Picasso, Reginald Marsh, and Jean Cocteau. He emulated his contemporaries Jasper Johns and Robert Rauschenberg, who were already established as artists, and supported them by purchasing their work. Occasionally Warhol helped set up window dressing jobs for them, which the two artists would do together under an assumed name.

At this time, the work of Johns, Rauschenberg, and others emerged as an alternative to the prevailing style of abstract expressionism. Warhol struggled to find his footing in this arena. His paintings of the late fifties depict comic book characters and advertising imagery; for these works, he deviated from his reliance on the mechanical in his printmaking and publishing processes by projecting an image onto canvas, tracing it, and painting it freehand. Taking the work to Ivan Karp at the Leo Castelli Gallery, he learned that Roy Lichtenstein was working in this same vein. But Warhol's relationship to images and process, established in his commercial career, set him apart from his contemporaries. Nan Rosenthal points to this important difference in attitude: "Warhol is suggesting in his words 'Pop comes from the outside' that making art is a collaborative not isolated process. And he is also pointing, in plain English, to the importance of getting an 'idea.'"[7] When Warhol returns to his consideration of the mechanical process of copying a photograph in making a print, the Art Director Andy becomes the Conceptual Artist Andy, steeped in a visual landscape of media images.

Notes

1. Nan Rosenthal, "Let Us Now Praise Famous Men: Warhol as Art Director," in *The Work of Andy Warhol*, ed. Gary Garrels (New York: Dia Art Foundation; Seattle: Bay Press, 1989), 42.

2. Donna De Salvo, "God Is in the Details: The Prints of Andy Warhol," in *Andy Warhol Prints: A Catalogue Raisonné 1962–1987* (New York: Distributed Art Publishers in conjunction with Ronald Feldman Fine Arts, Edition Schellman, and the Andy Warhol Foundation for the Visual Arts, 2003), 20.

3. Marco Livingstone, "Do It Yourself: Notes on Warhol's Techniques," in *Andy Warhol: A Retrospective*, ed. Kynaston McShine (New York: Museum of Modern Art, 1989), 65.

4. De Salvo, "God Is in the Details," 19.

5. Ibid., 21.

6. De Salvo, "The Genesis of Andy Warhol's Printmaking," in *Andy Warhol Prints*, 318.

7. Rosenthal, "Let Us Now Praise," 42.

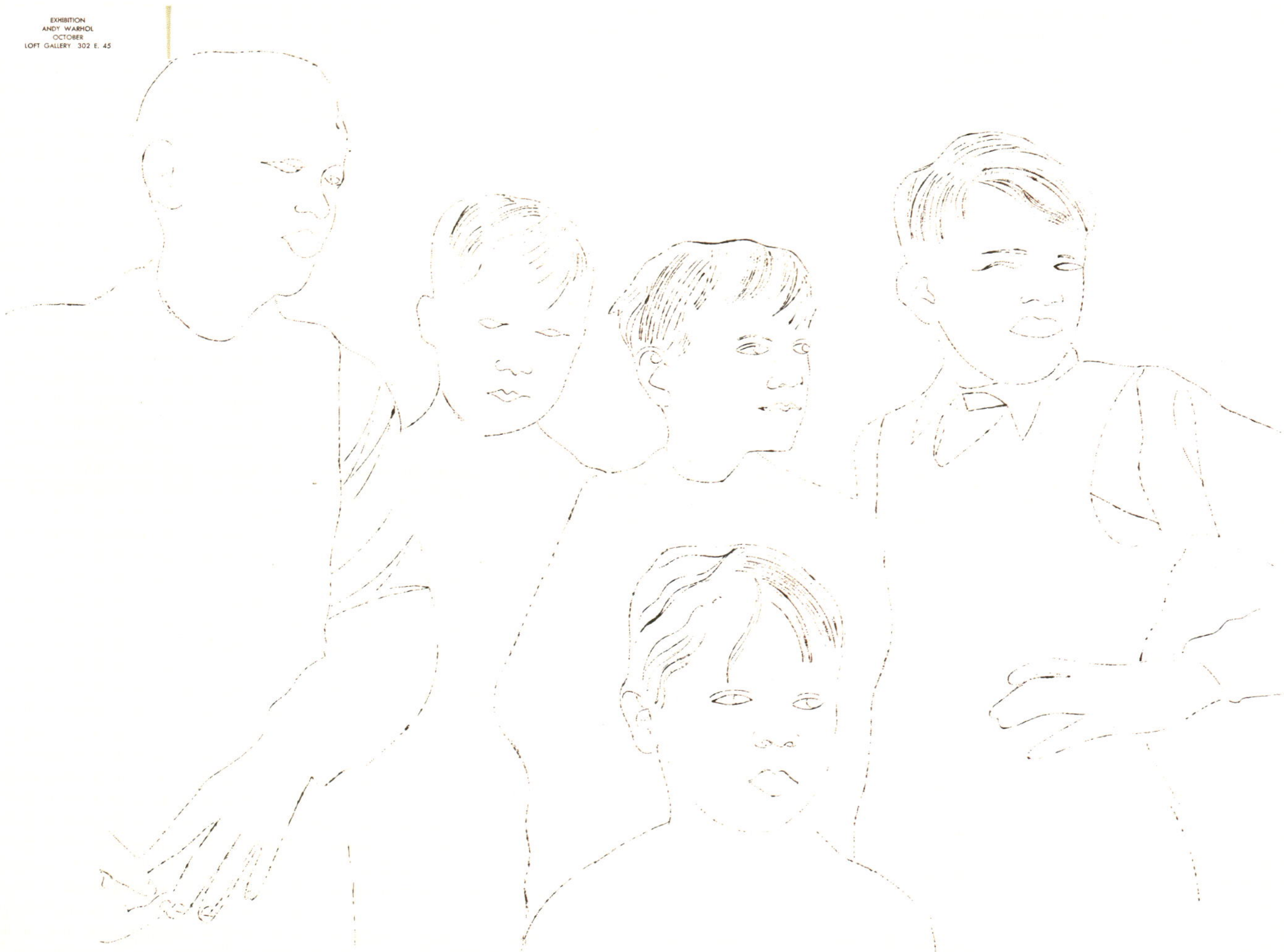


**5 Young Boys** (Loft Gallery announcement), 1954. Offset lithograph, 22⅛ x 29 in.

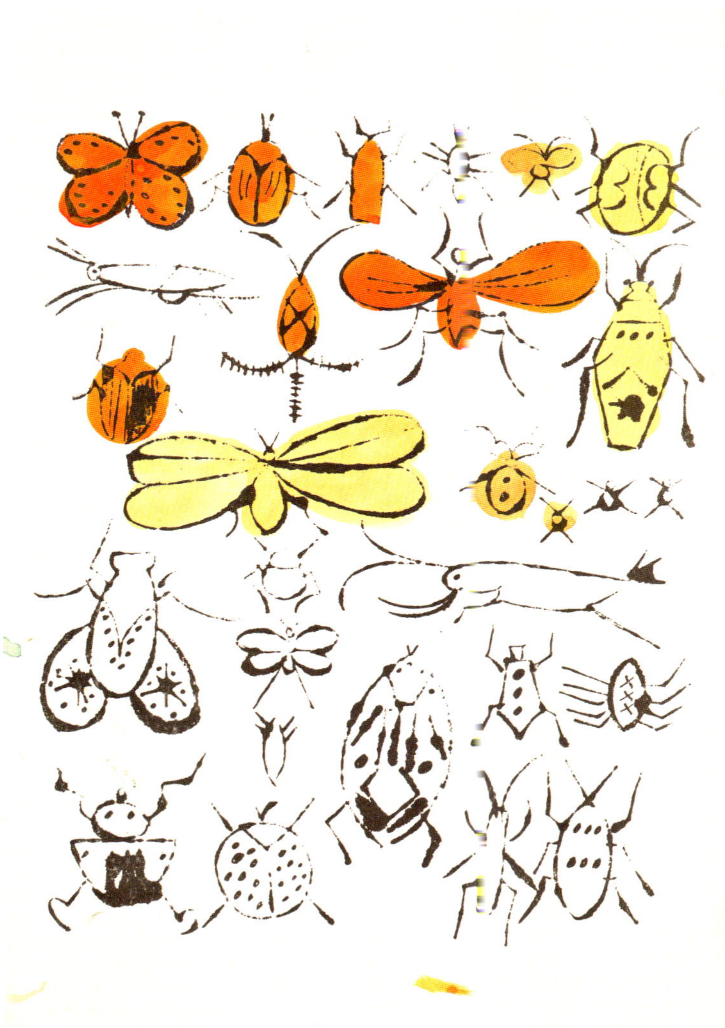

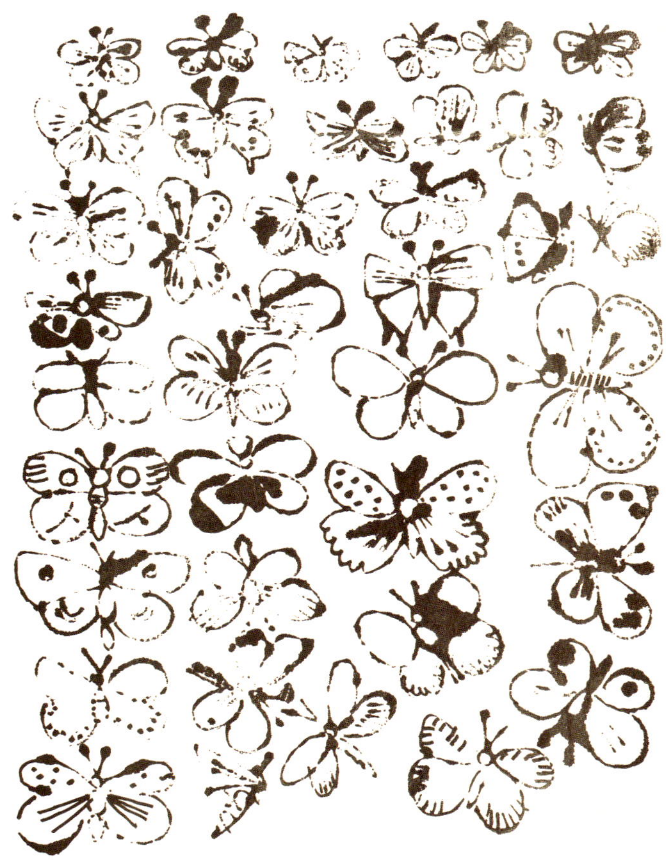

**Happy Bug Day**, 1954. Offset lithograph and watercolor, 14 x 9 3/8 in.

**Happy Butterfly Day**, 1955. Lithograph, 14 x 10 in.

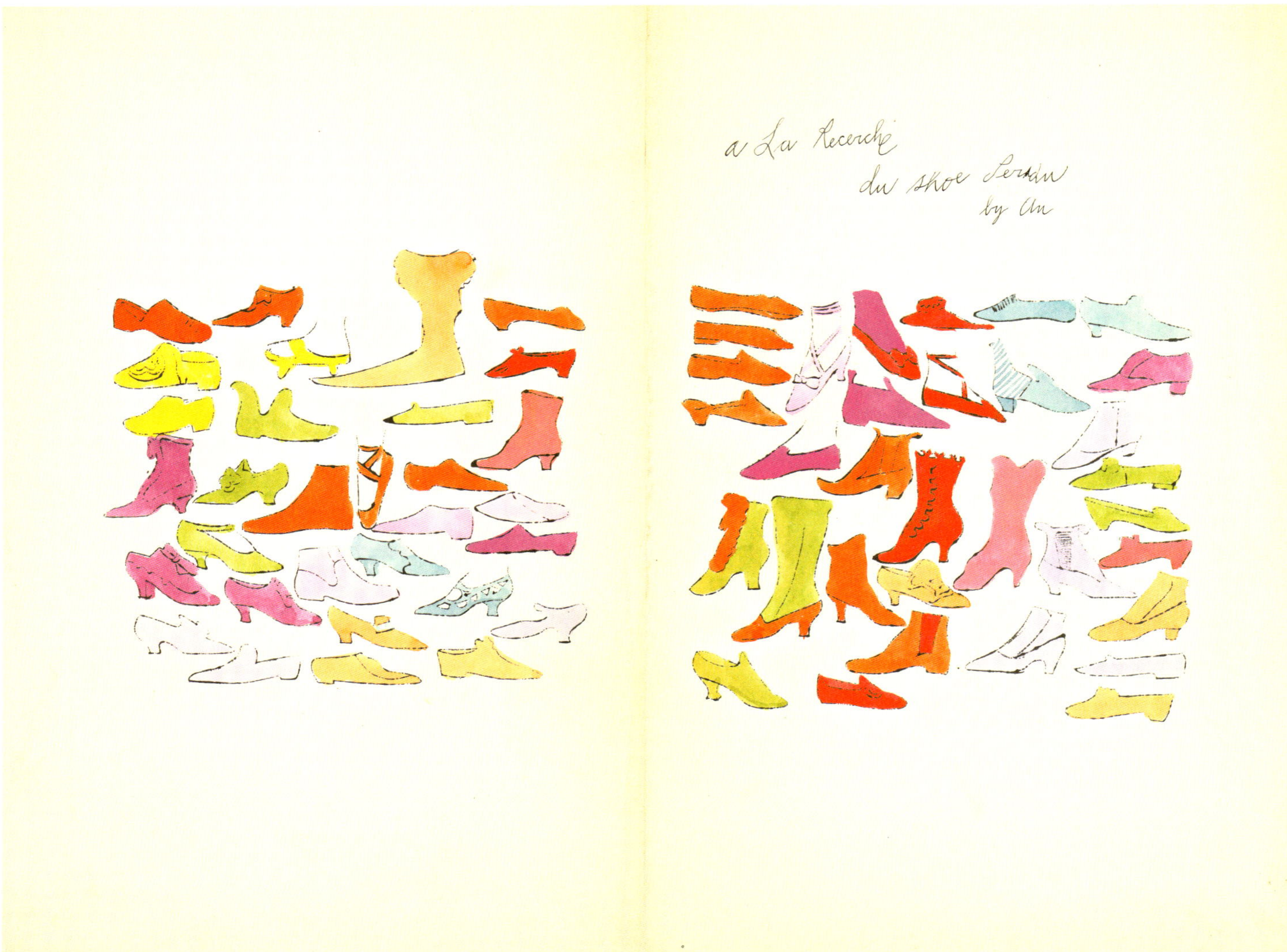

**À la recherche du shoe perdu**, cover, 1955. Offset lithograph and watercolor, 40¼ x 26⅛ in.

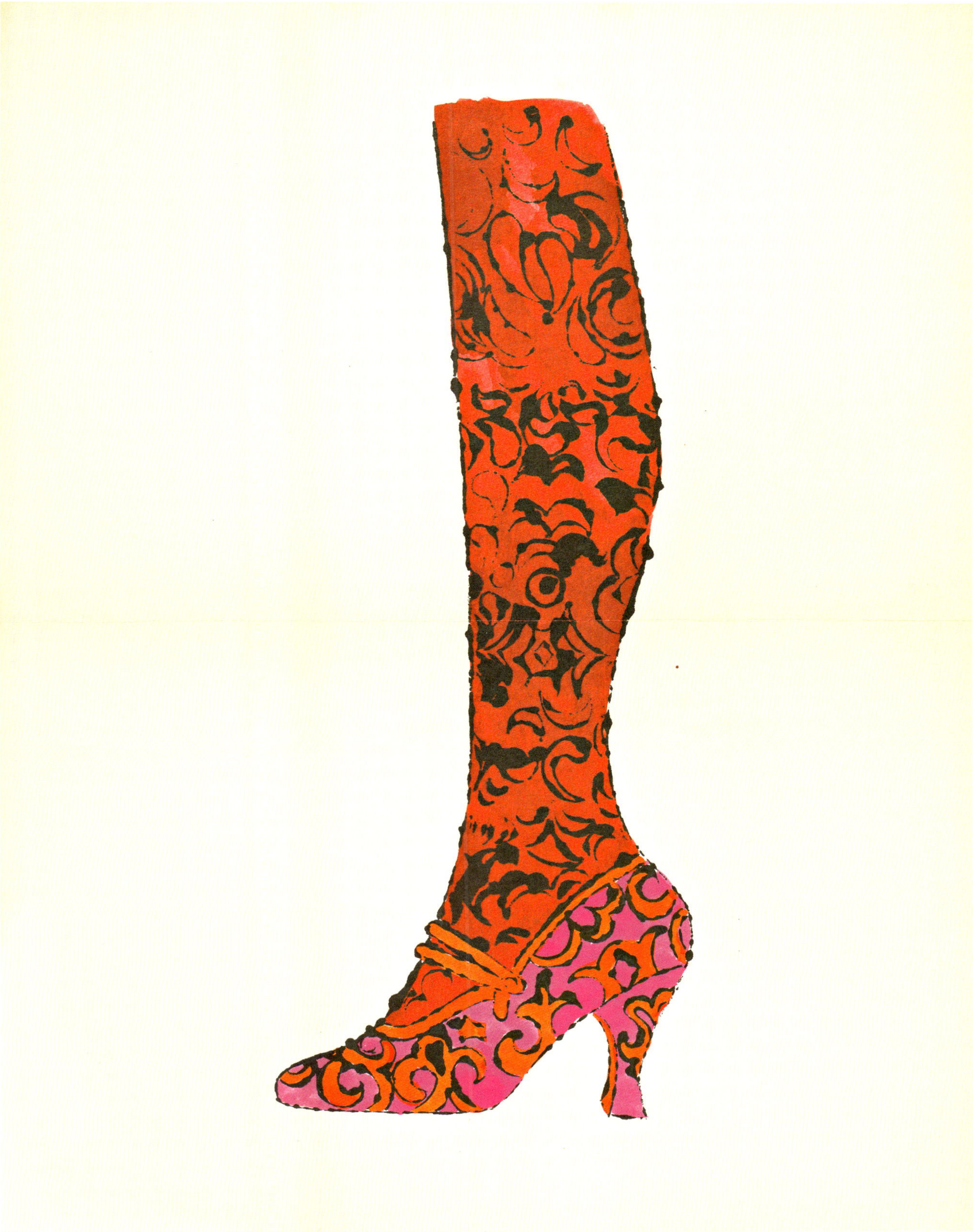

**Shoe and Leg**, 1955. Offset lithograph and watercolor, 25 x 19 in.

(following pages) **À la recherche du shoe perdu**, 1955. Offset lithograph and watercolor, each 9¾ x 13¾ in.

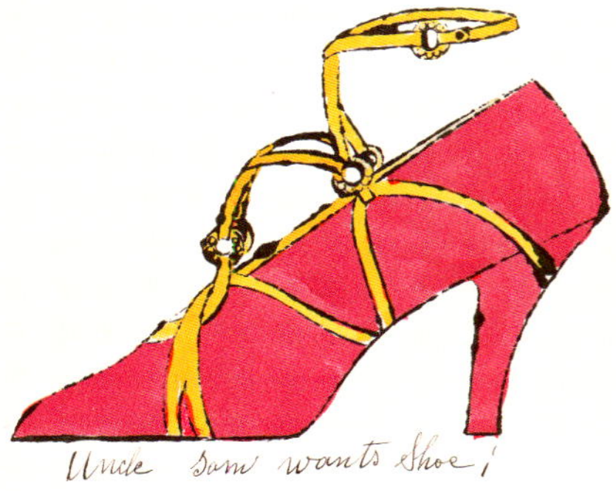
Uncle Sam wants Shoe!

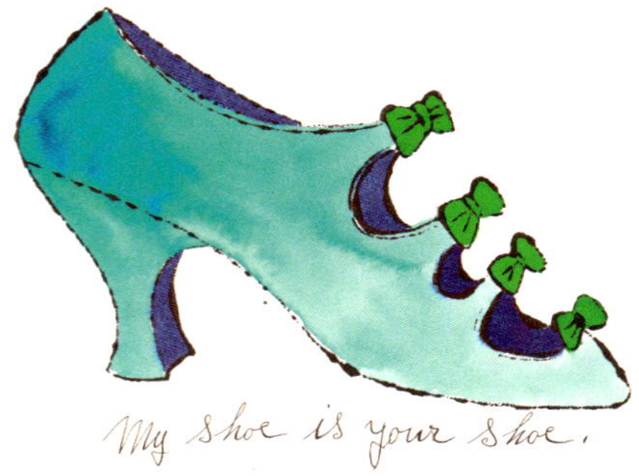
My shoe is your Shoe.

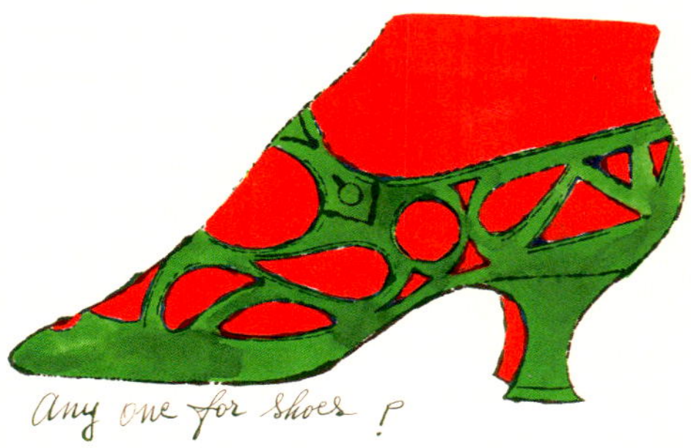
Any one for Shoes ?

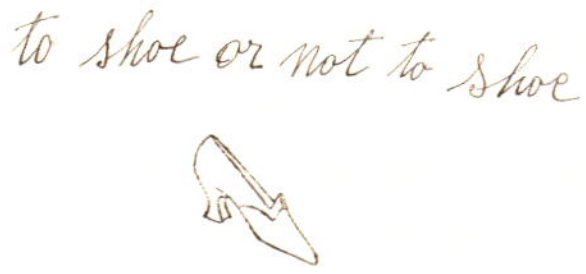
to shoe or not to shoe

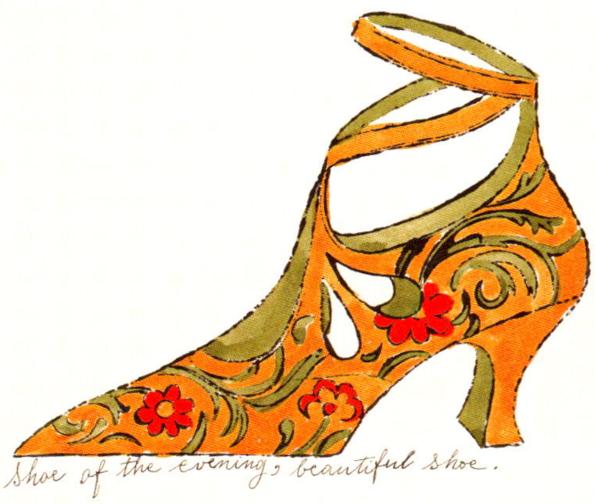
Shoe of the evening, beautiful shoe.

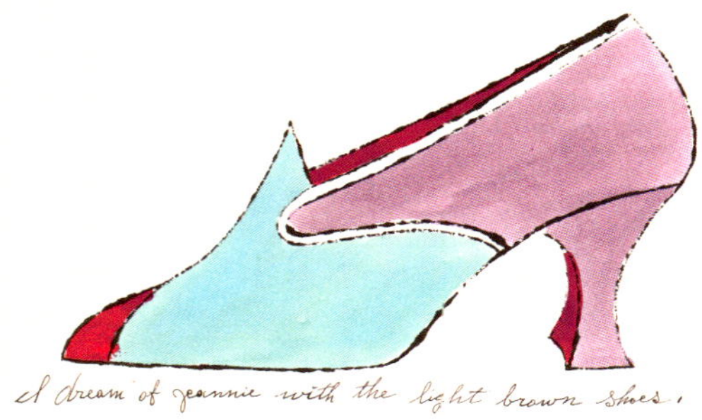
I dream of jeannie with the light brown shoes.

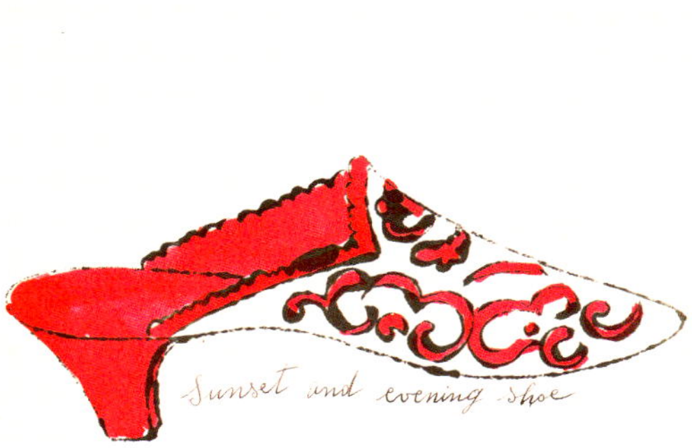
Sunset and evening shoe

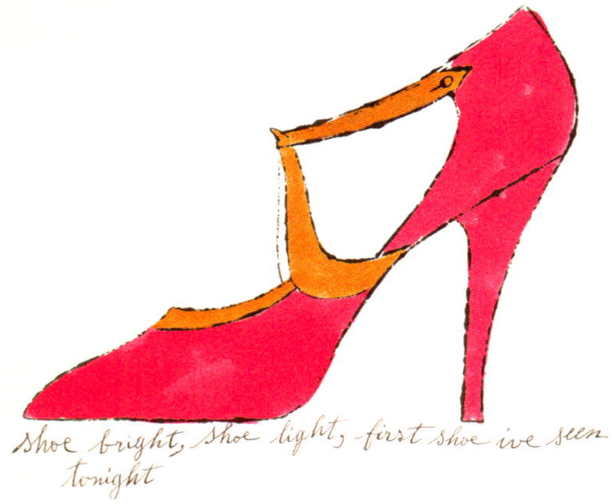
Shoe bright, shoe light, first shoe ive seen
tonight

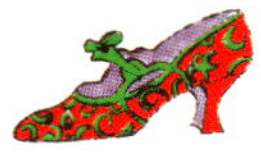

Beauty is shoe, shoe beauty...

Andy Warhol

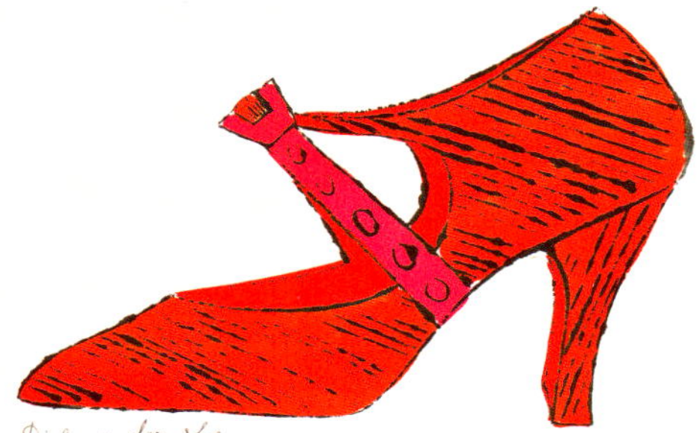

Dial M for shoe.

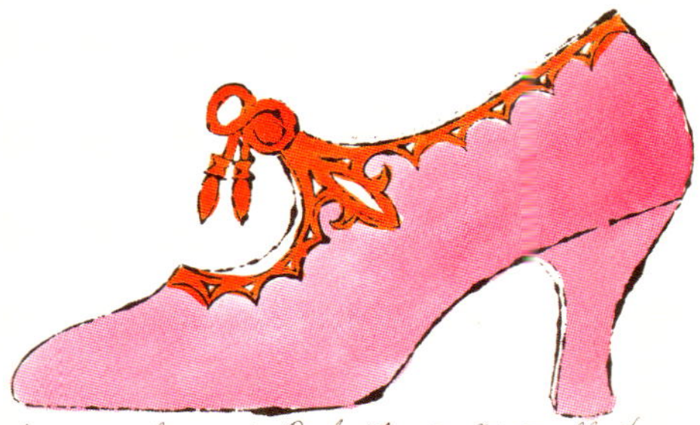

See a shoe and pick it up and all day long you'll have Good Luck

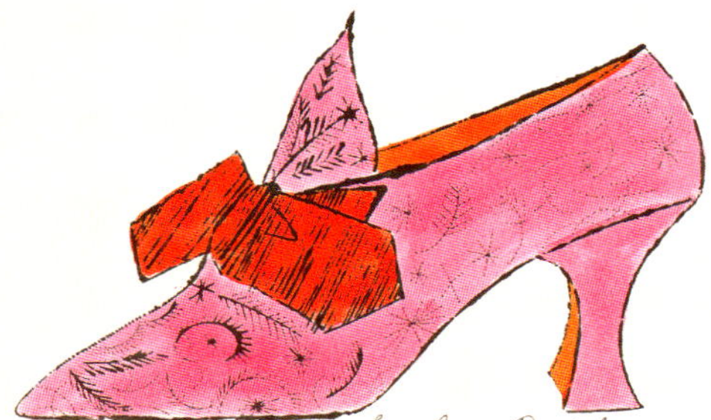

The autobiography of alice B. shoe.

In her sweet little alice blue shoes-

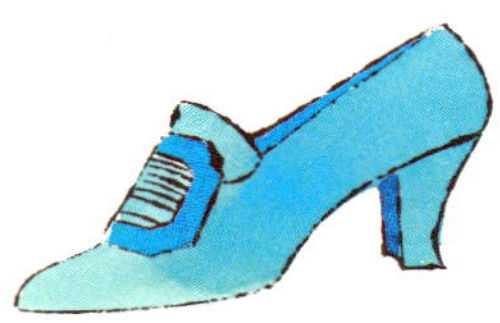

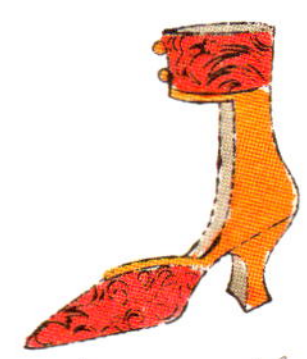

When I'm Calling Shoe.

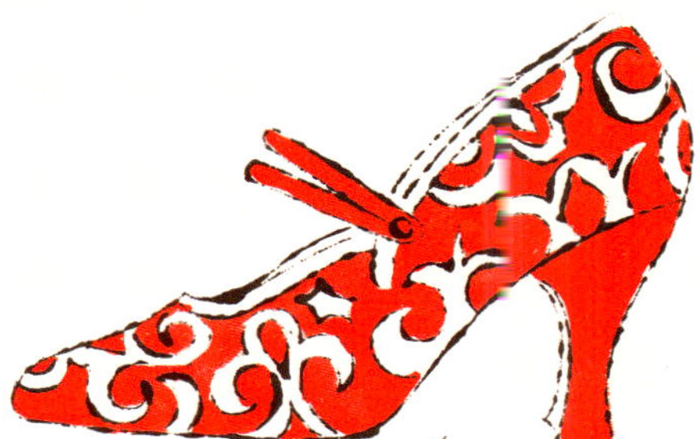

you can lead a shoe to water but you can't make it drink

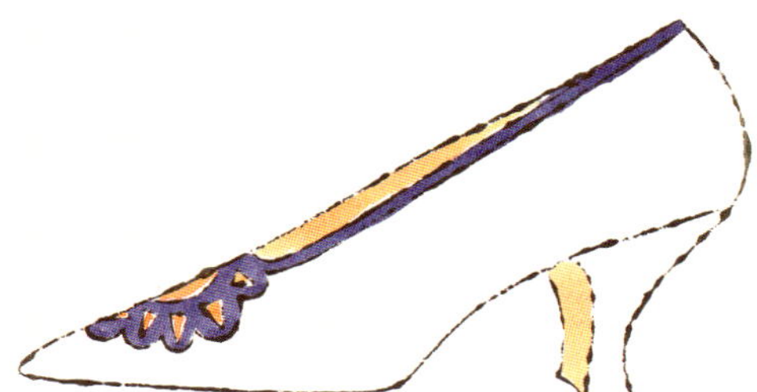

Shoe fly Baby

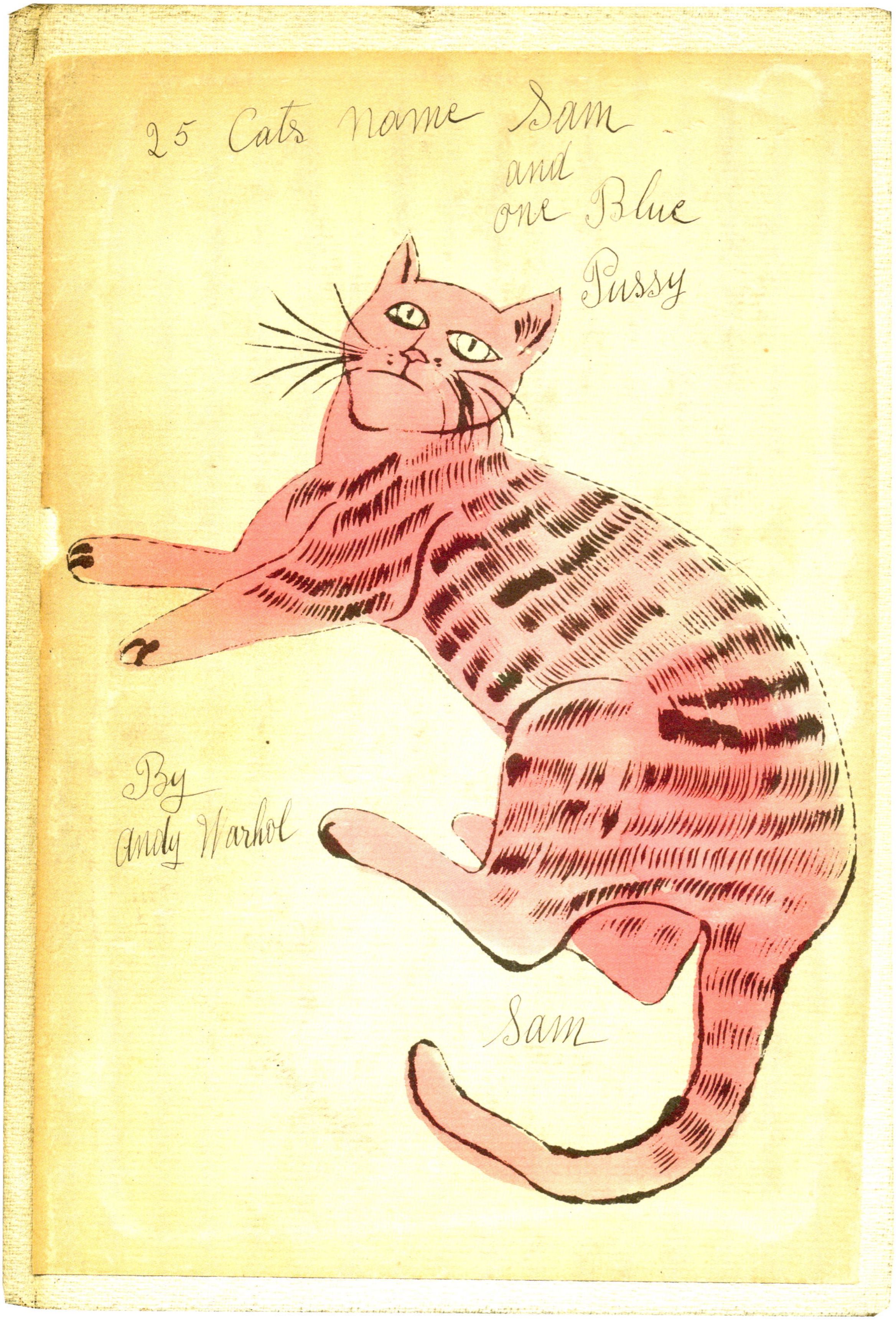


**25 Cats Name[d] Sam and One Blue Pussy**, cover, 1954. Offset lithograph and watercolor, 8 15⁄16 x 5 7⁄8 in.

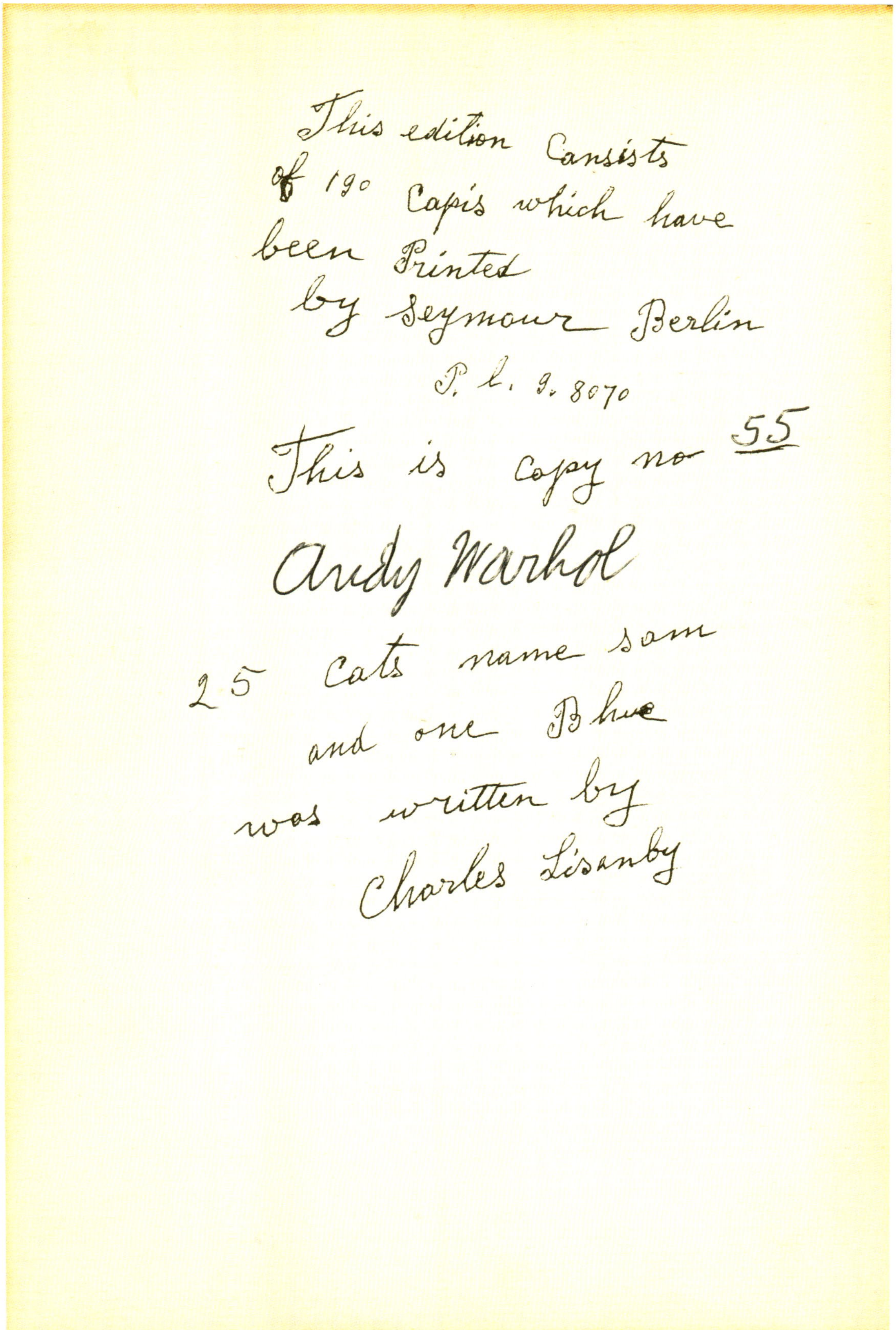
This edition Cansists
of 190 Capis which have
been Printed
by Seymour Berlin
P. L. 9. 8070
This is copy no 55
Andy Warhol
25 Cats name sam
and one Blue
was written by
Charles Lisanby

**25 Cats Name[d] Sam and One Blue Pussy**, colophon, 1954. Offset lithograph and watercolor, 9 x 5 ⅞ in.

(following pages) **25 Cats Name[d] Sam and One Blue Pussy**, 1954. Offset lithograph and watercolor, each 9 x 5 ⅞ in.

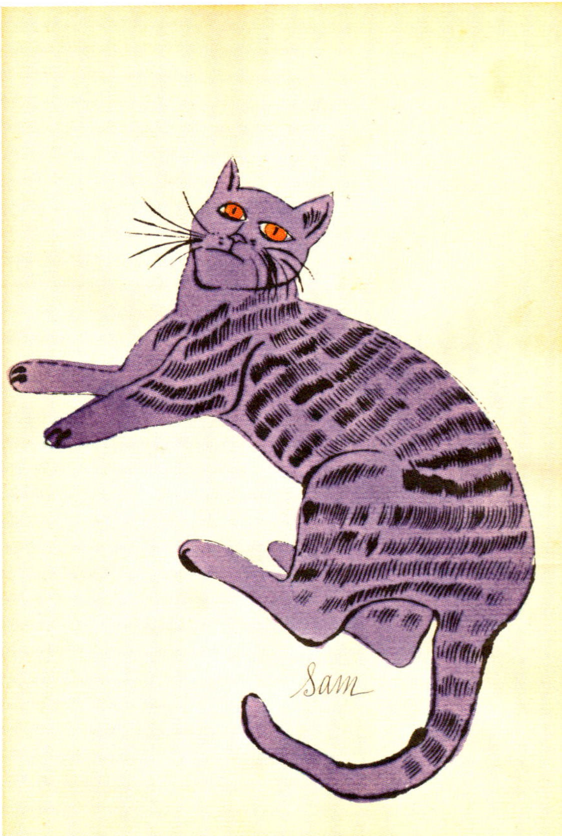
Sam

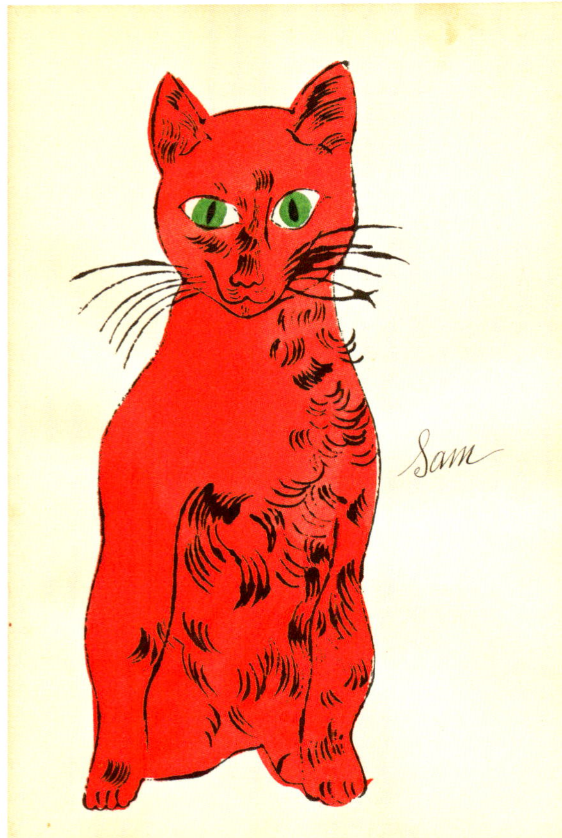
Sam

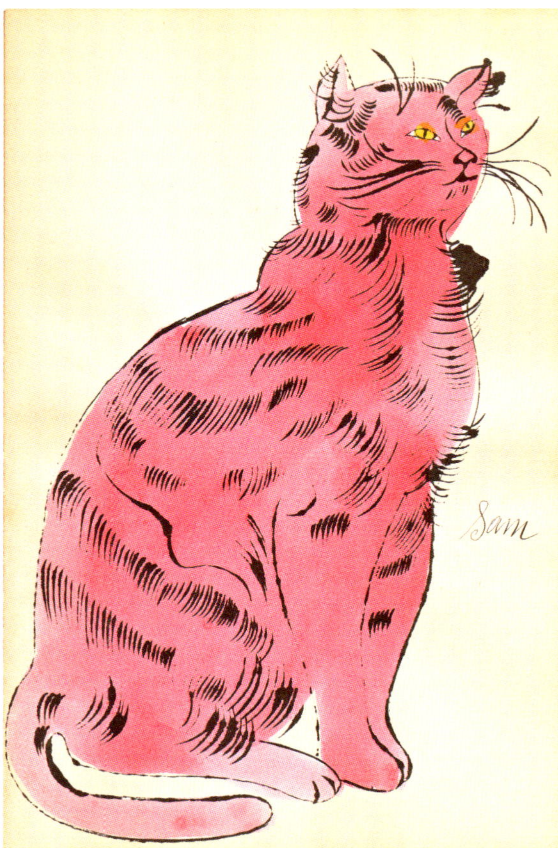
Sam

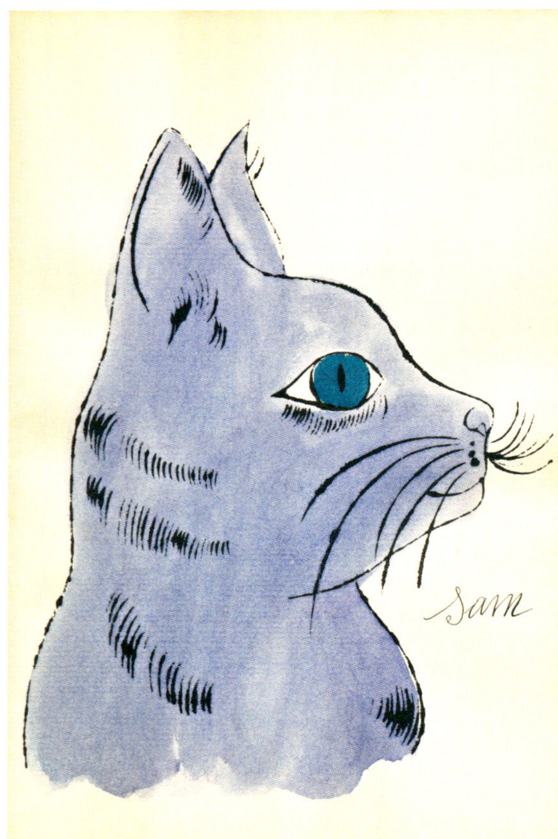
Sam

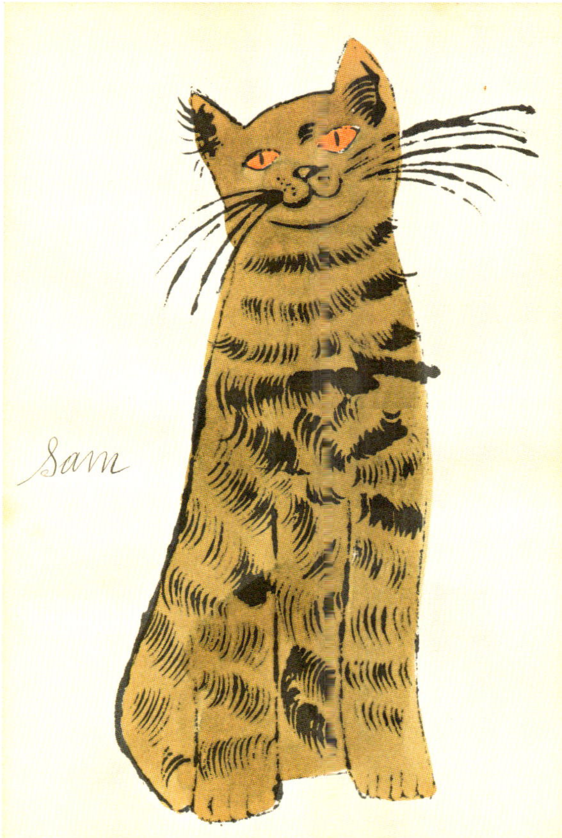
Sam
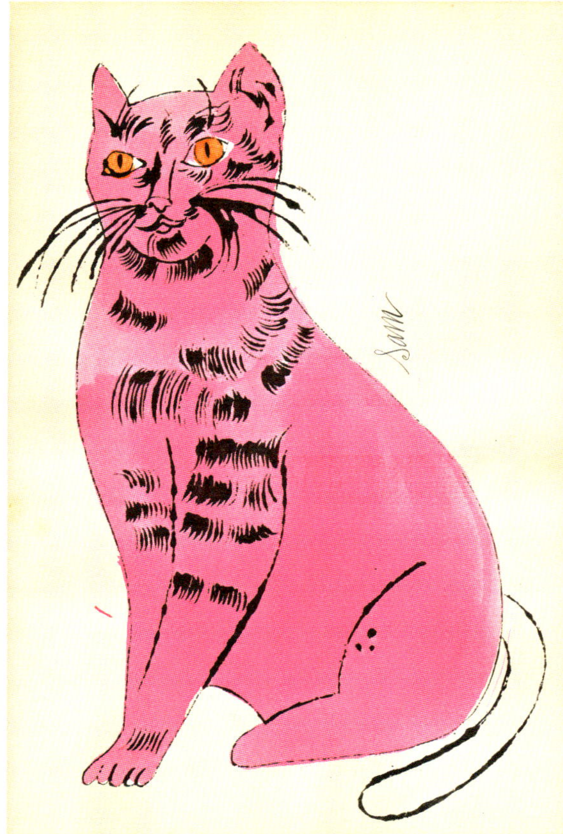
Sam
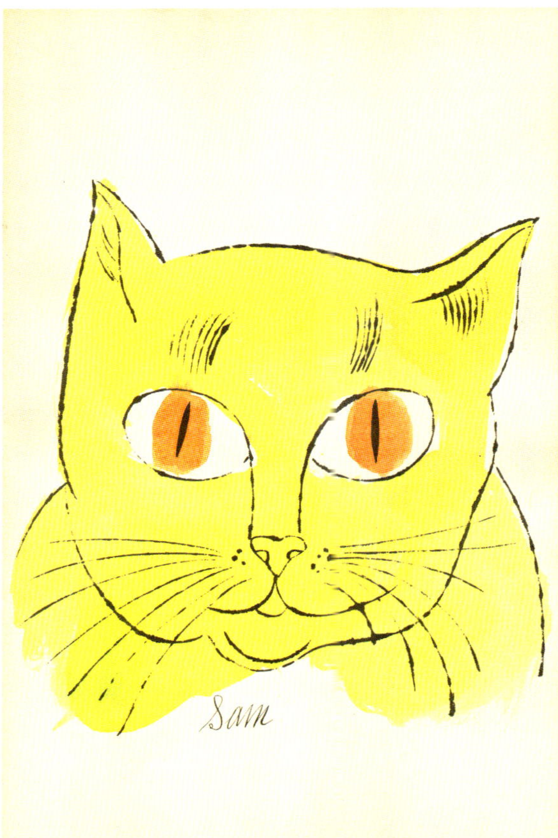
Sam
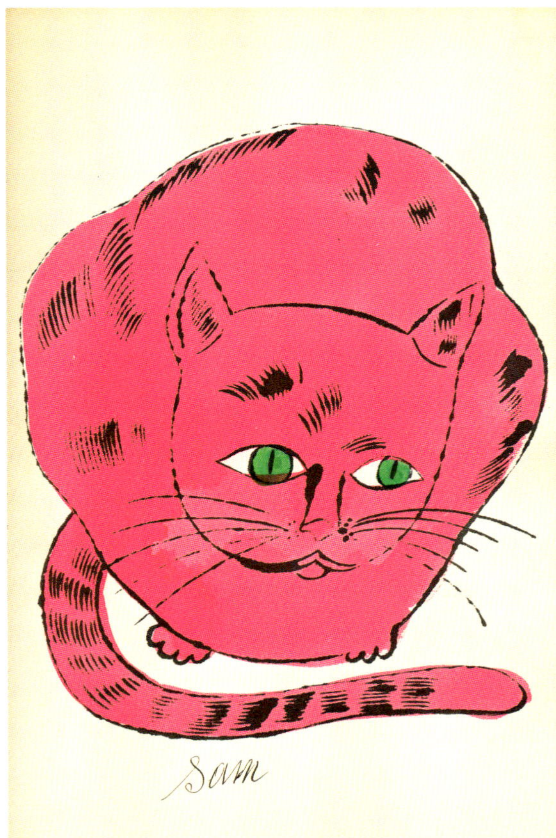
Sam

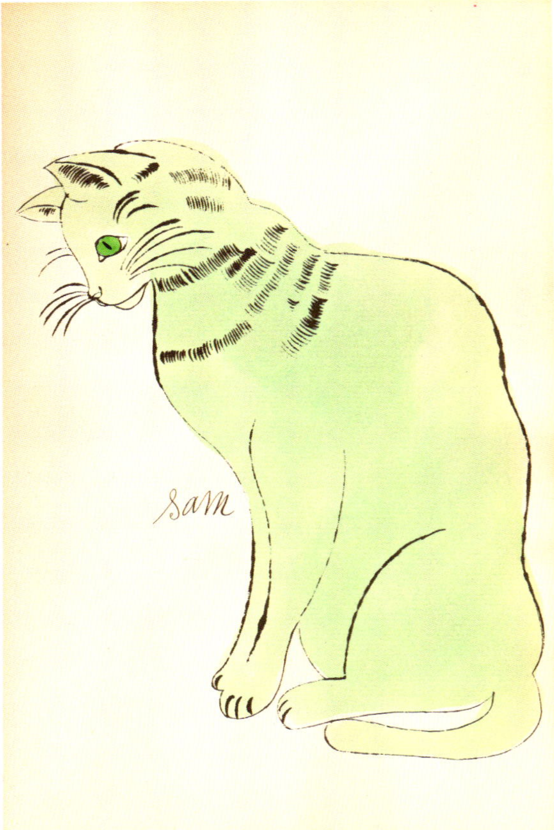
Sam

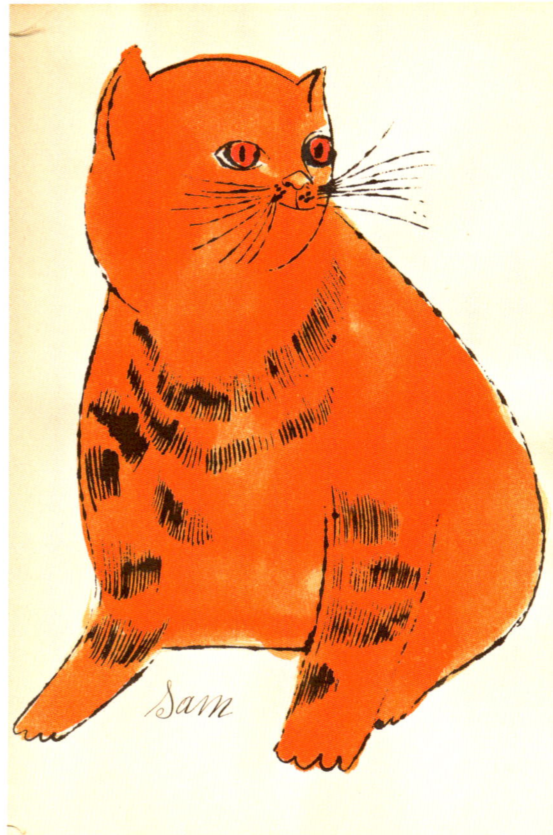
Sam

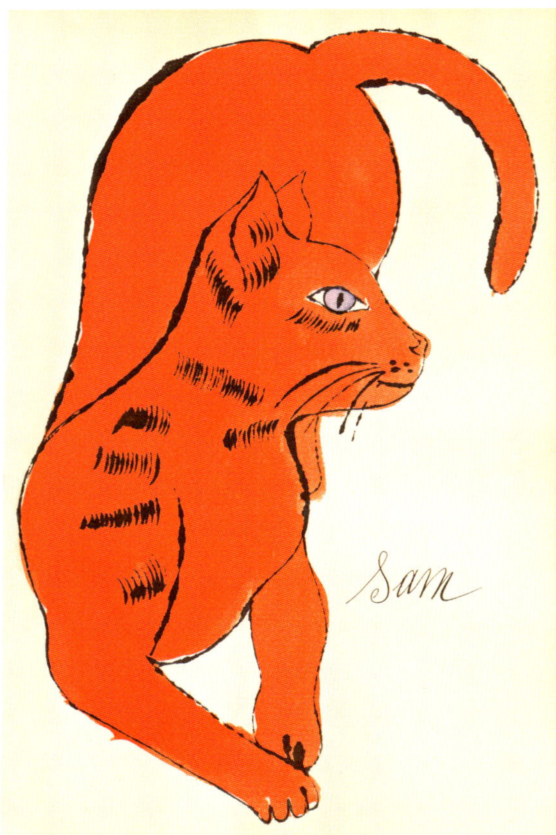
Sam

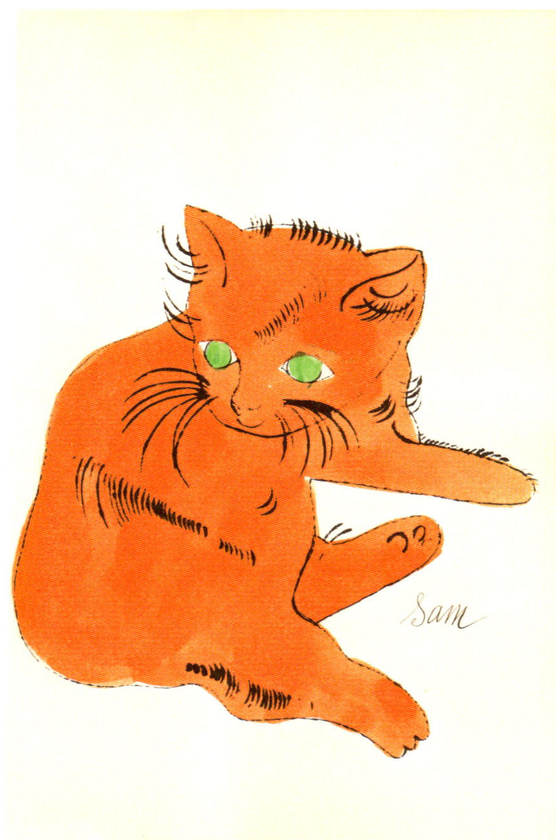
Sam

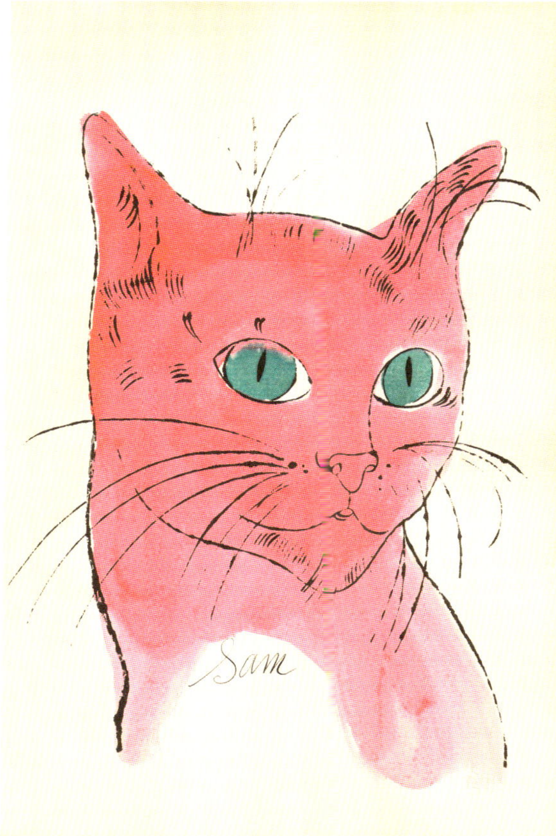
Sam

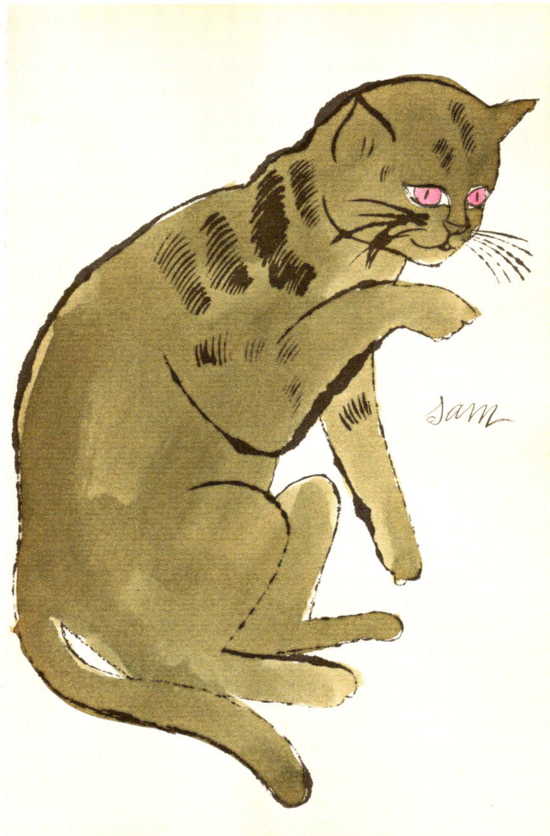
Sam

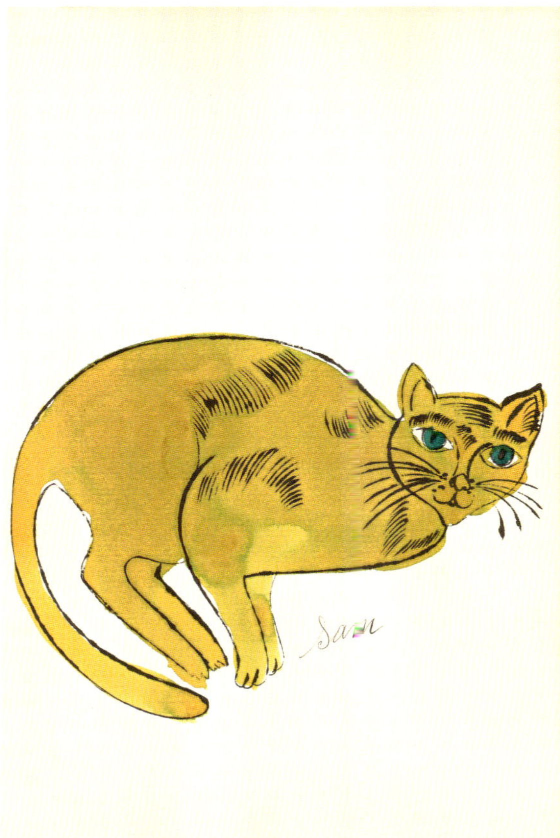
Sam

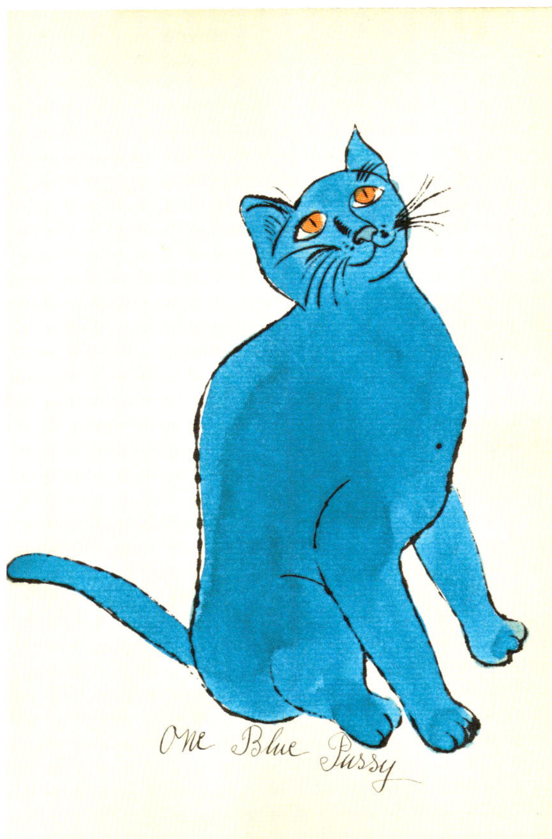
One Blue Pussy

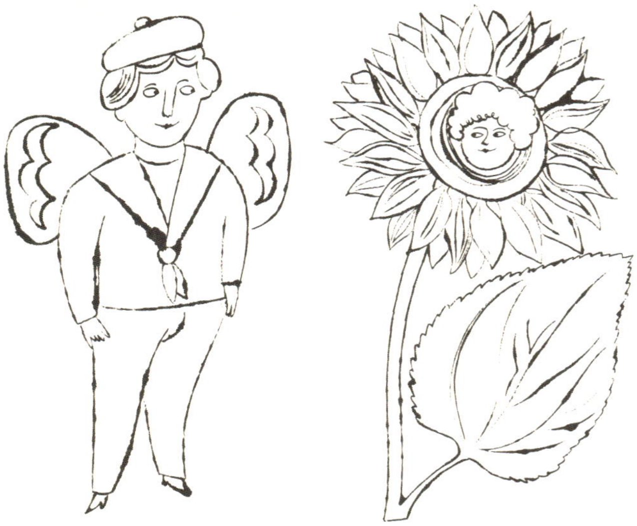

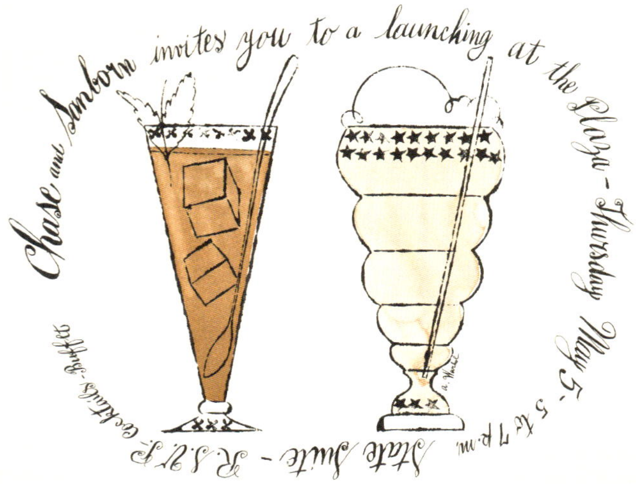


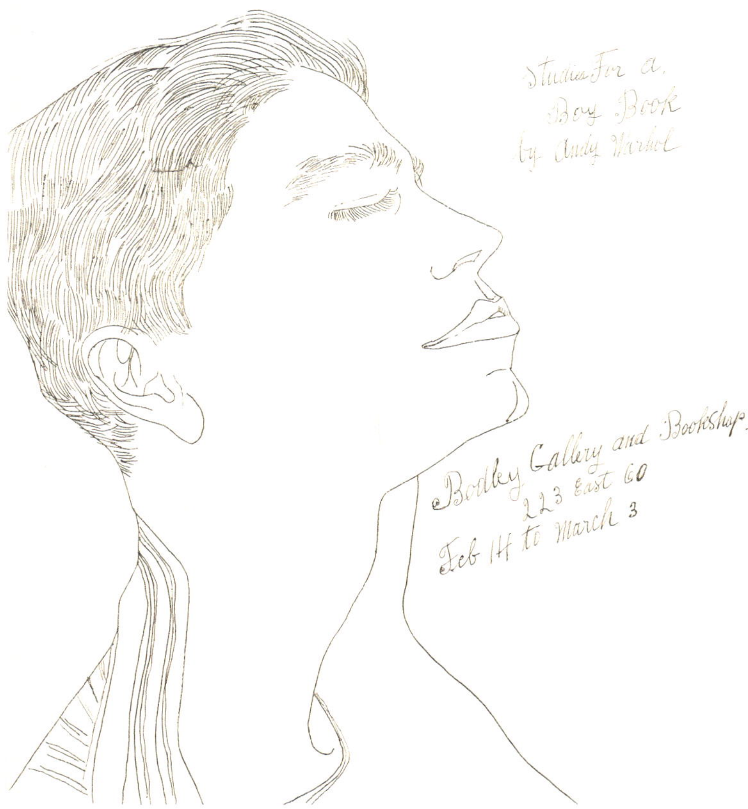


**In the Bottom of My Garden**, 1955. Offset lithograph and watercolor, 8 ½ x 11 in.

**Launching at the Plaza** (with reply card), 1960. Offset lithograph, 8 ½ x 11 in.

**Studies for a Boy Book** (Bodley Gallery announcement), 1957. Offset lithograph on paper, 15 ⅞ x 13 ½ in.

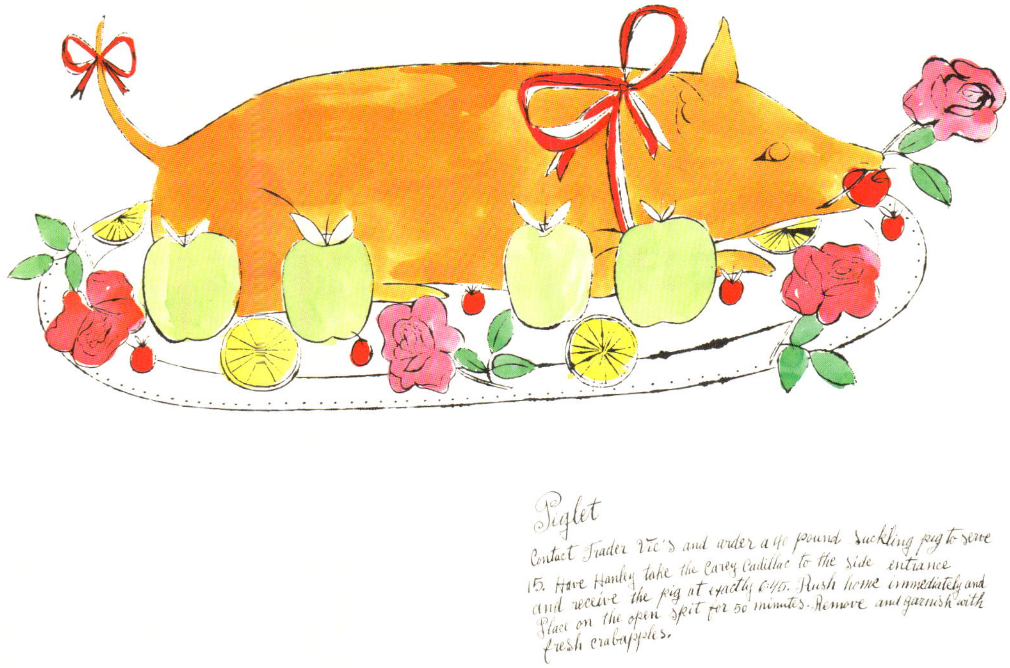


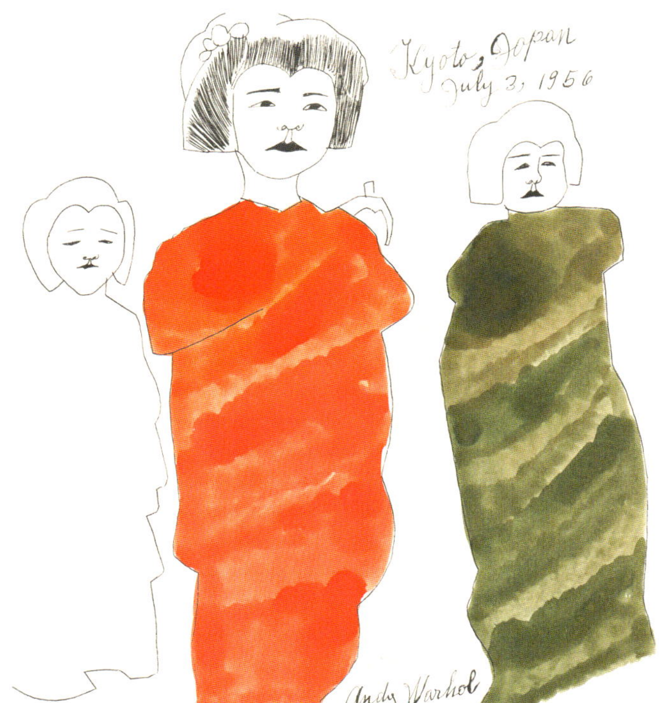


**Wild Raspberries by Andy Warhol and Suzie Frankfurt: Piglet**, 1959. Offset lithograph and watercolor, 17 1/8 x 21 1/2 in.

**Kyoto, Japan, July 3, 1956**, 1956. Offset lithograph and watercolor, 17 3/8 x 14 3/8 in.

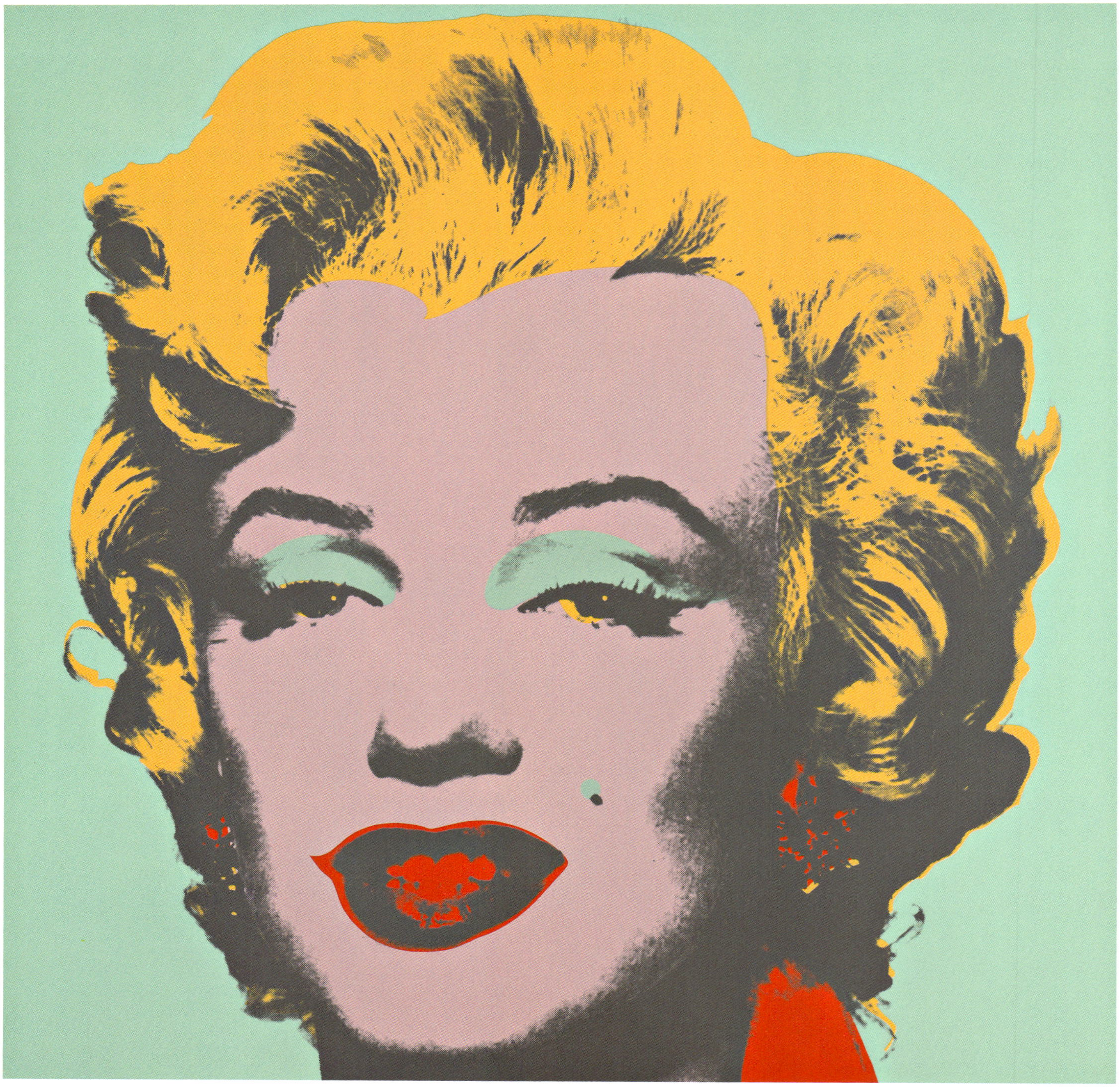

# The Factory and Factory Additions: 1962–1974

Until 1962, Warhol had been staging shows of illustrations and paintings in small galleries. Hungry for more recognition, Warhol actively sought the attention of New York's art elite with his paintings based on advertisements and comic book characters, and those works allowed him to leap from the world of graphic design into the circle of more powerful galleries, artists, and curators. Drawing from his interests and experience as a commercial artist, Warhol found readymade sources in everyday products, photographs published in newspapers and magazines, and celebrity promotional images multiplied in the darkroom for distribution to fans. The work that quickly garnered him fame and notoriety—painted silkscreen canvases and experimental films—echoed these mechanical, reproducible processes and distinguished Warhol from his pop art peers.

Warhol called his studio "the Factory," adopting the mainstream language of business for his counter-cultural cohort. He assembled a group of artists, musicians, misfit socialites, and "Superstars." The bohemians of this factory thrived on desire, sex, drugs, music, and fashion, and their unfettered experiences fed their collaborative creative production.[1] Warhol was the mechanical eye and ear that captured it all in films, photographs, and audio recordings.

In the midst of it all, Warhol employed his art director–like approach to manufacturing paintings. With his breakthrough Campbell's soup cans and Brillo boxes from 1962, Warhol had turned to silkscreening

**Marilyn Monroe (Marilyn)**, 1967. Screenprint, 36 x 36 in.

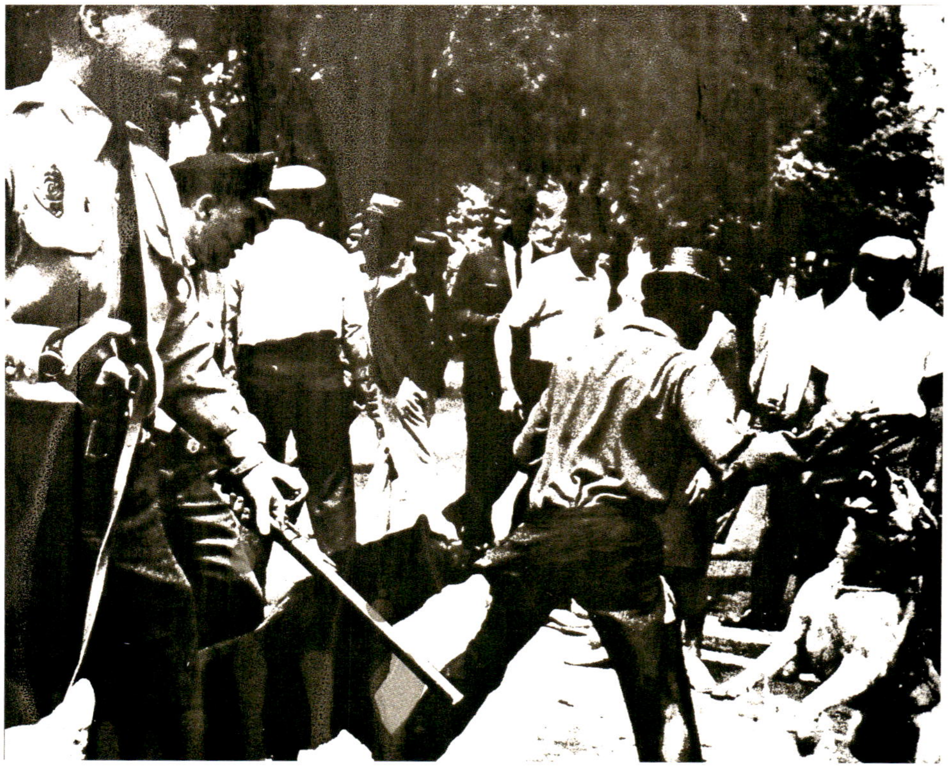

**Birmingham Race Riot**, 1964. Screenprint, 20 x 24 in.

designs instead of hand painting onto canvas. Silkscreen printing is a stencil process in which areas of a mesh screen are blocked with a glue or varnish. Ink is applied over the mesh with a squeegee, and the ink passes through the uncovered areas of the screen onto the support. In using a photograph to create the stencil, a printmaker first coats parts of the screen with photoreactive chemicals, then places a photographic transparency on top of the screen and exposes it to light to create the stencil.

Warhol's early successes with the silkscreen paintings brought him invitations to participate in print portfolios. Printmaking was undergoing a renaissance in the 1950s and 1960s as fine-art presses like Gemini G.E.L., ULAE, and Chiron Press grew in stature in the art world, providing artists with new creative outlets and the art market with new commodities. Warhol's working method at the Factory was already parallel to the relationship between the artist who generated the ideas for prints and the technicians who executed them. Silkscreen processes in particular provided Warhol a direct means to transfer existing imagery onto paper or canvas. Robert Rauschenberg also utilized this process to great extent, focusing on images as poetic elements within larger compositions. Warhol, on the other hand, preferred to take the media images at face value.

In 1964, the curator Sam Wagstaff Jr. of the Wadsworth Atheneum in Hartford, Connecticut, invited Warhol to participate in the portfolio project *Ten Works by Ten Painters*. Wagstaff's selection of artists represented his view of significant artistic tendencies of the day. The portfolio placed Stuart Davis, Ellsworth Kelly, Robert Motherwell, George Ortman, Larry Poons, Ad Reinhardt, and Frank Stella, most

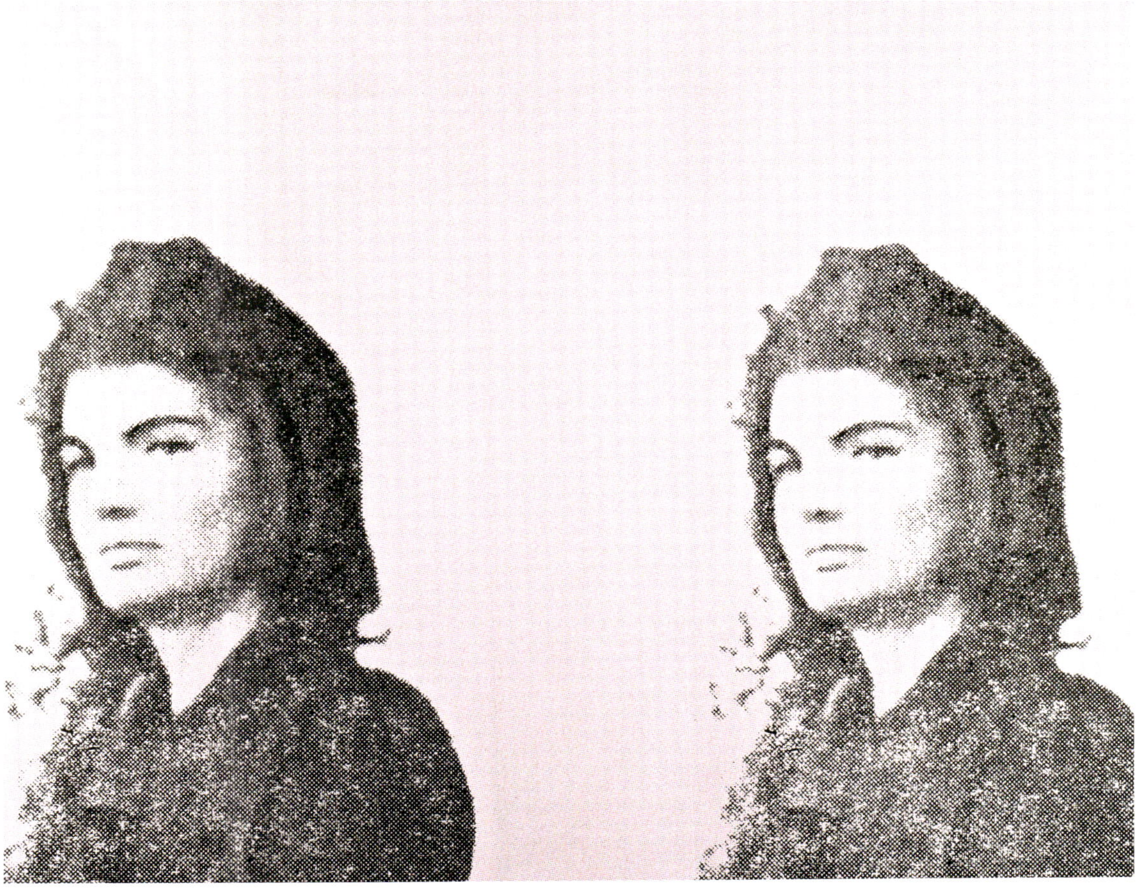

**Jacqueline Kennedy II (Jackie II)**, 1966. Screenprint, 24 x 30 in.

working in abstraction, alongside the pop artists Robert Indiana, Roy Lichtenstein, and Warhol. Warhol's contribution was markedly different from the others; he appropriated and reproduced a photograph by Charles Moore, published in *Life* magazine the year before, depicting police dogs attacking a black civil rights demonstrator in Birmingham, Alabama. *Birmingham Race Riot* (1964, opposite) thrust a timely and searing image circulated by popular media into a series of works conceived as distanced from everyday experience by virtue of their abstract compositions.

The choice to use Moore's photograph was consistent with Warhol's selection of disturbing media images at this time. Many depicted or signified death: grisly car accidents, an electric chair—even his iconic image of Marilyn Monroe can be seen as a death mask marking the actress's suicide in 1962. Prints based on journalistic images emphasize photography's ability to freeze action, to arrest a moment in time. Yet Warhol removes them from the context of the news report that establishes their meaning. He instead shifts the focus by cropping the source image of *Birmingham Race Riot* to isolate the violence and the crowd's aghast witness of it, or by removing traces of location or situation from *Jacqueline Kennedy I, II,* and *III* (above, and pp. 46, 47) to tell a tragic story through one riven, recognizable face. Warhol exploited "the preconceived image":[2] the prints reverse the sources' ephemeral essence—to be consumed, then discarded—by immortalizing a moment through selective art direction.

The three prints depicting Jackie Kennedy appeared in *11 Pop Artists*, a set of portfolios commissioned by the Philip Morris company for exhibitions in the United States and abroad. The three works together show the first lady in a progression from a young, glamorous wife at her husband's side to a widow isolated in her grief. The final print reveals a grid of images, a montage of news photographs that encapsulate the tragedy of John F. Kennedy's assassination. While other works in the portfolios depicted contemporary life through products and fashion, Warhol's prints were the only ones to reference events of the day. The political connotations stand out, as do the starker compositions based on the gray scale of the photographic source material. The organizer's intention to circulate the portfolio as an exhibition adds further dimension to Warhol's choice of a media image, plucked from its original circulation pattern and inserted into another one. Furthermore, the exhibition plan was a propaganda move designed by Ruder Finn, Philip Morris's public relations arm, with the help of the United States government to promote American culture in Europe and Latin America, important spheres of influence in the burgeoning Cold War era.[3] Warhol's selection of images that call up a troubling episode in recent American life and politics complicated the plan to spread a positive image of US culture abroad.

A common rhetoric associated with printmaking is its democratizing effect, as a populist counterbalance to the rarity of original works of art. Artists' publishing multiple prints equates to more viewers experiencing them in galleries and more collectors purchasing them. With his business acumen, Warhol recognized the economic advantage and set up his own publishing enterprise, Factory Additions, in 1966. That year, Warhol ironically proclaimed his retirement from painting with an exhibition at Leo Castelli Gallery featuring *Cow* wallpaper and *Silver Clouds*, an immersive environment created of prints and multiples. He aimed to devote himself to filmmaking, and Factory Additions enabled him to capitalize on his fame and raise money for his film production by publishing print versions of his most famous works. From 1967 to 1970, he released four portfolios—*Marilyn Monroe* (1967, pp. 38, 52–55), *Campbell's Soup I* (1968, pp. 82–83), *Campbell's Soup II* (1969, pp. 84–85) and *Flowers* (1970, pp. 77, 86–89)—sets of ten prints in large editions of 250 printed by a commercial outfit, Salvatore Silkscreen Co., Inc.

In tandem with the economic benefit of multiplicity, the Factory Additions prints furthered Warhol's engagement with the ubiquitous, serialized nature of media images that he first set out to explore in his paintings. With the rising influence of minimal art's value of standardized forms and machine-made materials and conceptual art's emphasis on ideas and systems, seriality as a format was well explored in the mid-1960s. While Warhol's new print projects made a strong impression through mechanical reproducibility, they counteracted the visually inert, duplicating forms of grids and other ordering structures propagated at the time.[4] Warhol's approach complicated the media's distribution of repeatable images as well, as he introduced high-tone visual variation into the sameness. For Warhol, desire for theatrical color (selected for his approval by his print publisher David Whitney) and utterly flat surfaces alter the source image in ways that enhance the visual impact of his prints. Instead of the rhythm of the same form repeated over and over, the variations in color and slippage in registration of the ten Marilyn prints, for example, push the composition toward dissonance when they are viewed together.

Flipping the internal logic of the systems of media image production reached a high point at the Factory, both in films and in the approach to printmaking of Factory Additions. The variations from print to print give life to the static images in ways that suggest temporality, like a set of film frames passing in sequence.[5] This action connects the prints to Warhol's experiments in films, especially *Sleep* (1963), *Empire* (1964), and *Screen Tests* (1964–66), which also attempt to alter perceptions of time, in the case of the films, by stilling the moving image.

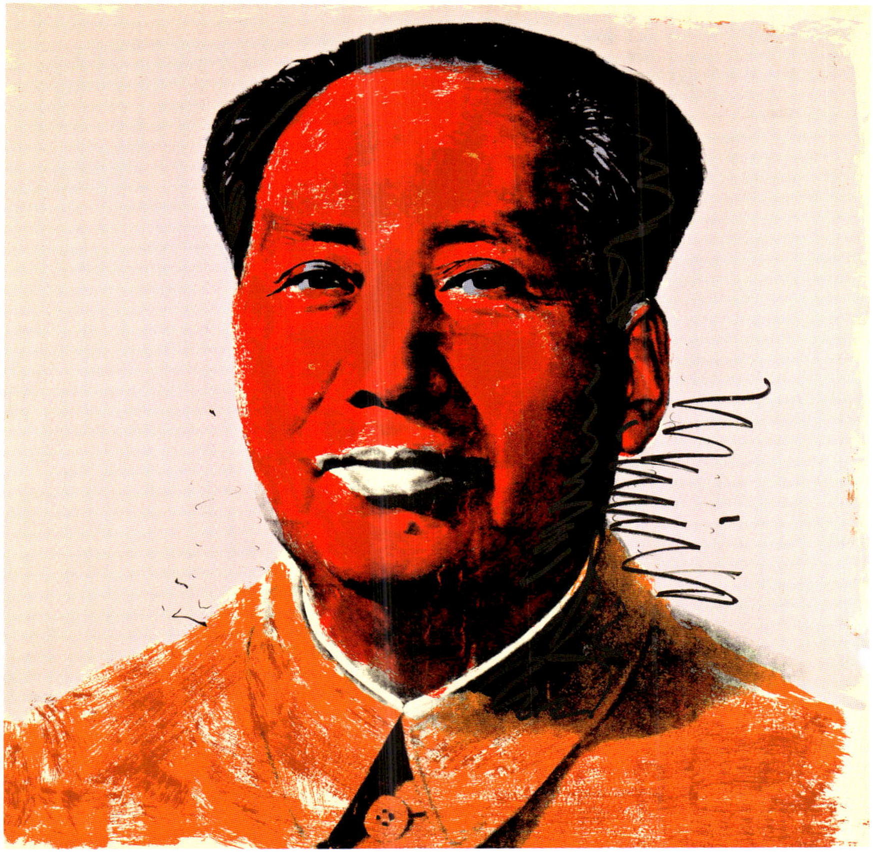 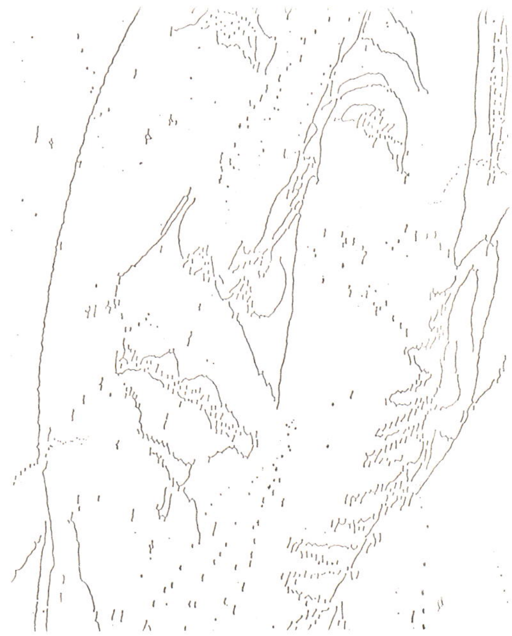

**Mao**, 1972. Screenprint, 36 x 36 in.
**Untitled**, 1973. Xerox print on typewriter paper, 11 x 8 ½ in.

On June 3, 1968, the radical feminist writer Valerie Solanas entered the Factory, shot Warhol and his associate Mario Amaya, and attempted to shoot Fred Hughes, Warhol's manager and business partner. Warhol nearly died as a result. His recovery was long and arduous, and it changed the course of his artistic production. Factory Additions continued during his convalescence, with projects progressing on two versions of the Campbell's soup cans (1969) and *Flowers* (1970). The source imagery for the *Flowers* paintings of 1966, on which the print series was based, was a photograph lifted from a 1964 issue of *Modern Photography*. The image's author, the photographer Patricia Caulfield, sued Warhol, eventually receiving royalties as part of the settlement. It wasn't the first time Warhol had been sued over copyrighted images; another case involved Charles Moore's Birmingham images from *Life* magazine.[6] Afterward, Warhol became more careful in securing the rights to reproduce existing imagery from printed media sources, but he shifted decisively toward using Polaroid photographs taken by him or his assistants.[7]

In 1972, President Richard Nixon traveled to China, the first US president to visit the People's Republic. That same year, Warhol decided to work with the perhaps most widely reproduced and circulated image at the time—the portrait of China's leader taken from his book *Quotations from Chairman Mao Tse-Tung*. Also known as the "Little Red Book," it was published and distributed across China from 1964 through 1976, the years of the Cultural Revolution. The US political attempts to normalize relations with the largest communist nation created an array of camera-ready media moments that Warhol could have reworked. Yet when asked about his use of the iconic portrait, Warhol evasively quipped, "I thought it would be fun to take on Mao as a fashion figure."[8]

Beginning with the *Mao* series (pp. 43, 61, 95–99), Warhol and his Factory worked on silkscreen prints and paintings more or less simultaneously—the lag between the painting projects and their print versions decreased sharply as he saw the potential for wider distribution and greater income. He also produced wallpaper with the same likeness of Mao; shown together in Paris in 1974, the paintings hung on a field of the same face, a multiplying army of Maos. To the bright colors and off-registration printing, Warhol reintroduced line drawing, interjecting the flourish of the artist's hand to the official portrait. This gesture carried on as the signature style for the commissioned portrait prints that dominated the last decade of his career.[9]

In this twelve-year span, Warhol executed two projects that exist only as prints: the 1968 portfolio *Flash—November 22, 1963* (pp. 65–70) and *Sunset* (1972, opposite and pp. 63, 100–101). The *Flash* portfolio covers the assassination of President John F. Kennedy through the media's words and images. Warhol created essentially a large illustrated book with compositions collaging news photos from television and print and campaign poster images tucked into paper folders printed with the Teletype reportage of the events in Dallas on that day. (See Richard H. Axsom's in-depth analysis of that work in this catalogue.)

*Sunset* is a series of 632 unique prints executed in an array of mesmerizing color variations that never repeat. The architect Philip Johnson commissioned the series in 1972 for the Hotel Marquette in Minneapolis, where 472 of the prints formed a wallpaper-like installation. The source image reportedly dates to 1966, when the de Menil family commissioned Warhol to make a film of a sunset to be projected in the Rothko Chapel in Houston. Along with the photographic media images he had long used, the instant imaging of Polaroids and televisual technology pushed Warhol's art in new directions from this point on. Warhol favored a square format for his prints; Polaroids, instant photos, and television sets all shared that shape. If the *Sunset* image was taken from a film, it must have been cropped to fit this format. As film stills, the multitude of sunsets freezes that single moment in time, repeating an ephemeral still point until it is beyond recognition as an exceptional event. In each print, the variation in the individual screenprinted colors resembles the visual noise of television static, lending confusion to the state of the frozen image—are we looking at the same moment broadcast through many consoles? The simple horizontal layers of the sunset image prefigure Warhol's exploration of abstraction that would come in the late seventies and eighties.

After *Sunset*, Warhol let go of seriality in favor of sequence, as if to abandon the attempt to insert temporality to the frozen time of still images. Subsequent work seems to embrace time's passage akin to the progression of images in moving pictures. He also recognized the greater marketability of portraiture and themed portfolio commissions and turned decisively toward the "Business Art" model that characterizes the last decade of his artistic production.

**Sunset**, 1972. Screenprint, 34 x 34 in.

Notes

1. Thierry de Duve, "Andy Warhol, or the Machine Perfected," trans. Rosalind Krauss, *October* 48 (Spring 1989): 3.

2. Gerard Malanga, "A Conversation with Andy Warhol," *Print Collector's Newsletter* 1, no. 6 (1971): 126.

3. Richard Maxwell, *Culture Works: The Political Economy of Culture* (Minneapolis: University of Minnesota Press, 2001), 31.

4. John Coplans, "Early Warhol," *Artforum* 8 (March 1970): 54.

5. Ibid., 59.

6. Laura Gilbert, "No Longer Appropriate?," *Art Newspaper* 235 (May 2012), http://old.theartnewspaper.com/articles/No-longer-appropriate/26378.

7. Patrick Smith, *Andy Warhol's Art and Films* (Ann Arbor, Michigan: UMI Research Press, 1986), 187.

8. Riva Castleman, *The Prints of Andy Warhol* (Paris: Flammarion, 1990), 21.

9. Donna De Salvo, "God Is in the Details: The Prints of Andy Warhol," in *Andy Warhol Prints: A Catalogue Raisonné 1962–1987* (New York: Distributed Art Publishers in conjunction with Ronald Feldman Fine Arts, Edition Schellman, and the Andy Warhol Foundation for the Visual Arts, 2003), 26.

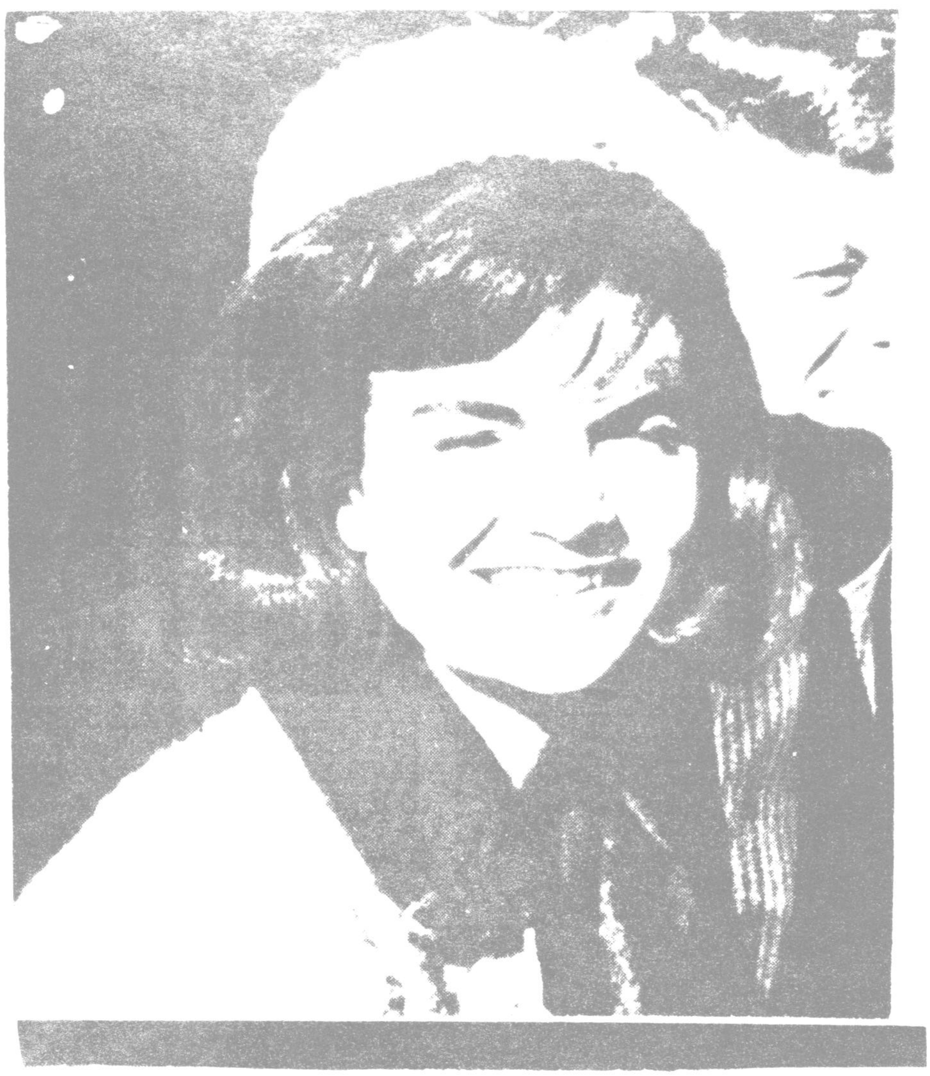

**Jacqueline Kennedy I (Jackie I)**, 1966. Screenprint, 24 x 20 in.

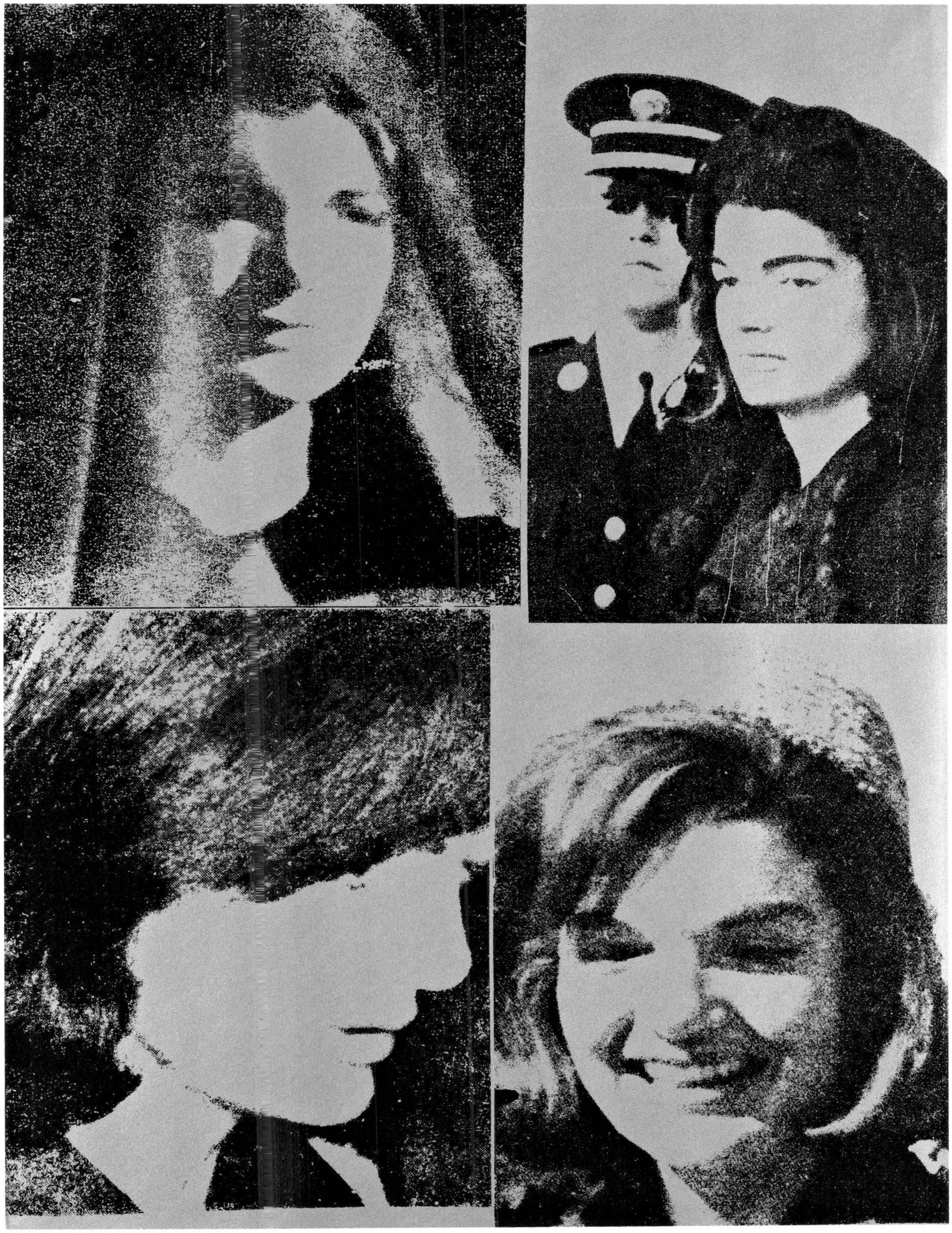

**Jacqueline Kennedy III (Jackie III)**, 1966. Screenprint, 40 x 30 in.

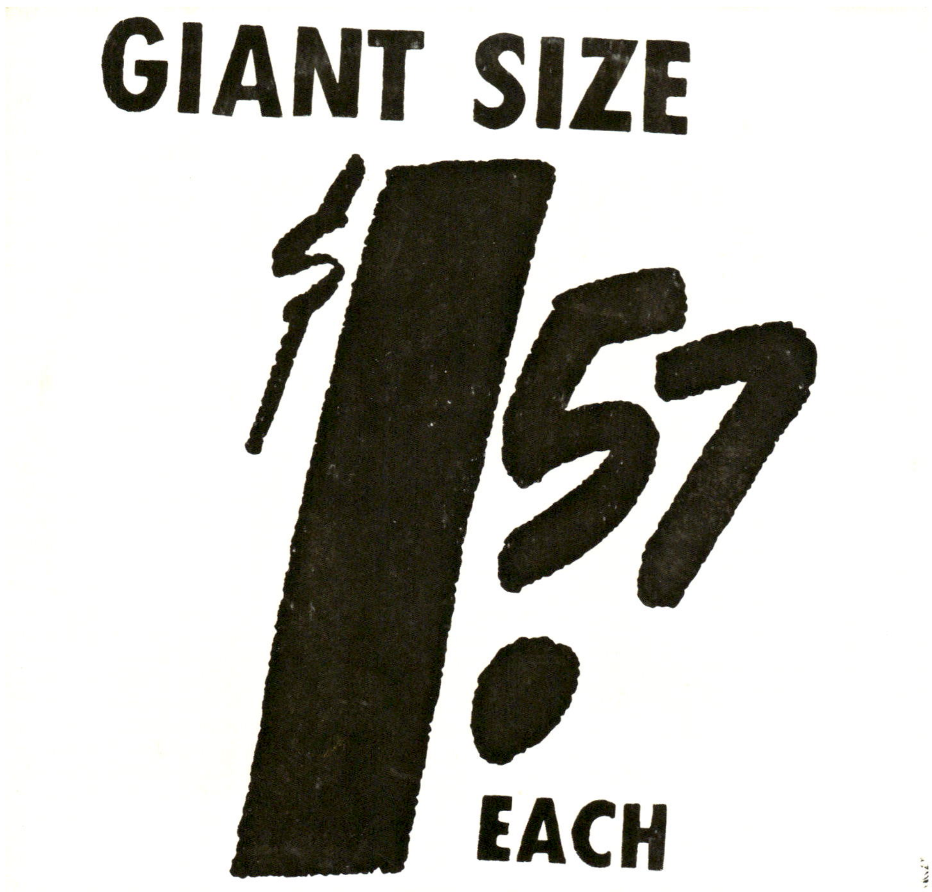


**$1.57 Giant Size**, 1963. Screenprint on coated record cover stock, 12¼ x 12¼ in.

**S&H Green Stamps**, 1965. Offset lithograph, 23 x 22¾ in.

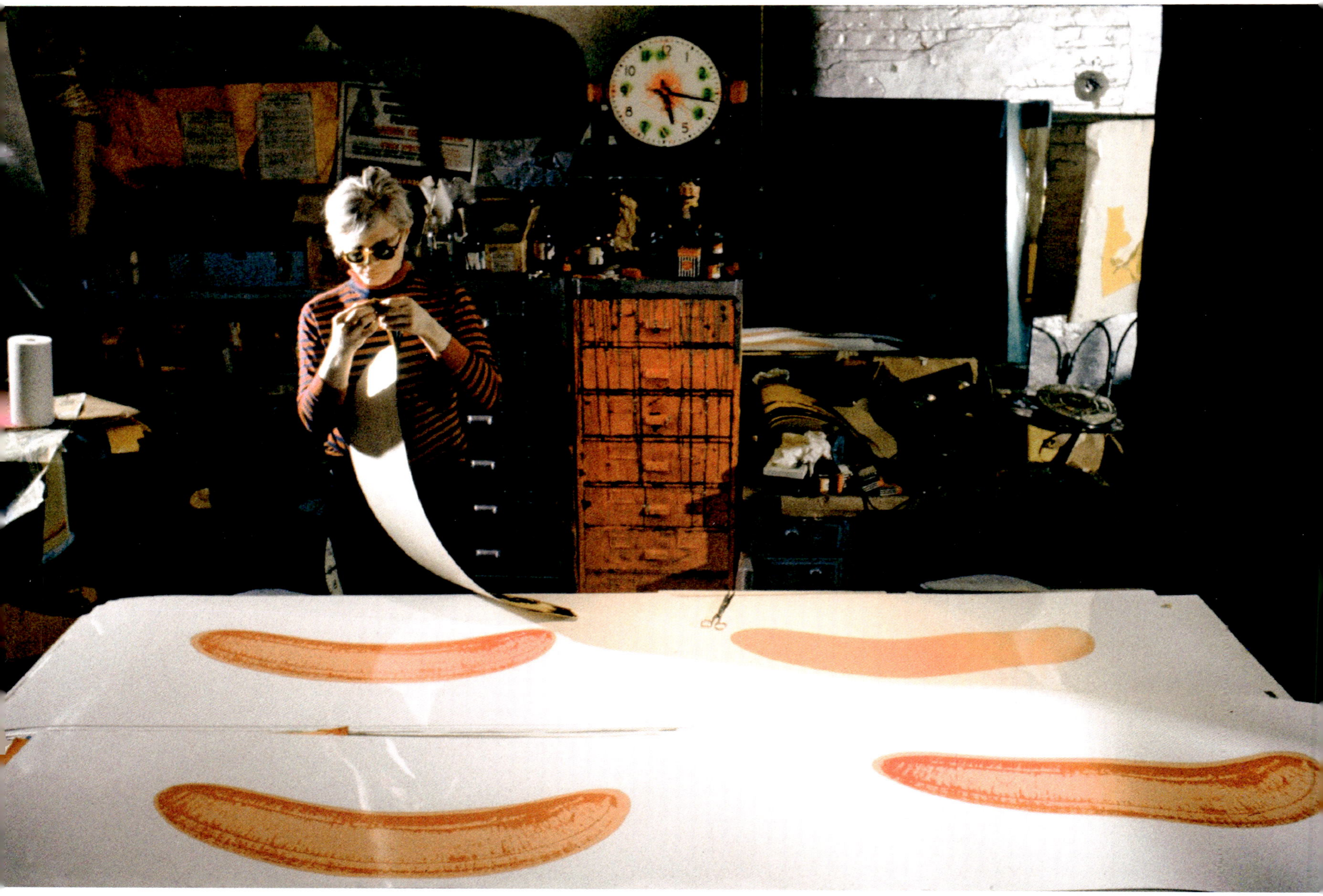

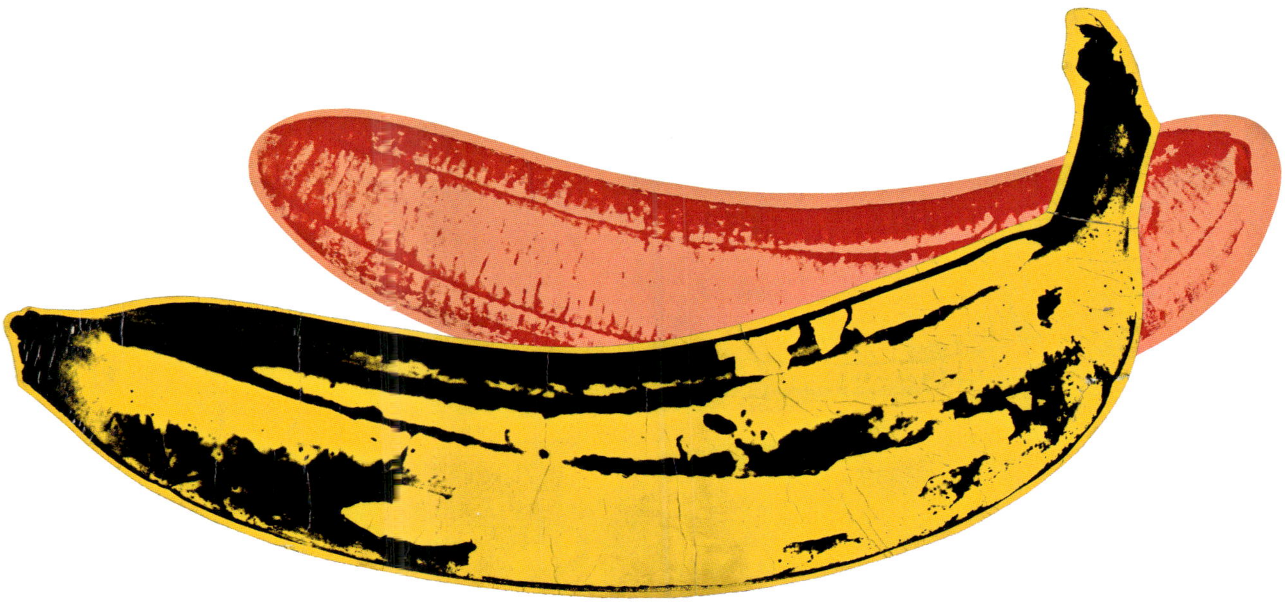

**Banana**, 1966. Two screenprints on styrene and laminated plastic, 24 x 53 ¼ in.

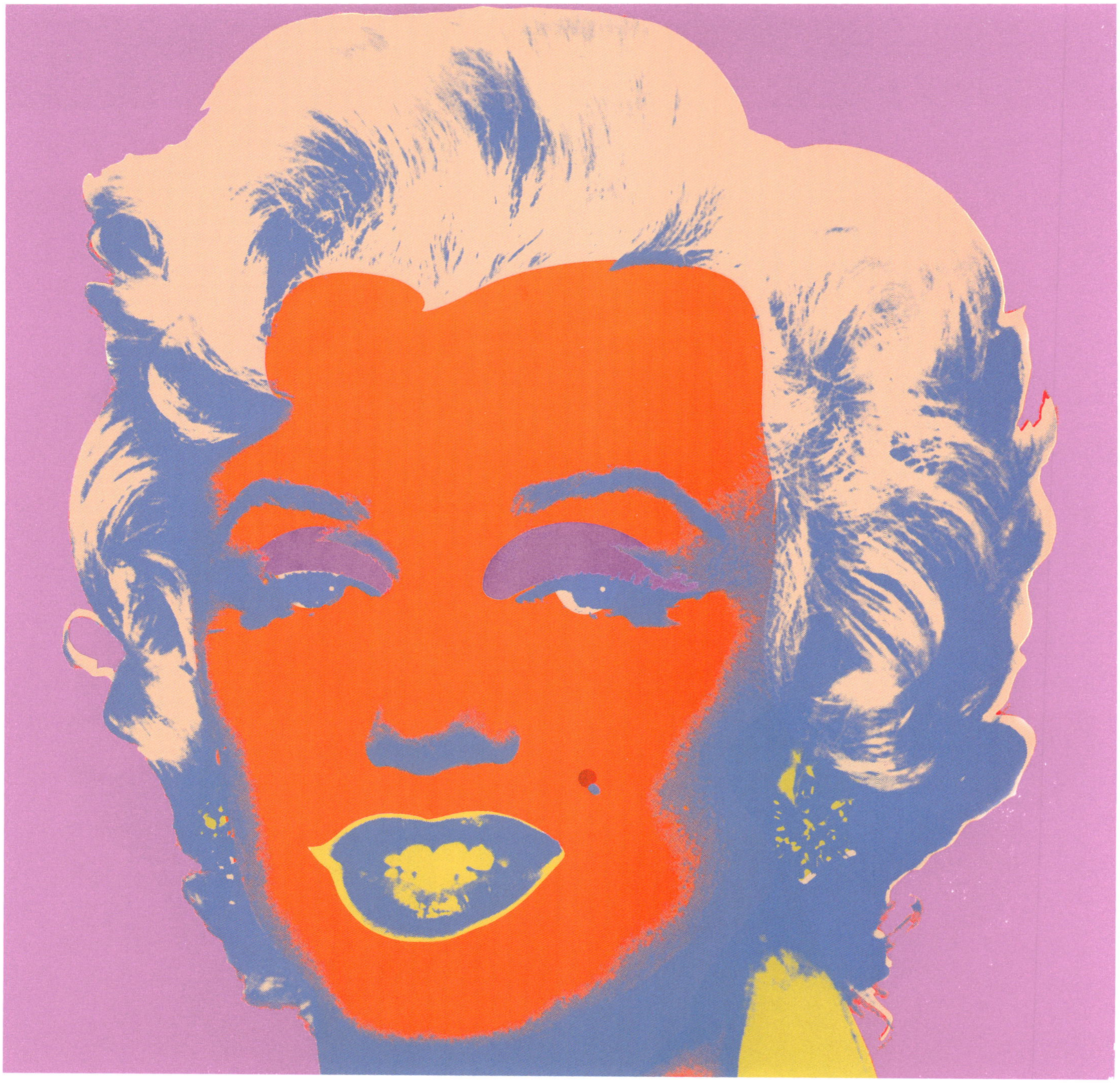

**Marilyn Monroe (Marilyn)**, 1967. Screenprints, 36 x 36 in.

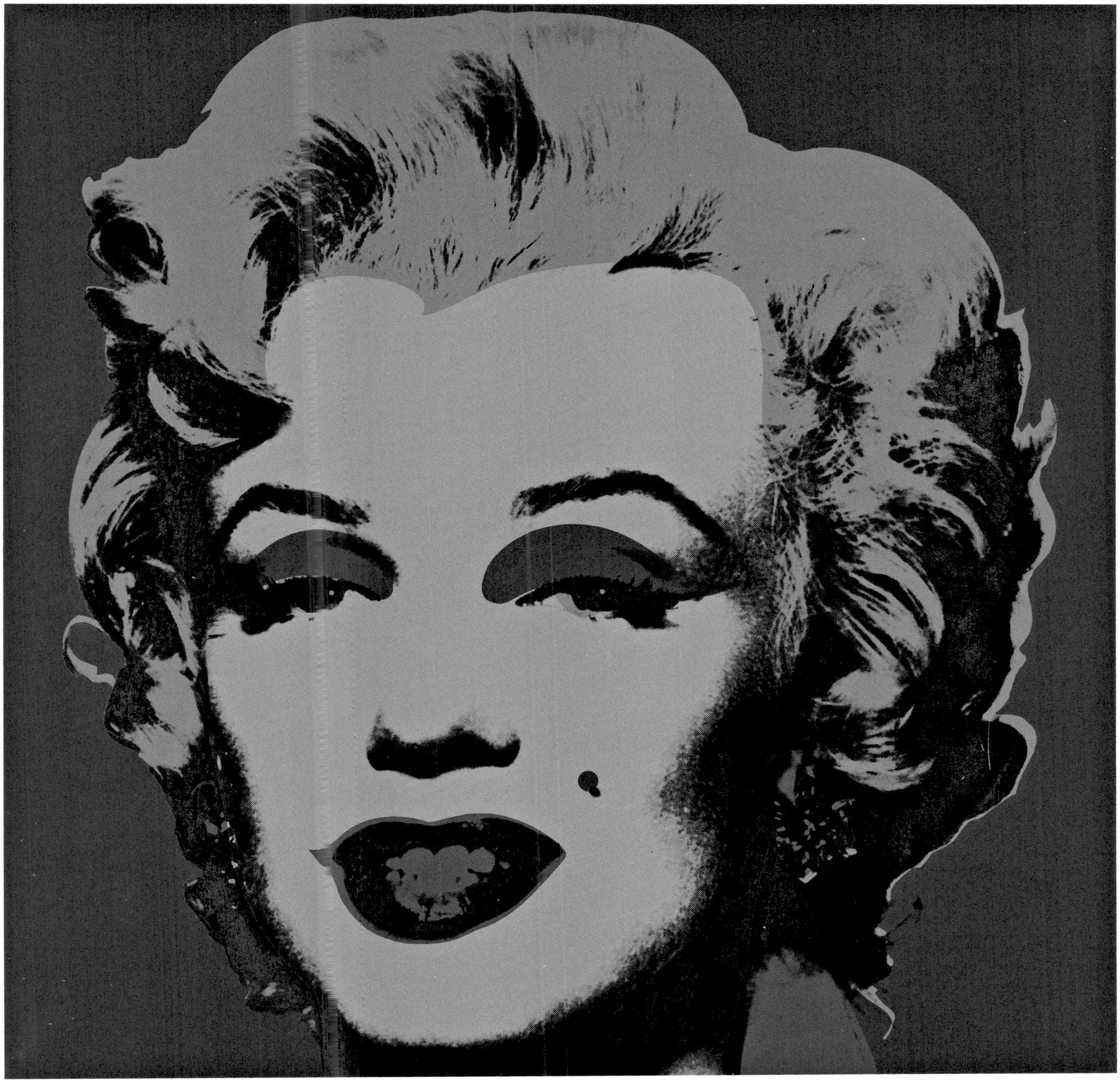

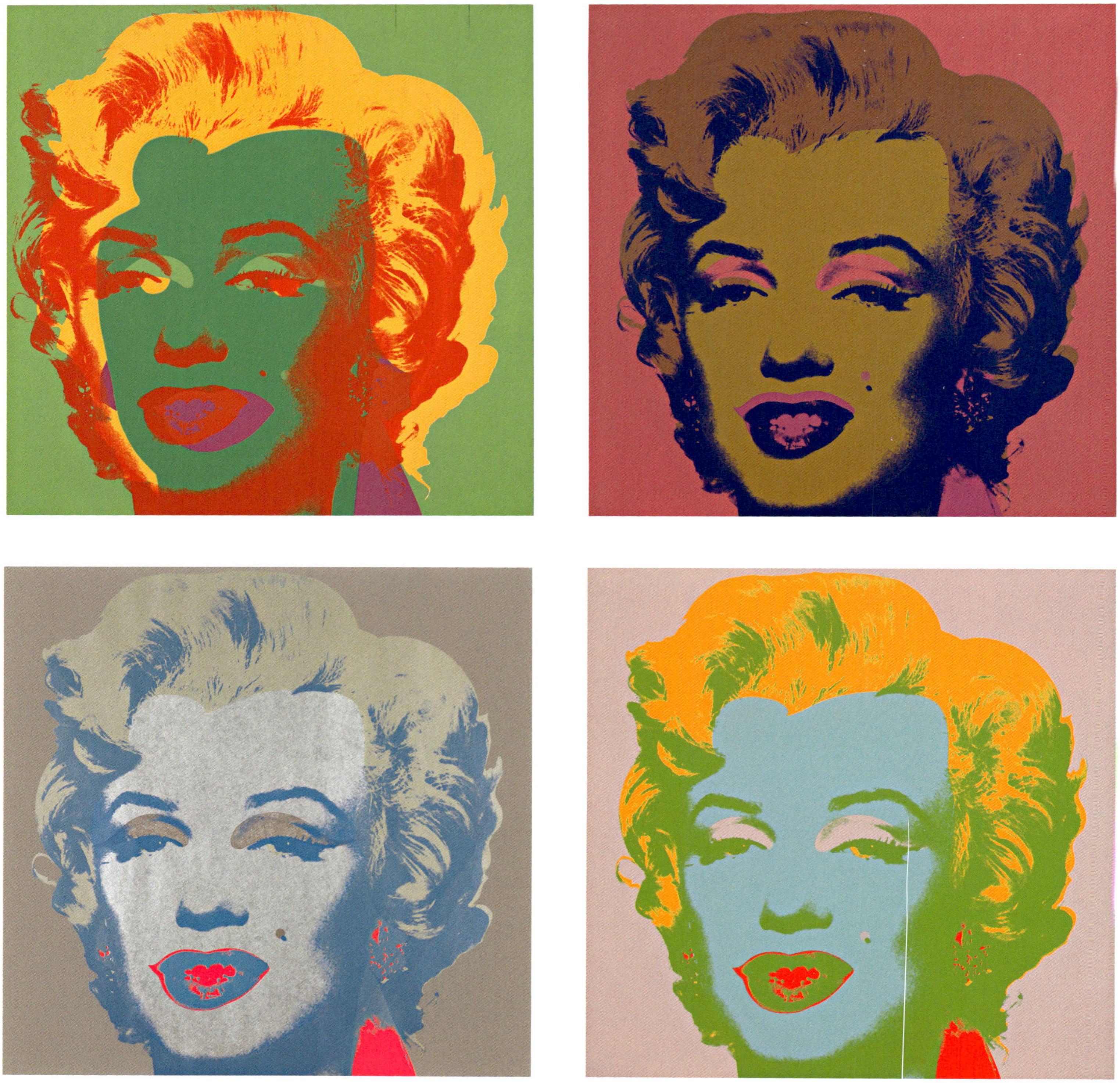

**Marilyn Monroe (Marilyn)**, 1967. Screenprints, each 36 x 36 in.

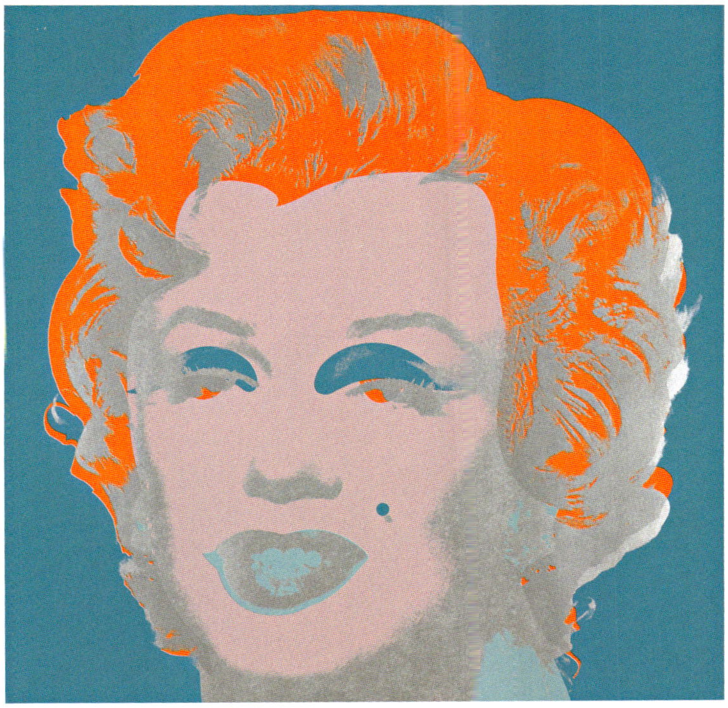

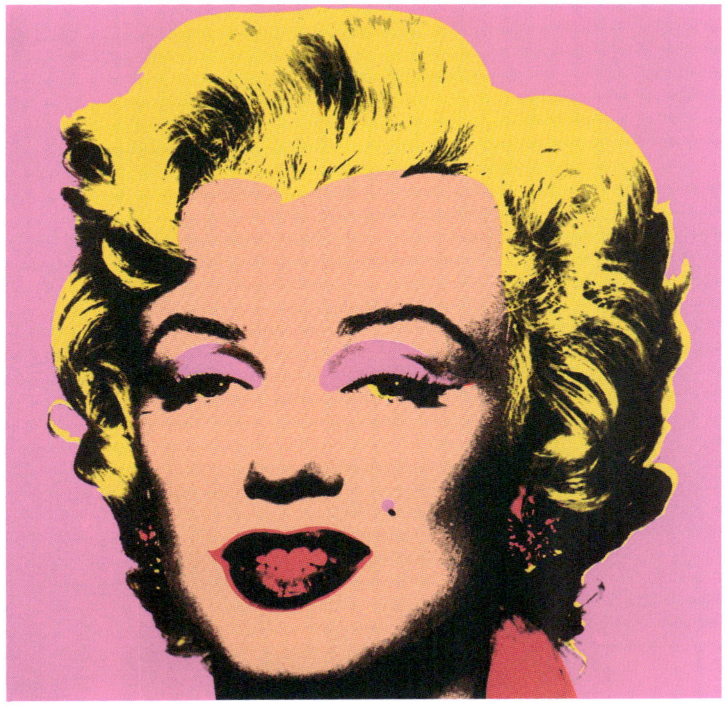

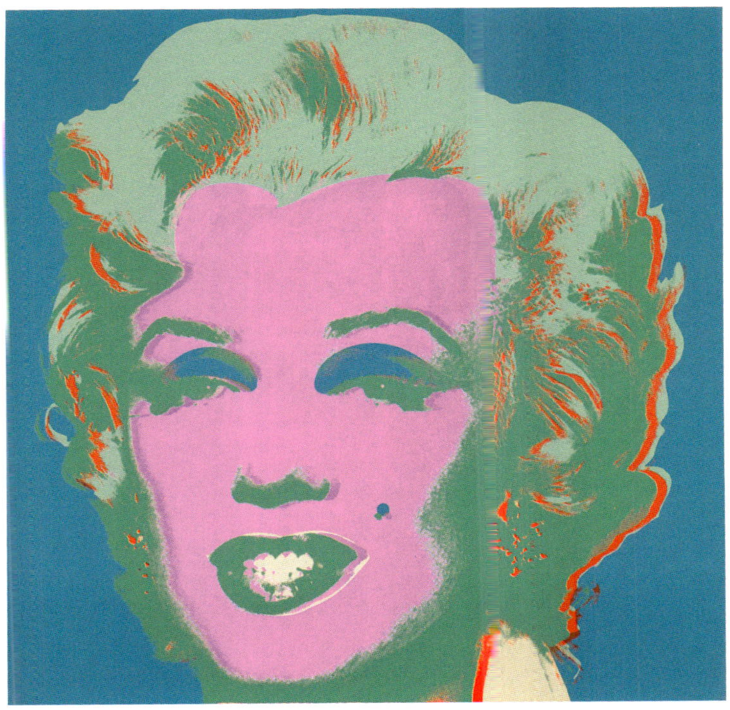

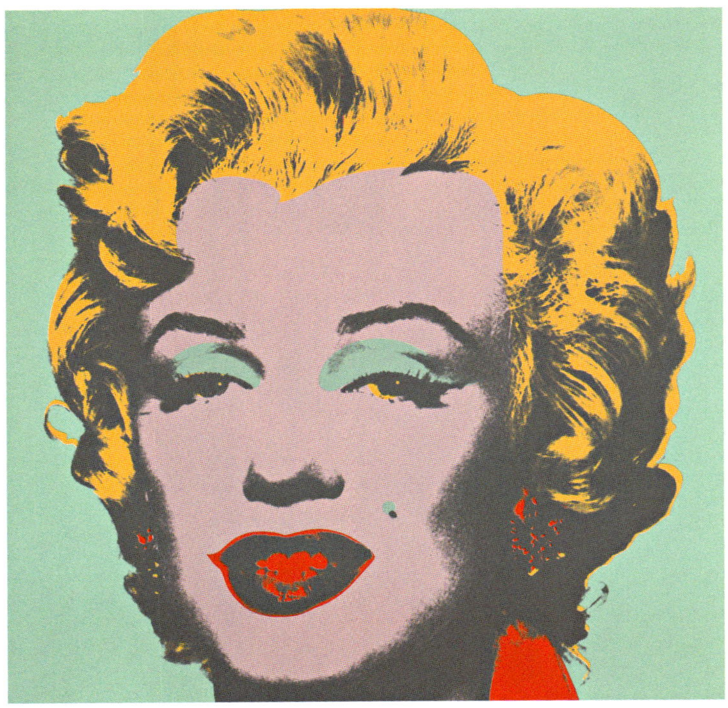

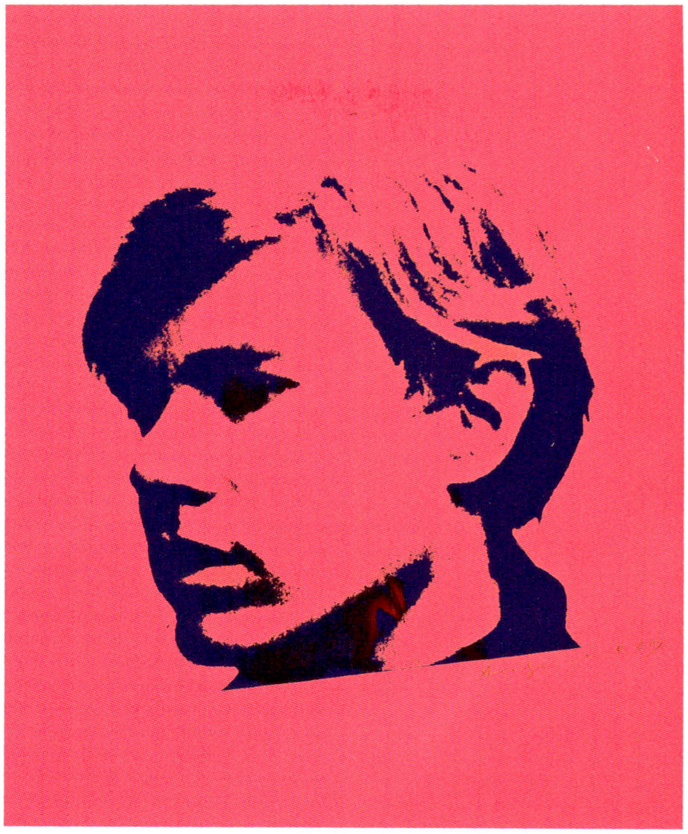

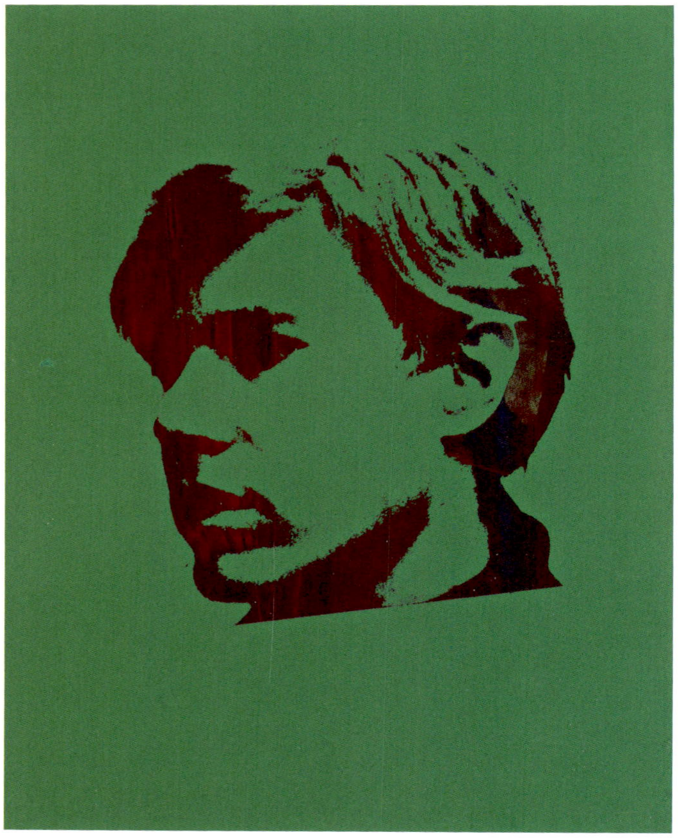

**Self-Portrait**, 1967. Screenprint, $19\frac{7}{8}$ x $12\frac{7}{8}$ in.

**Self-Portrait**, 1967. Screenprint, 18 x $11\frac{3}{4}$ in.

(opposite) **Flash—November 22, 1963**, front cover, 1968. Screenprint on cloth mounted on cardboard, $22\frac{1}{2}$ x $22\frac{3}{8}$ in.

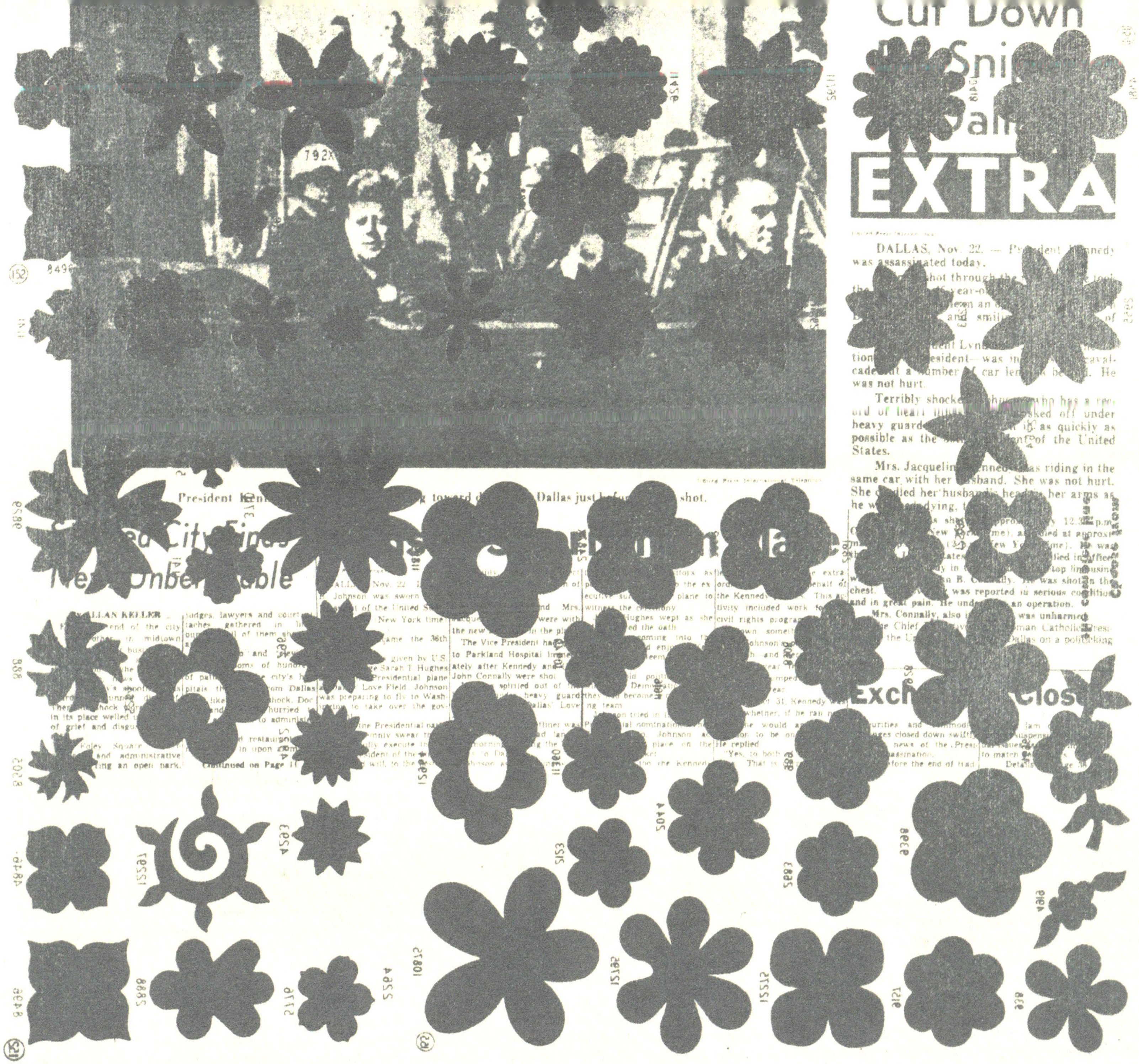
EXTRA
DALLAS, Nov. 22. — President Kennedy was assassinated today.
was not hurt.
States.
Exch
Continued on Page 11

# Lament for a Dead President: Andy Warhol's *Flash—November 22, 1963*

**RICHARD H. AXSOM**

An idiosyncratic and deeply personal response to the assassination of President John F. Kennedy, *Flash—November 22, 1963* is one of Andy Warhol's most important and ambitious print series.[1] Relatively unknown and not as widely published or exhibited as other of the artist's print series, the *Flash* portfolio assumes a unique place in Warhol's art as a narrative work and in his editioned print oeuvre as an artist's book.[2] Published in 1968 by Racolin Press, Inc., of Briarcliff, New York, it consists of eleven screenprints placed in separate paper folders with Teletype reports of the assassination and its aftermath screenprinted on them (pp. 65–70). Phillip Greer, a poet and a friend of Warhol's, selected and sequenced texts from the Associated Press to replicate newswire copy in Teletype style.[3] The folders are held as "pages" between hinged cardboard covers mounted with cloth, overprinted front and back with light to dark silver inks. Conceived as a deluxe artist's book, itself contained in a clear acetate slipcase, Warhol's *Flash* portfolio is

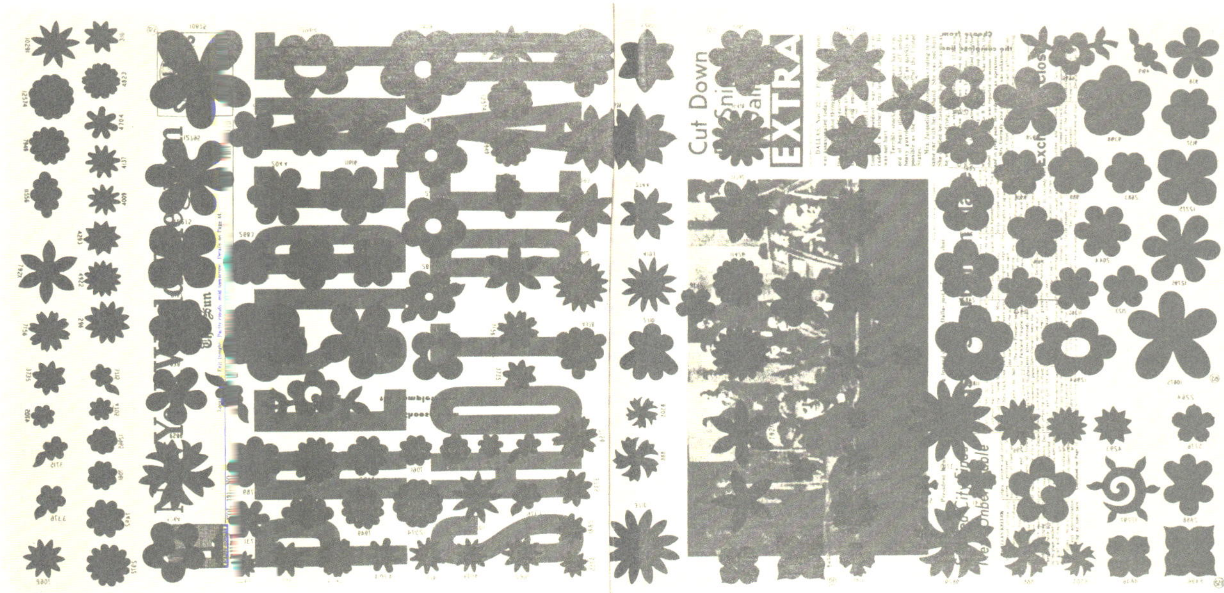

FIRST DAY -- 11/22/63

FIRST LEAD KENNEDY
DALLAS, NOV. 22 -- PRESIDENT AND MRS. KENNEDY ARRIVEDX HERE
TODAY IN THE SECOND DAY OF THEIR SWING THROUGH TEXAS.
FOLLOWING TUMULTUOUS RECEPTION IN SAN ANTONIO, HOUSTON AND
FORT WORTH YESTERDAY, THE PRESIDENT WAS XXXX SCHEDULED TO SPEAK
TODAY TO A DEMOCRATIC LUNCHEON, AFTER A MOTORCADE TO THE DALLAS
TRADE MART.
THOUSANDS OF TEXANS XXXXX RIMMED THE LANDING AREA AT LOVE FIELD
AS THE PRESIDENT'S PLANE, AIR FORCE ONE, TOUCHED DOWN AT 11:37 A.M.(CST).
EDL152ACS

FLASH
DALLAS -- SHOTS AT KENNEDY MOTORCADE.
CJ1235PCS

BULLETIN -- PRECEDE KENNEDY
DALLAS, NOV. 22 -- THREE SHOTS WERE FIRED AT PRESIDENT KENNEDY'S
MOTORCADE IN DOWNTOWN DALLAS TODAY. XXXXXXXX THE PRESIDENT'S CAR.
WITH MRS. KENNEDY AND GOV. AND MRS. JOHN B. CONNALLY, JR., SPED
OFF IMMEDIATELY IT WAS UNCLEAR WHETHER THERE WERE ANY CASUALTIES.XXXX
XXXXXXXXXXXXXXXXX
CJ1236PCS

BULLETIN -- 1ST ADD SHOTS
XXXXXX THE SHOTS RANG OUT AS THE PRESIDENT'S CAR WAS APPROACHING
AN OVERPASS EN ROUTE TO THE TRADE MART, WHERE HE WAS TO DELIVER A
SPEECH. THEY APPEARED TO COME FROM BEHIND THE MOTORCADE. (PICKUP
1ST LEAD.....FOLLOWING TUMULTUOUS XXXX TO END)

**Flash—November 22, 1963**, cover, 1968. Screenprint on cloth mounted on cardboard, 22 ½ x 44 ¾ in.

**Folder with Teletype text**, 1968. Screenprint on paper, 21 ½ x 21 ¼ in.

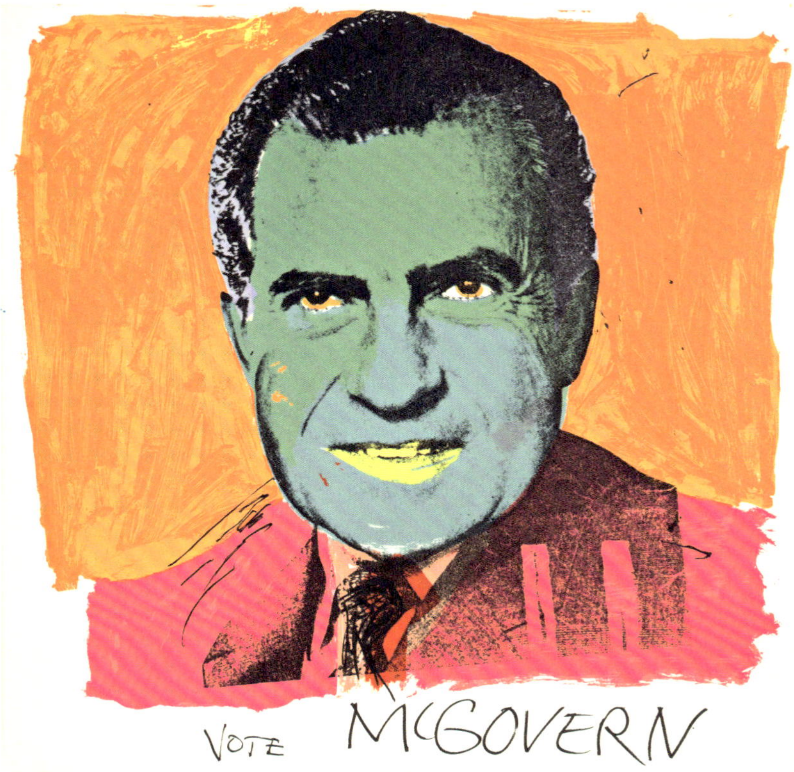


**Vote McGovern**, 1972. Screenprint, irregular composition; 41 5/16 x 41 1/8 in. (105 x 104.4 cm); sheet: 42 x 41 5/16 in. (106.7 x 106.6 cm). Museum of Modern Art, Gift of Philip Johnson. (415.1973) © The Andy Warhol Foundation for the Visual Arts/ARS, NY
Photo credit: © The Museum of Modern Art/Licensed by SCALA/Art Resource, NY

unique in its presentation among the artist's other print series, whose paper or cardboard containers are nondescript. The nature of the project as a book also accounts for the smaller sheet size of the prints—20 7/8 x 20 7/8 inches—in contrast to the large scale of the major print series, which would have been an unwieldy choice.[3]

In addition to Warhol's great themes of consumer society, celebrity, and mortality—visualized with compelling subjects, vibrant color, and seductive design—a political dimension courses through his paintings and prints that is equally significant.[4] There are portraits of world political figures that include American presidents, presidential candidates, communist dictators, and an English queen. The artist's *Vote McGovern*, an editioned screenprint, is a classic poster in American political history (1972, above). Warhol replaced the face of George McGovern with that of Richard Nixon, McGovern's opponent in the 1972 presidential race. Set against a harsh orange background, it is colored bilious green and deathly blue—the face of Satan itself.

Outside of the political portraits, other types of subjects carry political commentary, which as treated by Warhol can be wrenching and disturbing. This body of the artist's political works is never overtly polemical—it is always nuanced, distanced, yet powerful. For *Birmingham Race Riot* (1964, p. 40), Warhol took an infamous photograph that had appeared in *Life* magazine and polarized its blacks and white into an agonizing racial metaphor. Political themes are also sustained in a series of major portfolios that include *Electric Chair* (1971, pp. 62, 90–93), *Mao* (1972, opposite and pp. 43, 95–99), and *Sunset* (1972, pp. 45, 63, 100–101), and later, *Endangered Species* (1983, pp. 6, 162–67).[5] The *Sunset* prints, in particular,

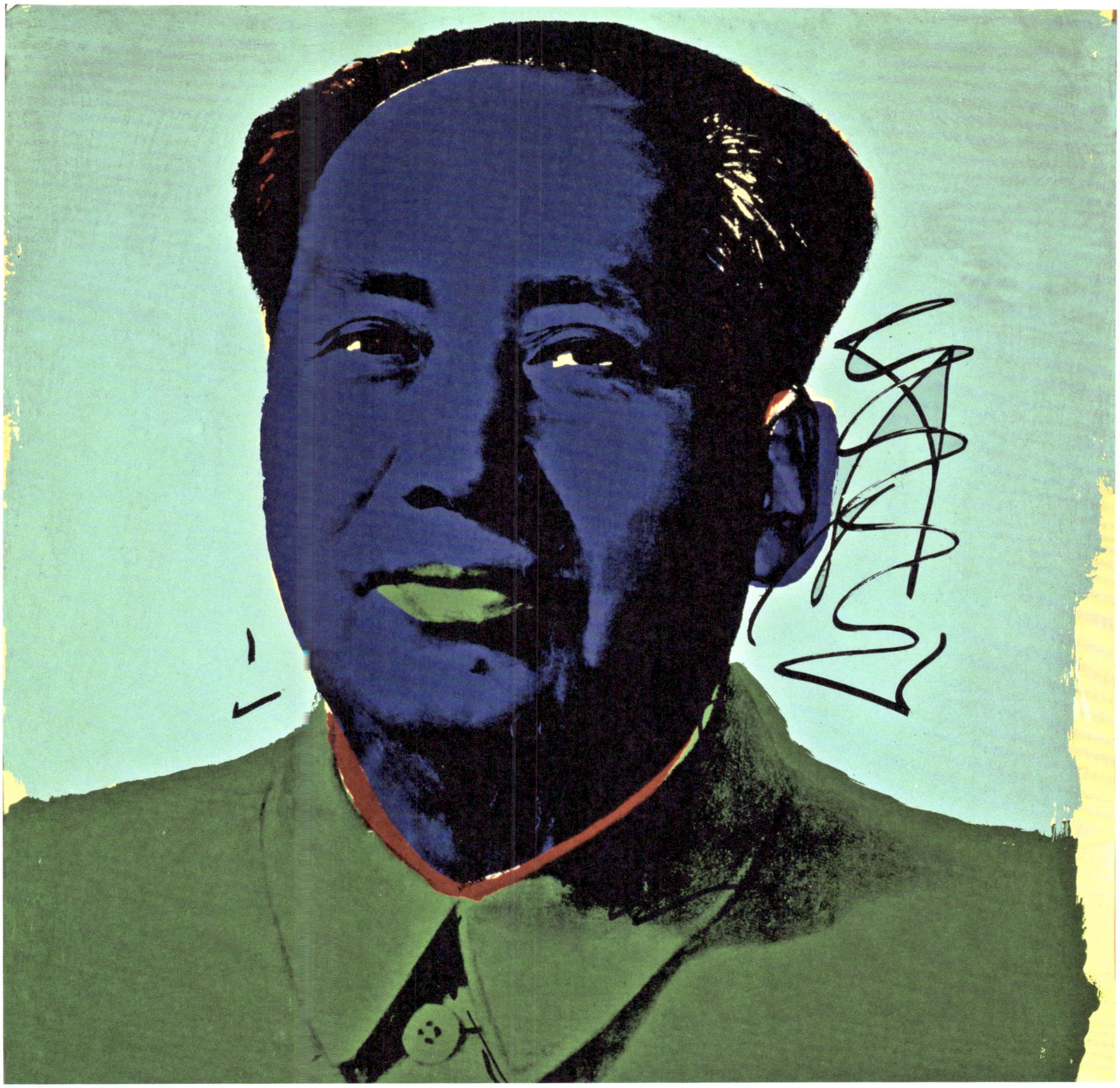

**Mao**, 1972. Screenprint, 36 x 36 in.

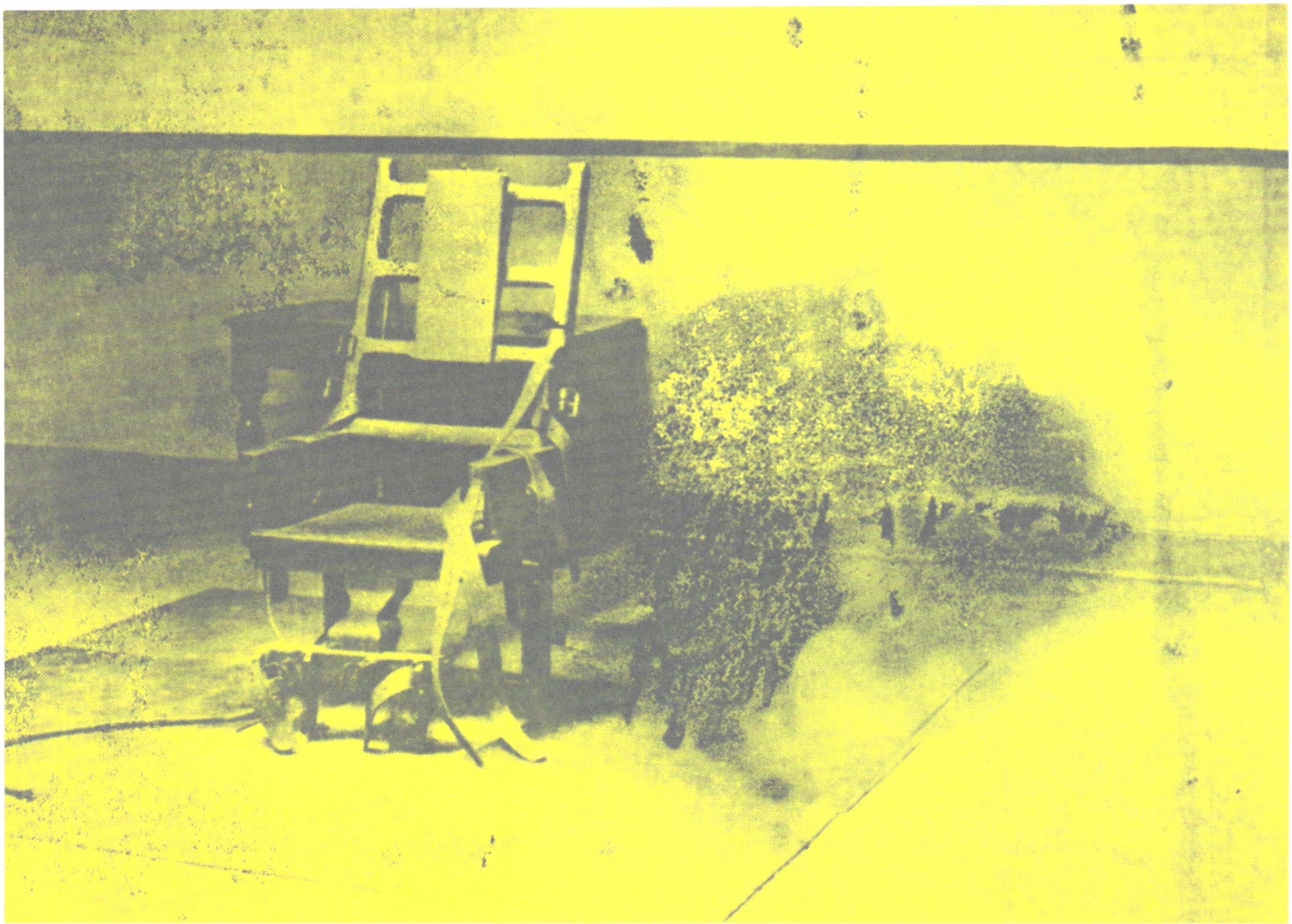

**Electric Chair**, 1971. Screenprint, 35 ½ x 48 in.

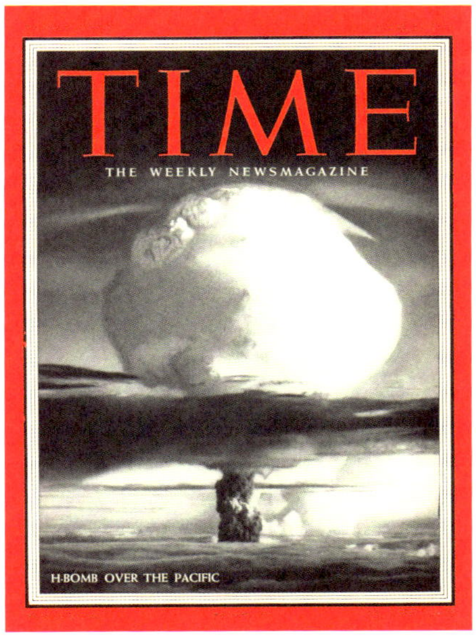


**Sunset**, 1972. Screenprint, 34 x 34 in.
**H-Bomb over the Pacific**, *TIME* magazine, cover, April 12, 1954

are disconcerting in their camouflaged meanings. On the one hand, they are scenic images of a single setting sun, printed in an edition of 632 uniquely colored screenprints that was commissioned for a luxury hotel in Minneapolis. On the other hand, though never advertised as such, they also suggest hydrogen bomb blasts, linked in imagery to the abundant photographs of nuclear tests in the South Pacific that began to be published in the popular media in the early 1950s (see above right). Each detonation was given a name. One particular explosion occurred over Christmas Island in 1962. A bright, truncated disk appeared in a dark sky, seen against unnatural-looking bands of clouds. The name of that test was *Sunset*.[6] Warhol's series is a subversive critique of American privilege and complacency—masquerading as sofa art. Everything is not so simple. This remains the case for the *Flash* portfolio.

Original source material for the eleven screenprints in *Flash* was drawn from popular media that included a campaign poster, an advertisement, televised images, and photographs taken from newspapers and magazines.[7] Much of the imagery carries a televised quality that cues how most Americans witnessed the national trauma—though they would have viewed it in black and white, not Warhol's glaring color. Flickering, grainy images and scan lines further the link in the prints. The Kennedy assassination was the first major news story tracked primarily on television as events unfolded, almost immediately in live coverage.

Until 1974, Warhol's print series, with the exception of *Flash*, consisted of a single image—Marilyn Monroe, Campbell's soup cans, hibiscus flowers, an electric chair, a sunset, and Mao Tse-tung, repeated and serialized usually in ten color variations. In *Flash*, however, there are no repeated frames. Each is a distinct

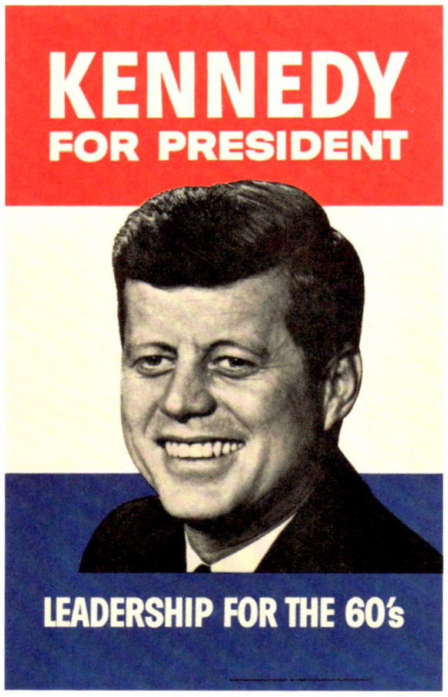


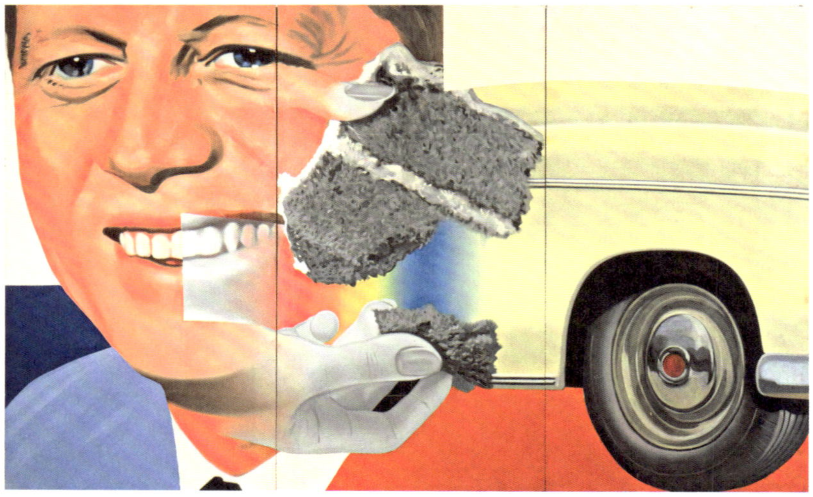

**Kennedy for President** (campaign poster), designed by Donald Wilson, 1960. Lithograph, 41 x 28 in.

James Rosenquist, **President Elect**, 1960–61. Oil on Masonite, 89¾ x 144 in. (228 x 366 cm). Musée National d'Art Moderne, Centre Georges Pompidou, Paris, France, Inv. AM1976-1014. © James Rosenquist/Licensed by VAGA, New York, NY
Photo credit: © CNAC/MNAM/Dist. RMN-Grand Palais

cell in its own right. There is one image, though, that is serialized eight times in five of the eleven prints. It is a close-up of President Kennedy's face, in various scales and color treatments, drawn from a ubiquitous poster from the 1960 presidential campaign (above left). On the poster, a black-and-white photograph of a smiling Senator Kennedy rests on a tricolored banner of red, white, and blue: "Kennedy for President" appears in block capitals above and "Leadership for the 60's" below. It is the same portrait of Kennedy that appears in James Rosenquist's *President Elect* (1960–61, above right), a celebratory tribute to the beginning of Kennedy's journey to the presidency.[8]

The layered meanings of Warhol's imagery lie, of course, in the artist's alterations of his appropriated photographic, filmic, and televised source materials. There is a broad range of manipulations that includes disconnections of imagery: close-ups, croppings, abrupt variations in scale, discordant juxtapositions of image, reversals, superimpositions, montages, distortions, negative photographic imagery, blurred imagery, strong blacks and whites, and bold color.

Color, which can be searing and disconcerting, is primarily monochrome in nine of the prints, with paired colors in two others. It is so saturate and intense that it can overpower the photographic imagery. From a relatively short viewing distance, all content disappears into a sequence of mostly abstract color squares, Warhol's analogue for how the media can block out meaning in its repeated exposure of events and barrages of information.

*continued on page 71*

**The sequence of prints in the portfolio tells the Kennedy story in a nonlinear progression. Time and place are disjunctive from the summer of 1960 to the events of November 22, 23, 24, and 25, 1963. Following is a brief synopsis of the eleven prints.**

(pages 65–70) **Flash—November 22, 1963**, 1968. Screenprints, each 20⅞ x 20⅞ in.

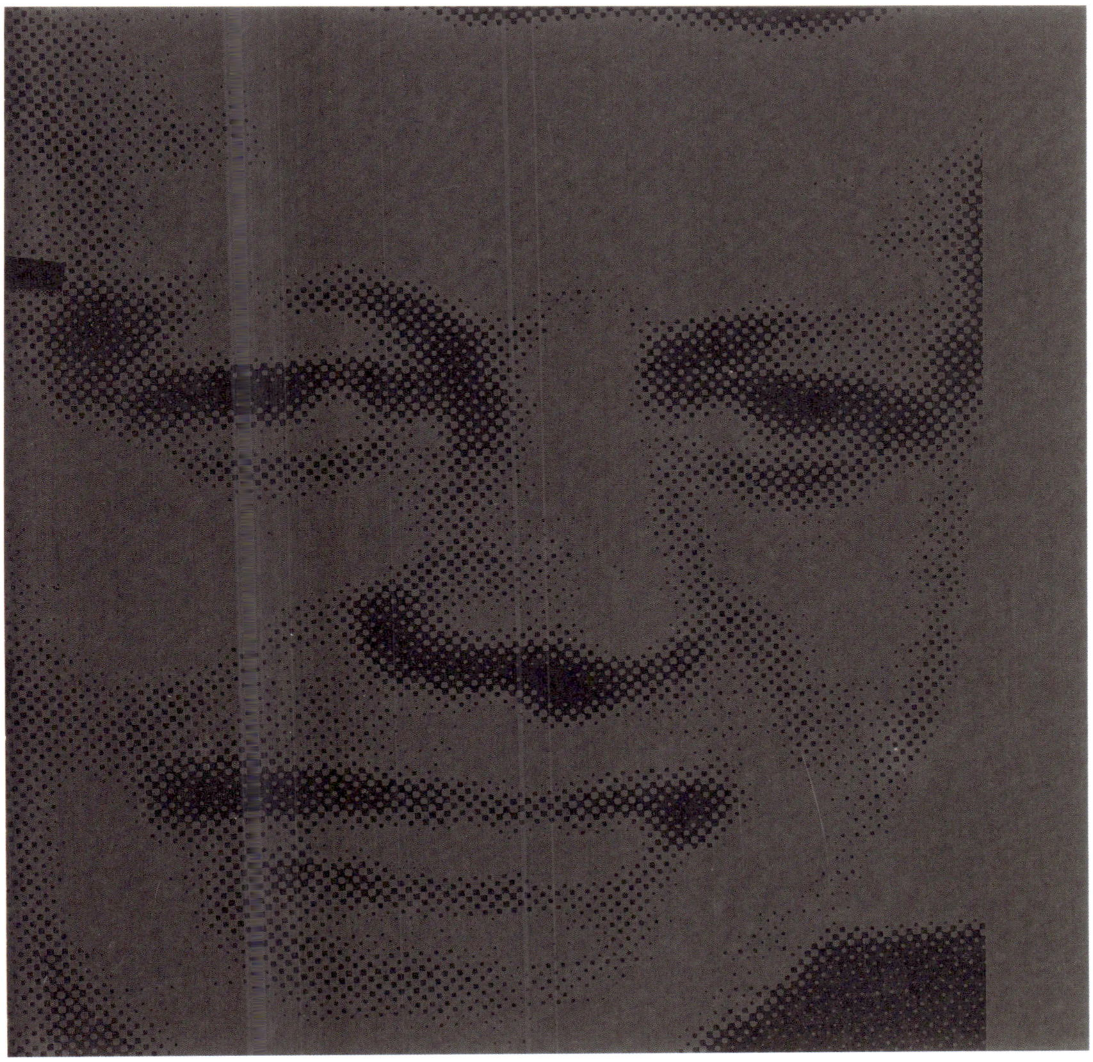

**An extreme close-up in black monochrome of Senator Kennedy's face. The visibility of halftones indicates a photographic image as the source.**

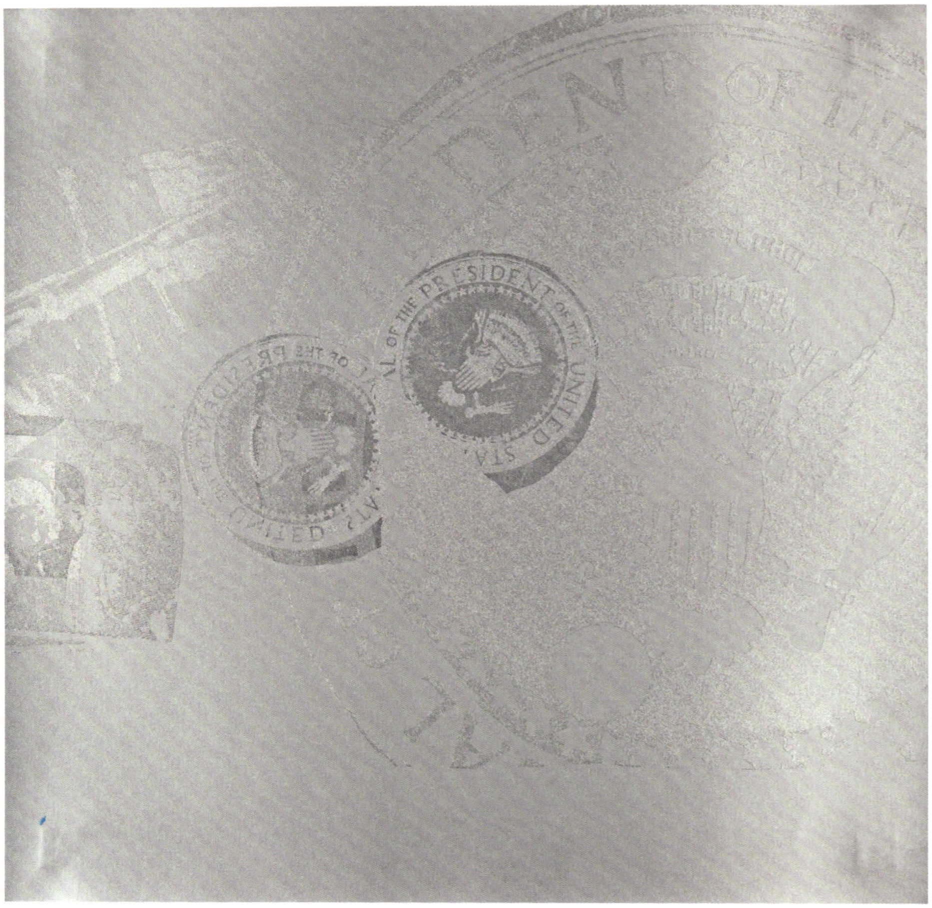

A cropped close-up of the Seal of the President of the United States in silver-gray monochrome, with two superimposed smaller images of the same seal. The three circular seals echo three smaller dark gray discs that suggest bullet holes shot through the larger seal. To the left of the two seals is an iconic photograph of Jacqueline Kennedy, beside President Kennedy, smiling to cameras from the open limousine of the presidential motor-cade moments before the assassination.

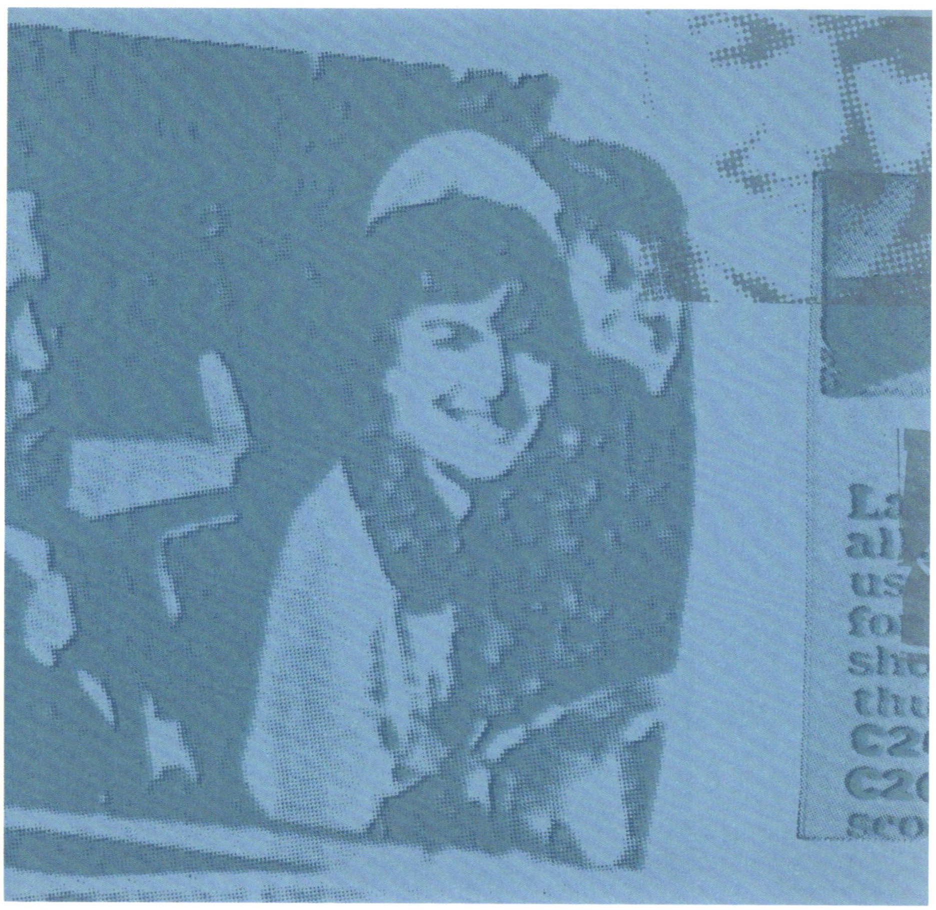

Full sheet in blue of the same photograph of the first lady in the open limousine.[9]

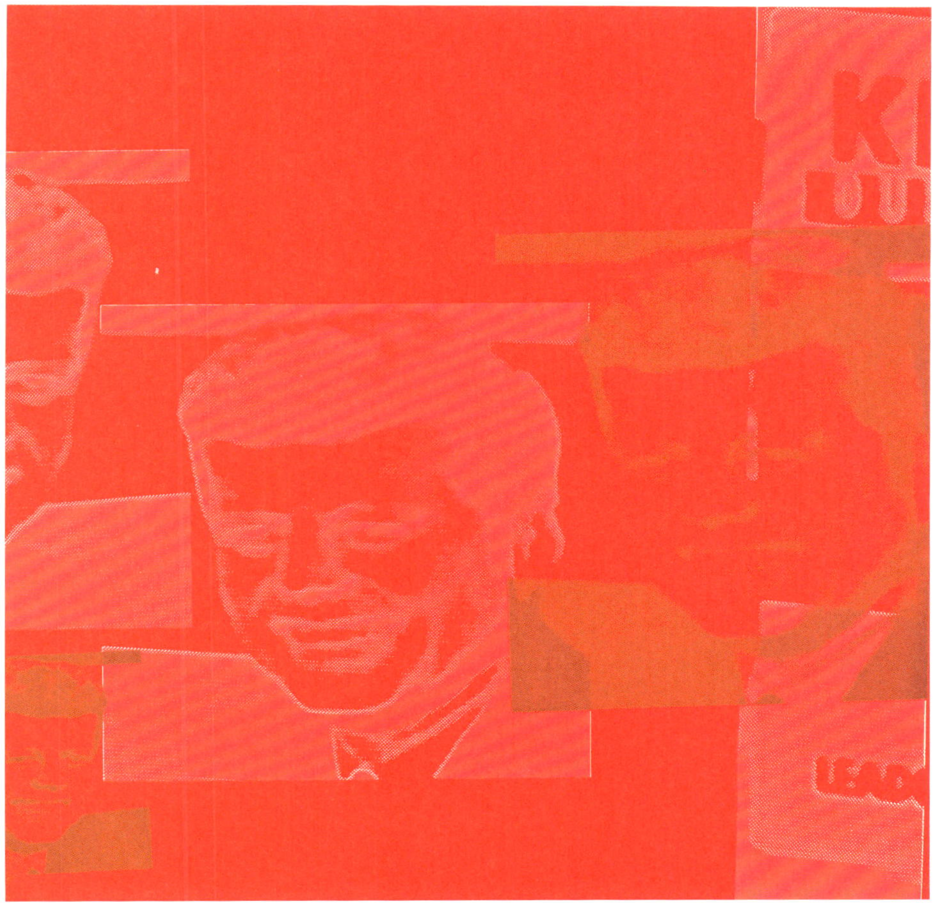

**Two photographic negative images of the Kennedy face from the 1960 campaign poster printed in monochrome red.**

**Printed in magenta ink, a photograph of Lee Harvey Oswald, moments before Jack Ruby shot him dead. A film clapboard, with unfilled fields for scene, take, sound, director, and date, is superimposed.**

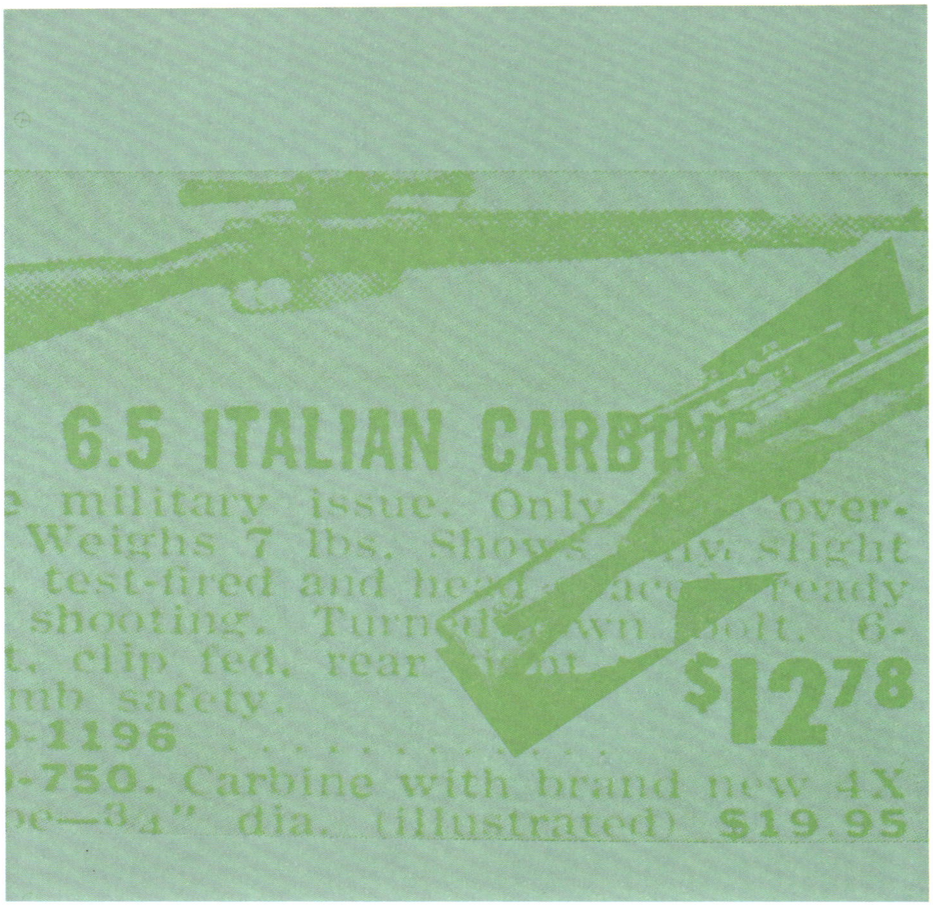




Green advertisement for a 6.5 Italian carbine rifle (Mannlicher-Carcano rifle) with a cropped photograph of the actual murder weapon used by Oswald overlaid at the top.

White image with three adjacent headshots of Kennedy taken from the 1960 campaign poster.

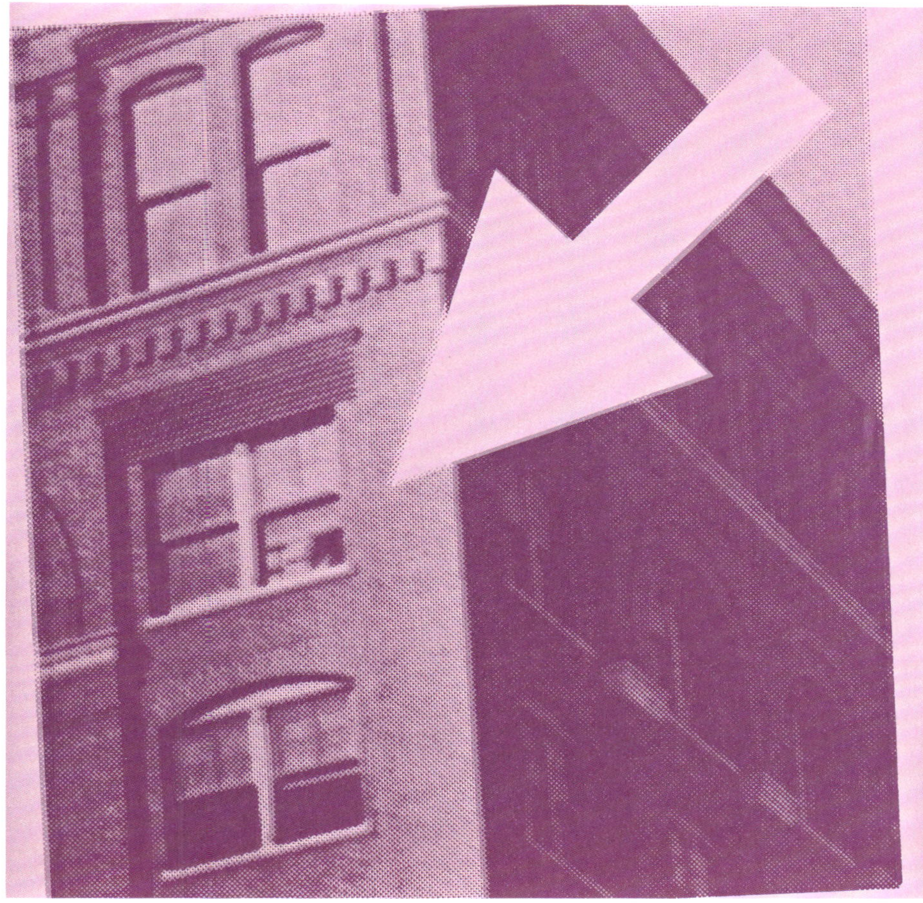

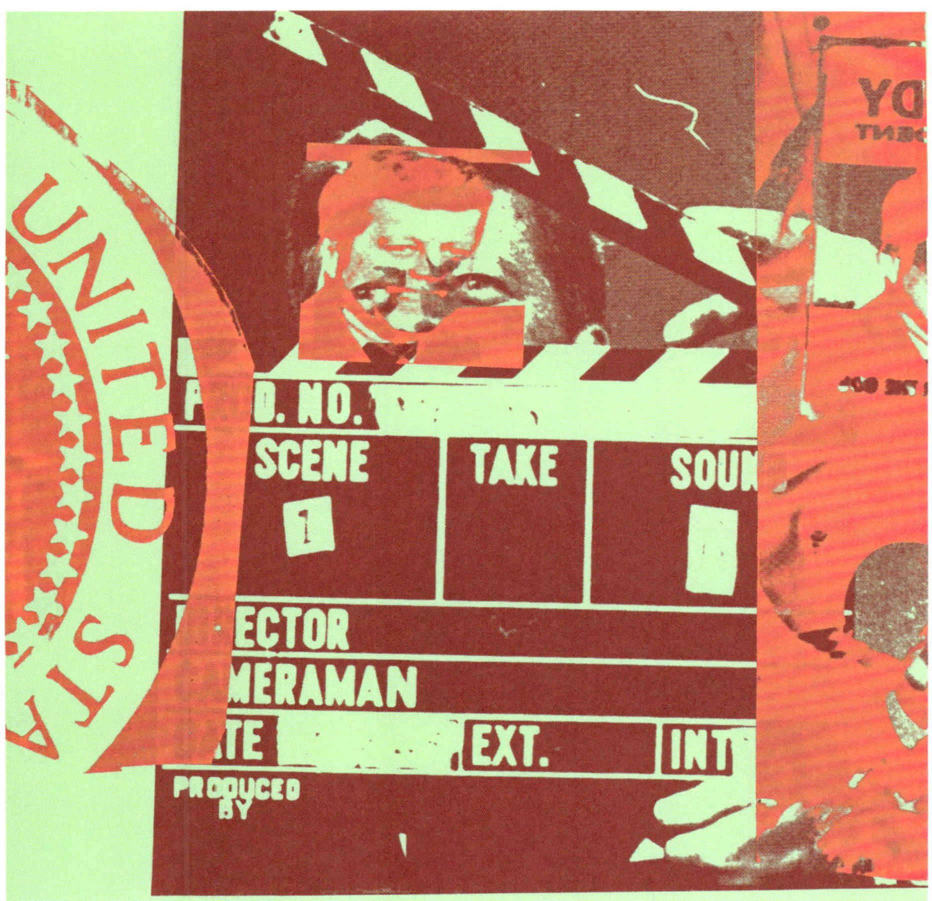


**Pale and medium purple photographic image of the Texas School Book Depository building in Dallas. A superimposed directional arrow points to the window on the sixth floor from which Oswald shot and killed President Kennedy.**

**In red and green, the same filmmaking clapboard superimposed on the campaign poster face of Kennedy adjacent to a cropped image of the presidential seal.**

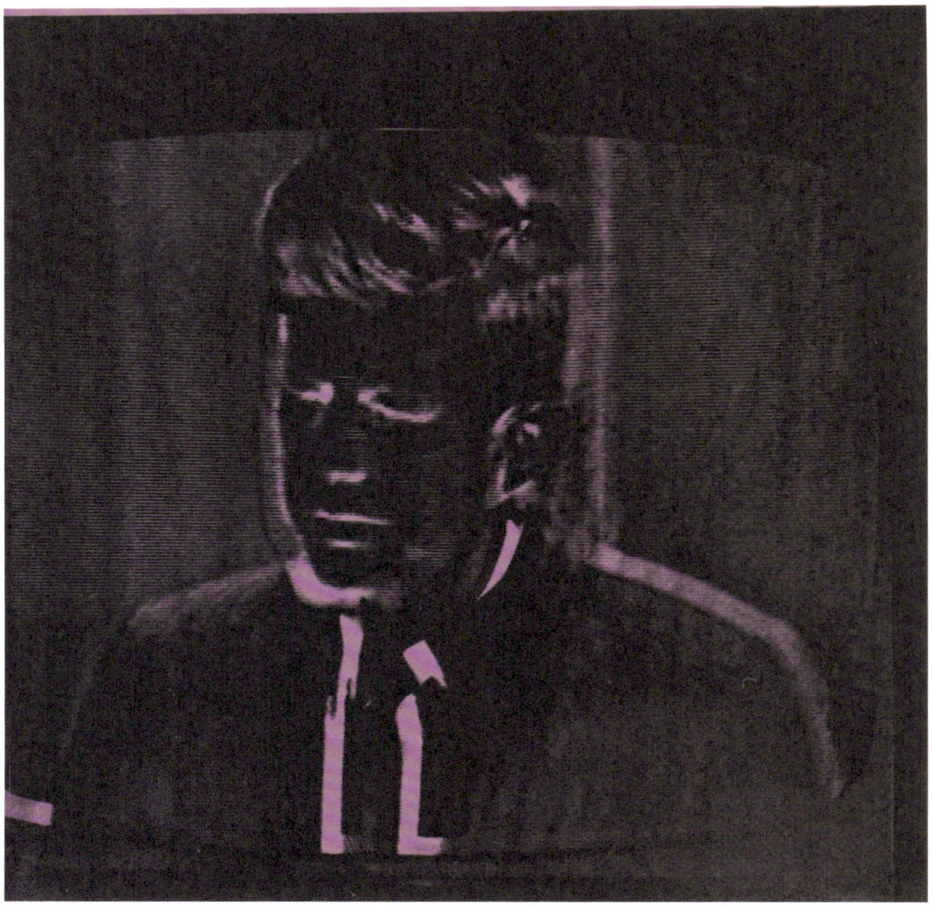

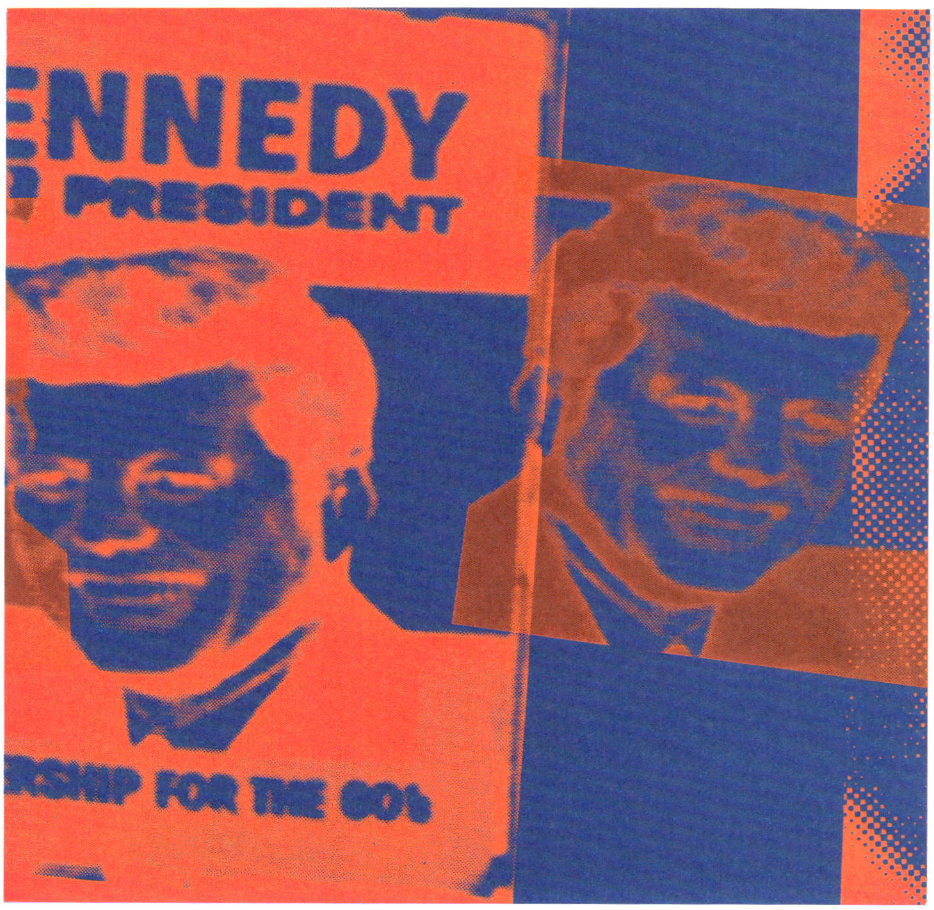


Black frame with scanlines and neon pink outlines of President Kennedy, taken from a televised image of the president addressing the Congress of the United States on May 25, 1961, and announcing NASA's plans for a manned American moon landing by the end of the decade.

Polarized negative images in red and blue of Kennedy's face on the 1960 campaign poster.

As noted at the time by many commentators, the distancing effect and repetition of televised news coverage of the Vietnam War made Americans numb to its horrors. Warhol's use of color in *Flash* makes the same point in his commentary on the media frenzy surrounding the Kennedy assassination.[10] Warhol's blinding color also complements the title of the portfolio and its dual meanings: news flash or breaking news and camera flash—the abrupt and glaring illumination of subjects.

Warhol's *Flash* tells the story of Kennedy's assassination with the artist's images and Greer's texts. It is, however, recounted in two parallel narratives, not one. *Flash* is remarkable as the only instance of storytelling in Warhol's prints or paintings. And the dual narrative structure is unorthodox. The more traditional linear narrative, with some scrambling of chronology, lies in the eighteen pages of Teletype texts variously printed on the folders, both front and back, which contain the eleven screenprints. They tell the tragic story, beginning on November 22 with the president and first lady's arrival on Air Force One at Love Field in Dallas and ending with the burial of Lee Harvey Oswald on November 25. The style of the Teletype reportage is typical of the genre: succinct, objective, and clinical.

> FLASH
> DALLAS—SHOTS AT KENNEDY MOTORCADE
> CJ1235PCS

This journalistic aspect of *Flash* is bolstered by the portfolio's book cover, which when opened flat reveals the front page of the *New York World Telegram* for November 22, 1963, with a harsh tabloid headline in large caps: **PRESIDENT SHOT DEAD**. Nearly obscured as it is with an overlay of silver floral shapes, it is all the more powerful.

The narrative sequence of the prints, on the other hand, is nonchronological and covers another time frame, from the 1960 presidential campaign to the murder of Oswald. The vivid imagery is strikingly different from the texts printed in black ink on the gray-white folders. Most frames in the prints are as disconnected in composition as the nonlinear sequence of events is in the unusual storytelling. The greatest contrast in the prints is between the aggressive, nearly monochromatic color in eight of them, which blocks most of the imagery from immediate recognition, and the stark black, silver, and white monochrome of the other three. Warhol's double narratives—image and text—are dramatic visual and emotional foils for each other.

Again, the prints are a nonlinear snapshot chronology of Kennedy's presidency from 1960 to 1963. The repetition of imagery and obliterating color speak to the deadening effect of media saturation. Sensitivities are blunted. The Teletype texts are, ironically, otherwise. Although objective and deadpan on the surface, the reportage arouses painful, subjective responses in those who lived through the events and for those who only know them secondhand. However impersonal the style of reporting is, the flashes and bulletins can break hearts.[11]

> AS SOON AS THE PLANE'S ENGINES STOPPED, ATTORNEY
> GENERAL ROBERT F. KENNEDY, THE SLAIN PRESIDENT'S
> BROTHER, BOUNDED UP THE STEPS AND INTO THE CABIN.
> WITHIN A FEW MINUTES, HE REAPPEARED AT THE DOORWAY
> WITH MRS. JACQUELINE KENNEDY AND THE TWO WATCHED, HAND
> IN HAND, AS THE COFFIN WAS LOWERED TO A WAITING NAVAL
> AMBULANCE...

-6-

THE CEREMONY TOOK PLACE WITHIN MOMENTS AFTER THE COFFIN CONTAINING THE BODY OF SLAIN PRESIDENT JOHN F. KENNEDY WAS LOADED ABOARD THE PLANE. MRS. JOHNSON, MRS. KENNEDY AND A GROUP OF WHITE HOUSE AIDES ATTENDED THE OATH-TAKING, WHICH WAS ADMINISTERED BY FEDERAL JUDGE SARAH T. HUGHES, WHO WAS APPOINTED TO OFFICE BY PRESIDENT KENNEDY IN OCTOBER, 1961.

KT250PCS

WASHINGTON, NOV. 22 -- THE XXXX AIR FORCE JET CARRYING PRESIDENT LYNDON B. JOHNSON AND THE BODY OF ASSASSINATED PRESIDENT JOHN F. KENNEDY LANDED AT ANDREWS AIR FORCE BASE SHORTLY AFTER 6 P.M. (EST).

THE PLANE WAS MET BY AN HONOR GUARD OF AIRMEN IN DRESS UNIFORM, WITH RIFLES AND BAYONETS, AND BY HIGH-RANKING GOVERNMENT OFFICIALS.

AS SOON AS THE PLANES ENGINES STOPPED, ATTORNEY GENERAL ROBERT F. KENNEDY, THE SLAIN PRESIDENT'S BROTHER, BOUNDED UP THE STEPS AND INTOTHE CABIN. WITHIN A FEW MINUTES, HE REAPPEARED AT THE DOORWAY WITH MRS. JACQUELINE KENNEDY AND THE TWO WATCHED, HAND IN HAND, AS THE COFFIN WAS LOWERED TO A WAITING NAVAL AMBULANCE, TO BE TAKEN TO BETHESDA NAVAL HOSPITAL.

MRS. KENNEDY, HERX DRESS AND STOCKINGS STILL SMEARED WITH HERX HUSBAND'S BLOOD, APPEARED COMPOSED. SHE RODE IN THE AMBULANCE TO THE HOSPITAL.

CD515PCS

NITE LEAD KENNEDY

DALLAS, NOV. 22 -- PRESIDENT JOHN F. KENNEDY WAS ASSASSINATED HERE TODAY.

-16-

AT THE CATHEDRAL, THE PROCESSION STOPPED FOR THE REQUIEM MASS, WHICH ENDED AT XXXX 1:15 P.M. AFTER THE PROCESSION OF PRELATES FOLLOWED THE CROSS UP THE AISLE, THE PALLBEARERS CARRIED PRESIDENT KENNEDY'S COFFIN BEHIND THEM. THEN MRS. KENNEDY, HOLDING CAROLINE'S HAND, CAME OUT OF THE CHURCH AND WAITED WHILE THE CASKET WAS PLACED ON THE CAISSON. ERECT AND UNMOVING, BUT OBVIOUSLY WEEPING BEHIND HER BLACK XXX VEIL, MRS. KENNEDY FINALLY MOVED DOWN THE STEPS AND INTO A WAITING LIMOUSINE, FOLLOWED BY OTHER MEMBERS OF THE KENNEDY FAMILY. CARDINAL CUSHING WAS WEEPING AS HE LEFT THE CHURCH. GEN. EISENHOWER AND MR. TRUMAN BOTH STOPPED FOR BRIEF WORDS WITH MRS. KENNEDY BEFORE THEY RODE TOGETHER IN THE PROCESSION.

WHEN THE CORTEGE WAS FINALLY FORMED -- THE KENNEDY FAMILY GROUP WAS SO LARGE THAT PRESIDENT AND MRS. JOHNSON, RIDING DIRECTLY BEHIND THEM, WERE IN THE 10TH CAR -- SLOW MOVEMENT TO ARLINGTON BEGAN, REACHING THE CEMETERY MORE THAN AN HOUR LATER. JUST AS THE CORTEGE REACHED THE GRAVESITE, 50 AIRFORCE JETS -- REPRESENTING THE 50 STATES -- ROARED OVERHEAD, FOLLOWED BY THE PRESIDENT'S PERSONAL PLANE, AIR FORCE ONE.

**Folders with Teletype text**, 1968. Screenprints on paper, each 21½ x 21¼ in.

THEN MRS. KENNEDY, HOLDING CAROLINE'S HAND, CAME OUT OF THE CHURCH AND WAITED WHILE THE CASKET WAS PLACED ON THE CAISSON. ERECT AND UNMOVING, BUT OBVIOUSLY WEEPING BEHIND HER BLACK VEIL...

PRESIDENT JOHN FITZGERALD KENNEDY WAS BURIED TODAY IN ARLINGTON NATIONAL CEMETERY. THE SLAIN PRESIDENT WAS LAID TO REST ON A GRASSY SLOPE WITHIN VIEW OF THE LINCOLN MEMORIAL AND THE CAPITOL

JUST AS THE CORTEGE REACHED THE GRAVESITE, 50 AIRFORCE JETS—REPRESENTING THE 50 STATES—ROARED OVERHEAD, FOLLOWED BY THE PRESIDENT'S PERSONAL PLANE, AIR FORCE ONE.

THE SERVICE WAS OVER. MRS. KENNEDY, WITH ROBERT KENNEDY ALONGSIDE, WALKED SLOWLY BACK TO THE LIMOUSINE FOR HER RETURN TO THE WHITE HOUSE. SHE ALMOST TRIPPED ONCE, BUT RECOVERED HER BALANCE UNASSISTED.

The typed, ordered lines of the Teletype copy and the staccato and disjointed rhythms of the prints create a dissonance in style and content. It is generated by Warhol's juxtaposition of the public sphere of popular media and its desensitizing repetitions and manipulated constructions of societal realities with the private sphere of personal emotion—in the case of the Kennedy assassination, unmediated grief.

The dramatic foils in structure and expressive character of the two narratives in *Flash* can be understood by Warhol's public stance on the assassination, verbalized in his oft-quoted statement on the media coverage of the event and by a telling anecdote that recounts an incident that happened in 1963 in the Factory, in its original location on East Forty-Seventh Street in Midtown Manhattan. Warhol said of President Kennedy's death:

> I'd been thrilled having Kennedy as president. . . . He was handsome, young, smart—but it didn't bother me that he was dead. What bothered me was the way television and radio were programming everybody to feel so sad. It seemed like no matter how hard you tried, you couldn't get away from the thing.[12]

Warhol's statement contradicts, with some qualification, his notion that repetition breeds indifference. Here he suggests that media manipulation can also extenuate emotions. The relentless sadness Americans felt was perpetuated by the media. If media repetition empties images of meaning, it can also engineer feelings. Warhol's indictment still stands. Most important in his statement were the provocative words that the president's death did not move him. This sentiment might seem natural for someone who claimed to be a machine.[13] Warhol's public persona was like that of Édouard Manet: detached observer and recorder of modern life. But, unlike Manet's, it dwelt upon the superficial: "If you want to know all about Andy Warhol, just look at the surface of my paintings and films and me, and there I am. There's nothing behind it."[14]

On the other hand, there are the Teletype texts that reveal another side of *Flash* and of Warhol himself that rounds out, by implication, a fuller appreciation of the portfolio. If dry in tone, the texts simultaneously generate strong feelings, at odds with the surface coolness and detached tenor of the prints. This unexpected flipside of *Flash* comes from Warhol himself. His provocative dismissal of Kennedy's death and his accusation of the media's programming Americans to be sad are complicated by his documented response to the announcement of Kennedy's death. One of Warhol's friends, the poet John Giorno, later asked:

> Where were you in '63 when JFK was shot? I was with Andy Warhol. We sat on the Tiffany couch among the clutter, watching the live TV coverage from Dallas. We heard Walter Cronkite say: "President Kennedy died at 2:00 pm on November 22, 1963." We started hugging each other, pressing our bodies together and trembling. I started crying and Andy started crying. We wept big, fat tears. It was the symbol of the catastrophe of our own lives.[15]

Warhol's anguish was genuine. *Flash* is, paradoxically, both impersonal and deeply human. It exposes a cleft in Warhol's public stance. Furthermore, the cool and detached Warhol does not square with an important aspect of his private life. He was a devout member of the Byzantine Catholic Church, hardly a cynic about interiority and the spiritual.[16]

Warhol and Greer created the *Flash* portfolio in 1968, six years after the Kennedy assassination. Why the delay and why the subject, especially since the artist had extensively treated the event in a series of painted and printed portraits of Jacqueline Kennedy in 1963 and 1964, based on photographs associated with the assassination (pp. 41, 46, 47)? To date, no plausible explanations have come up. Although there are suggestions that the project was simply retrospective, these seem to pale when the year in which Warhol created *Flash* is considered: 1968. It was the most unsettling year of the turbulent 1960s.

If the assassination of President Kennedy marked the beginning of America's loss of innocence, much had happened since that fateful day to further fray the American Dream. Only the landing on the moon of American astronauts in the summer of 1969 would later somewhat redeem a decade of political and social quagmire. The congestion of horrors in 1968 was unbearable. The year was marked by political assassinations, civil unrest, racial tensions, American crimes against humanity, and increasingly fervent antiwar demonstrations, initiated earlier by a countercultural generation of college students.

> *January–February: Tet Offensive: Relative failure of President Johnson's massive assault in North Vietnam leads to questioning by an increasing number of Americans of US policy in the Vietnam War.*
>
> *March 16: My Lai Massacre, Vietnam. Mass killing of 504 unarmed civilians by US Army soldiers; Robert F. Kennedy declares his candidacy for president in the 1968 presidential campaign.*
>
> *March 31: Under pressure for his handling of the Vietnam War, President Lyndon B. Johnson announces that he will not run in the 1968 presidential election.*
>
> *April 4: Assassination of Martin Luther King Jr.*

*April 4–8: 168 civil rights riots break out across the country, following the King assassination.*

*June 6: Assassination of Senator Robert F. Kennedy.*

*August 28: Chicago Democratic National Convention; police provoke riots in their attempt to control 10,000 protesters, many of them students.*

The years leading up to 1968 were demoralizing. So much had devolved since 1963 that, in retrospect, the Kennedy assassination seemed to be a harbinger of America's fall from grace. Perhaps Warhol felt it was time to reclaim that event as a dark genesis moment. The assassination, however, had remained on the artist's mind, as attested by *Since* (a. k. a. *Kennedy's Assassination*), an unfinished film Warhol directed and produced in 1966. Improvised and comedic in tone, its repeated actions addressed the media's exploitation of the events of late 1963.

The periodic publication in *Life* magazine of frames from the Zapruder film of the assassination kept the horrors alive. The twenty-six-second film was shot by Abraham Zapruder, a spectator, with his 8mm home-movie camera. It captures the president's motorcade as it turned into Elm Street in Dealey Plaza and the very second when Oswald's bullet struck Kennedy's head. Immediately after the assassination, thirty frames in black and white appeared in the November 29 issue of *Life*. The magazine later published color frames in the October 2, 1964, and November 25, 1966, issues—both devoted to the report of the Warren Commission, which investigated the assassination. The general public did not see the actual film until it was broadcast on national television in the early 1970s. It is tempting to see some influence on the *Flash* portfolio in the bright colors and blurred and eccentric compositions of the Zapruder frames.

It is not known exactly when Warhol began working on the *Flash* portfolio—although certainly sometime in early 1968, possibly after February, when he moved the Factory to a new location on Union Square West. The assassination of Martin Luther King Jr. in April is an important contender for what could have been the immediate reason for Warhol to revisit Kennedy's death. Ironically, on June 3, in the middle of the project, the artist fell victim himself to an assassination attempt at the Factory. Valerie Solanas, an aggressive feminist, actress, writer, and casual member of the artist's team, shot Warhol. He was seriously wounded and barely survived: he spent two months in the hospital.[17] The trauma of the event could have only been exacerbated when, three days after the attempt on Warhol, Senator Robert F. Kennedy, a presidential candidate, was fatally shot during a campaign stop in Los Angeles. Given Warhol's close friendship with the Kennedy family since the John Kennedy presidency in the early sixties, Robert Kennedy's death must have been crippling.[18] A print based on a photograph of Robert Kennedy was proposed for *Flash* after, one would imagine, the assassination of President Kennedy's brother. It was abandoned.[19]

If immaterial to the initiation of *Flash*, Warhol's near-assassination still bears upon our reception to it and to the artist's own feelings as he later brought finishing touches to the portfolio after his stay in the hospital. The event itself and Warhol's recovery prompted a dramatic change in his life and art. The raucous, heady years of the Factory would be no more. The 1970s brought about a new era, with Warhol preoccupied with commissioned portraits of the rich and famous.

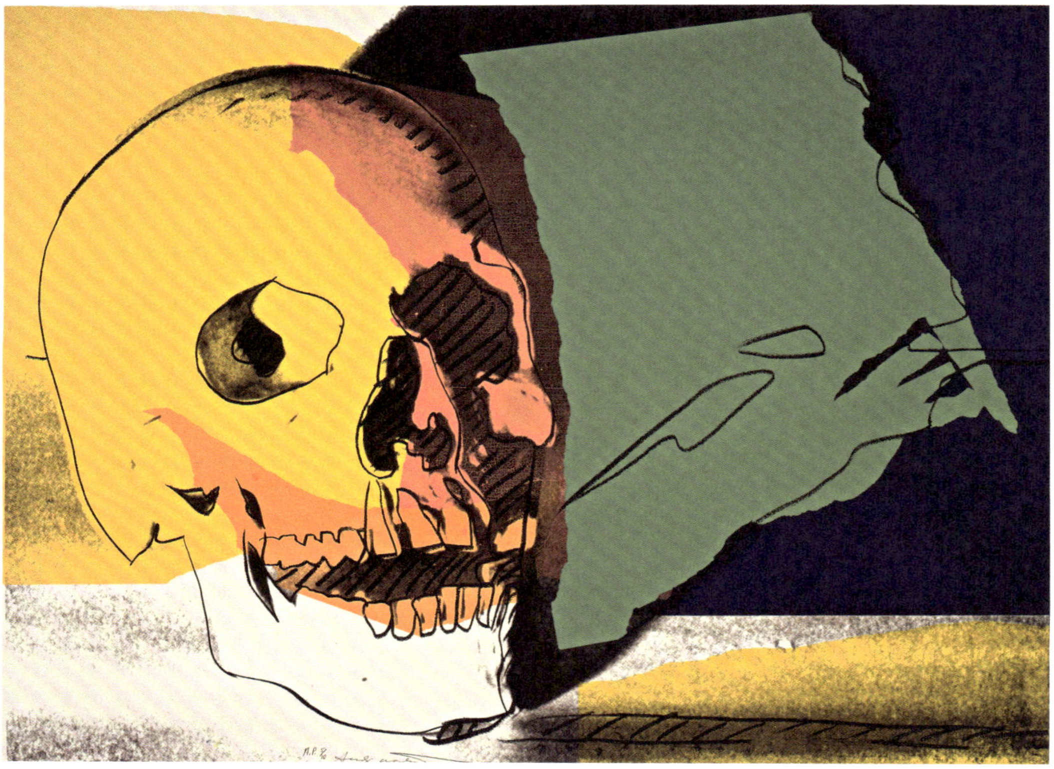

**Skull**, 1976. Screenprint, 30 x 40 in.

It is surprising that *Flash: November 22, 1963* is the only work of art from the period that addressed the assassination with such ambition and complexity. Warhol's brilliant and jarring conceit was to pair in a double narrative the media spectacle of Kennedy's death with the felt human tragedy of the event. *Flash* offers the dramatic arc of Kennedy's presidency: from the exuberant and successful 1960 campaign to the highlight of his presidency in 1961, when he announced to Congress that Americans would be on the moon by the end of the decade, and, finally, to his horrendous murder. This was a remarkably short period of three years that has the markings of epic misfortune.

The mythical implications of the Kennedy presidency are unavoidable. Its story is on the scale of Greek tragedy. The distinguished American writer and classical scholar Daniel Mendelsohn explained such thoughts on the occasion of the fiftieth anniversary of the assassination: "It's not hard to see why. Athenian drama returns obsessively—as we do, every November 22—to the shocking and yet seemingly inevitable spectacle of the fallen king, of power and beauty and privilege laid low."[20] The *Flash* portfolio is a grand memento mori. It is tethered to the artist's *Death and Disaster* paintings and prints, and other later related series, in its theme of mortality. *Flash* takes up the subject—developed in seventeenth-century Dutch still-life painting, with symbols of skulls, unfinished banquets, and burning candles—of life's brevity and the inevitability of death. Death is woven through Warhol's art, unequivocally in the paintings and prints of tabletop skulls (above and pp. 127–29). Celebrity and fame are also tropes for transience—the passing of all things beautiful and seemingly immortal.

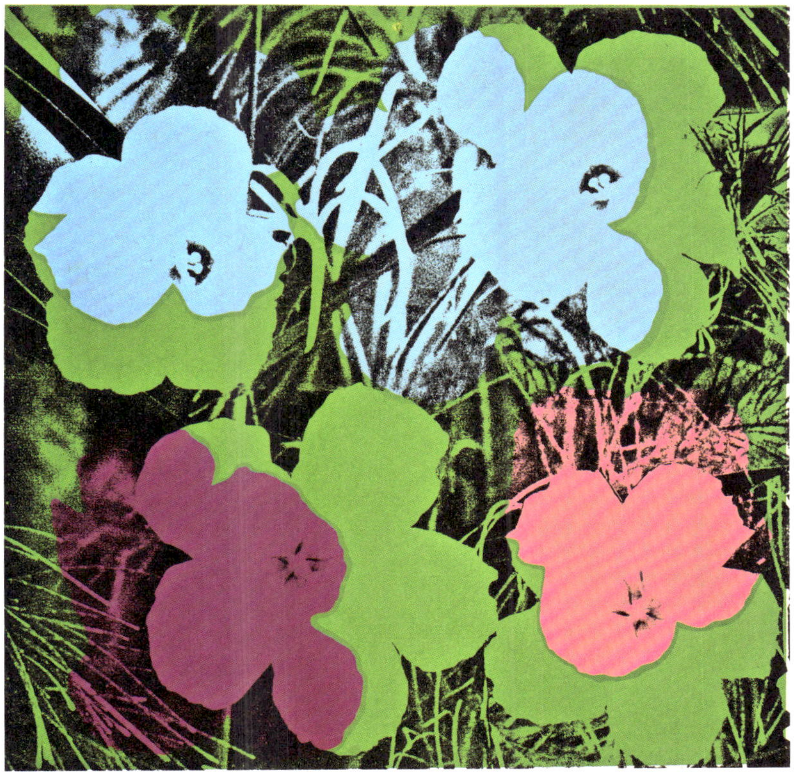

**Flowers**, 1970. Screenprint, 36 x 36 in.

The portfolio case carries over its entirety a loose grid of floral and foliate forms in various sheens of silver ink from light to dark. They are taken from a commercial sheet of graphic design samples.[21] Superimposed on the front page of the *New York World Telegram,* these abstracted and reflective shapes may soften the stark horror of the headline, but they also read as gunshots and splattered drops of blood. The floral motif is related to one of Warhol's most famous print series, the colorful and lyrical *Flowers,* a series of ten screenprints based upon a photograph of four hibiscus blooms (1970, above and pp. 86–89). In Dutch vanitas paintings, flowers are the most important embodiment of the memento mori theme: however beautiful, flowers are short-lived and will wilt and die. In China, hibiscuses symbolize the fleeting nature of beauty, fame, and personal glory. Flowers, the most appropriate of funereal tributes, strewn over the cover of the *Flash* portfolio as flowers on a grave, poignantly embellish Warhol's lament.

Warhol and Greer chose to conclude their wire-service coverage of the Kennedy funeral and burial with this bulletin:

> IN ALL THE SPEECHES, IN ALL THE EULOGIES, IN ALL THE COMFORTING MESSAGES, NOWHERE WAS THE WORLD'S SENTIMENT MORE CLEARLY EXPRESSED THAN IN A BRIEF DESCRIPTION ON THE BACK OF A PICTURE OF THE LATE PRESIDENT, WHICH WAS HANDED X AT XXXX ST. MATTHEW'S CATHEDRAL: "DEAR GOD, PLEASE TAKE CARE OF YOUR SERVANT, JOHN FITZGERALD KENNEDY."

## Notes

1. I would like to express my deep gratitude to Catherine Malone, collection manager of the Collections of Jordan D. Schnitzer and His Family Foundation; my research assistant, Anais Reyes, curatorial intern at the Madison Museum of Contemporary Art; and Brian Stusse, associate registrar at the Walker Art Center in Minneapolis, for their contributions to this essay. The *Flash* portfolio has been the sole subject of only one museum exhibition. In 1999, the Delaware Art Museum in Wilmington presented *Andy Warhol's "Flash—November 22, 1963."* It later had a featured role at the National Gallery of Art, Washington, DC, in the exhibition *Warhol: Headlines* in 2011, and in early 2013 it was exhibited along with the screenprint *Jackie II* (1966) at the Telfair Museums in Savannah, Georgia. Later that year the portfolio was at the center of *Flash Back—November 22, 1963*, organized by the Addison Gallery of American Art in Andover, Massachusetts. That exhibition examined the response of Warhol and other artists to the Kennedy assassination as it was refracted through the popular media. Other artists included Lutz Bacher, Wayne Gonzales, Marisol, Tina Mon, Ed Paschke, and T. R. Uthco and Ant Farm.

2. See the gallery guide for *Warhol by the Book*, an exhibition that was curated by Matt Wrbican and presented at the Andy Warhol Museum in Pittsburgh (October 10, 2015–January 10, 2016). A draft of the publisher's original contract describes the work as ultimately being a book; bound copies of the portfolio exist. The traditional artist's book brings together images and text, usually in a collaboration of an artist and a writer. From 1953 to 1955, Warhol produced several promotional and illustrated books in collaboration with friends who did hand coloring and often provided texts, including *À la recherche du shoe perdu* (c. 1955), with offset lithography, watercolor, and pen drawings and text by Ralph Pomeroy. Although not an artist's book proper, Kurt Benirschke's *Vanishing Animals* (1986) was illustrated by Warhol. The illustrations were reproductions of sixteen screenprints with collage provided by the artist. Warhol's commission followed the publication of his related *Endangered Species* portfolio of editioned and signed screenprints (1983). None of the species in the portfolio are duplicated in the book.

3. Next to nothing is known about the identity of Phillip Greer. Matt Wrbican, chief archivist at the Andy Warhol Museum, replied to my query that he has tried for some years to learn about Greer, to no avail. He understands there are archives for Racolin Press, the pubisher of *Flash*, but has been unable to access them.

4. It is only recently that the "political Warhol" has been addressed in the critical literature and in exhibition: *Pop Impressions: Europe/USA: Prints and Multiples from The Museum of Modern Art* (New York: Museum of Modern Art, 1999), catalogue text by Wendy Weitman; *Andy Warhol: Social Observer* (Philadelphia: Pennsylvania Academy of the Fine Arts, 2000), catalogue text by Jonathan P. Binstock et al.; and *Andy Warhol: Pop Politics* (Manchester, New Hampshire: Currier Museum of Art, 2008), catalogue text by Sharon Matt Atkins. In comparison to American pop art, international pop was more overtly political in its subjects. But Warhol's art holds, by far, the most political content of all the titular American pop artists. This holds true despite major works with powerful themes by other artists: Jim Dine, *Drag—Johnson and Mao*, 1967; Ed Kienholz, *Portable War Memorial,* 1968; Roy Lichtenstein, *Blam*, 1962; Claes Oldenburg, *Lipstick (Ascending) on Caterpillar Tracks*, 1969; and James Rosenquist, *F-111*, 1964–65.

5. Vlada Tcharyeva argues in her master's dissertation *The Political in Andy Warhol's Life and Work* (University of London, 2013) that beyond the overt political imagery, the entire oeuvre of Warhol is rife with the political. In his critique of museum installations, Holland Cotter takes a broadened view of political issues in the cultural and social history of art and collecting. He concludes that all art is "political to its core." See "Placement Is Politics in Brooklyn Museum Reinstallation," *New York Times*, May 19, 2016, http://www.nytimes.com/2016/05/20/arts/design/placement-is-politics-in-brooklyn-museum-reinstallation.html?rref= collection/sectioncollection/arts.

6. This interpretation of the *Sunset* portfolio is taken from an unpublished manuscript by Stephen Dull, "Andy Warhol's *Sunset.*" Precedents in Warhol's paintings for nuclear holocaust imagery include *Red Airmail Stamps* (1962), with its forty-five plus repetitions of a Boeing B-52 strategic bomber set against a Soviet red ground, and *Atomic Bomb* (1965), with a photograph of a bomb exploding in the American Southwest repeated twenty-five times, each image progressively darkening to suggest total nuclear annihilation in the last blackened image.

7. Specifically, *New York Times*, November 24 and 25, 1963; and *Life* magazine, November 29 and December 6, 1963.

8. Ten of the two hundred editions of *Flash*, lettered A–J, have three additional screenprints with the 1960 campaign poster's face of Kennedy.

9. In 1963–64, Warhol produced a number of single- and multipanel paintings of Mrs. Kennedy both smiling and grieving, based on photographs taken of her in the presidential motorcade on the fateful day of November 22, 1963 (the photograph in *Flash*), on Air Force One during Lyndon B. Johnson's swearing in as the thirty-sixth President of the United States, and during the funeral cortege up Pennsylvania Avenue. He also created three screenprints,

*Jackie I, Jackie II,* and *Jackie III,* in 1966 for the portfolios *11 Pop Artists I, 11 Pop Artists II*, and *11 Pop Artists III*, respectively. All of the "Jackie" paintings and prints were part of Warhol's *Death and Disaster Series* (1962–66).

10. Although color television in the United States had precedents in the 1950s, it wasn't until the mid-1960s that full-time network broadcasts in full-color television became the norm. Color television was expensive. Most Americans experienced the Kennedy assassination in black-and-white photographic and televised coverage.

11. Before beginning my research on *Flash*, I had never read through the Teletype texts. Carefully making my way through them at the Walker Art Center, I was unexpectedly deeply moved. Who would think that a work of art by Andy Warhol could bring tears to one's eyes?

12. Andy Warhol and Pat Hackett, *POPism: The Warhol '60s* (New York: Harcourt Brace Jovanovich, 1980), 77.

13. Warhol's wish appears in his famous statement: "The reason I'm painting this way is that I want to be a machine, and I feel that whatever I do and do machine-like is what I want to do." G. R. Swenson, "What Is Pop Art? Answers from 8 Painters, Part 1," *ARTnews* 62 (November 1963): 15.

14. Gretchen Berg, "Andy Warhol, My True Story," *Los Angeles Free Press* (March 17, 1967), as quoted in *Andy Warhol: A Retrospective* (New York: Museum of Modern Art, 1990), 457.

15. *Andy Warhol 365 Takes*: *The Andy Warhol Museum Collection* (New York: Abrams in association with the Andy Warhol Museum, 2004), 223.

16. The human side of Warhol is argued in *Warhol: Headlines* (Washington, DC: National Gallery of Art; New York, Prestel, 2011), catalogue texts by Molly Donovan, et al.

17. Alexandra Schwartz, "Andy Warhol and *Flash*," *MoMA* 2 (Winter 1974–75): 6.

18. On Warhol's ties to the Kennedy family, see Atkins, *Andy Warhol, Pop Politics,* 15n2.

19. Although thematically appropriate, it could have been left out for diffusing the sharp focus in the portfolio on the assassination of John F. Kennedy. Molly Donovan suggests that *Flash* was completed in early 1968. But that would not account for why the photograph of Robert Kennedy was considered for inclusion in the portfolio, an idea most likely entertained after his assassination in early June 1968. See "Where's Warhol? Triangulating the Artist in the Headlines," in *Warhol: Headlines*, 17.

20. Daniel Mendelsohn, "J.F.K., Tragedy, Myth," *New Yorker*, November 22, 2013, http://www.newyorker.com/books/page-turner/j-f-k-tragedy-myth.

21. This foliate motif first appears in the screenprint *Lincoln Center Ticket* (1967), again in the screenprint *Daily News* (c. 1967), and then in the screenprint *SAS Passenger Ticket* (1968). The *Lincoln Center Ticket* print presages Warhol's adoption of the foliate pattern for *Flash*.

(next page) **Flash—November 22, 1963**, back cover, 1968. Screenprint on cloth mounted on cardboard, 22½ x 22⅜ in.

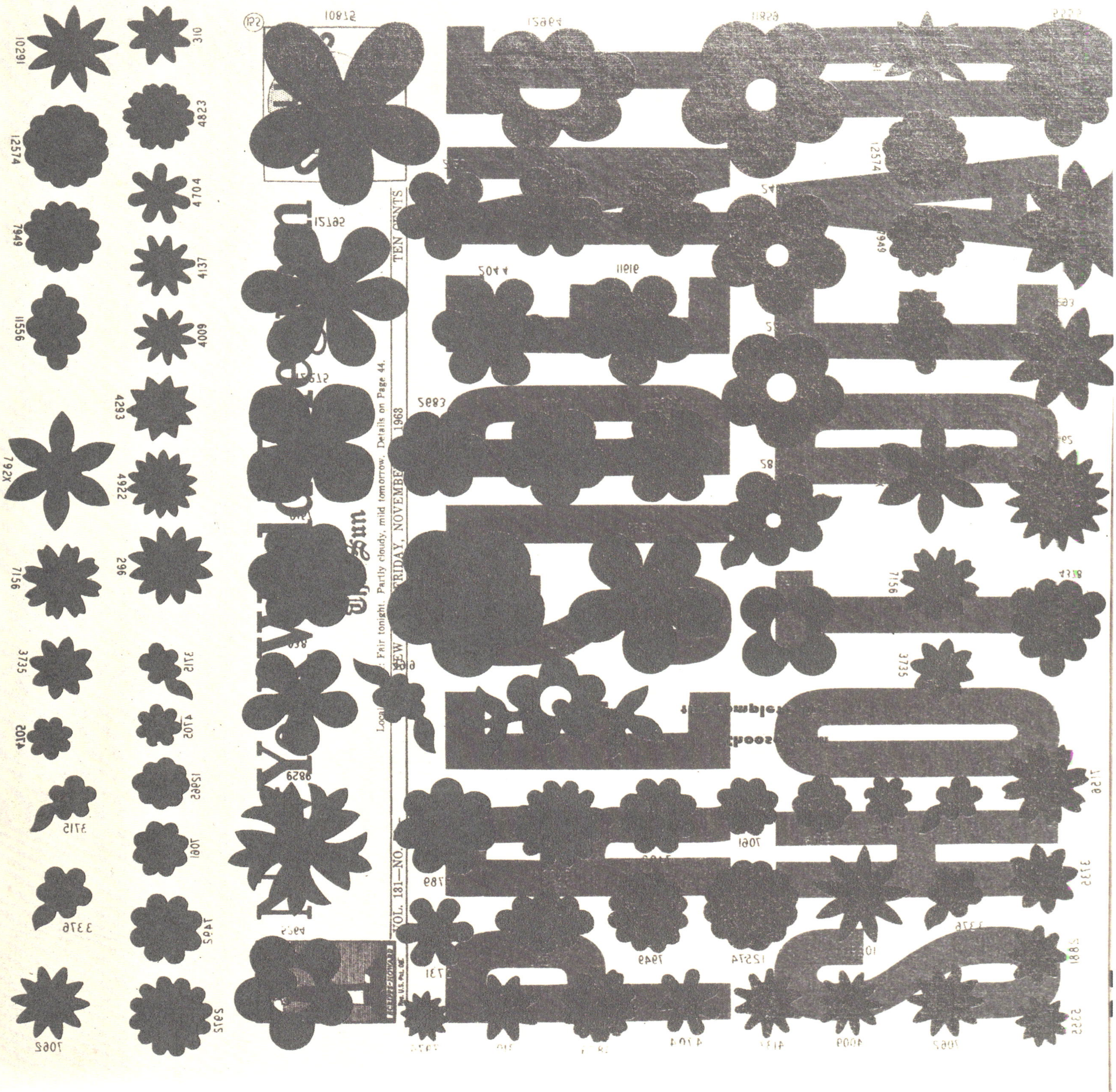

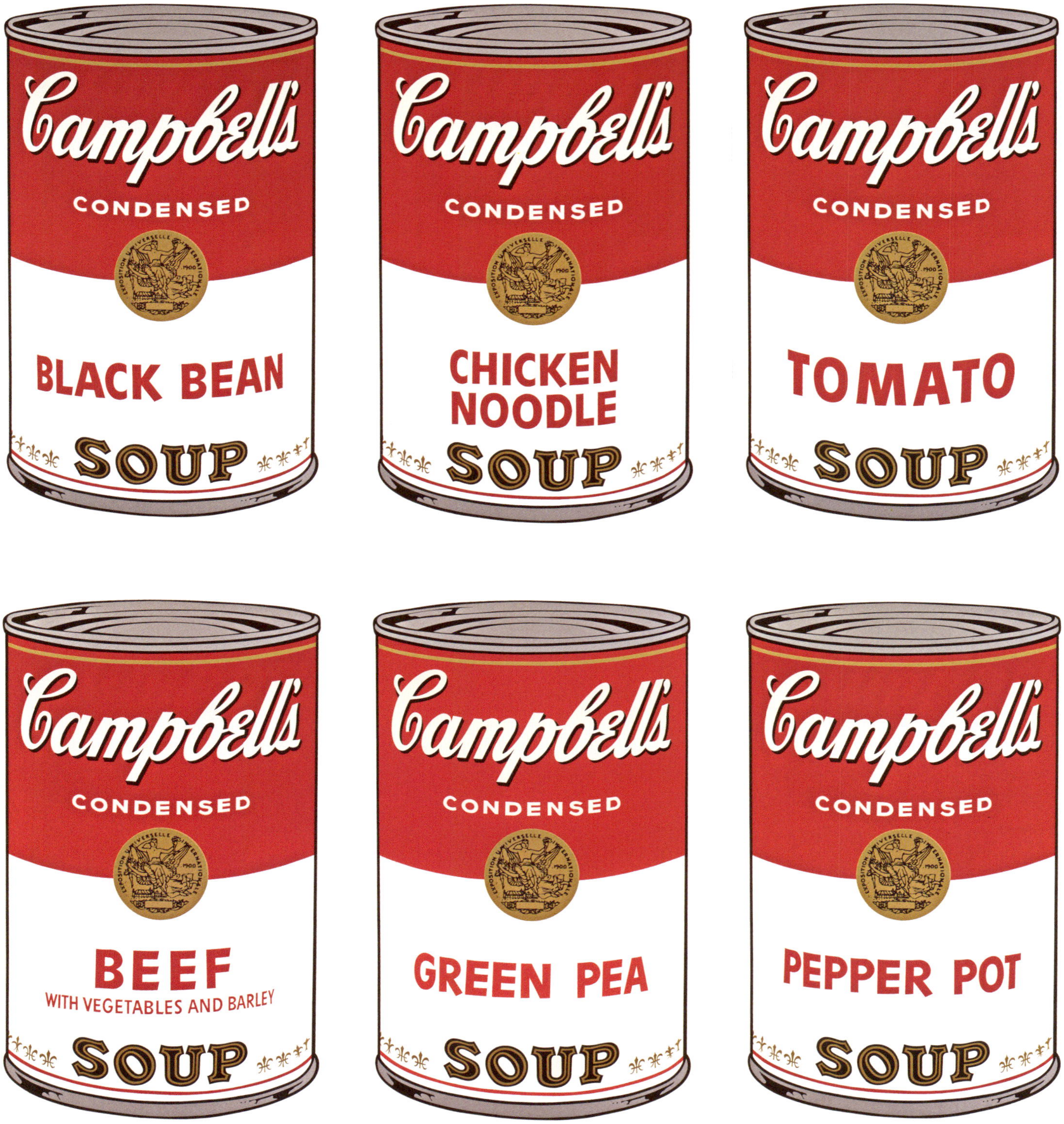


**Campbell's Soup I**, 1968. Screenprints, each 35 x 23 in.

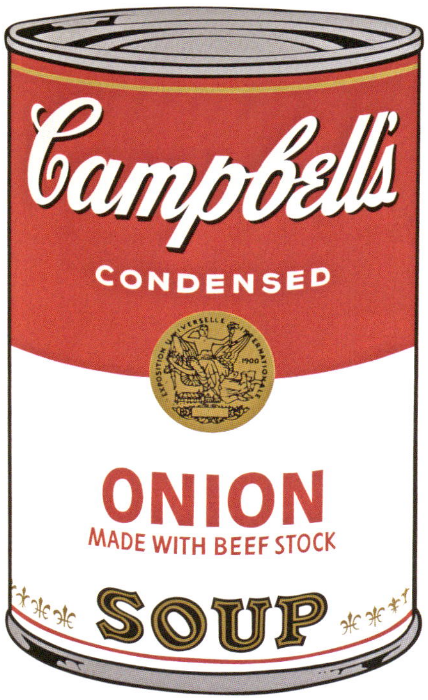
Campbell's
CONDENSED
ONION
MADE WITH BEEF STOCK
SOUP

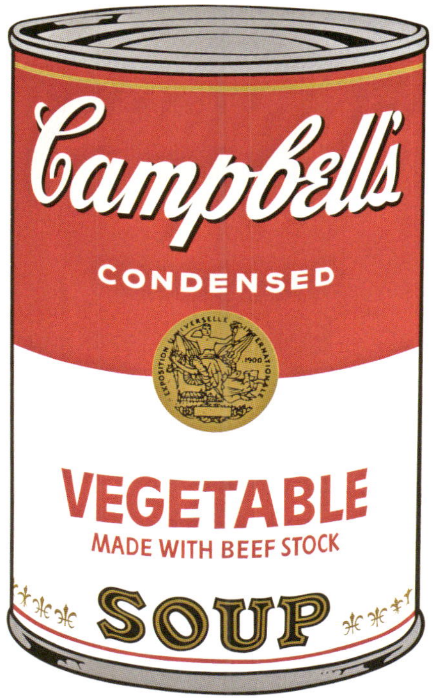
Campbell's
CONDENSED
VEGETABLE
MADE WITH BEEF STOCK
SOUP

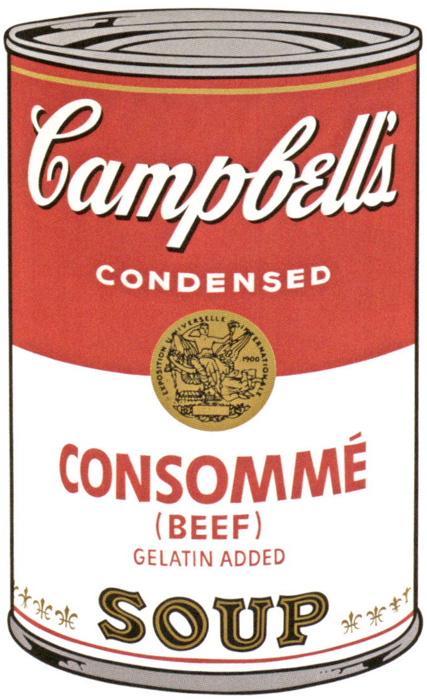
Campbell's
CONDENSED
CONSOMMÉ
(BEEF)
GELATIN ADDED
SOUP

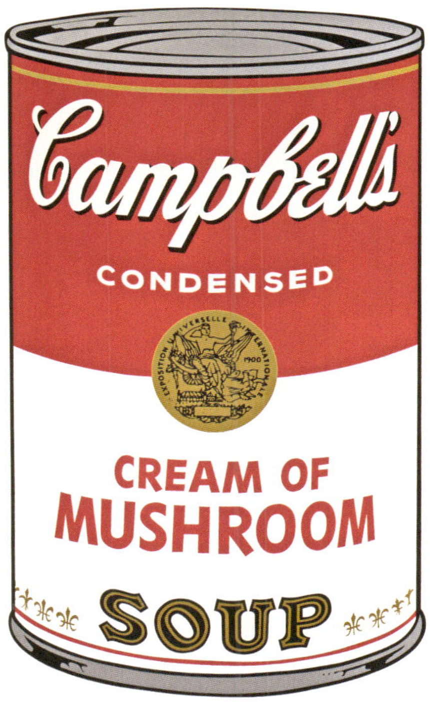
Campbell's
CONDENSED
CREAM OF
MUSHROOM
SOUP

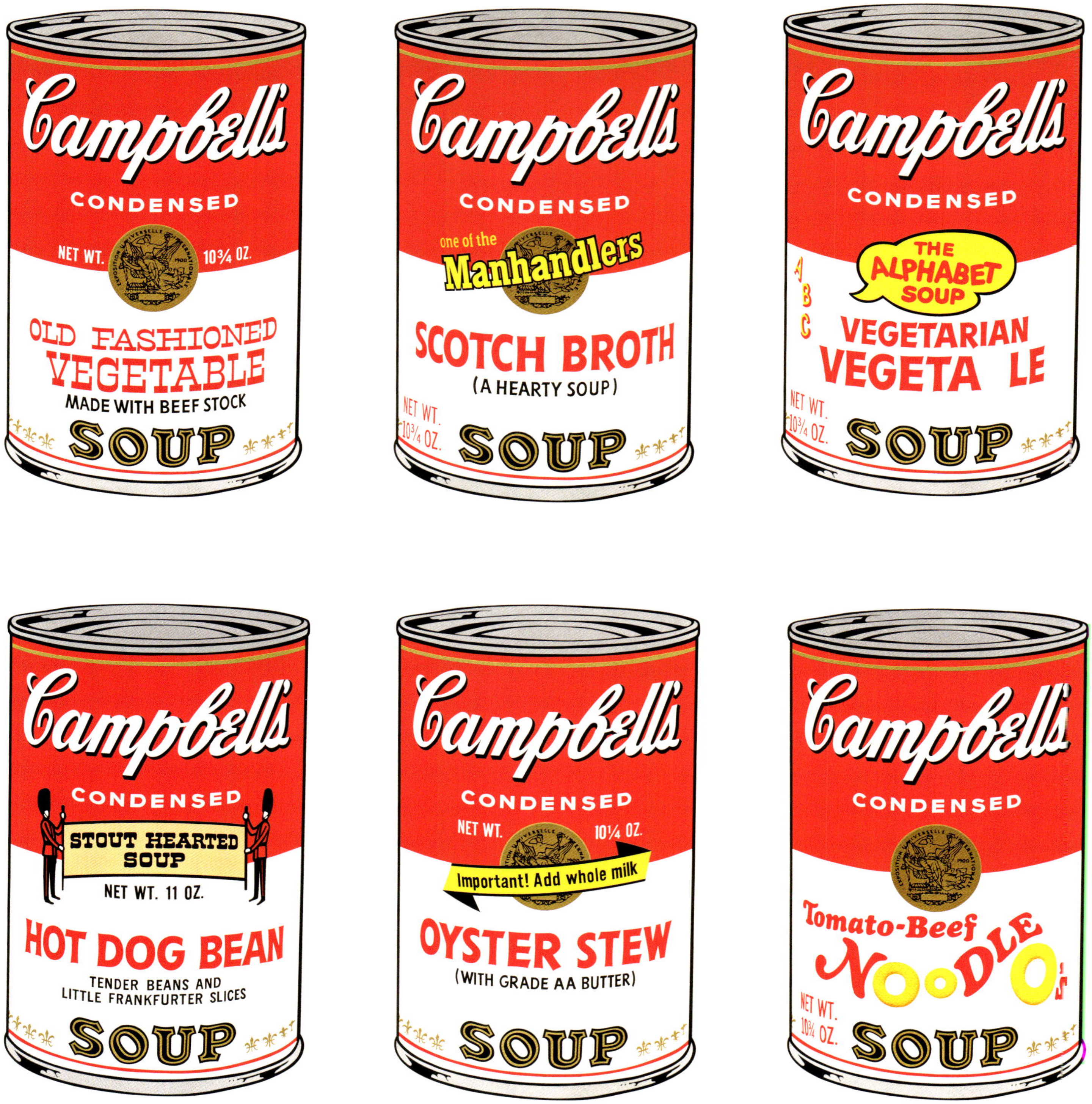


**Campbell's Soup II**, 1968. Screenprints, each 35 x 23 in.

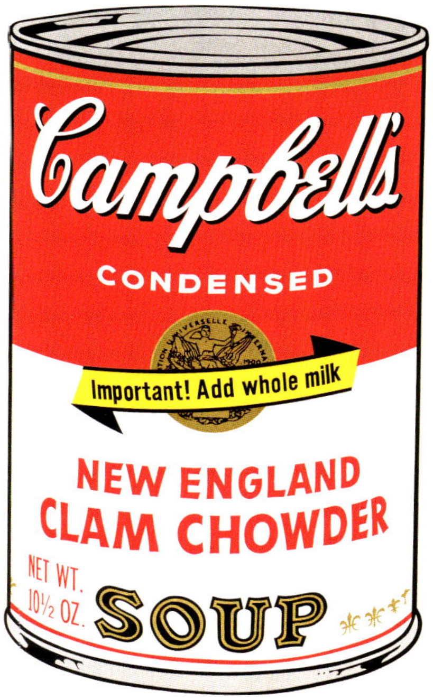
Campbell's
CONDENSED
Important! Add whole milk
NEW ENGLAND
CLAM CHOWDER
NET WT.
10½ OZ.
SOUP

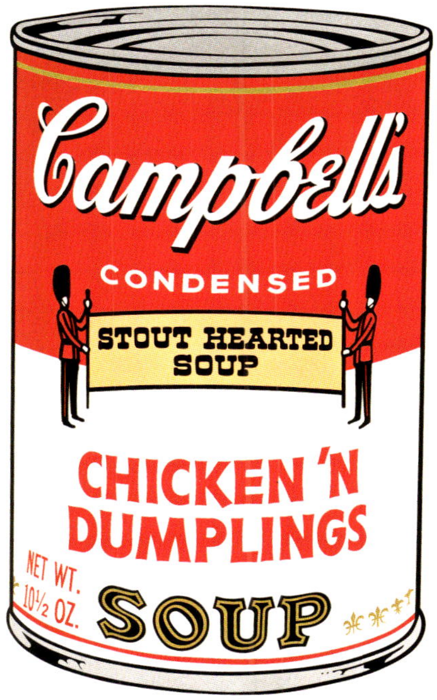
Campbell's
CONDENSED
STOUT HEARTED
SOUP
CHICKEN 'N
DUMPLINGS
NET WT.
10½ OZ.
SOUP

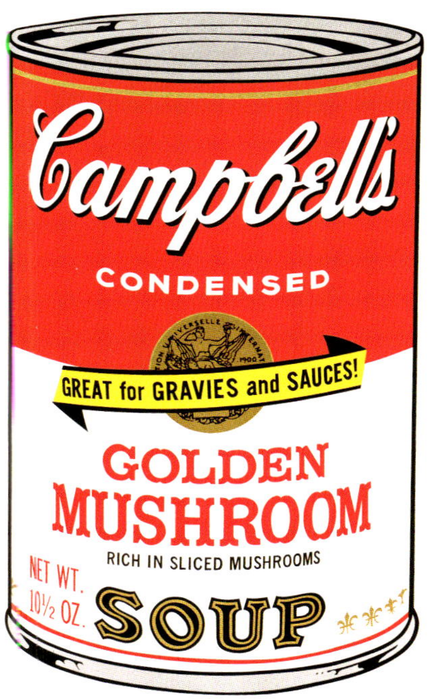
Campbell's
CONDENSED
GREAT for GRAVIES and SAUCES!
GOLDEN
MUSHROOM
RICH IN SLICED MUSHROOMS
NET WT.
10½ OZ.
SOUP

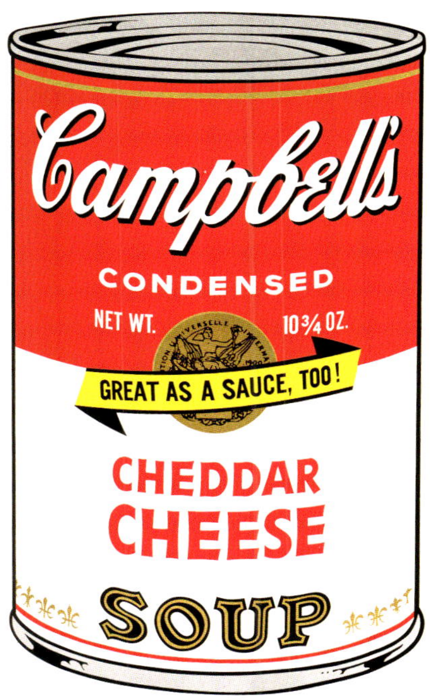
Campbell's
CONDENSED
NET WT.
10¾ OZ.
GREAT AS A SAUCE, TOO!
CHEDDAR
CHEESE
SOUP

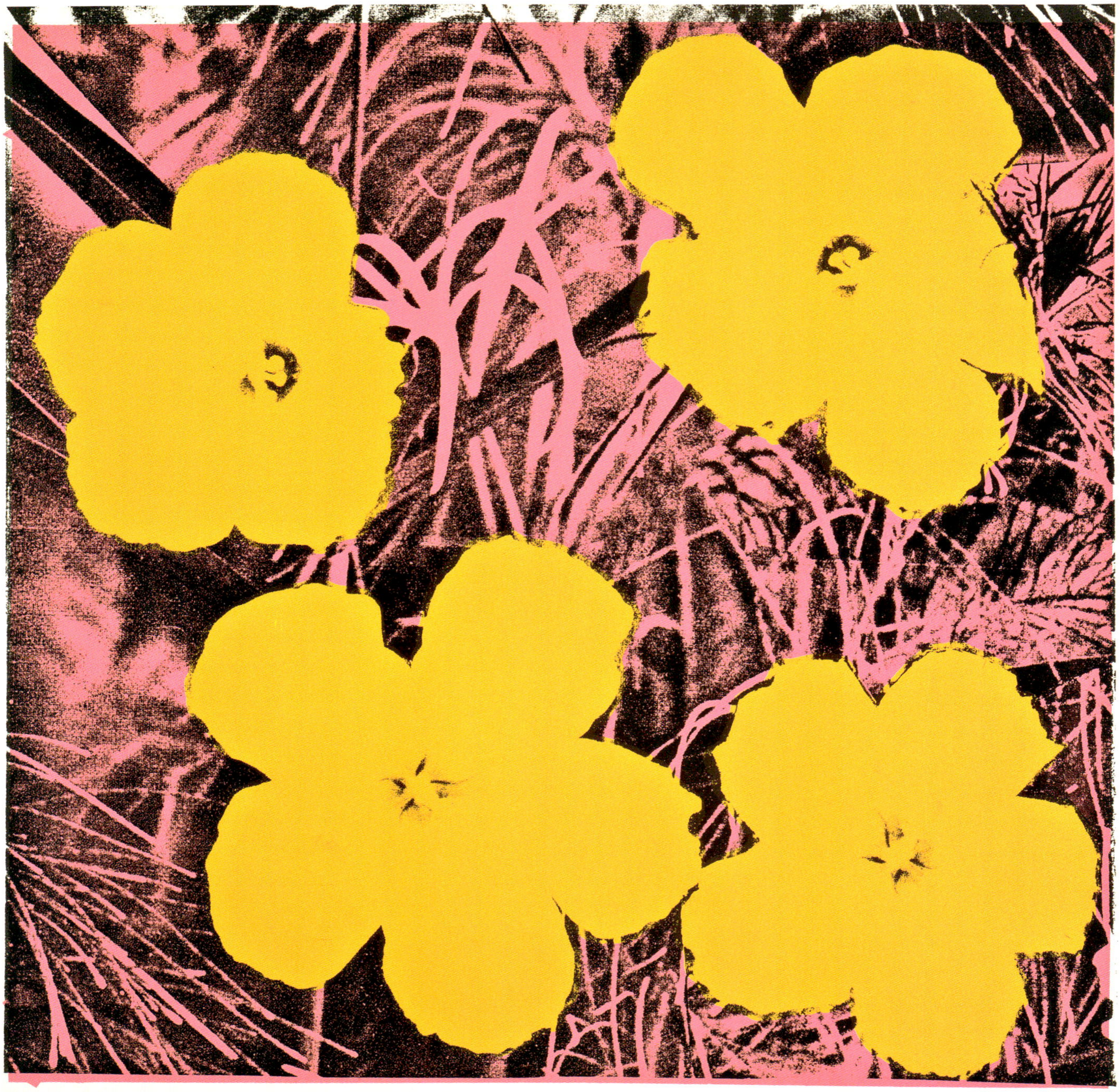

**Flowers**, 1970. Screenprints, each 36 x 36 in.

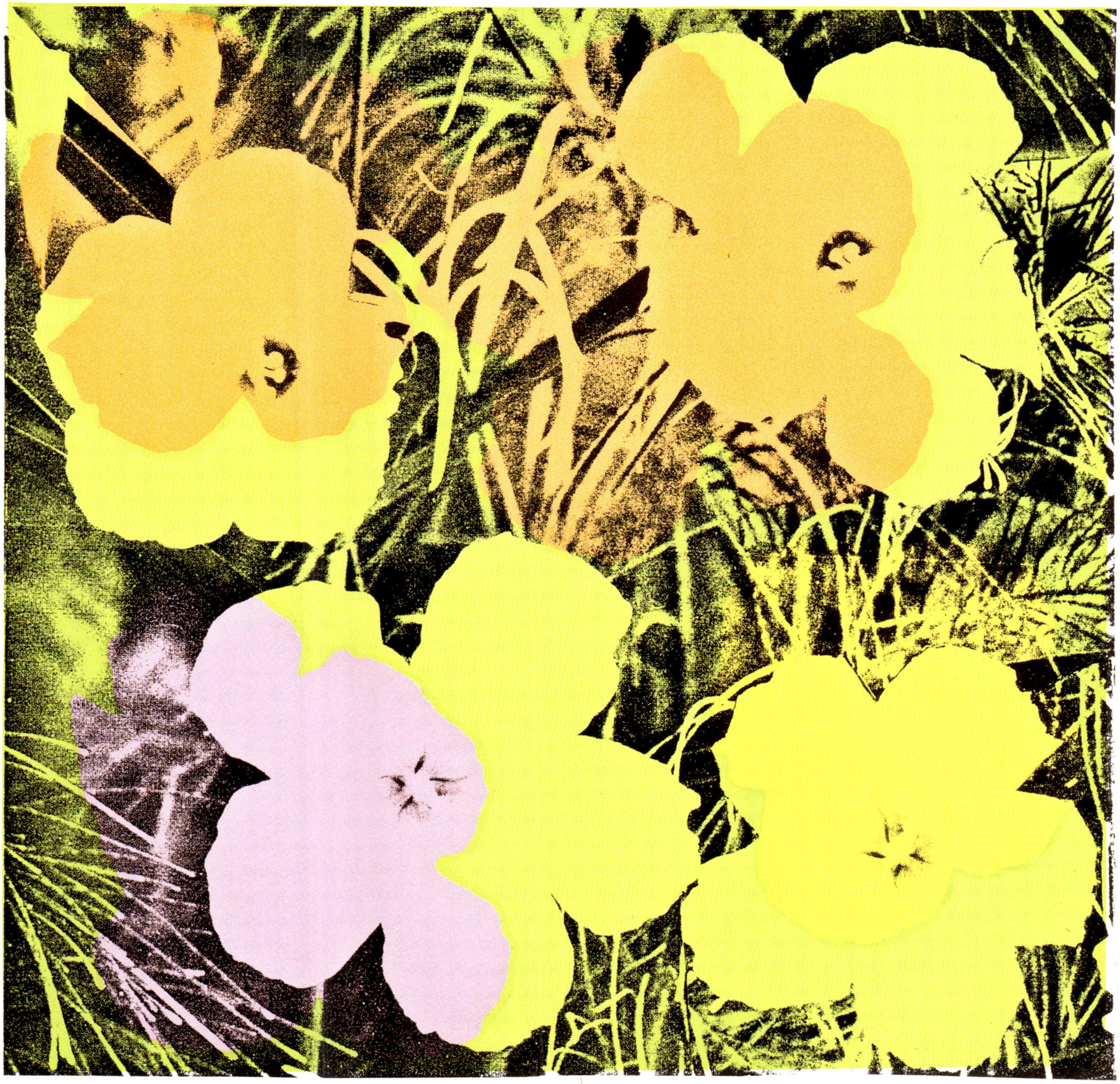

**Flowers**, 1970. Screenprint, 36 x 36 in.

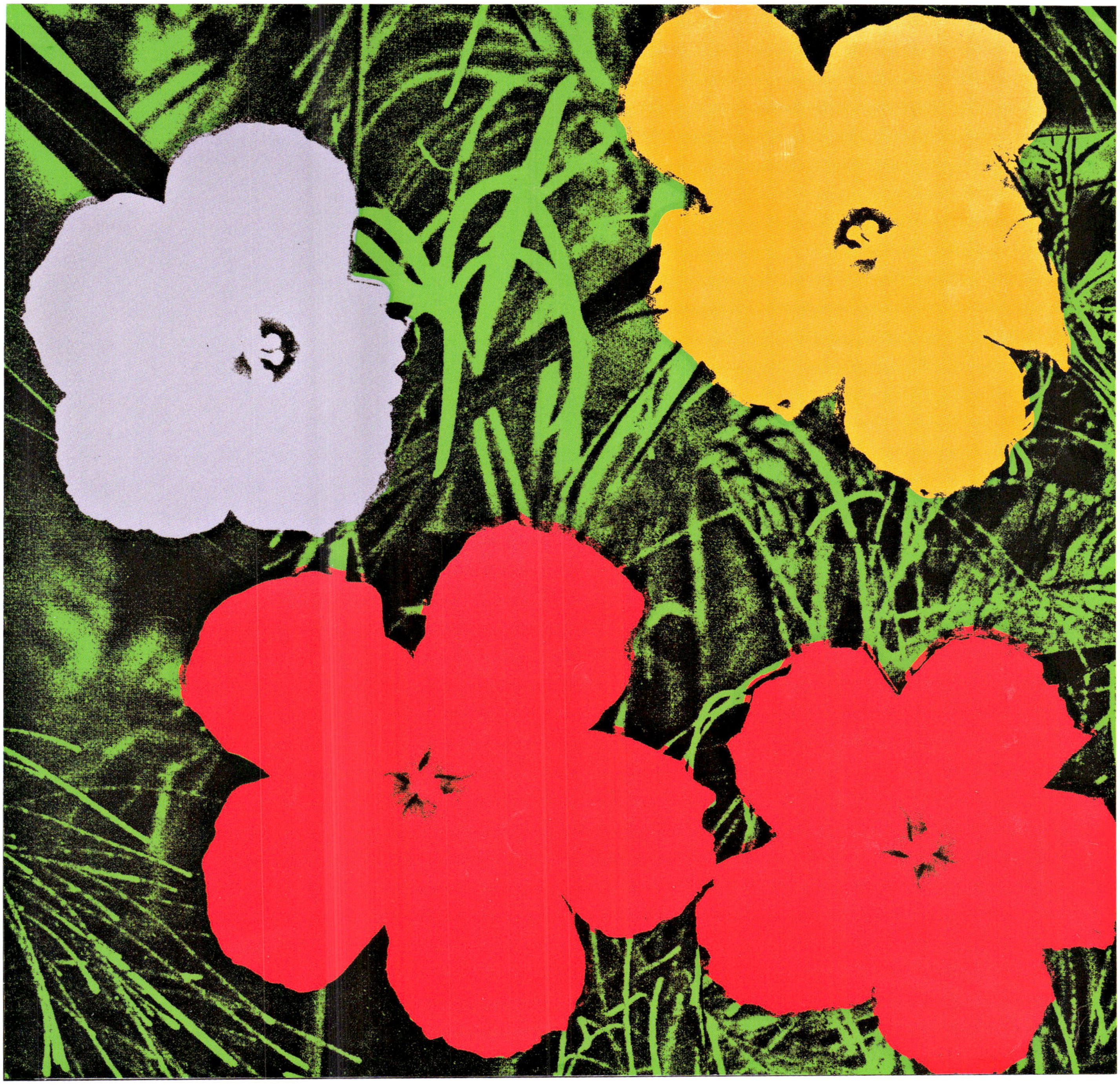

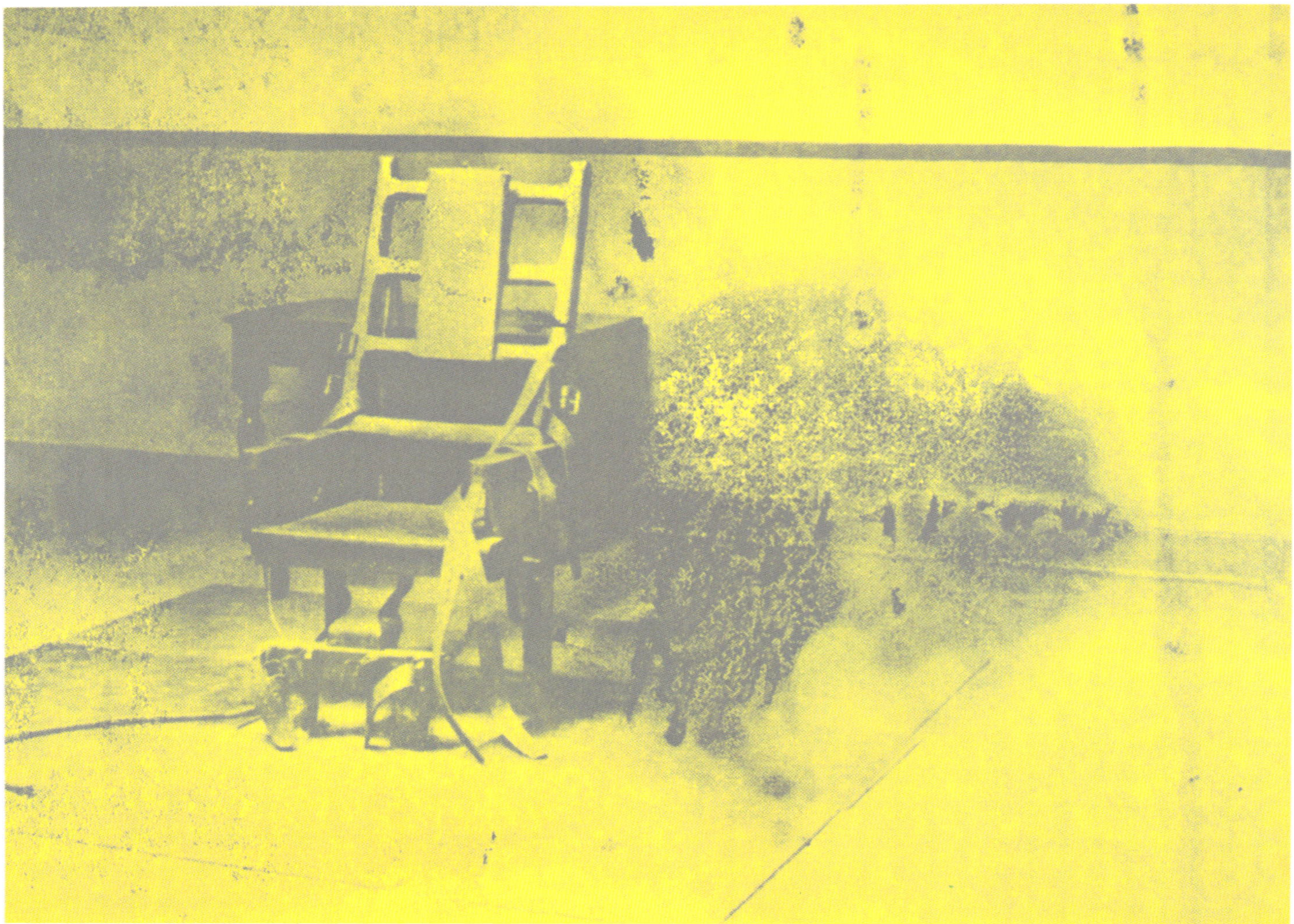

**Electric Chairs**, 1971. Screenprints, each 35½ x 48 in.

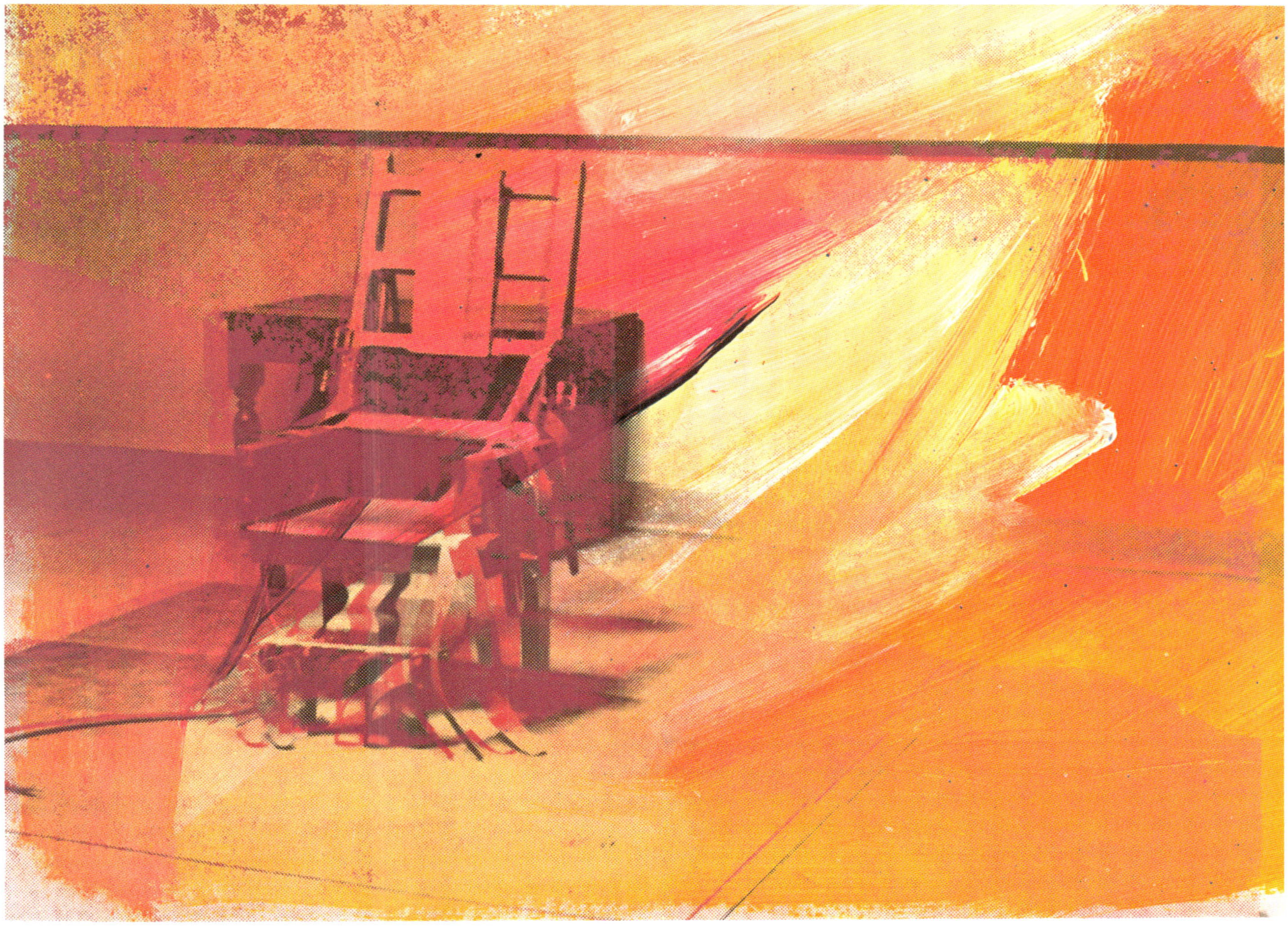

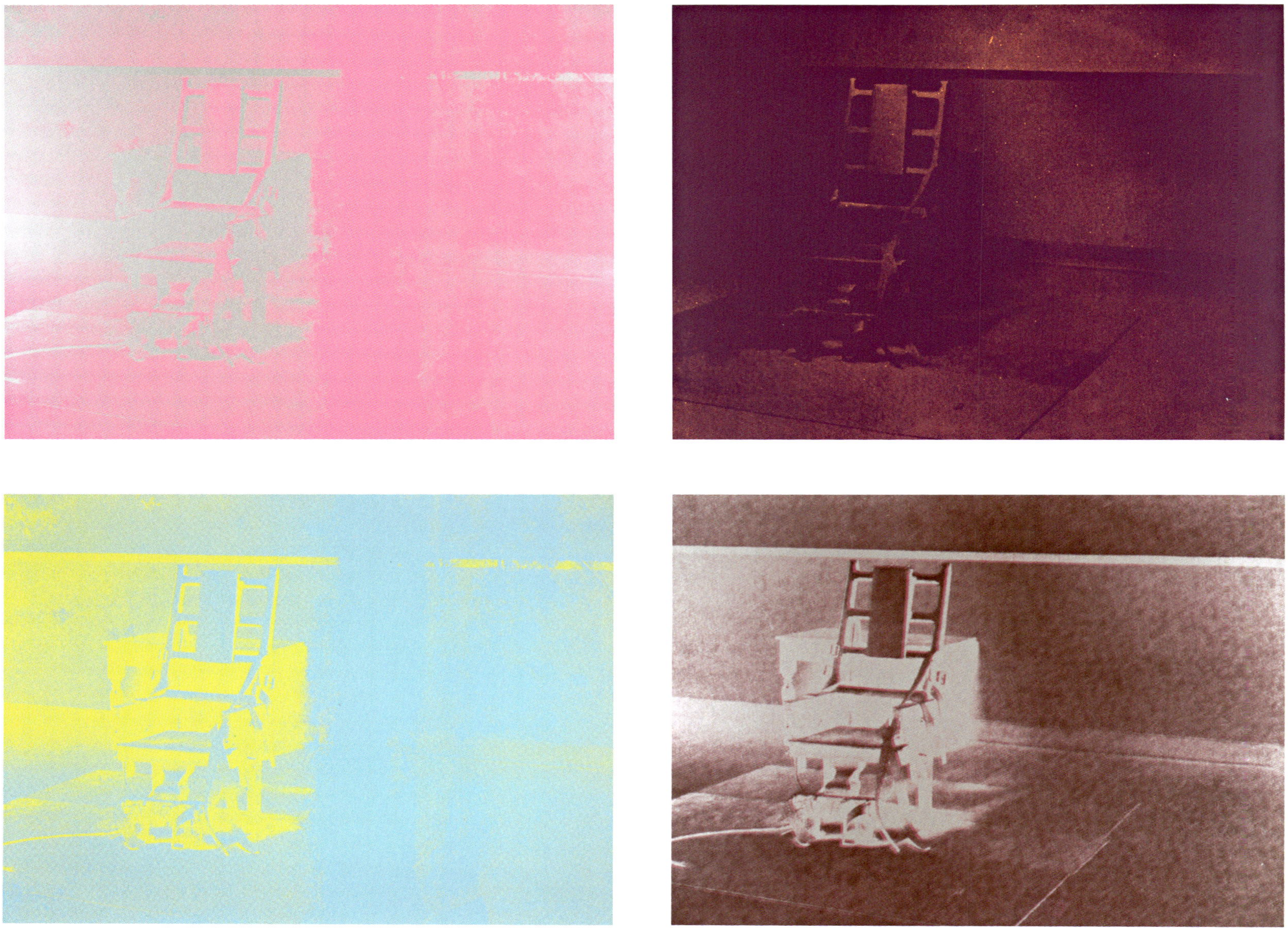

**Electric Chairs**, 1971. Screenprints, each 35½ x 48 in.

**Mao**, 1972. Screenprint, 36 x 36 in.

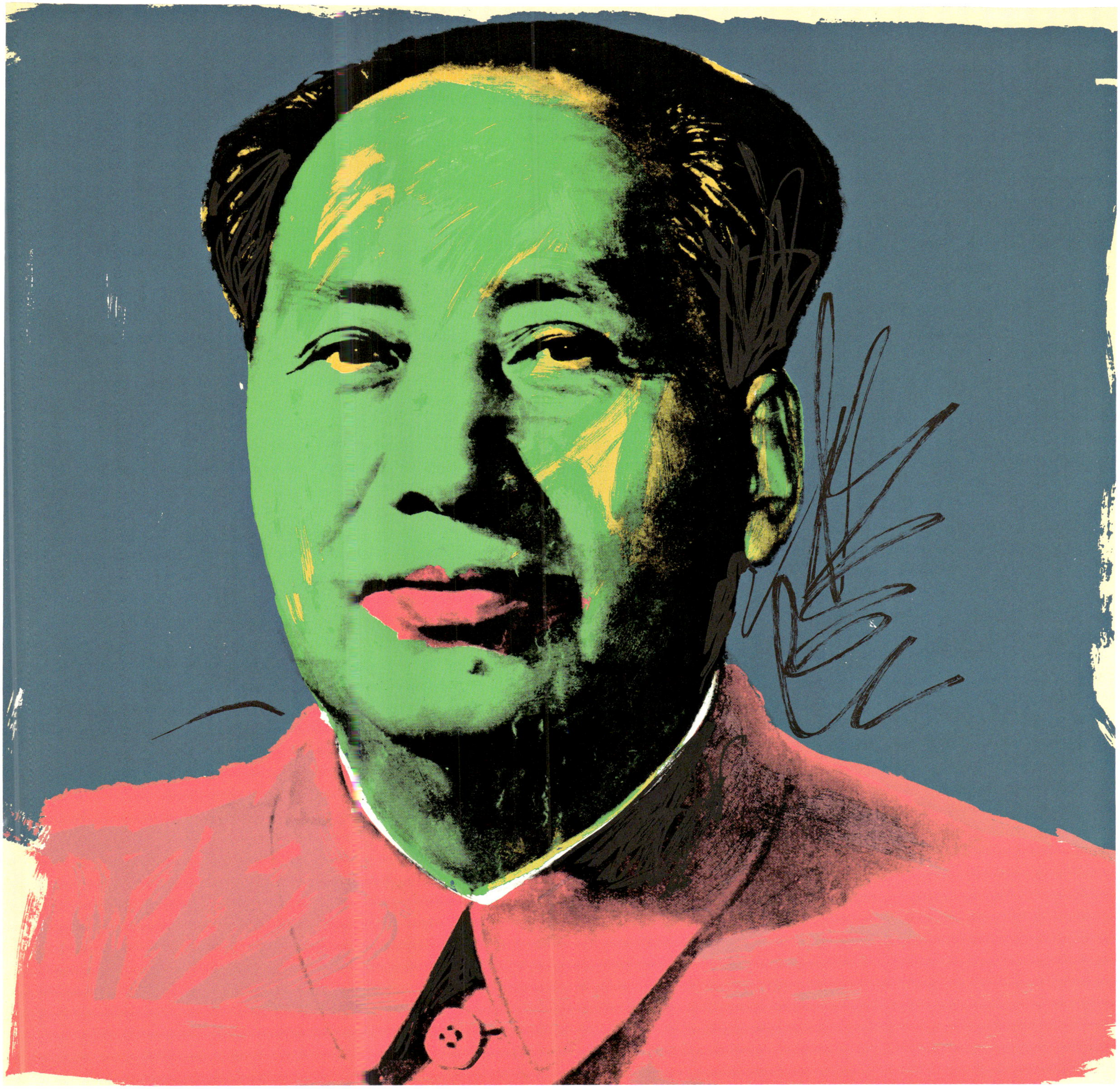

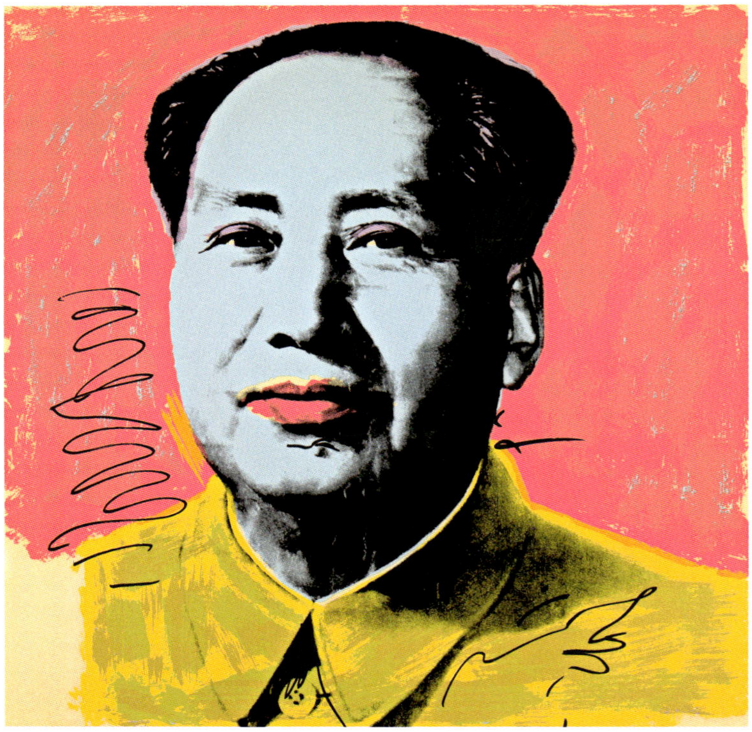
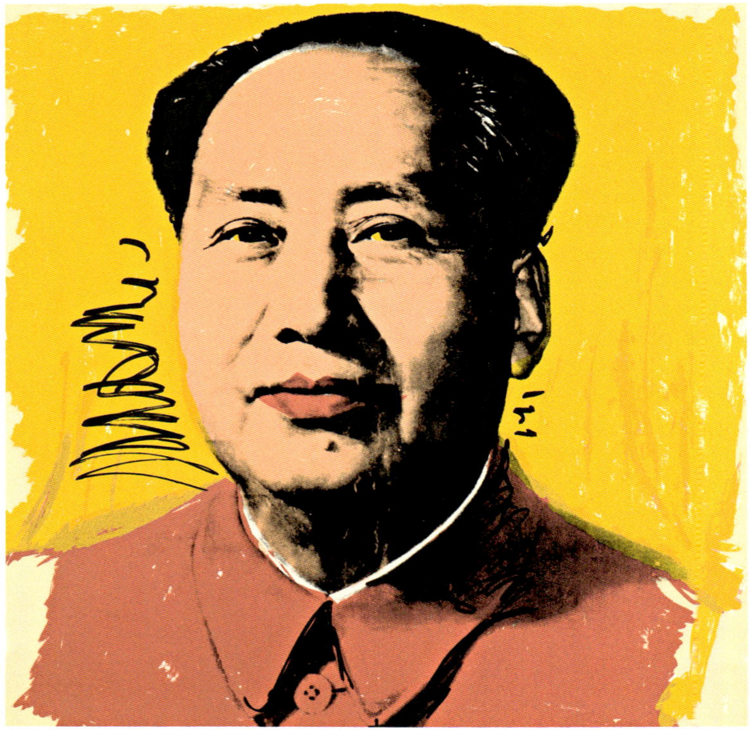

**Mao**, 1972. Screenprints, each 36 x 36 in.

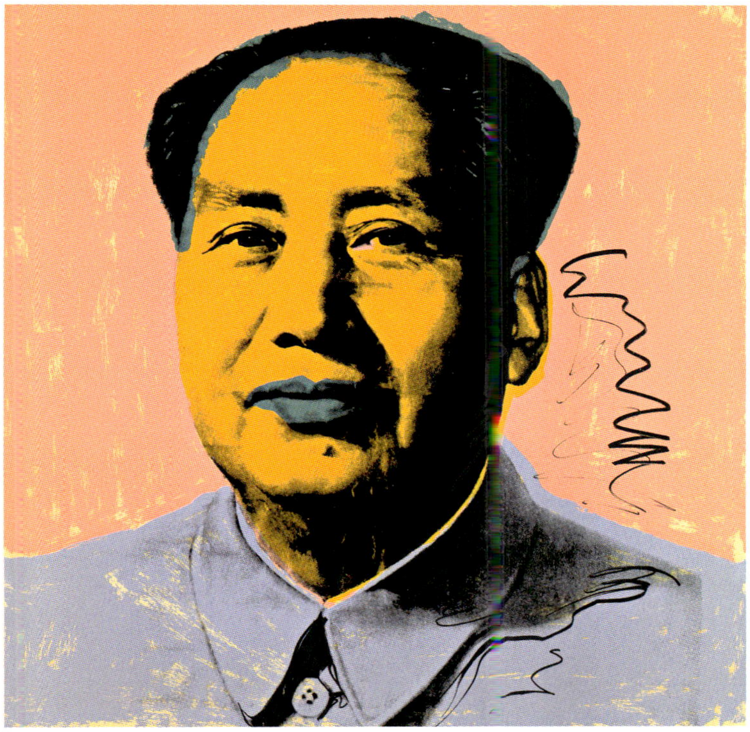

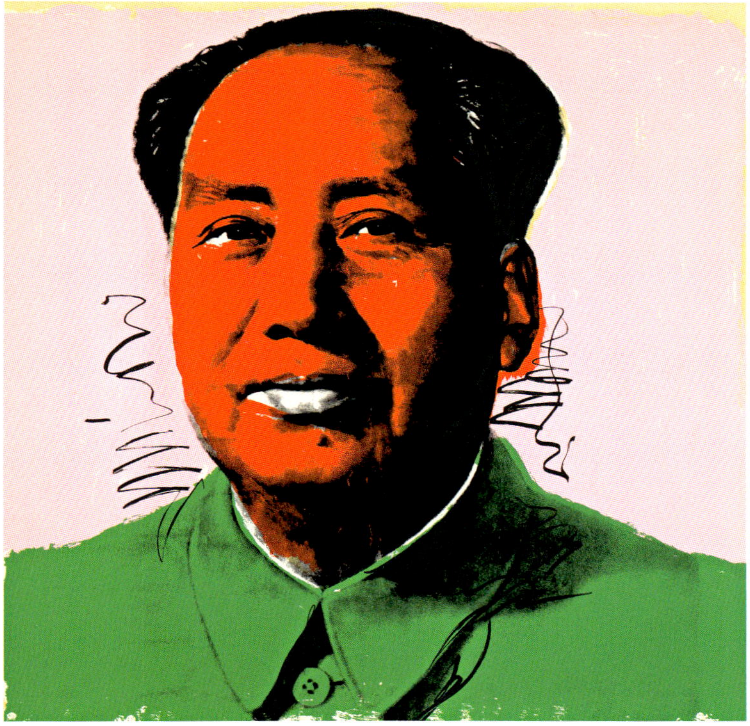

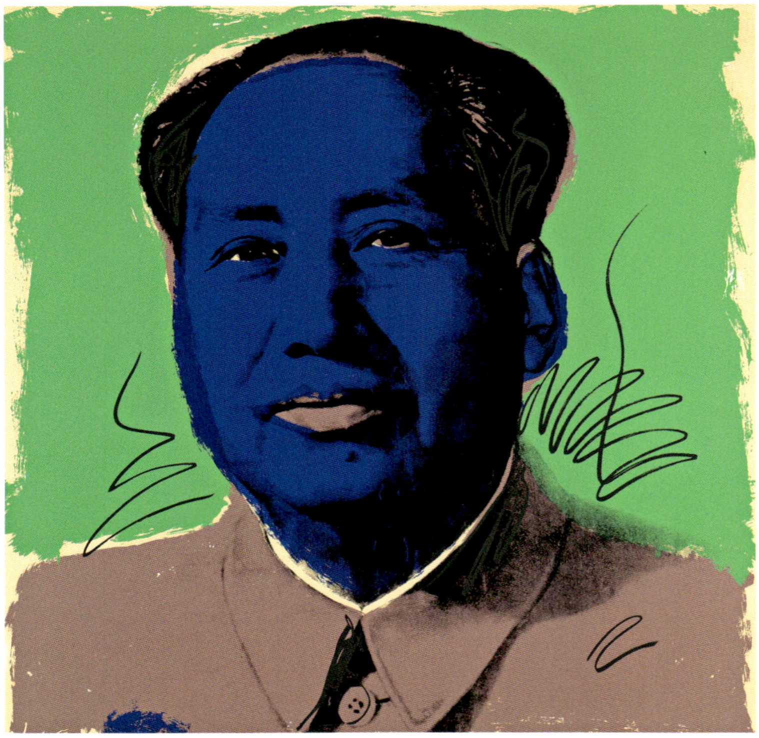

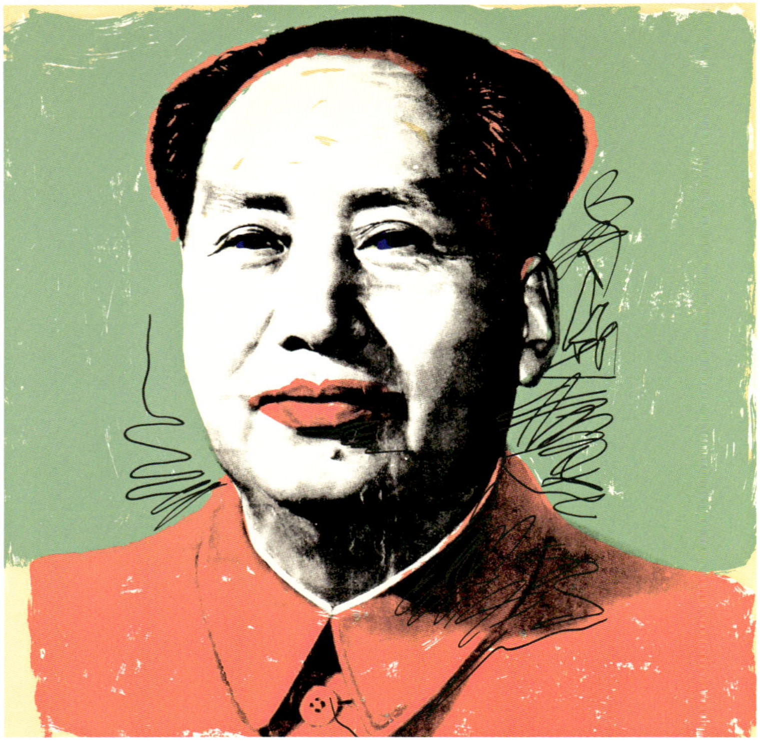

**Mao**, 1972. Screenprints, each 36 x 36 in.

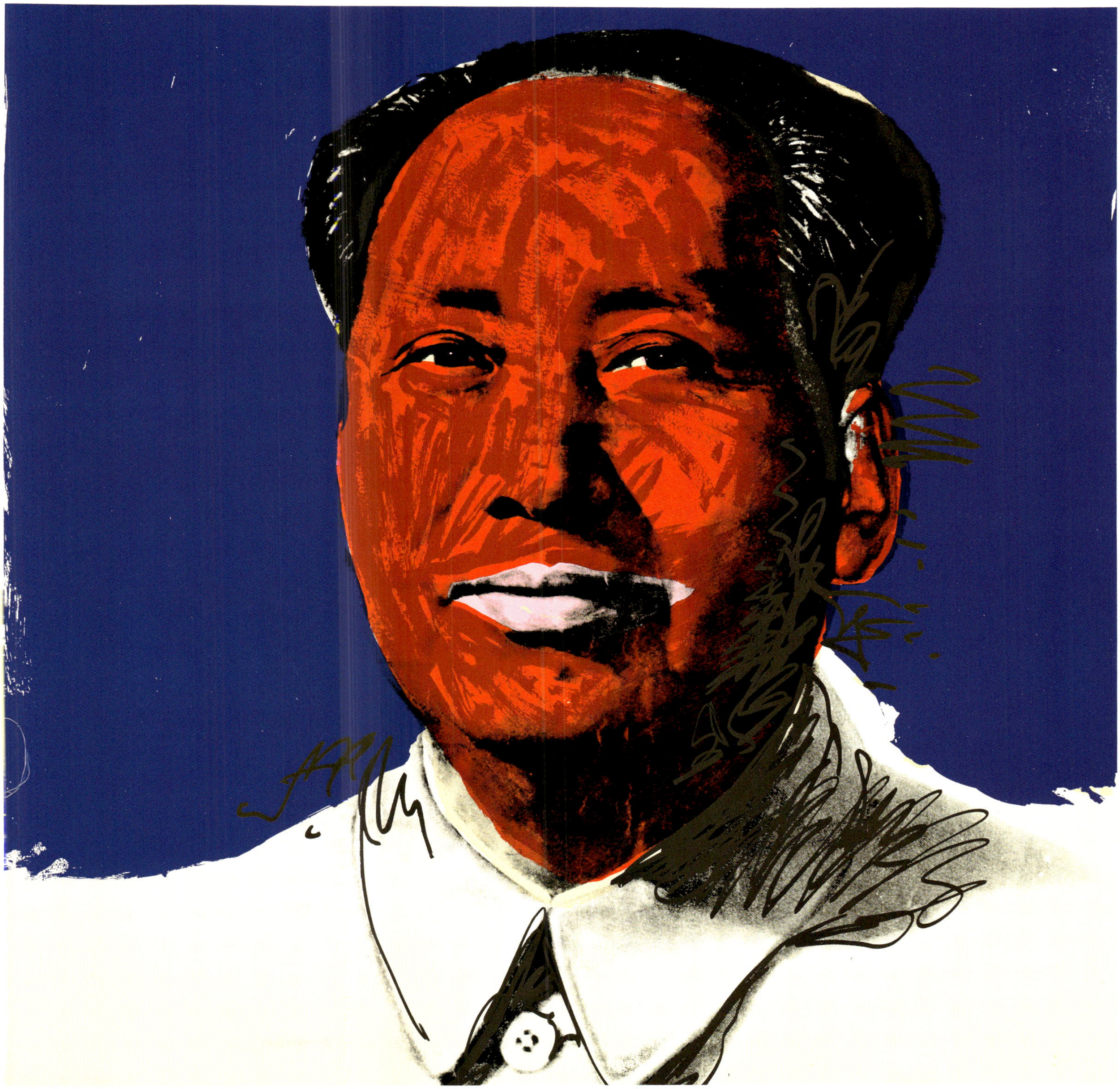

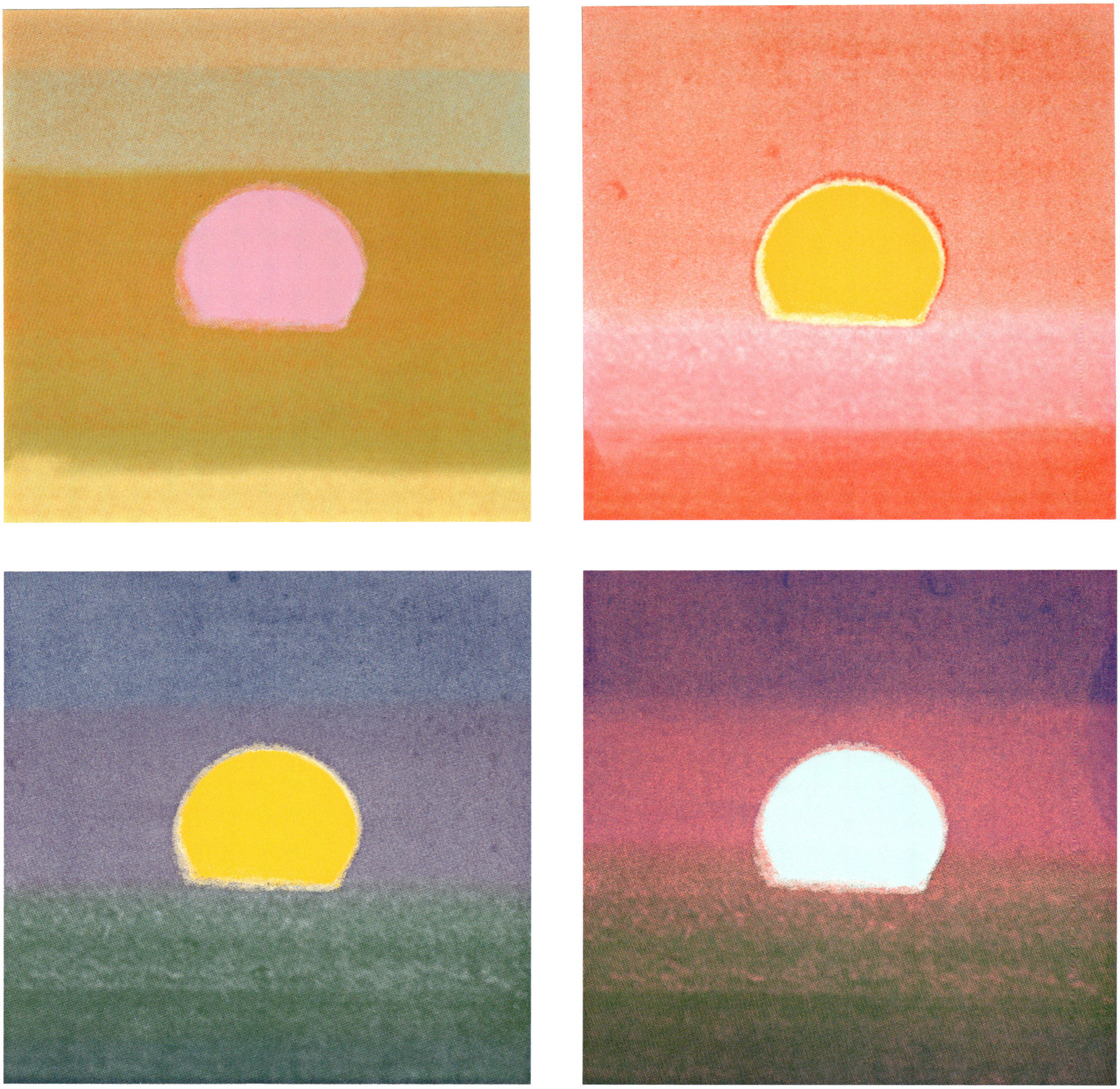

**Sunset**, 1972. Screenprints, each 34 x 34 in.

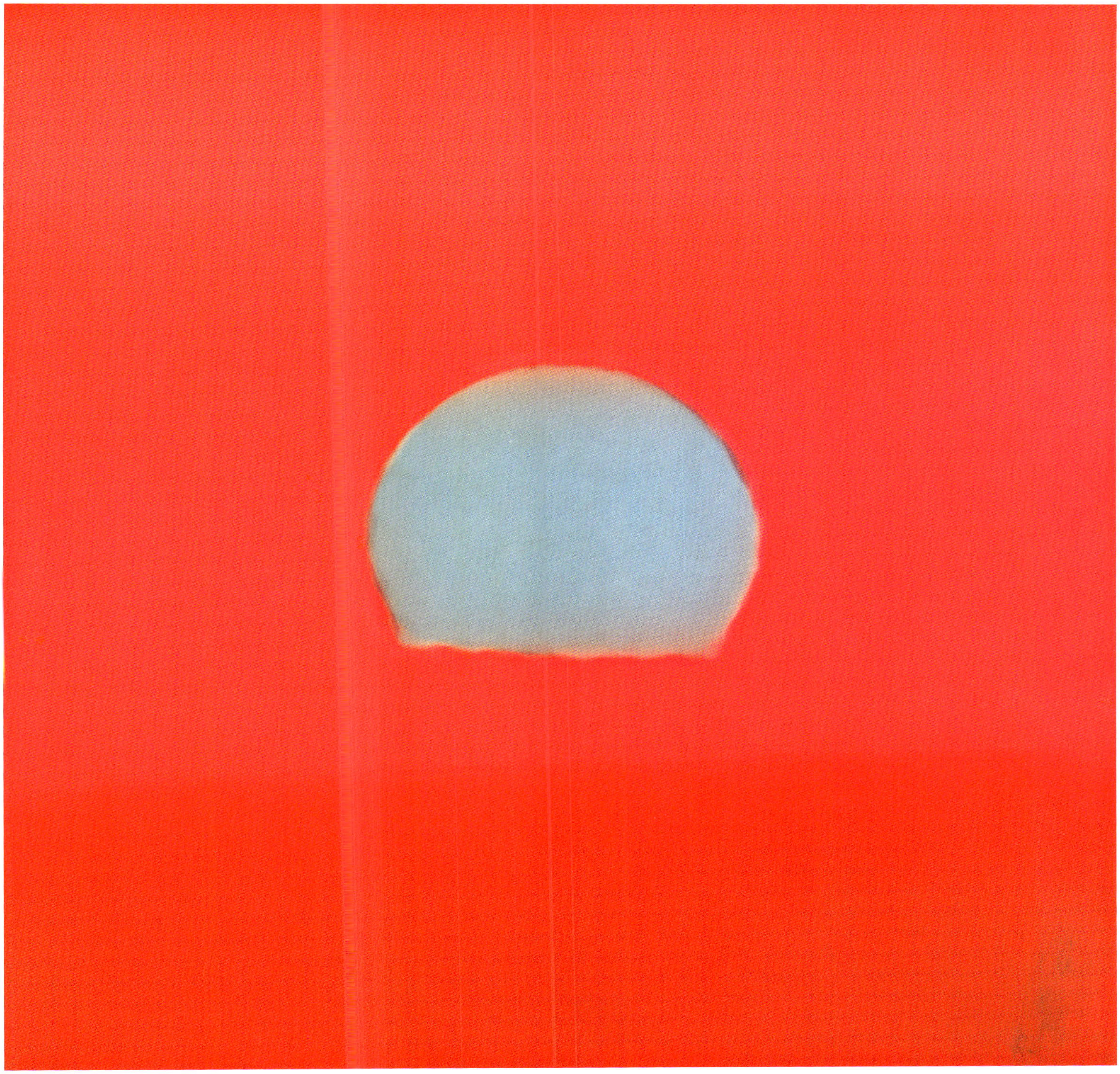

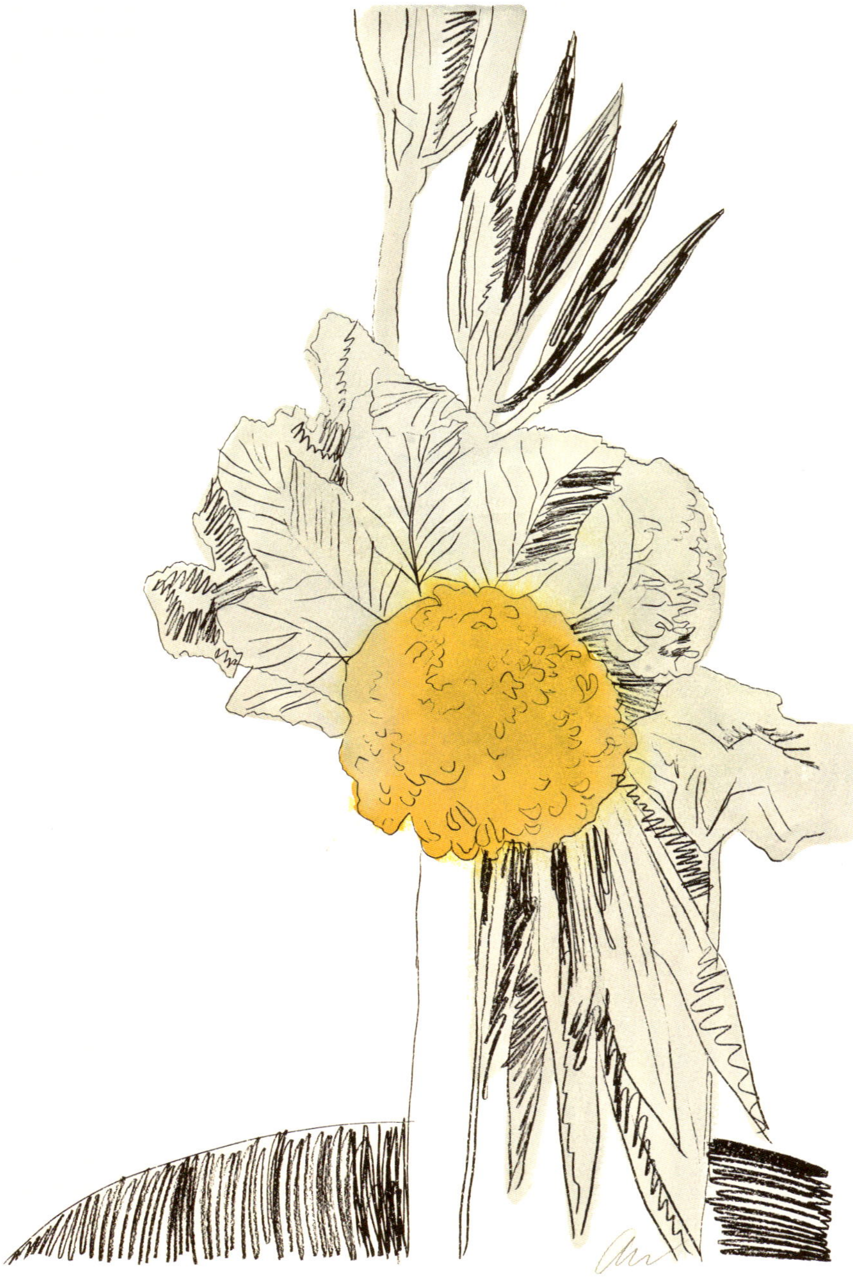

**Flowers (Hand-Colored)**, 1974. Screenprints, hand-colored with watercolor dye, each 40⅞ x 27¼ in.

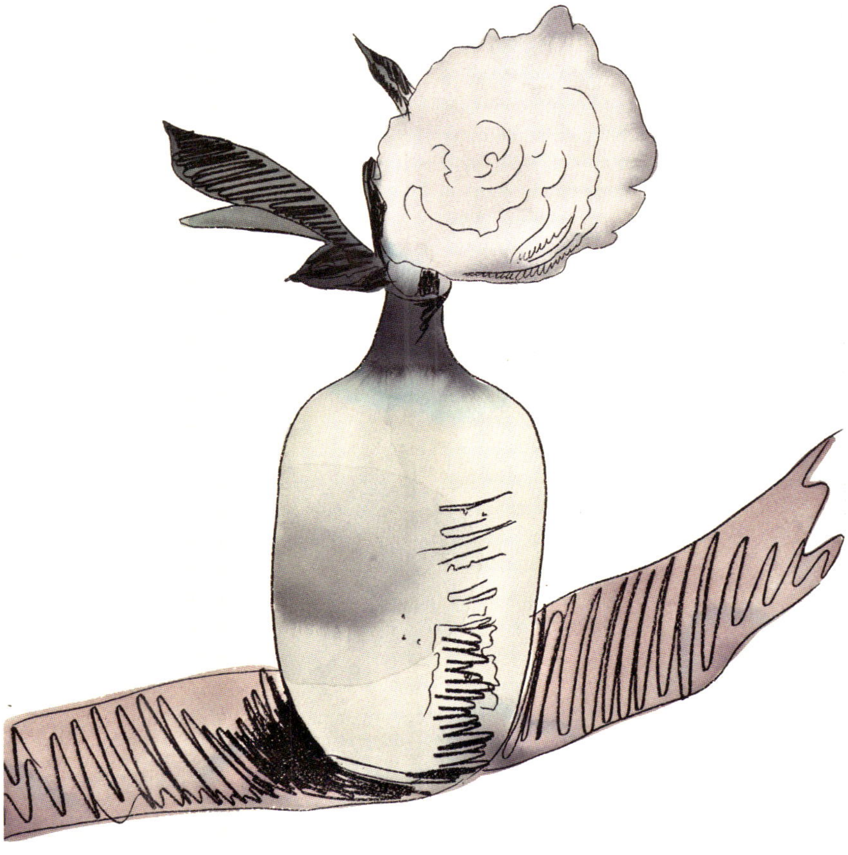

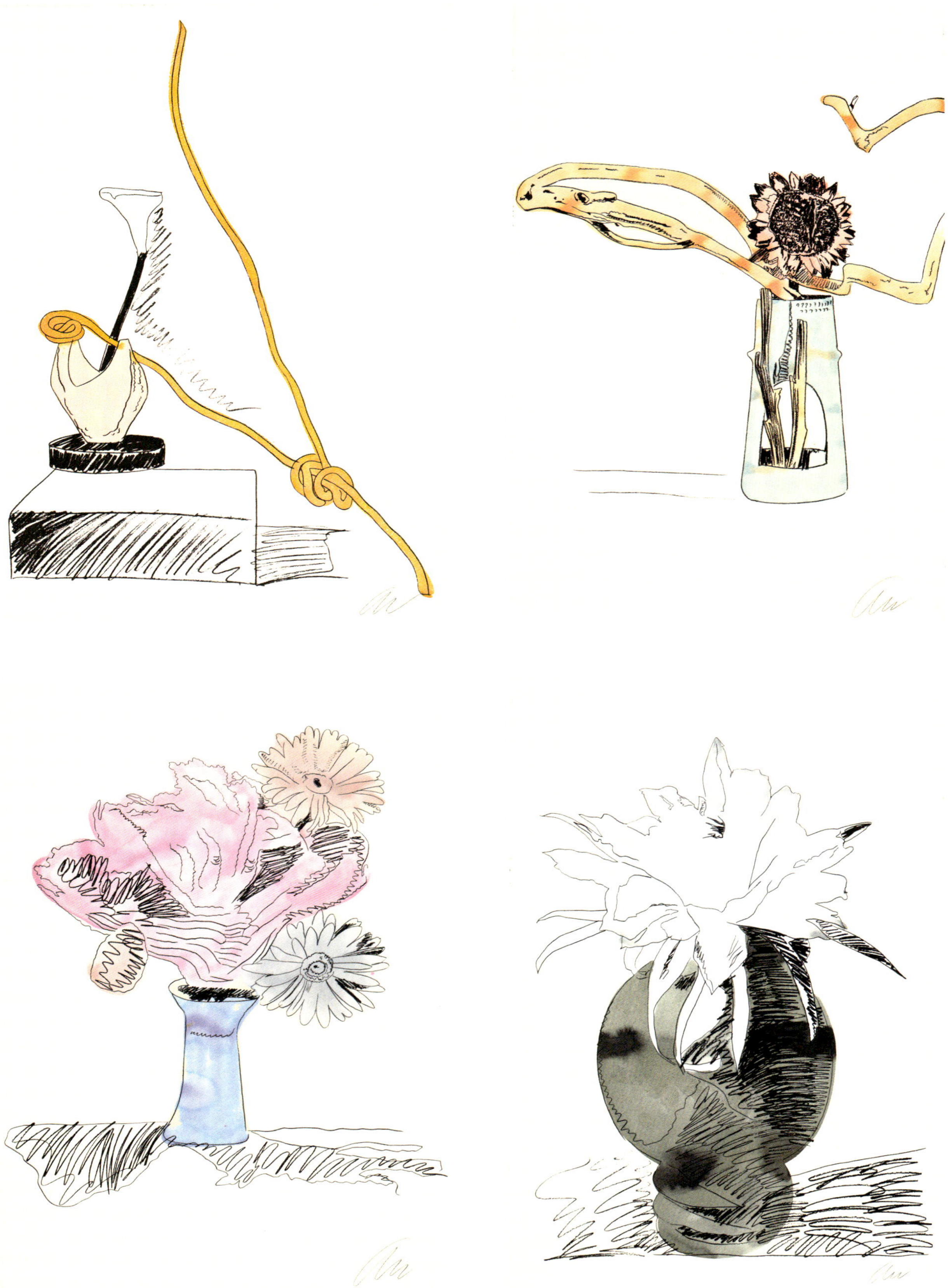

**Flowers (Hand-Colored)**, 1974. Screenprints, hand-colored with watercolor dye, each $40\frac{7}{8}$ x $27\frac{1}{4}$ in.

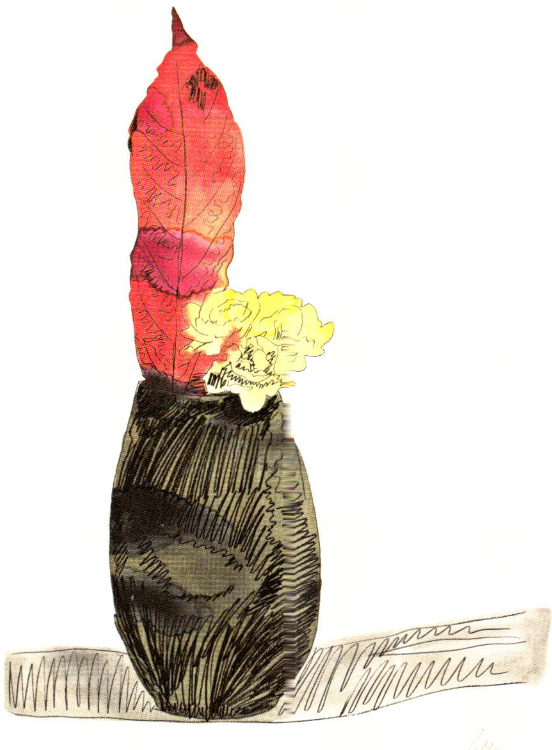

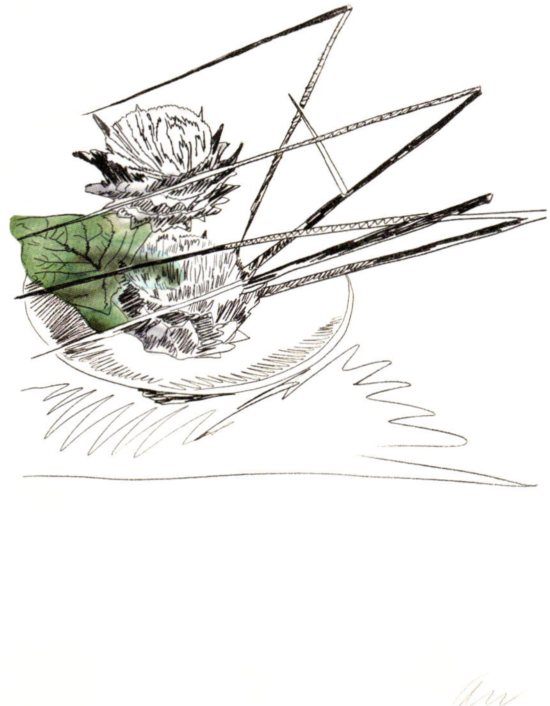

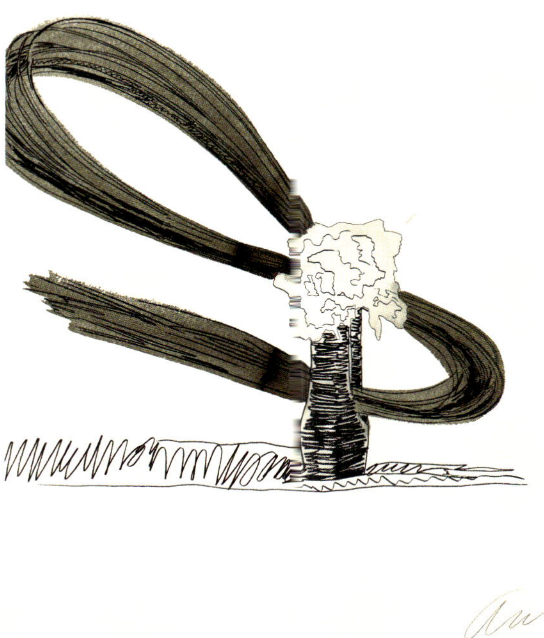

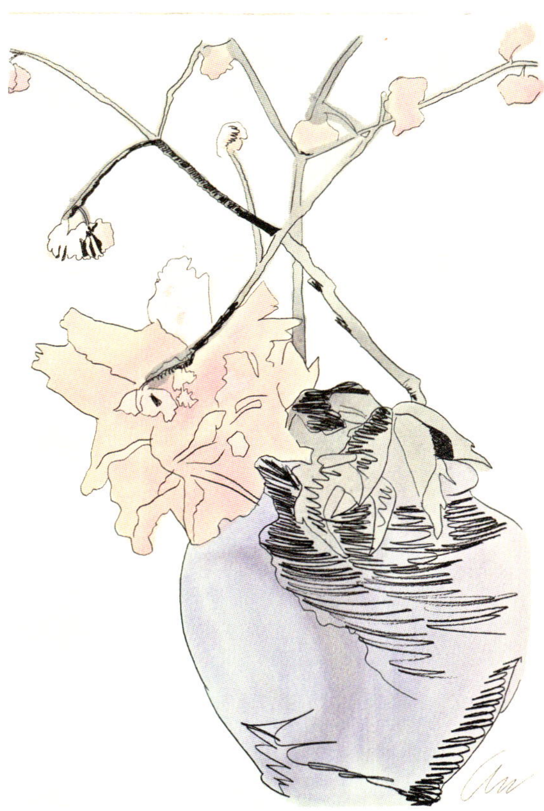

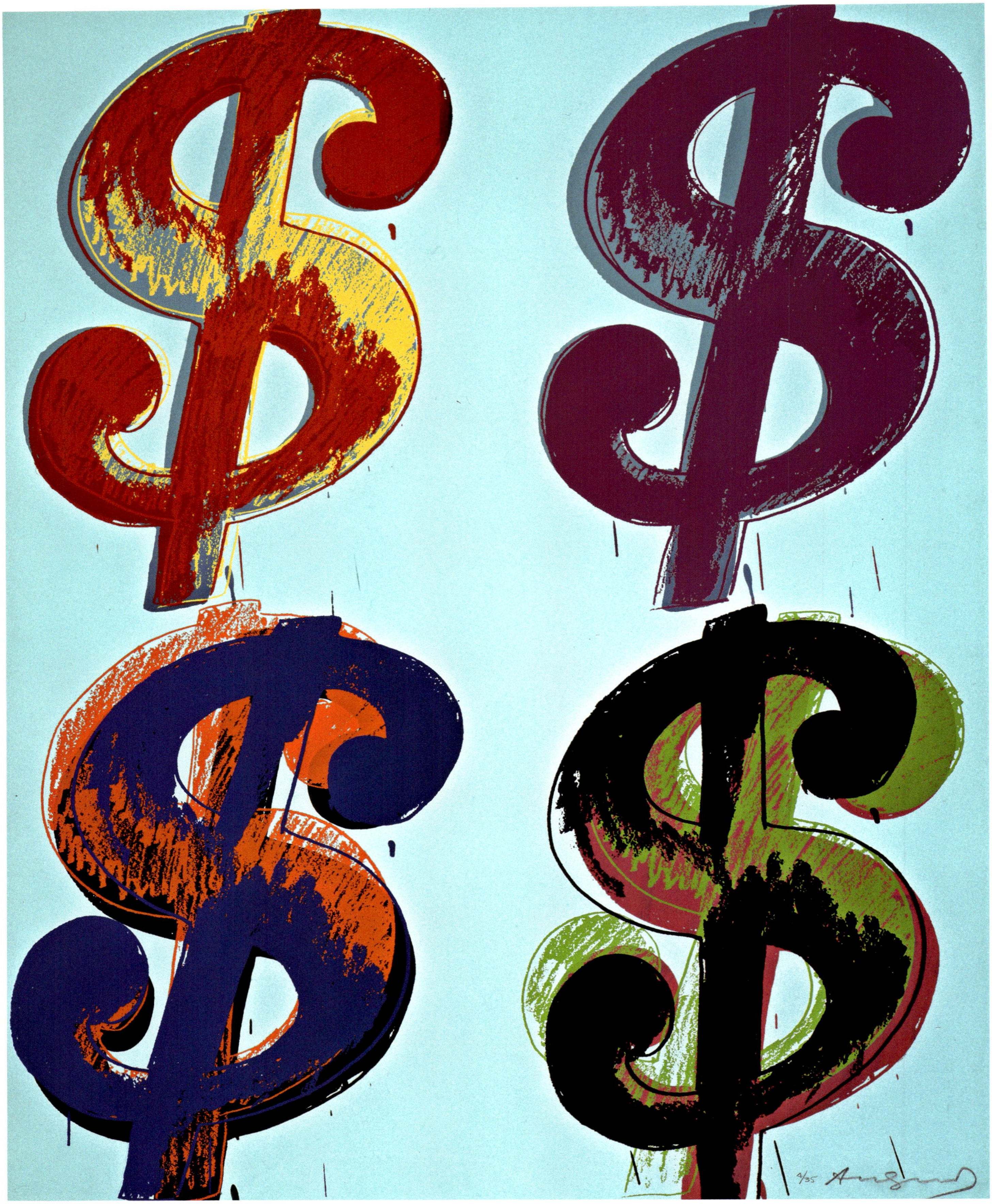

# Andy Warhol Enterprises, Inc.: 1975–1987

With his international art stardom firmly established in the 1960s, Warhol wanted to retire from painting and devote himself to making movies. This new direction required a change of scene. On the prodding of his business manager Fred Hughes and the film director Paul Morrissey, Warhol moved the Factory in early 1968 to an office building on Union Square. Divested of the silver foil walls and the party atmosphere, the second Factory was businesslike, with a more efficient operational structure, corporatized under the legal entity "Andy Warhol Enterprises, Inc." Warhol first used this identity in the 1950s for his commercial work, but, now revitalized, it covered many ambitious "Business Art" endeavors.

This move began before Solanas's attempt on his life in 1968, but that traumatizing event seems to have played a role in crystallizing this calculated route away from the underground scene. After his long recovery from the gunshot wounds, Warhol adopted a jet-set lifestyle that capitalized on his earlier successes; he surrounded himself with another subculture, this one of celebrities and patrons from the business world and high society. By the fall of 1974, Andy Warhol Enterprises moved into a suite of offices at 860 Broadway. The "crazy druggy people" that Warhol had formerly embraced as integral to his creative process were replaced by professionals who ran the various branches of the business.[1] Warhol had become a businessman, artist-executive, and media mogul with his hands in film production, *Interview* magazine,

**$ (4)**, 1982. Unique color screenprint, 40 x 32 in.

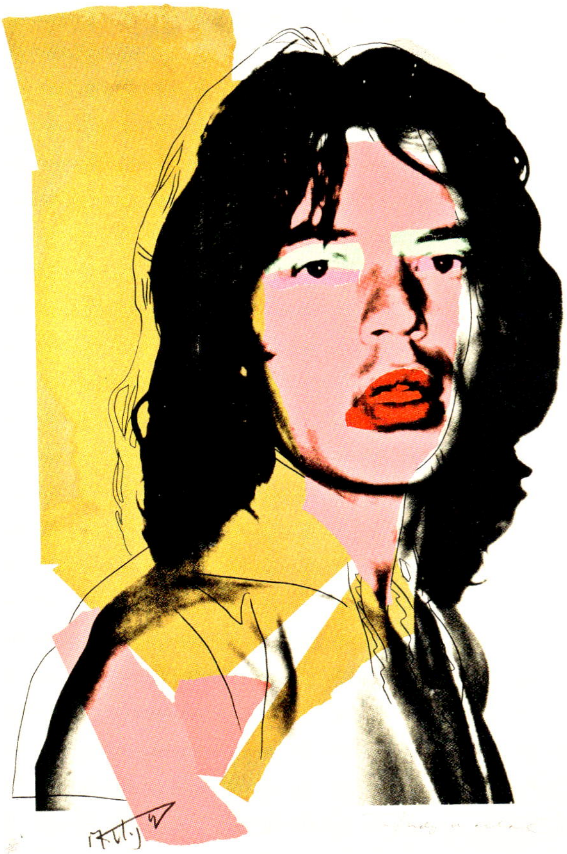

**Mick Jagger**, 1975. Screenprint, 43½ x 28¾ in.

print publishing, and an art studio. In *The Philosophy of Andy Warhol: From A to B and Back Again* (1975), Warhol explained his motivation:

> Business art is the step that comes after art. I started as a commercial artist, and I want to finish as a business artist. Being good in business is the most fascinating kind of art. After I did the thing called "art" or whatever it is called, I went into business art. I wanted to be an Art Businessman or a Business Artist. During the hippie era people put down the idea of business. They'd say "money is bad" and "working is bad." But making money is art, and working is art—and good business is the best art.[2]

As an artist presiding over a creative media company, Warhol's relationship to media images changed dramatically from his more critical usage in the 1960s. His career had come full circle from his days in advertising, as he returned to creating images that easily circulated in mainstream visual culture. Notably, his portraits—a significant source of income generated from private commissions—often flowed from one platform to another, as evidenced by *Mick Jagger* (1975, above and pp. 120–25) a published print project that appeared on an album cover several years later. This series of ten screenprints demonstrates the stylistic developments that made Warhol's portraiture distinctive and sought after and signals what would become an aesthetic associated with the disco era. Warhol returned to using blocks of color as distinct formal elements in the composition, a technique he had first employed in drawings in the 1950s.

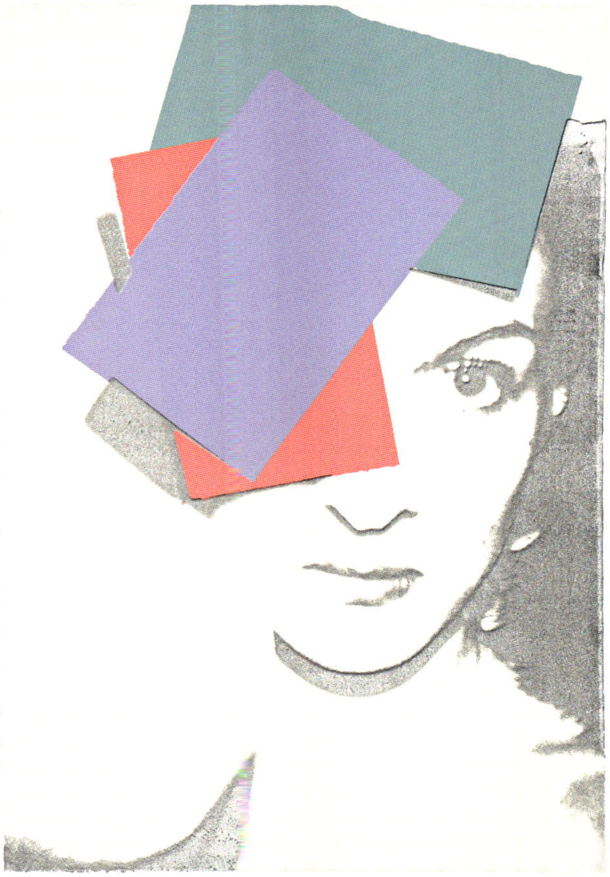

**Paloma Picasso**, 1975. Screenprint, 41 x 29½ in.

In his portrait of *Paloma Picasso* (1975, above), he experimented in the screenprint by combining the photographic source and squares of colored paper that flatten the composition and partially obscure Picasso's face.

Warhol took his experimentation one step further with *Ladies and Gentlemen* (1975, pp. 114–19), where torn pieces of paper overlay color and shape on the variously posed subjects in dramatic ways. Warhol often solicited ideas for his work, and he took encouragement for this series from the Italian art dealer Luciano Anselmino, who eventually published and exhibited the prints. The series features drag queens who were invited from the Gilded Grape nightclub in Greenwich Village to Warhol's studio, where he photographed them. Warhol was fascinated by transvestites and male-to-female transgender; Candy Darling, Ondine, and Holly Woodlawn were some of the stars of his films. Not only did he find them to be the epitome of the movie star's glamorous presence, but he was also drawn to the artifice and gender role-play associated with drag. "I guess it's interesting to try to be another sex."[3]

In the first half of the 1970s, Warhol's prints reveal more about his desire and his homosexuality than his two-dimensional work had since the 1950s. (The films made in the Factory explore sex explicitly and in this way stand apart from his work in print and painting.) Warhol's cameras, both film and Polaroid, allowed him to watch same-sex and heterosexual couples through a mediating remove. As his filmmaking enterprise was declining, prints and photographs became another outlet for manipulating and circulating this highly provocative form of media image. With the Polaroid as the intermediary, he could capture

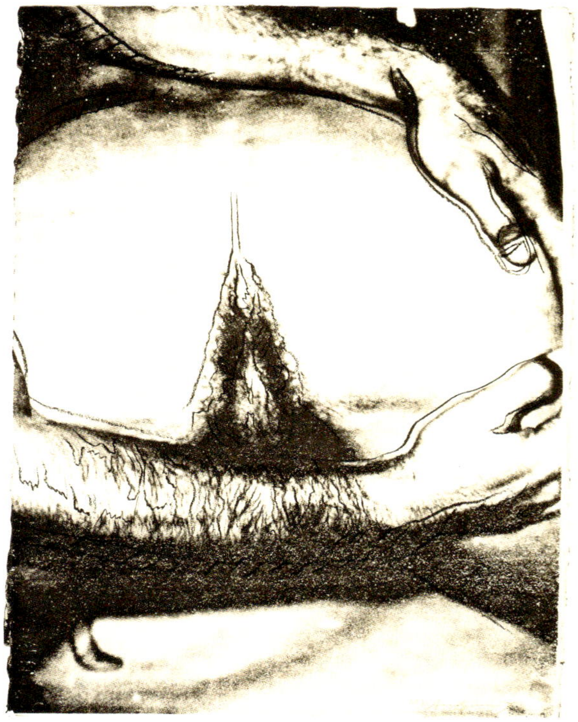

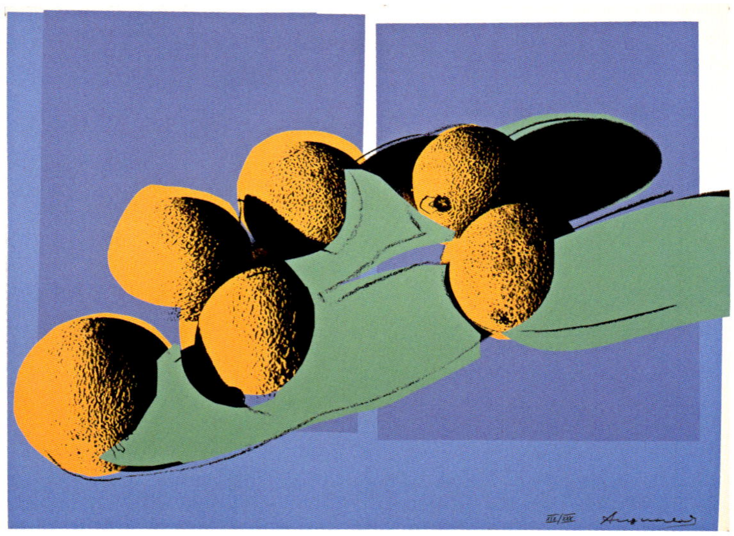

**Sex Parts**, 1978. Screenprint, 31 x 23¼ in.
**Space Fruit: Still Lifes, Cantaloupes I**, 1979. Screenprint, 30 x 40 in.

willing portrait subjects like Mick Jagger in seductive poses. A slender, shirtless Jagger captured in the Polaroids is already sexy; then Warhol, in his prints, emphasizes full lips and open mouth with hot colors, blacks out facial features as if to censor identity, and accents fine hands and long hair with drawn line. The 1978 six-print portfolio *Sex Parts* (above) goes further with its graphic portrayal of gay sex. Warhol invited men from bathhouses back to the studio for photo shoots involving sex; he shot close-up depictions of buttocks, penises, and torsos, referring to them, in coded fashion, as "landscapes."[4] In his prolific print output, this series, published in a small edition of thirty with five artist's proofs, is one of very few representations of physical manifestation of desire.

Referring to the sexualized male body as a landscape was another way Warhol distanced himself from the real and the physical. This sense of remove paralleled his exploration of abstraction in the subsequent prints *Space Fruit* and *Shadows*, both published in 1979. *Space Fruit* (above and pp. 142–45) forms a set of sparse still-life compositions based on photographs of various fruits lit at dramatic angles. Very little detail of the fruit is given to imply dimensionality. Large areas of solid color also serve to flatten the picture plane. This use of color gives equal weight to the objects and their shadows, leveling the difference between presence and absence. *Shadows* (opposite left and pp. 140–41) is a similar exercise in depicting what is not there.[5] Based on a photograph of darkened room, the many works in the series

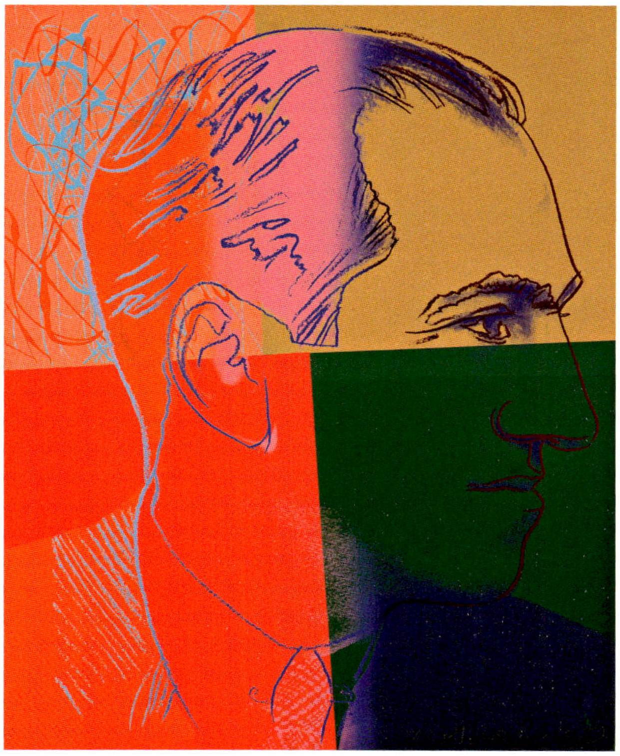

**Shadows I**, 1979. Screenprint with diamond dust, 43 x 30½ in.
**Ten Portraits of Jews of the Twentieth Century: George Gershwin**, 1980. Screenprint, 40 x 32 in.

hone in on shape and surface, rather than depict a perspective into an architectural space. Both series resonate with Warhol's darker obsessions with death and decay: when read metaphorically a still life or looming shadow becomes a memento mori, or reminder of one's eventual demise.

Both series also indulge the visual plenty associated with Warhol's rich surfaces, now including diamond dust, and their compositional complexity stands in counterpoint to the remaining program of the Business Art model—portrait commissions—taking place at the same time. The critics had a strong distaste for his outright commercialism, yet commissions kept coming. Warhol and his quirks, fetishes, and bohemian background had been accepted into an upper-class cultural domain where his slippery ability to avoid stating beliefs and his vapid guise became virtues to his business. From this "in" position, he managed to become a great cultural arbiter who, through *Interview* magazine, appearances at Studio 54 and on television, and his role as an ad pitchman, claimed the power of the media to designate what and who would rise to the top of the cultural imagination circa 1980.[6]

By 1980, Warhol entered into a partnership with the gallery owner Ronald Feldman and created a number of thematic portfolios. The subject matter was often suggested by Feldman, as was the case with their first endeavor, *Ten Portraits of Jews of the Twentieth Century* (1980, above right and pp. 150–55).

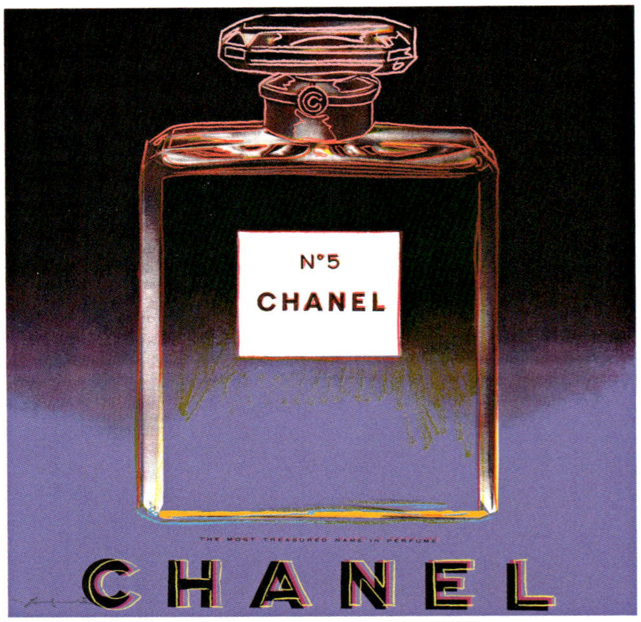


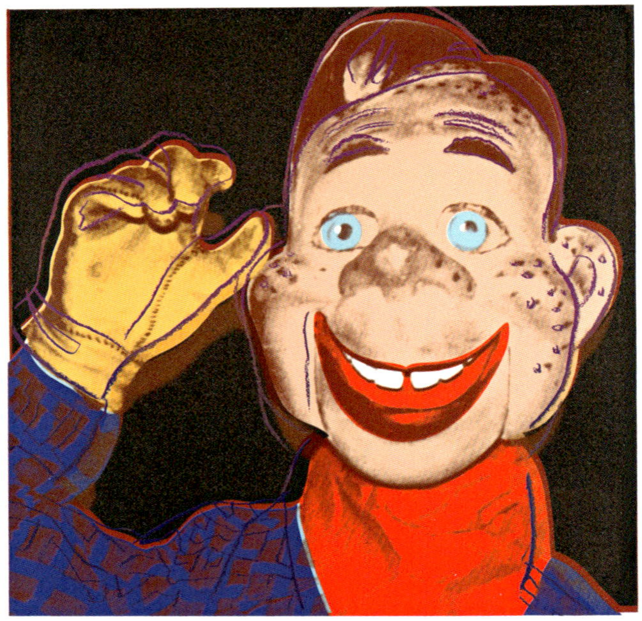

**Ads: Chanel**, 1985. Screenprint, 38 x 38 in.
**Myths: Howdy Doody**, 1981. Screenprint with diamond dust, 38 x 38 in.

The portraits of historical subjects from Albert Einstein to Gertrude Stein derived from existing images and mark a return to exploring extant material, sometimes drawn from media images, other times from books or other archival sources. The series also marks the time when prints were privileged, and paintings of the subjects would follow later.[7] Elsewhere in the art world, rising artists of the "Pictures Generation" reevaluated appropriation and the role images play in determining social mores and historical narratives. Warhol did not return to his earlier tactics with quite the same critical gusto. The 1985 *Ads* series (above left and pp. 170–73) reads as a celebratory, almost nostalgic look at iconic advertisements and logos from years past, alongside more recent campaigns for Volkswagen and the Macintosh computer. *Ads* follows the through line from Warhol's earliest commercial work, a study of the powerful appeal of the media's images as an alluring, seductive visual experience. An earlier series, *Myths* (1981), still problematized this attraction. A hybrid—some images were appropriated; many were staged photographs—the series depicts archetypes as a set of flawed characters. *Santa Claus* leers out from behind his costume; *Uncle Sam* wears an inscrutable expression; *Howdy Doody* (above right and p. 159), *Mickey Mouse,* and *Superman* are moralizing figures whose authority or authenticity appears to be called into question when assembled in this grouping. The black skin of *Mammy* (p. 158) disappears into the black background as she becomes an invisible character in what appears to contemporary eyes as a frank commentary on the position of African Americans in US cultural industry and society at large. Warhol himself appears as *The Shadow* (p. 160), a reference to the crime fighter of old-time radio drama. Instead of a hero, Warhol is a lurker in the wings, the artist as marginalized persona who sees and knows all.

The final years of Warhol's printmaking career were filled with portfolio commissions, with themes ranging from endangered species to details of Renaissance paintings. Often these works served other functions, sold to raise funds for political or awareness-raising campaigns. The late works complete a circle started with his first shoe ads and book covers, all inserted into a vast stream of visual information gaining meaning through context and circulation. Warhol's final print works, *Camouflage* (opposite and pp. 174–79), published posthumously in 1987, have been read as a metaphor for the enigmatic

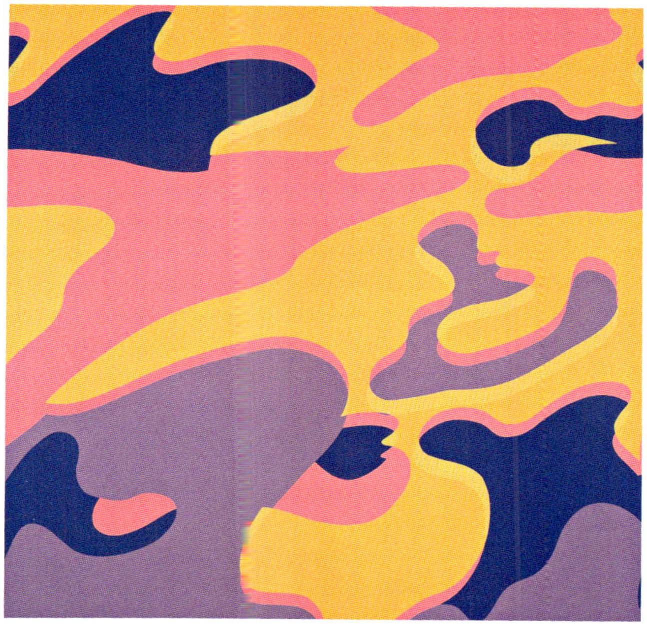

**Camouflage**, 1987. Screenprint, 38 x 38 in.

character that was Warhol, who never provided the public with a full view of himself.[8] Like his abstract *Shadows*, they empty the visual field of representation and signification, yet they are full of color and pattern intended to mesmerize the eye and ultimately distract us from comprehending what is concealed. Military camouflage patterns were once hand-painted, then mass-produced in repeating sections. The development of camouflage suggests the transformation of a traditional image based on visual observation into the technical image Vilém Flusser proposed, one created and propagated by machines without human intervention. Like Flusser's experimental artist, Warhol played against these images by infusing the patterns with animating color, taking away any function the original image had. Ultimately, Warhol's screenprints mimic the screens that media images appear on, but like *Camouflage*, they scramble the message the media desires to impart.

Notes

1. Arthur C. Danto, *Andy Warhol* (New Haven: Yale University Press, 2009), 121, 124.

2. Andy Warhol, *The Philosophy of Andy Warhol (From A to B and Back Again)* (New York: Harcourt Brace Jovanovich, 1975), 92.

3. Ibid., 98.

4. Joseph D. Ketner II, *Image Machine: Andy Warhol & Photography* (Nuremburg: Verlag für moderne Kunst, 2012), 57.

5. Benjamin Buchloh, "Drawing Blanks: Notes on Andy Warhol's Late Works," *October* 127 (Winter 2009): 11.

6. David Robbins, "Cigar Store Indian: Andy Warhol's *Cowboys and Indians*," *Arts Magazine* 60 (May 1986): 52.

7. Donna De Salvo, "God Is in the Details: The Prints of Andy Warhol," in *Andy Warhol Prints: A Catalogue Raisonné 1962–1987* (New York: Distributed Art Publishers in conjunction with Ronald Feldman Fine Arts, Edition Schellman, and the Andy Warhol Foundation for the Visual Arts, 2003), 30–31.

8. Ibid., 32.

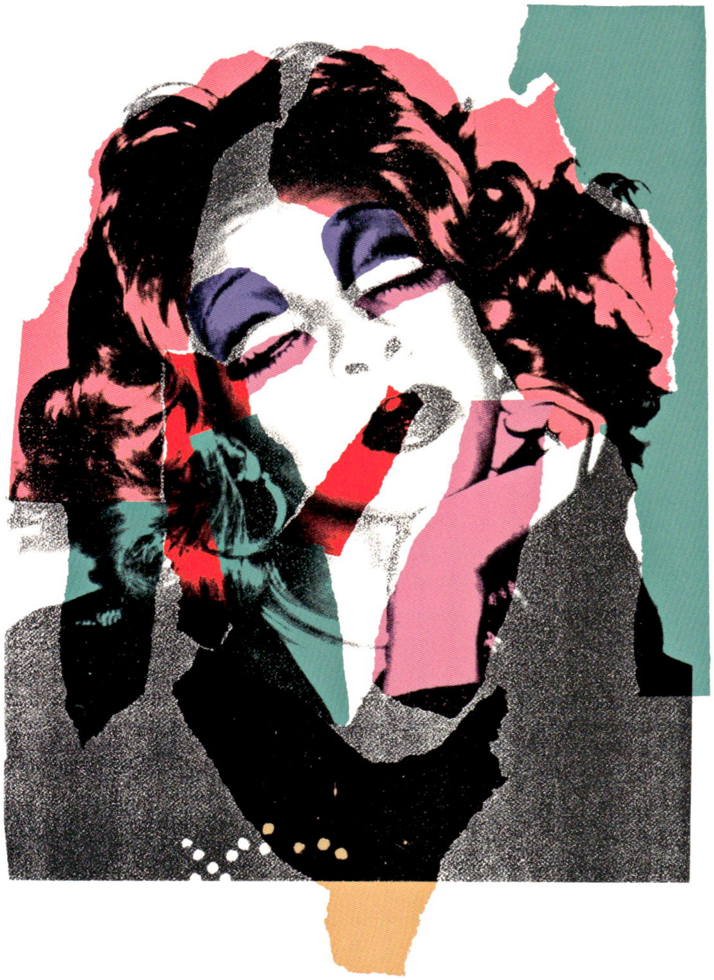

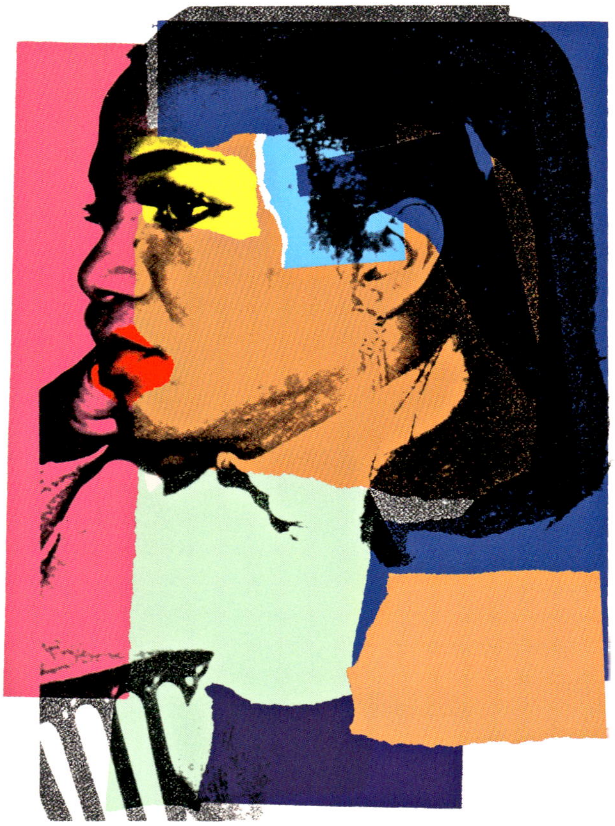

**Ladies and Gentlemen**, 1975. Screenprints, each 43½ x 28½ in.

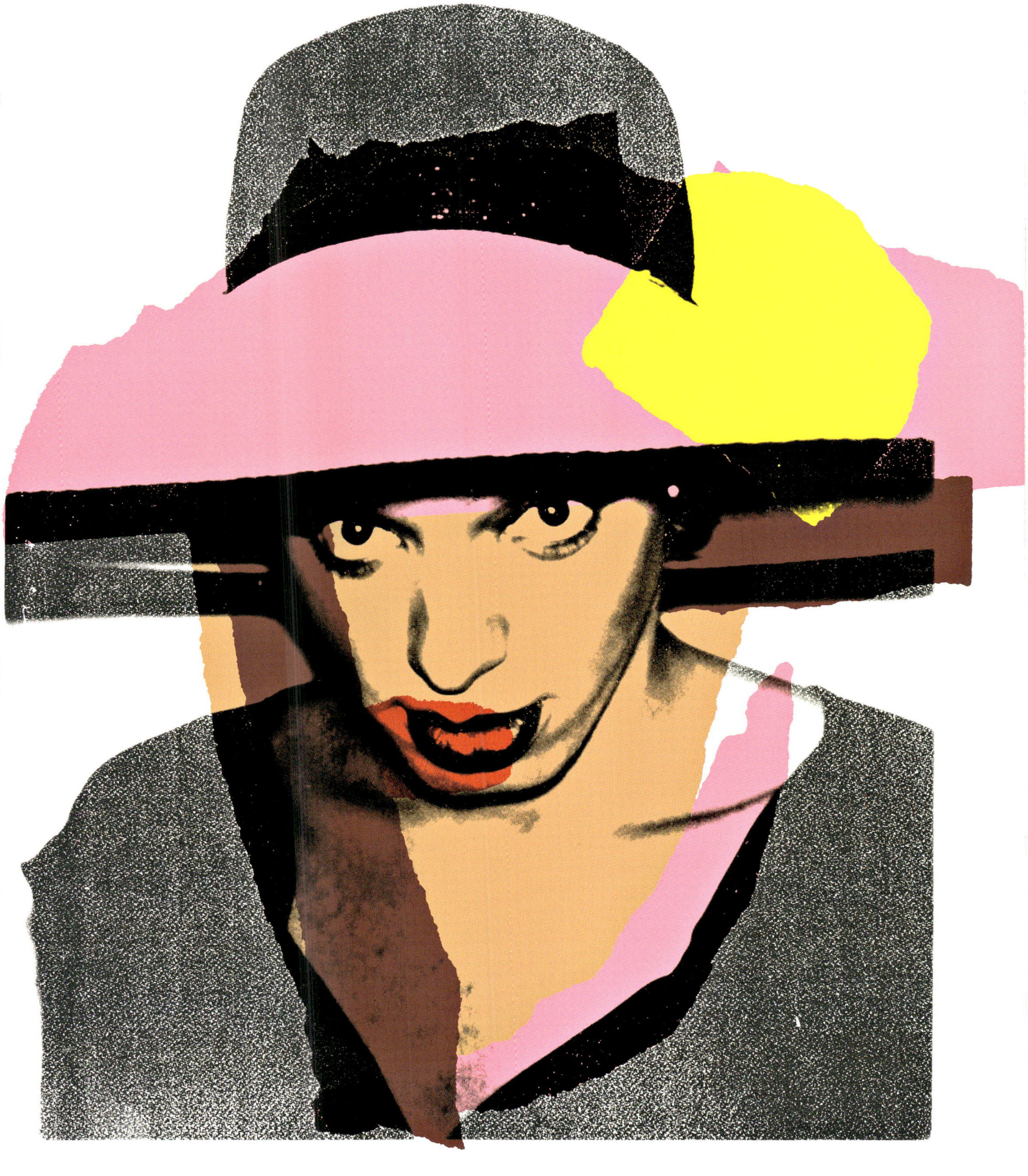

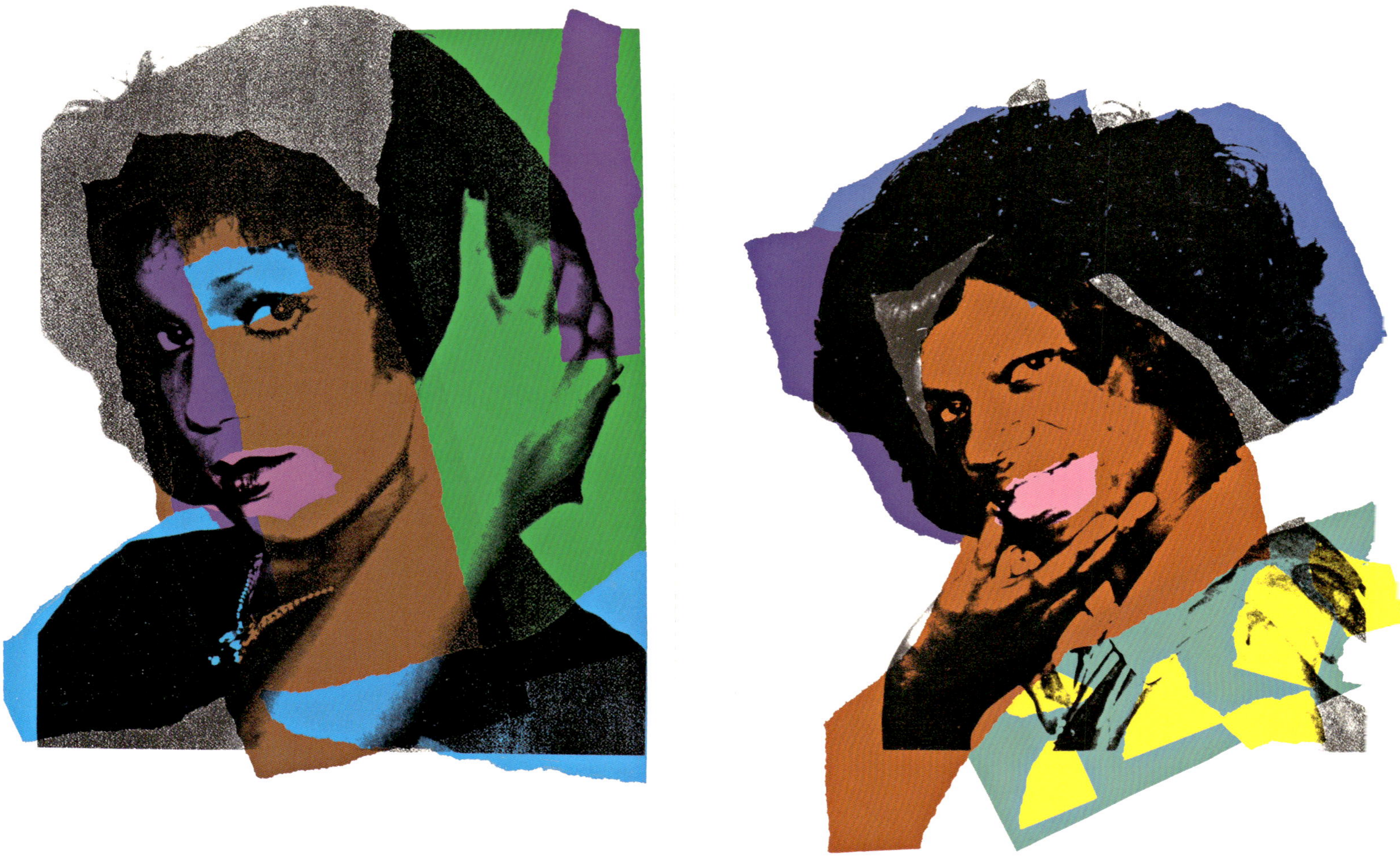

**Ladies and Gentlemen**, 1975. Screenprints, each 43½ x 28½ in.

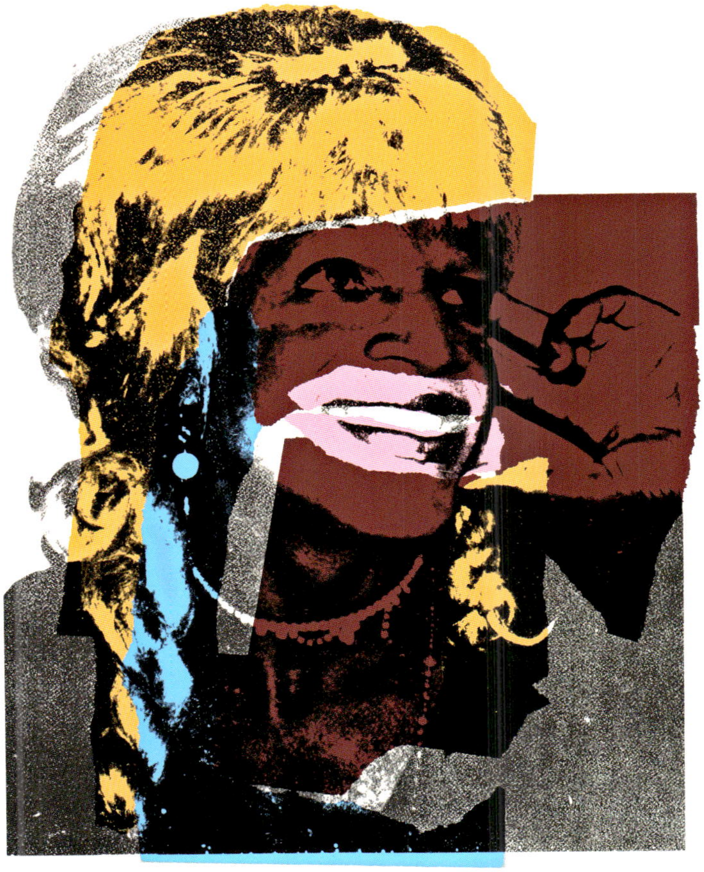

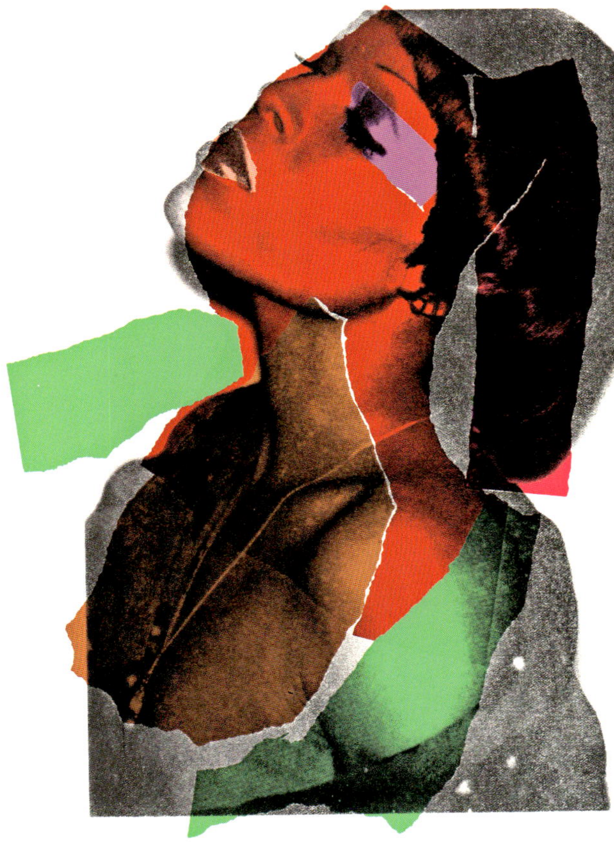

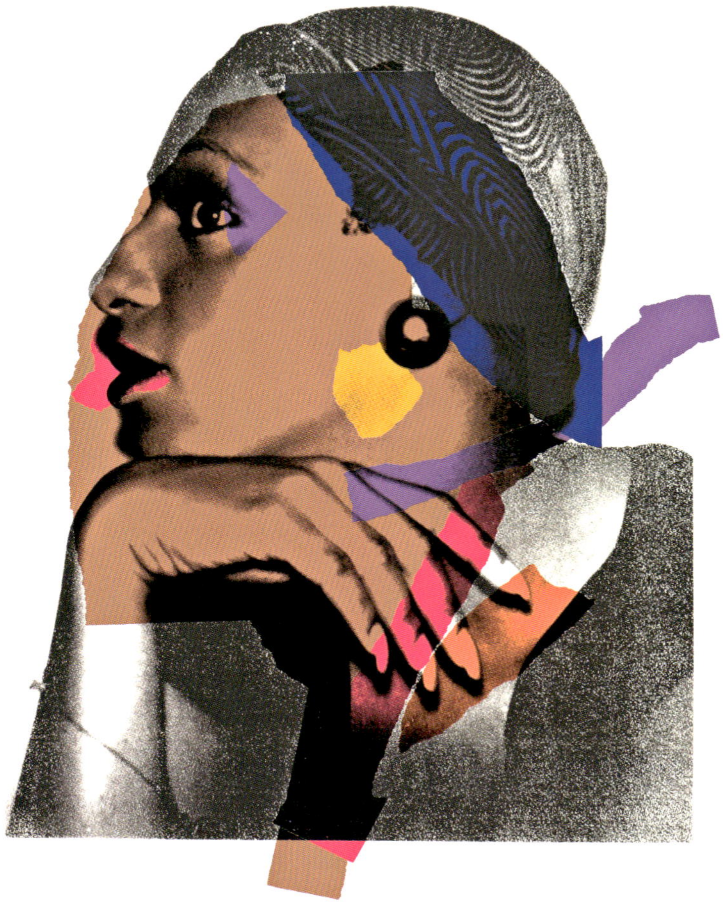

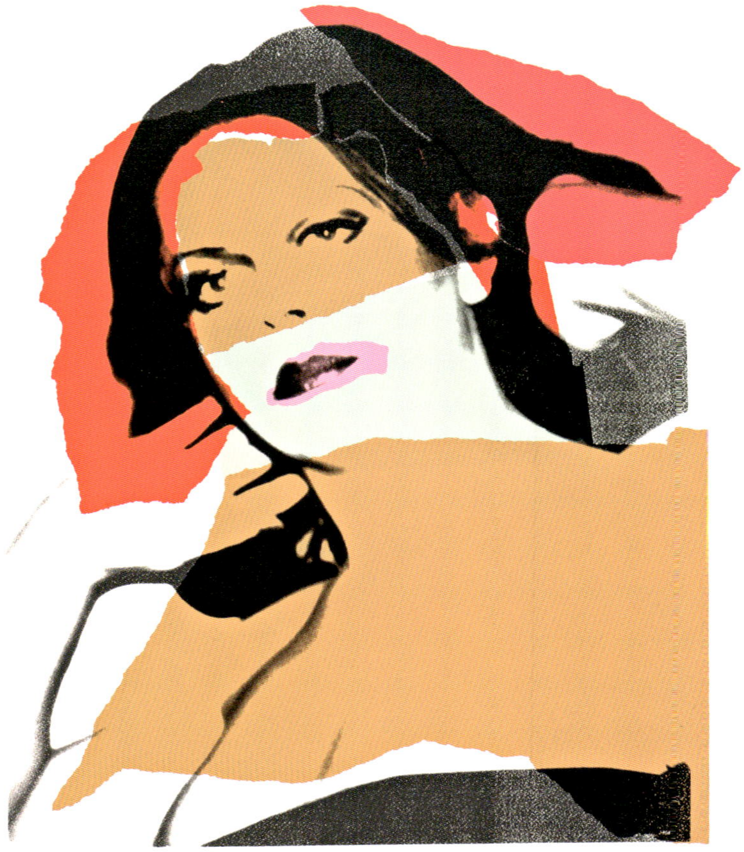

**Ladies and Gentlemen**, 1975. Screenprints, each 43½ x 28½ in.

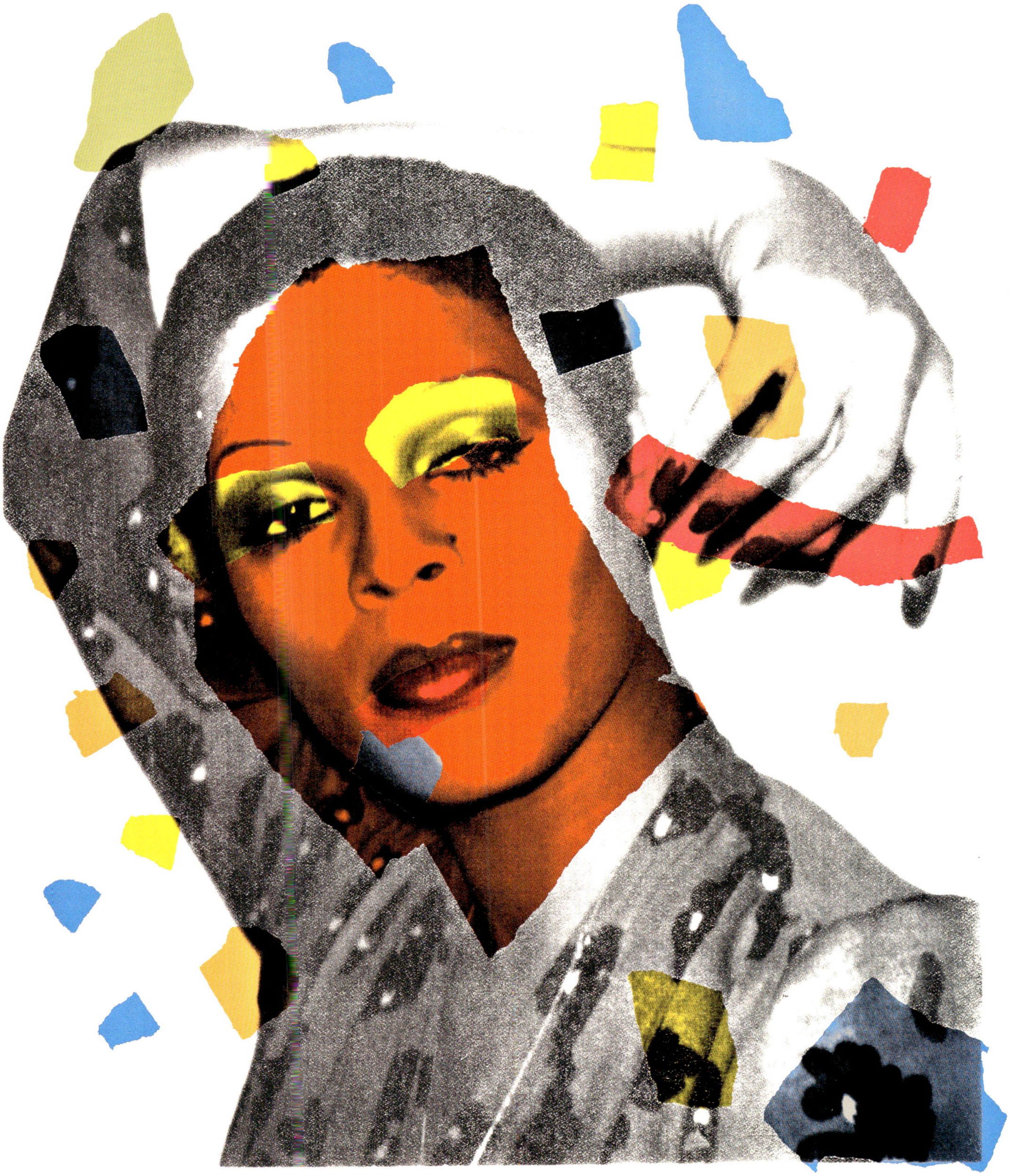

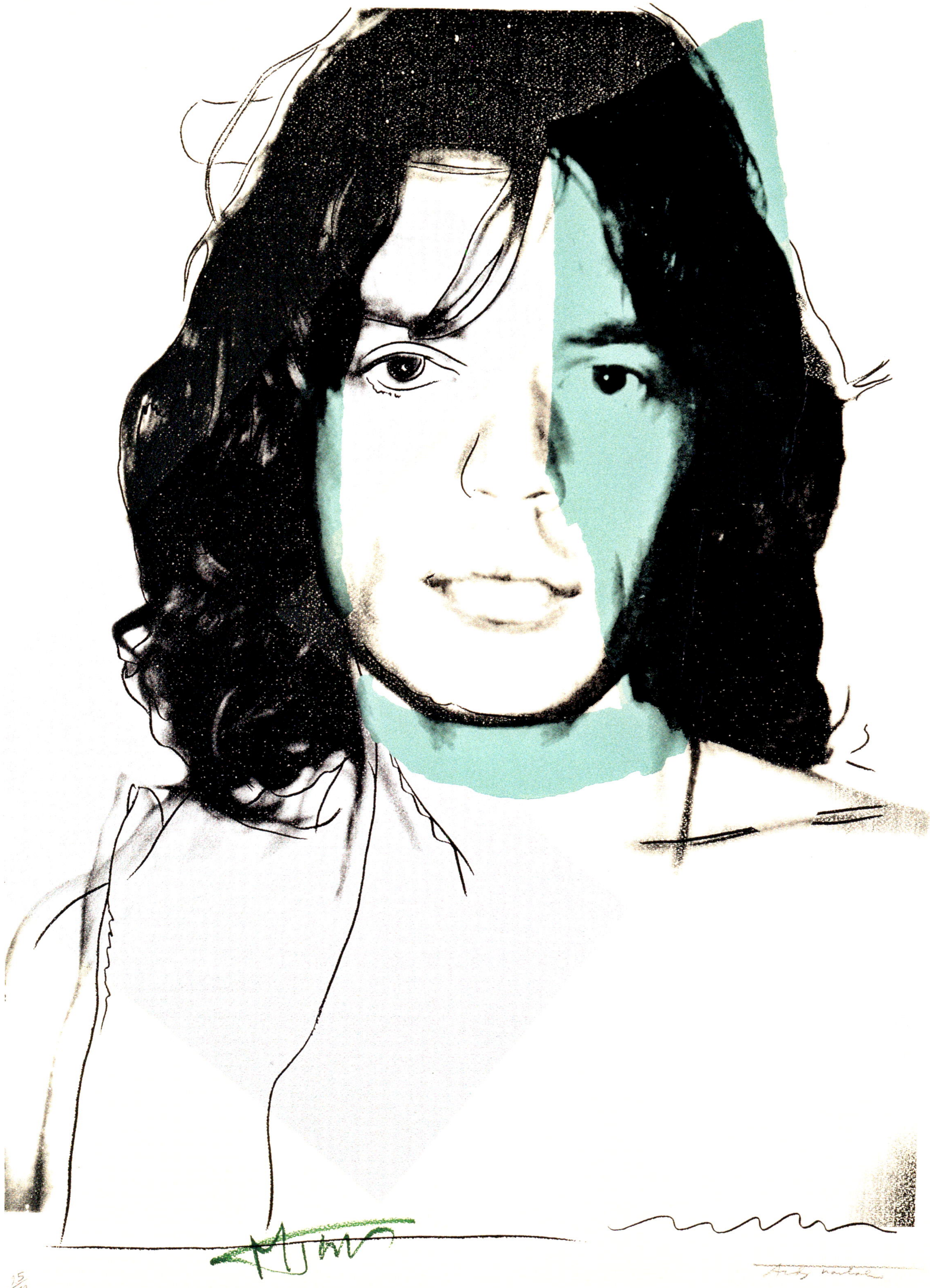

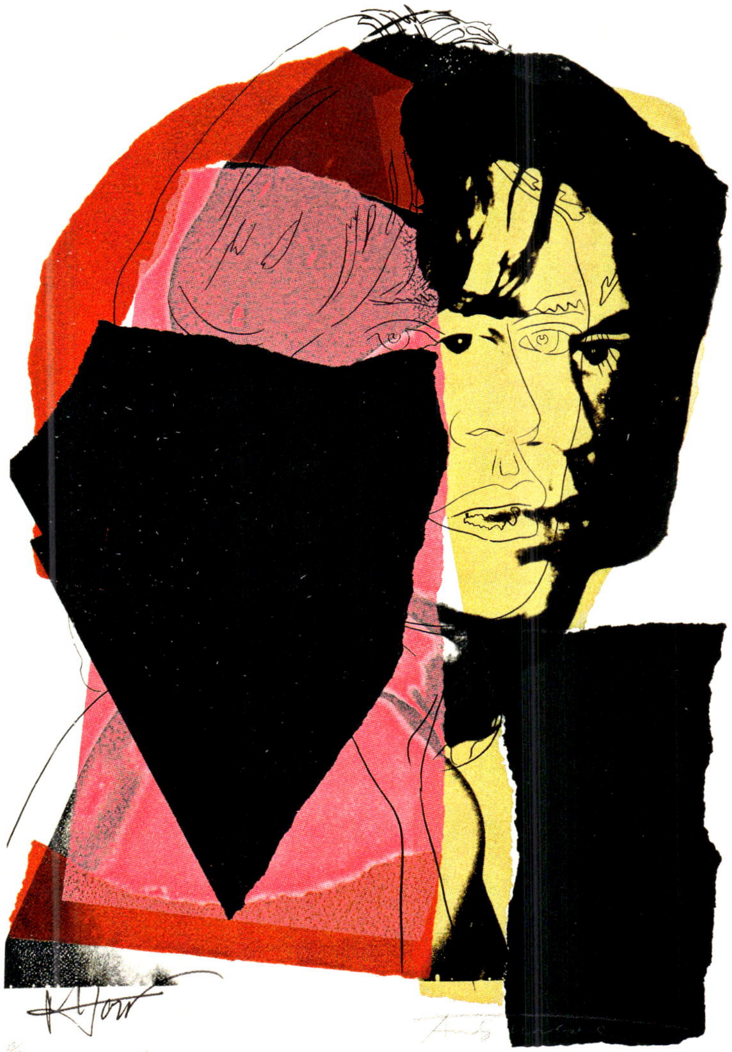

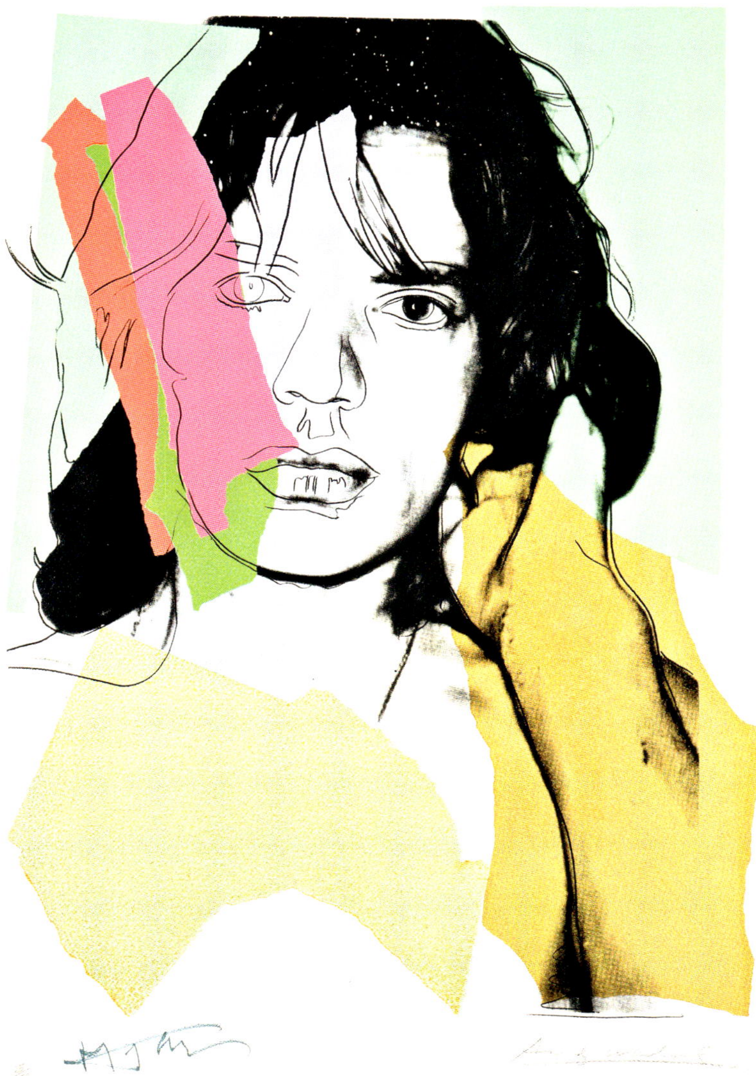

**Mick Jagger**, 1975. Screenprints, each 43½ x 28¾ in.

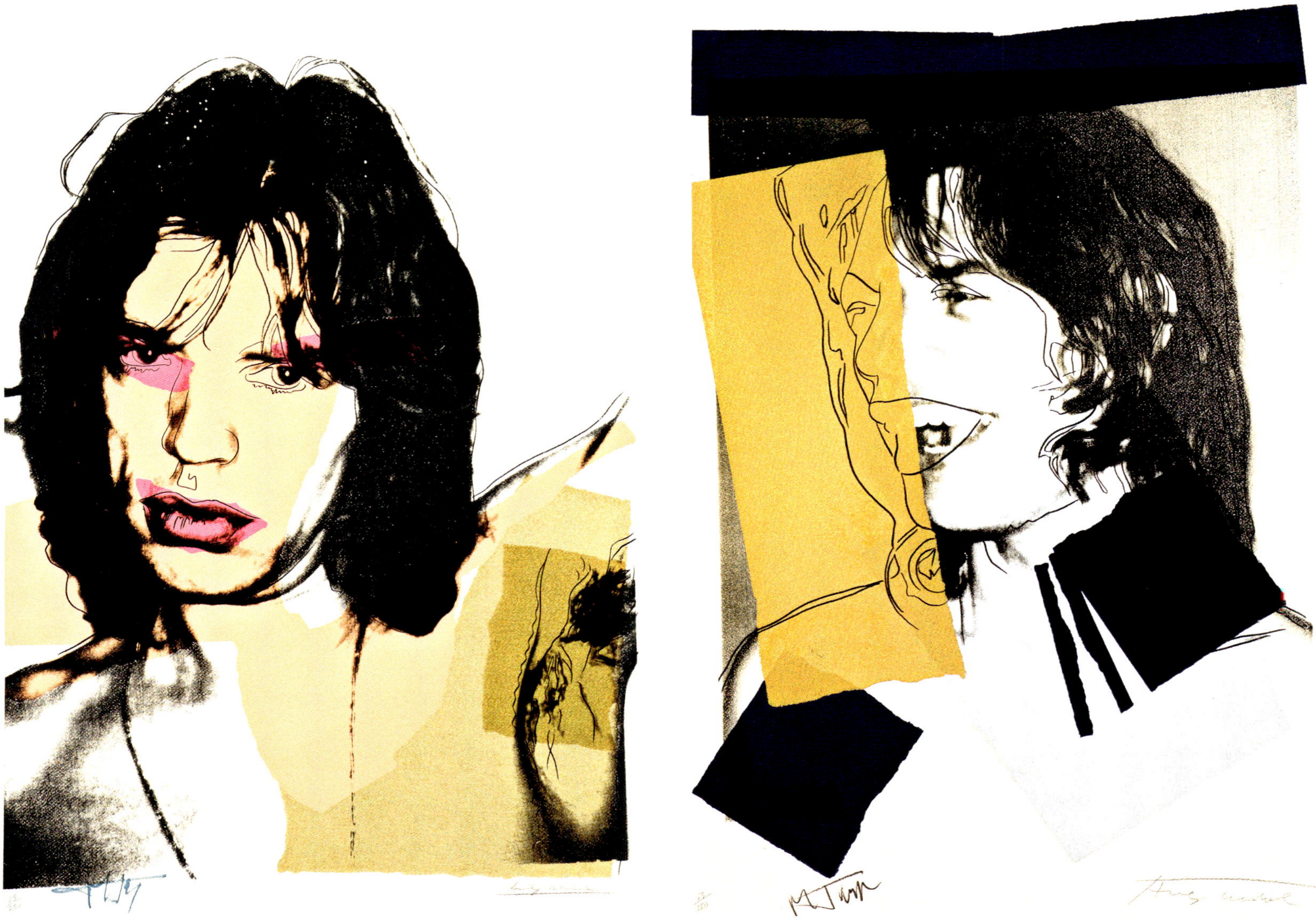

**Mick Jagger**, 1975. Screenprints, each 43½ x 28¾ in.

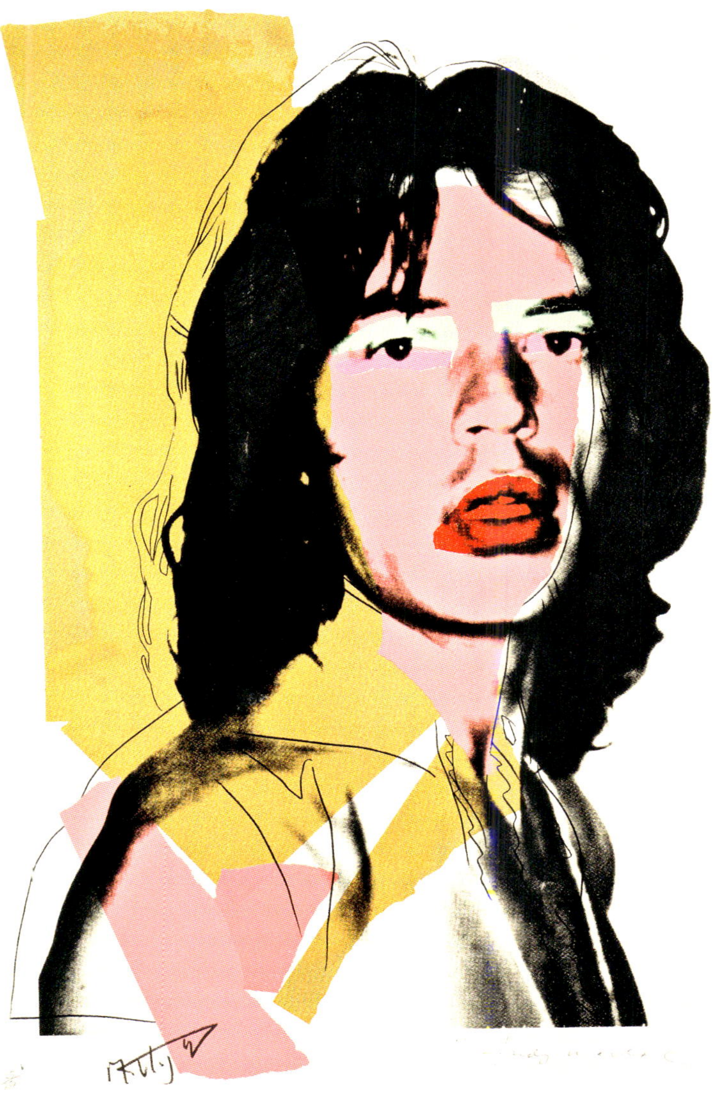

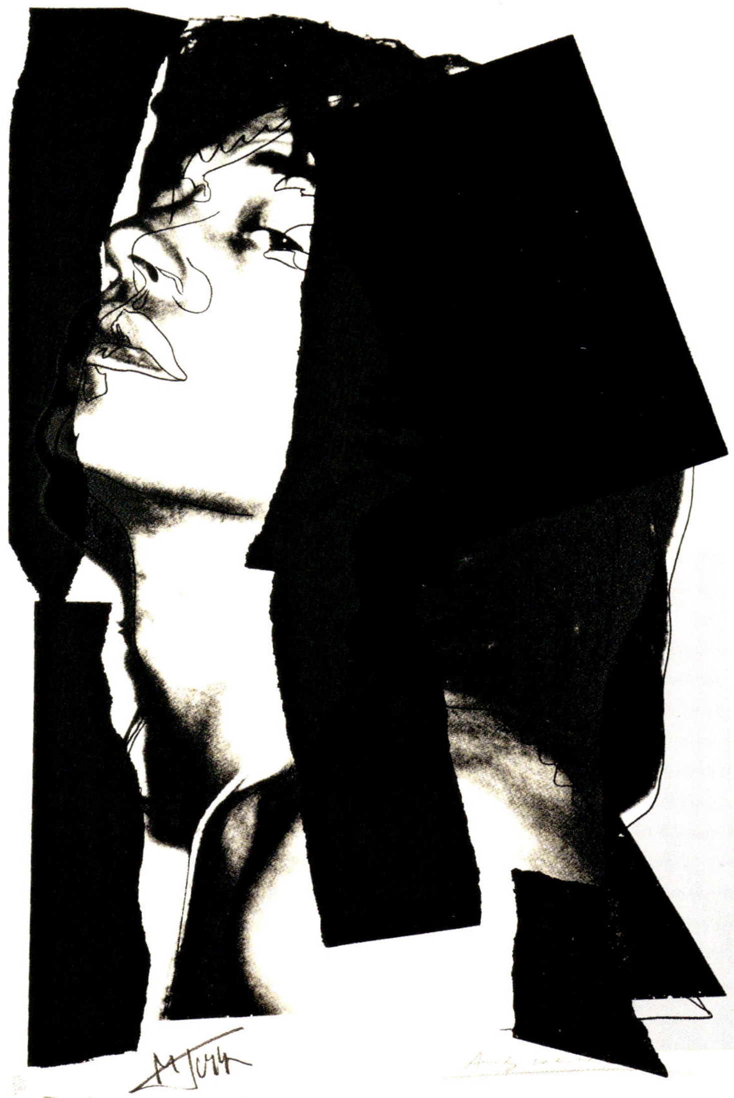

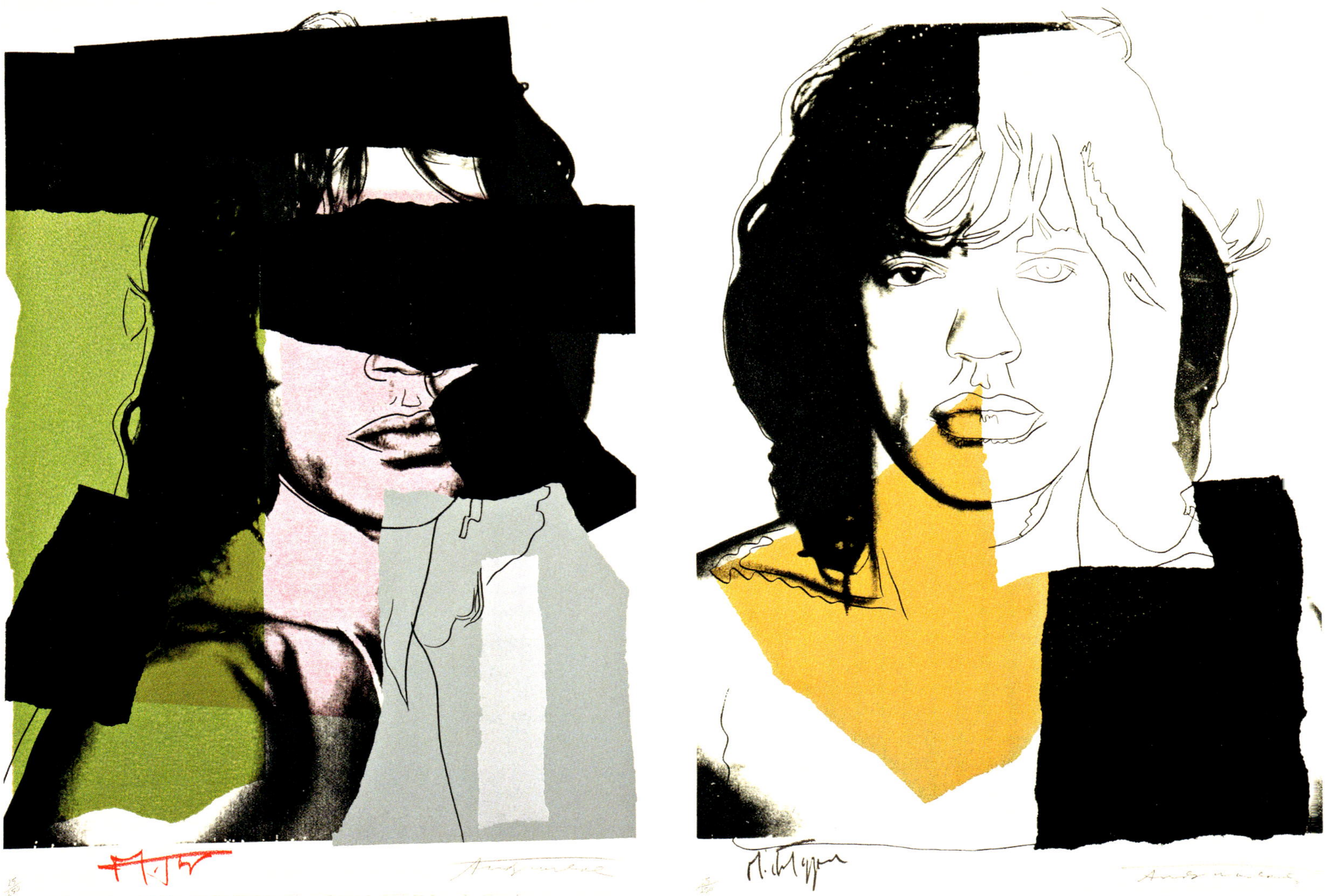

**Mick Jagger**, 1975. Screenprints, each 43½ x 28¾ in.

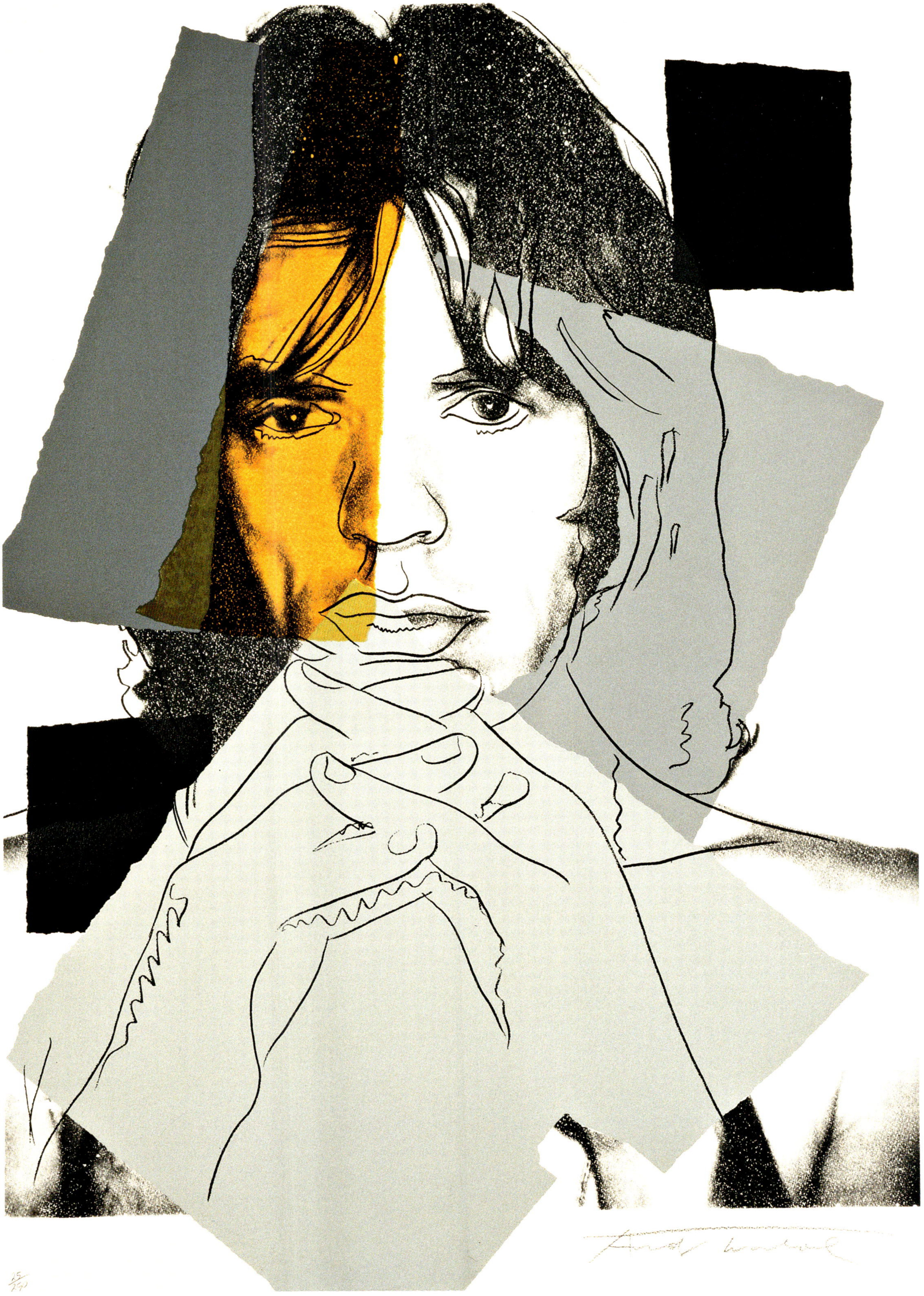

**Skull**, 1976. Screenprint, 20 x 27 in.

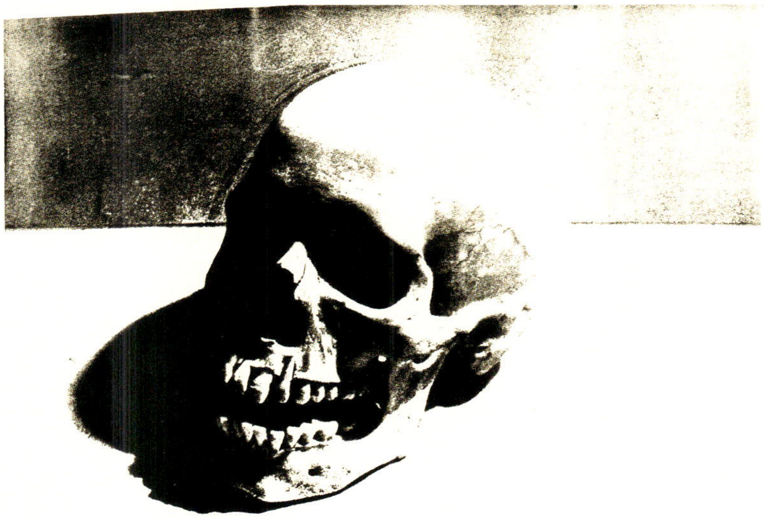

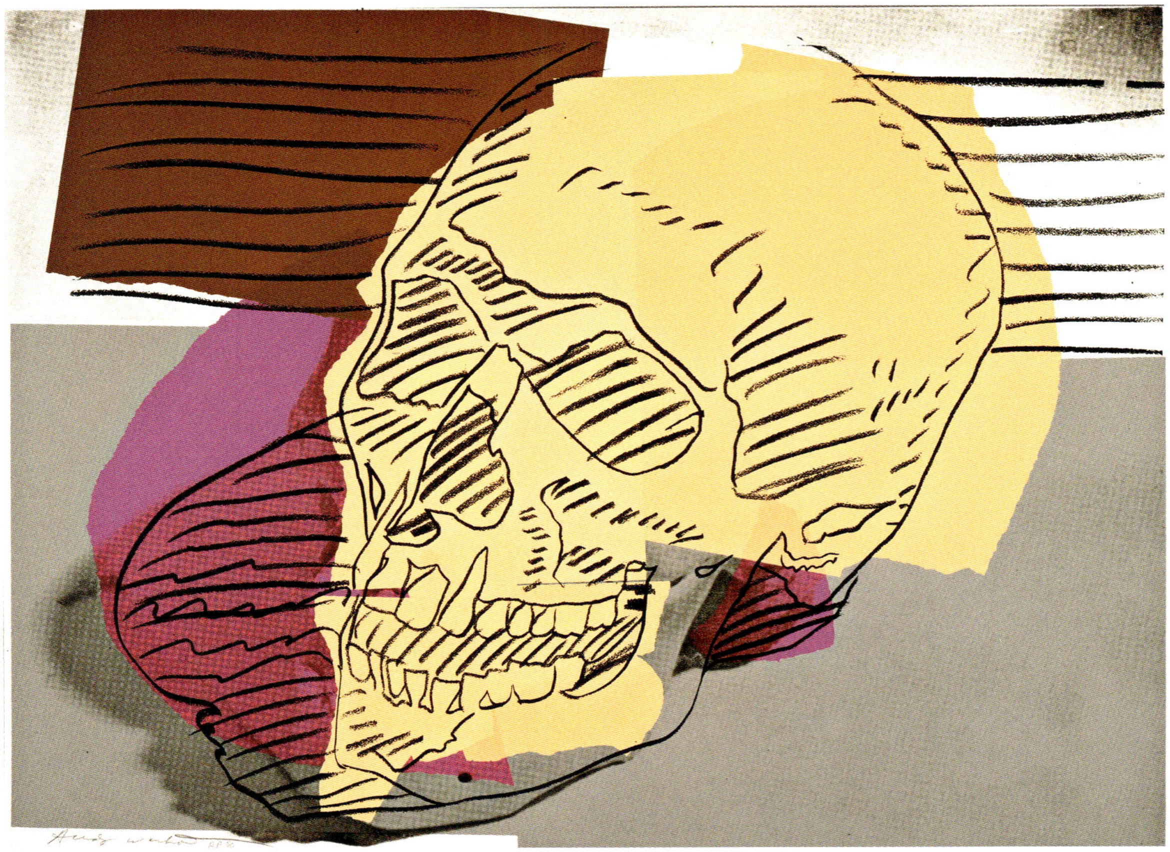

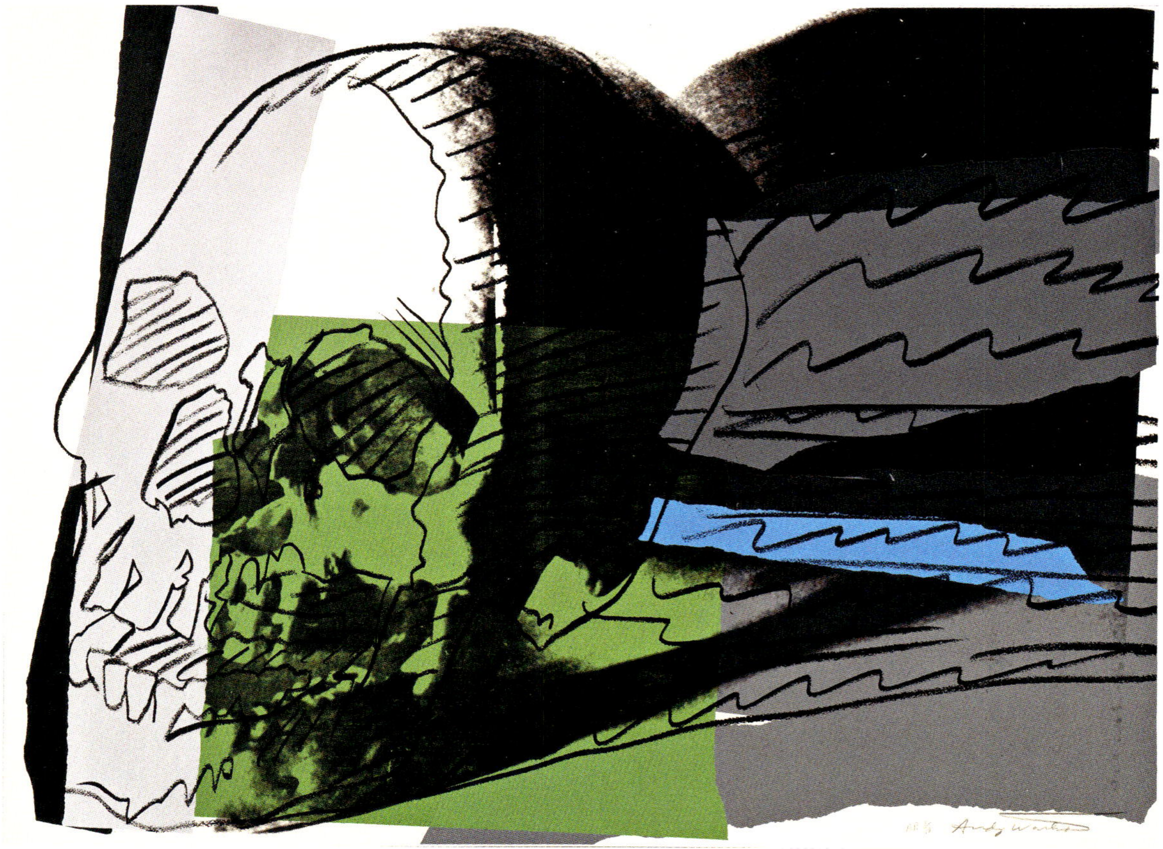

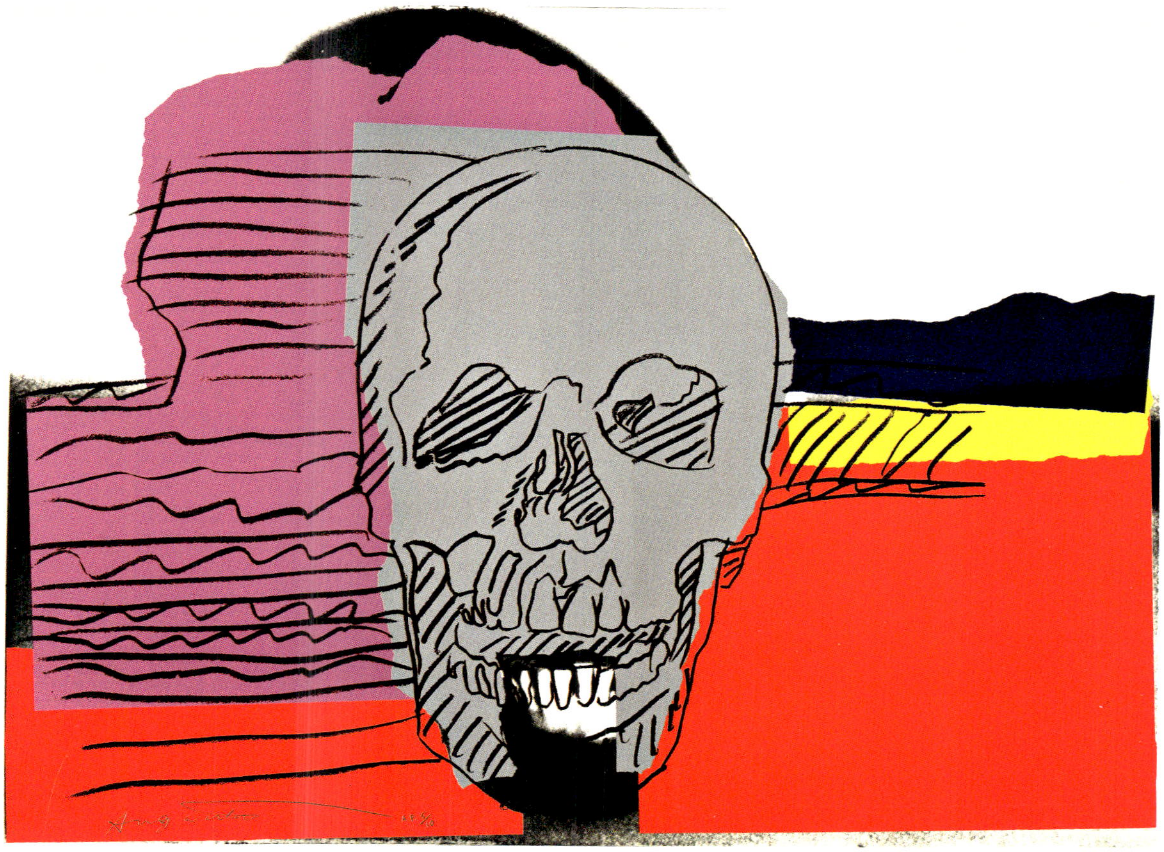

**Skulls**, 1976. Screenprints, each 30 x 40 in.

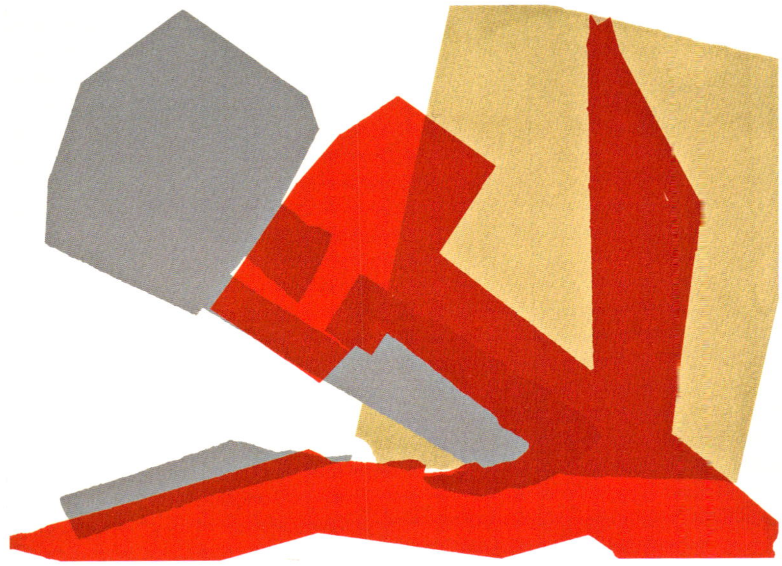
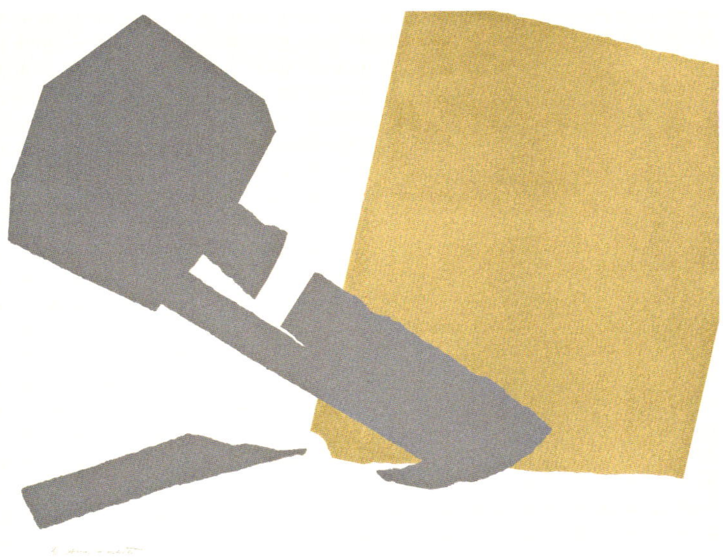
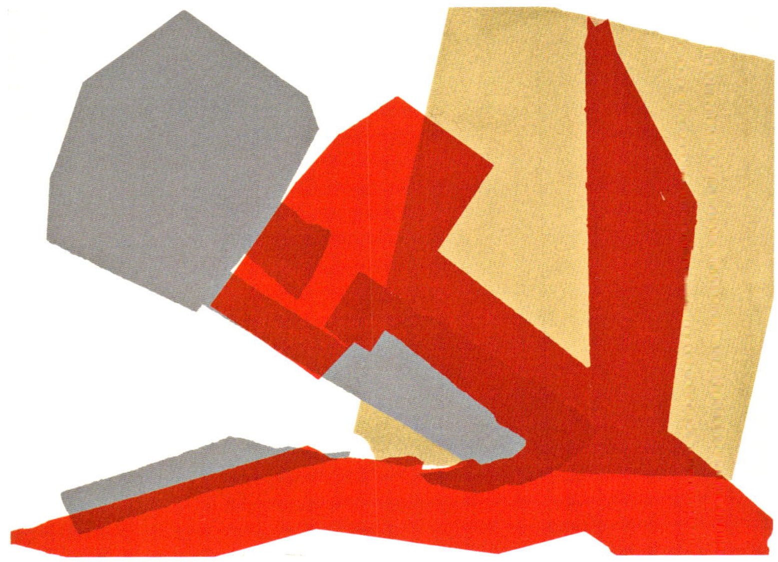
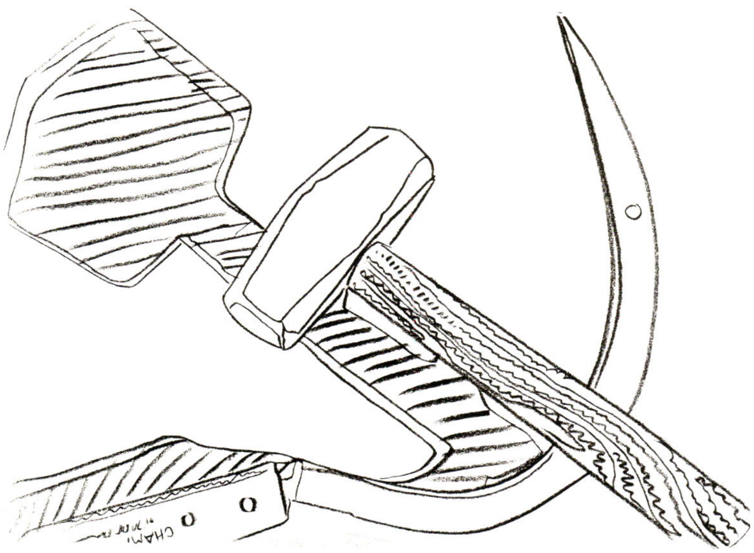
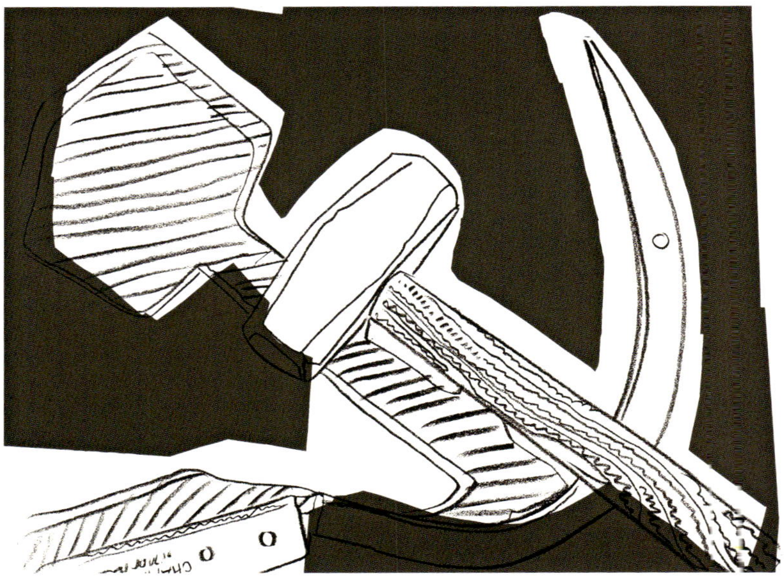

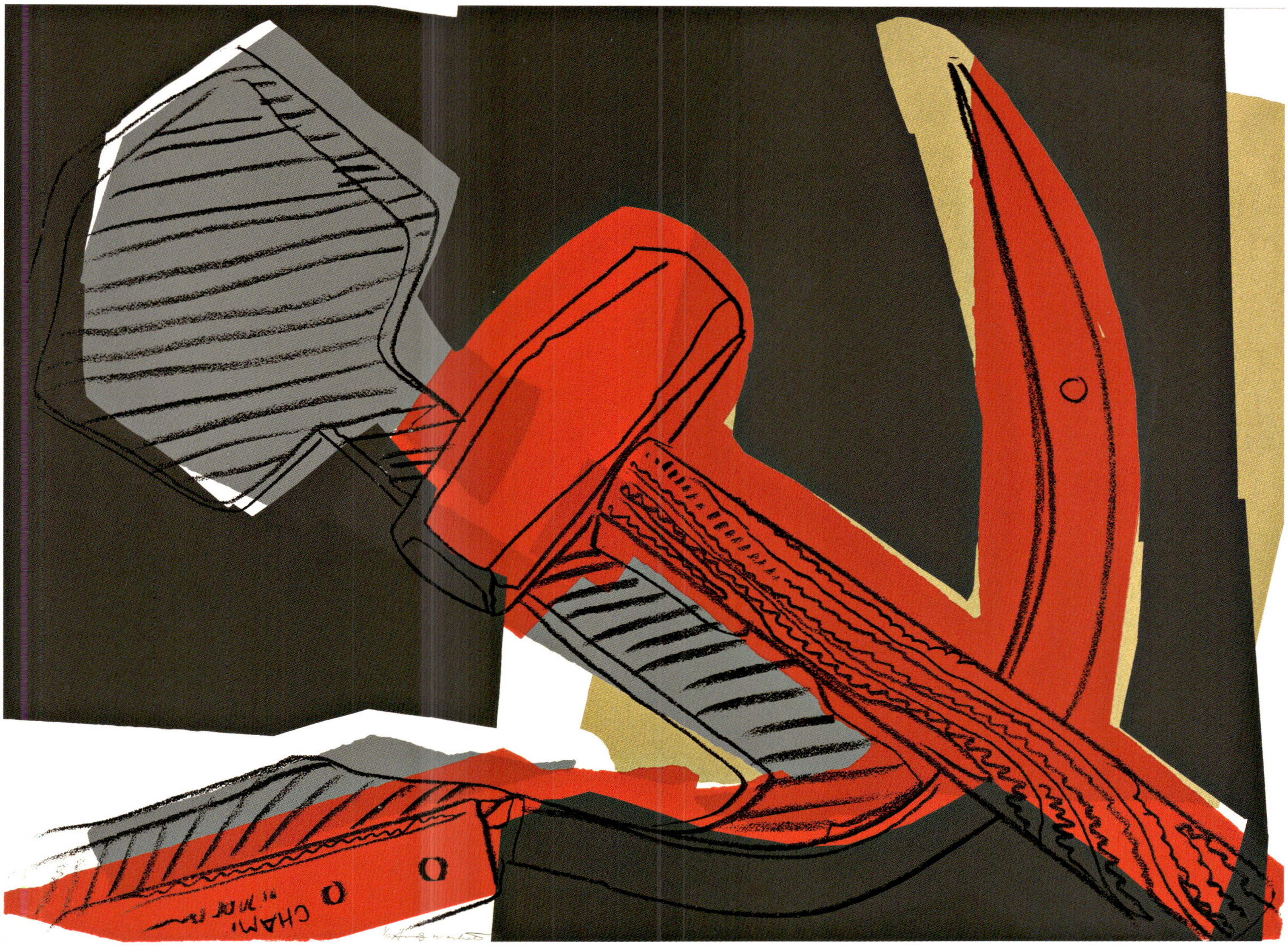

**Hammer and Sickle (Special Edition)**, 1977. Screenprints, each 30 x 40 in.

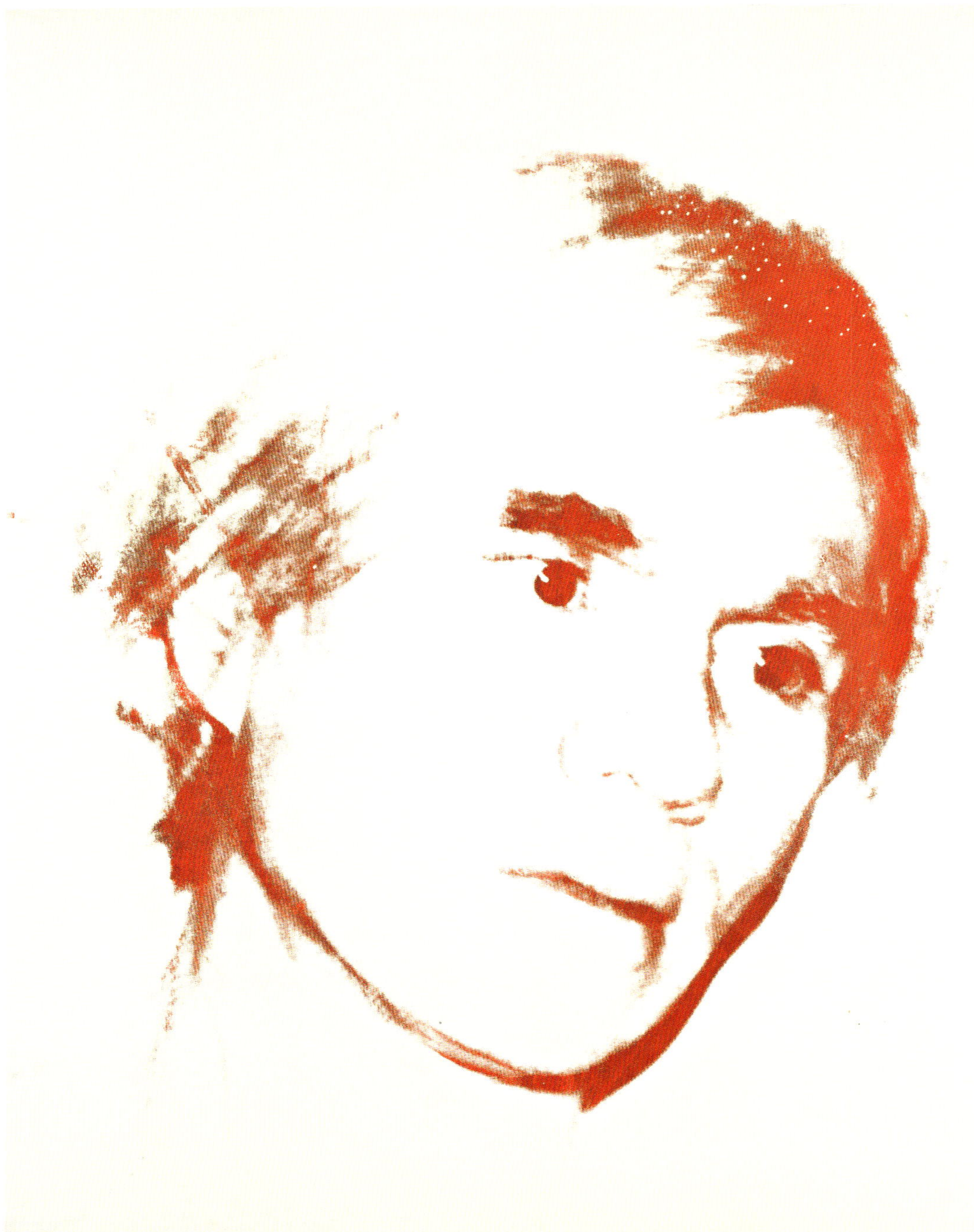

**Self-Portrait**, 1977. Screenprint, 45 x 35 in.

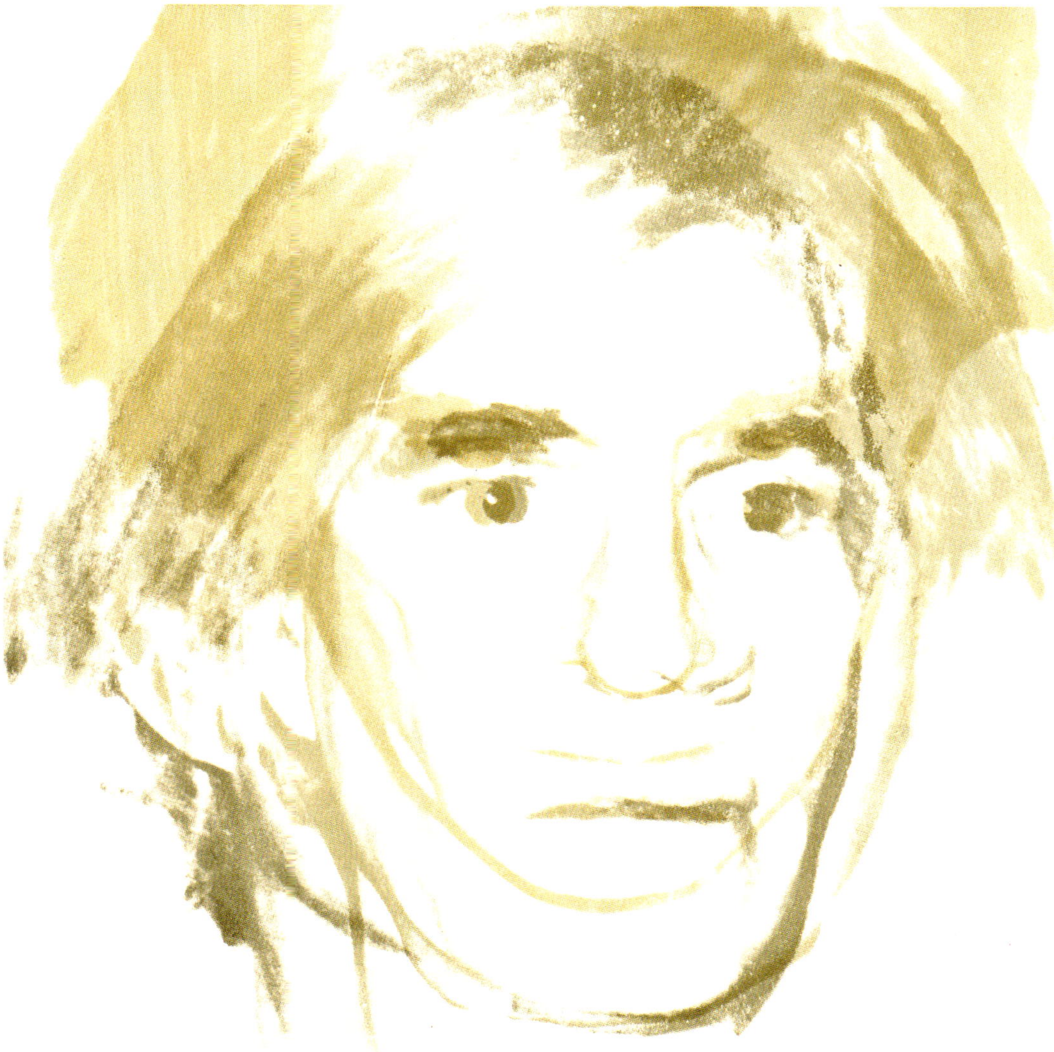

**Self-Portrait**, 1977. Screenprint, 45 x 35 in.

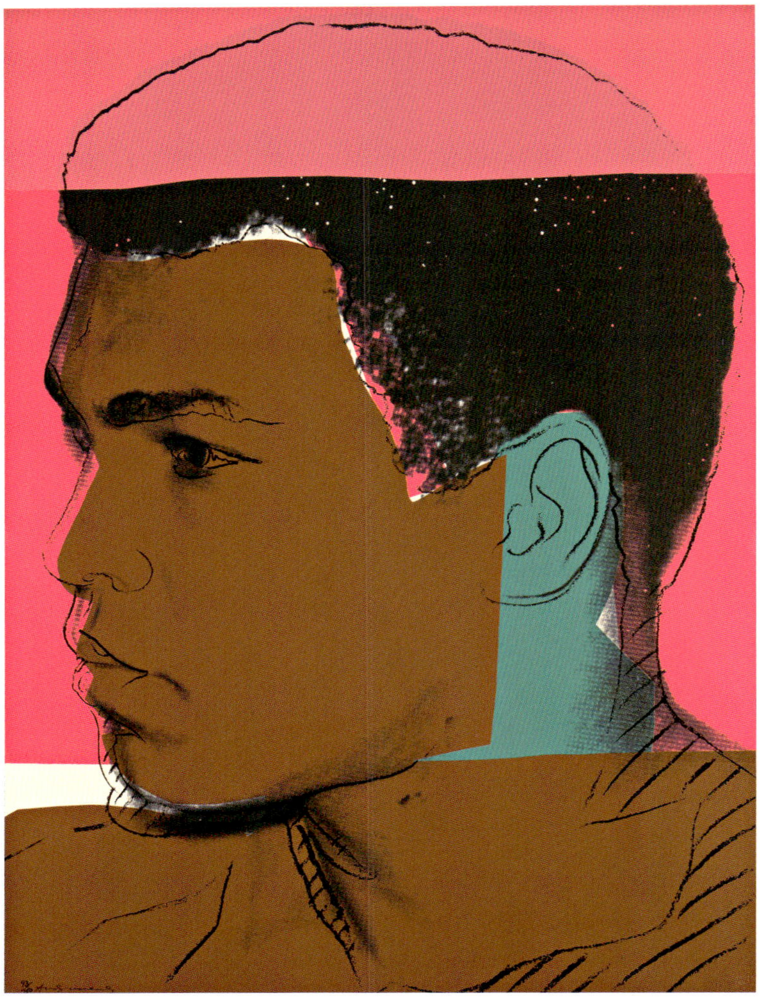

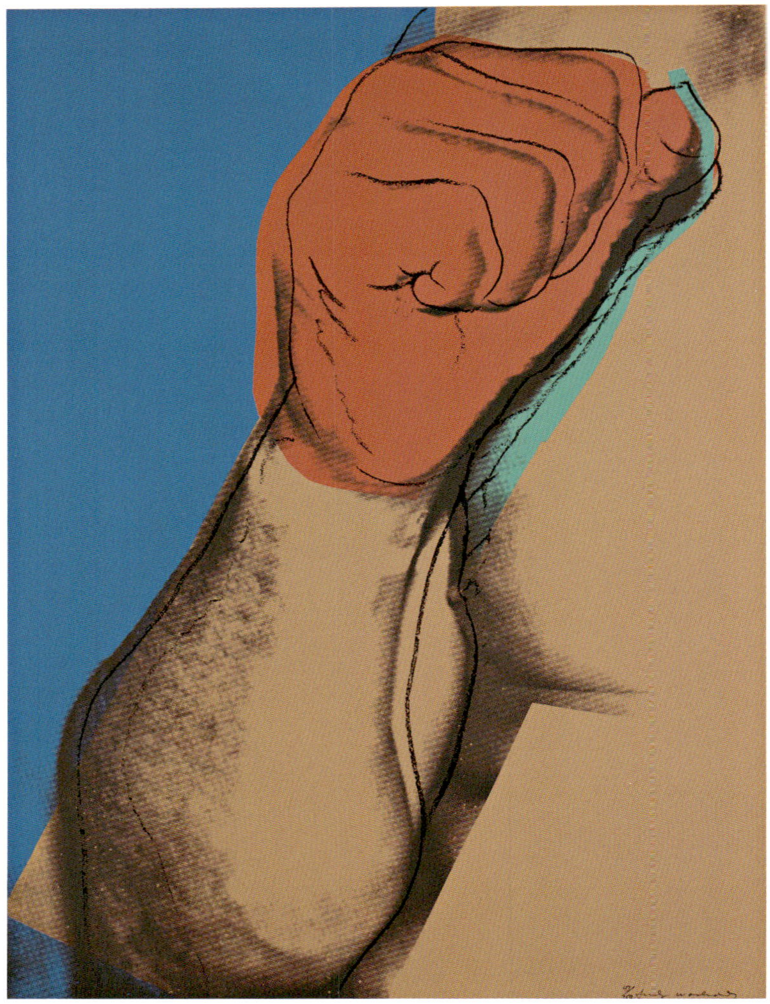

**Muhammad Ali**, 1978. Screenprints, each 40 x 30 in.

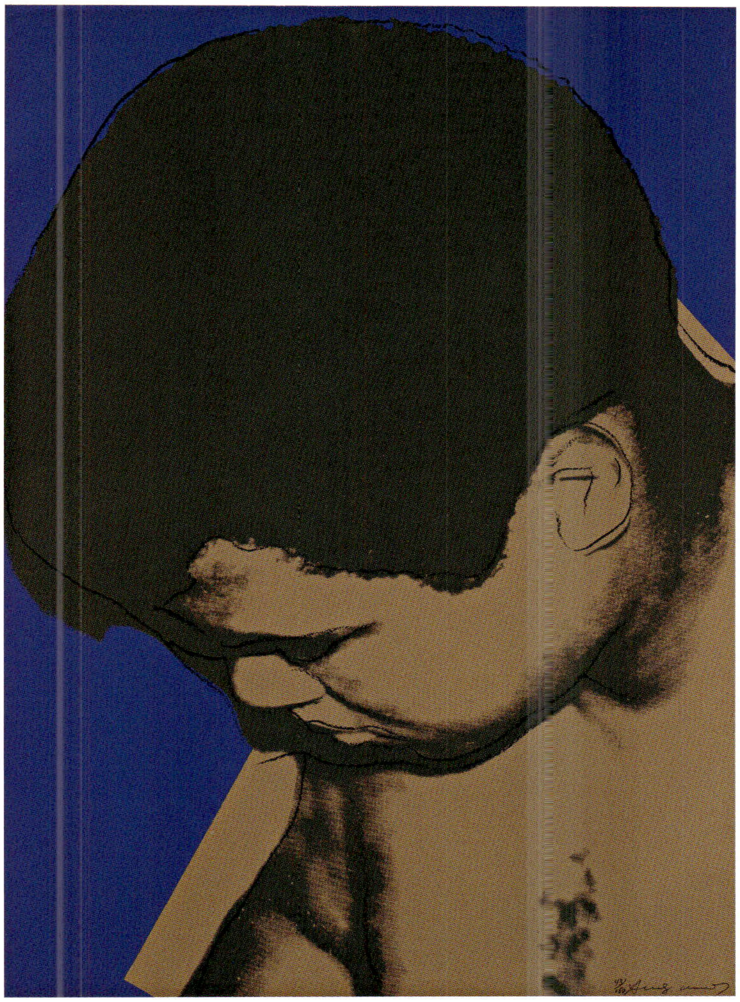

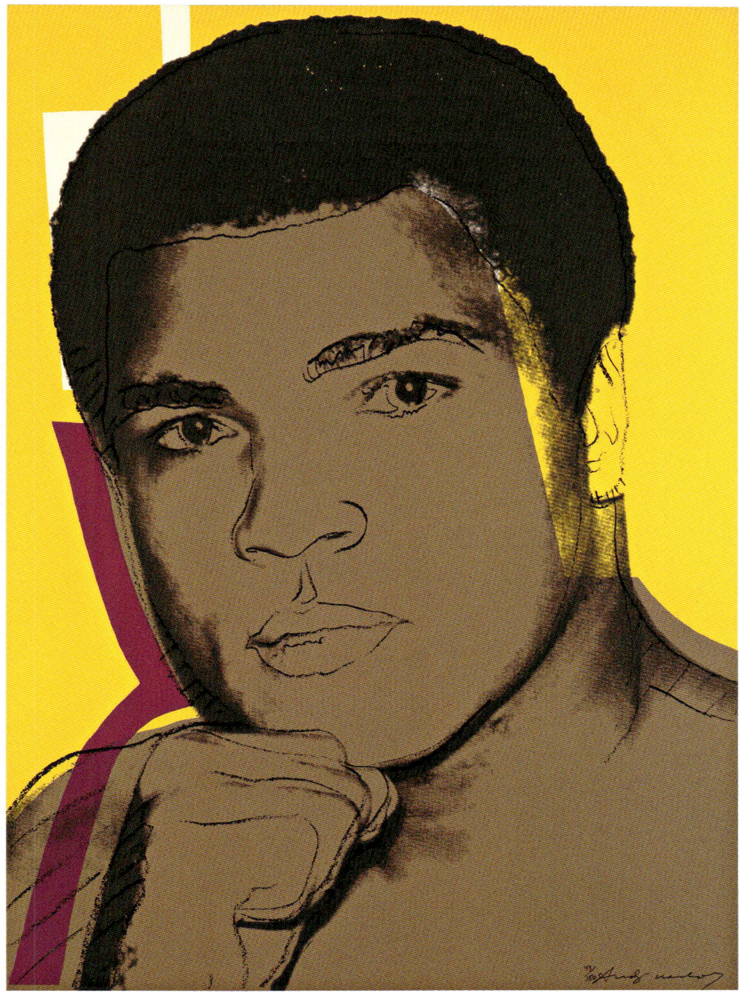

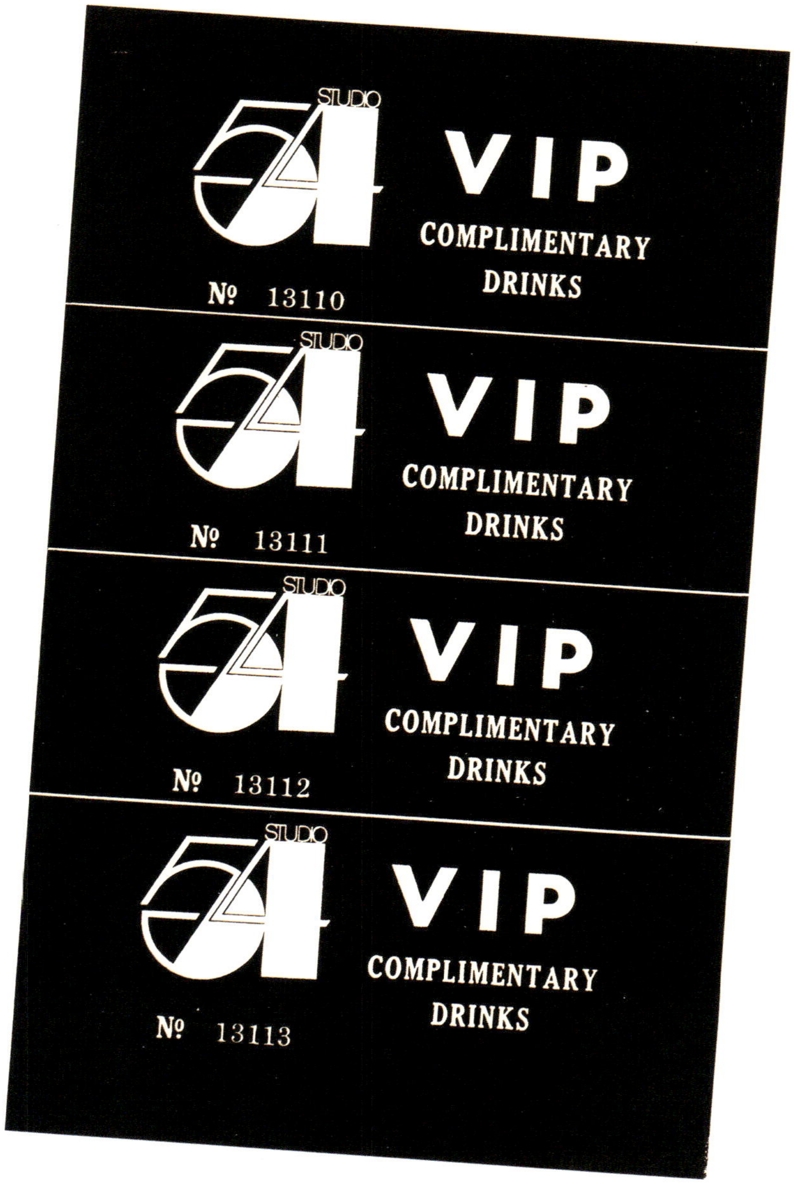


**Studio 54 Complimentary Drink Invitation**, 1978. Screenprint, 38⅜ x 25 in.

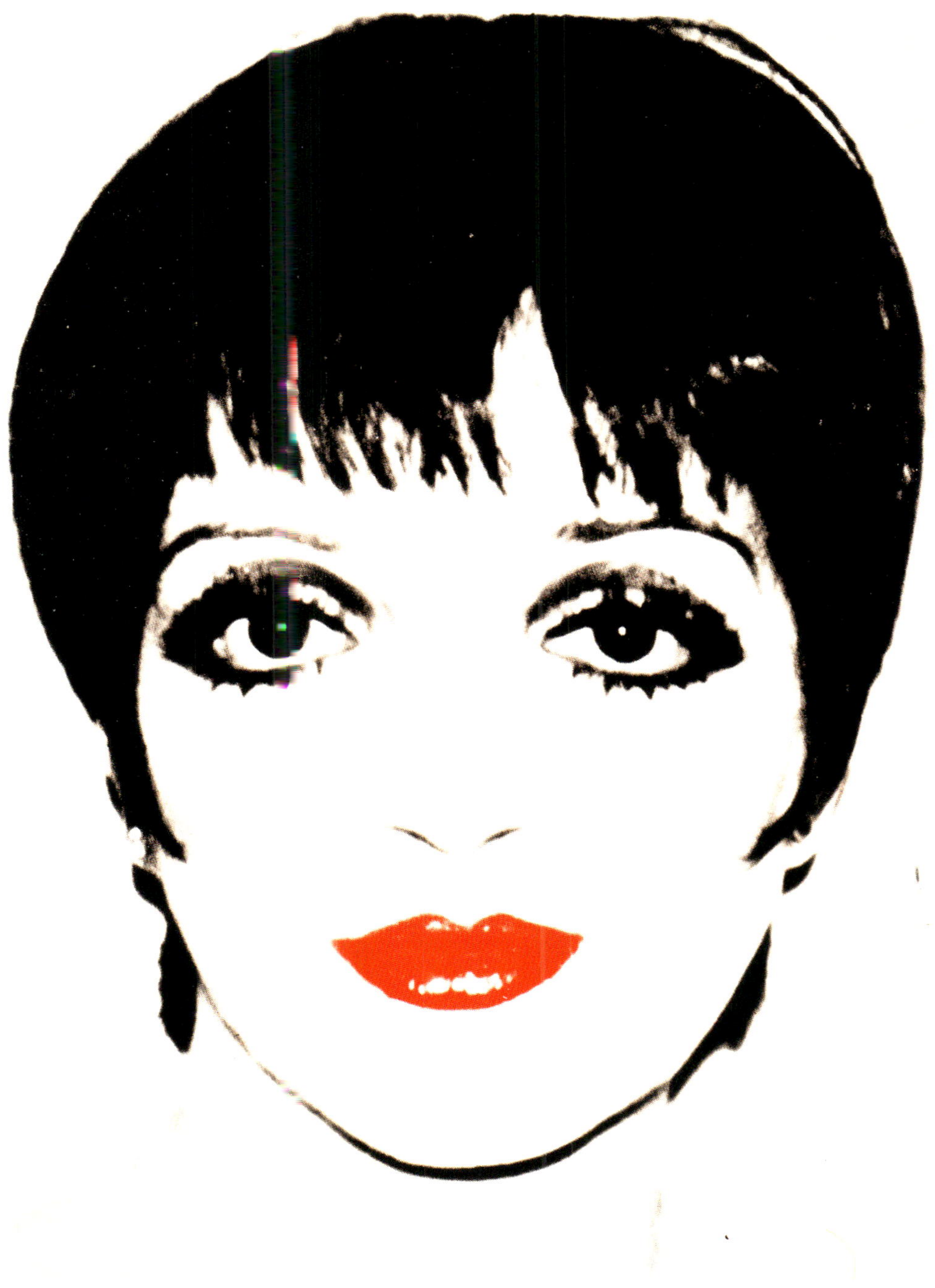

**Liza Minnelli**, 1978. Screenprint, 45 x 35 in.

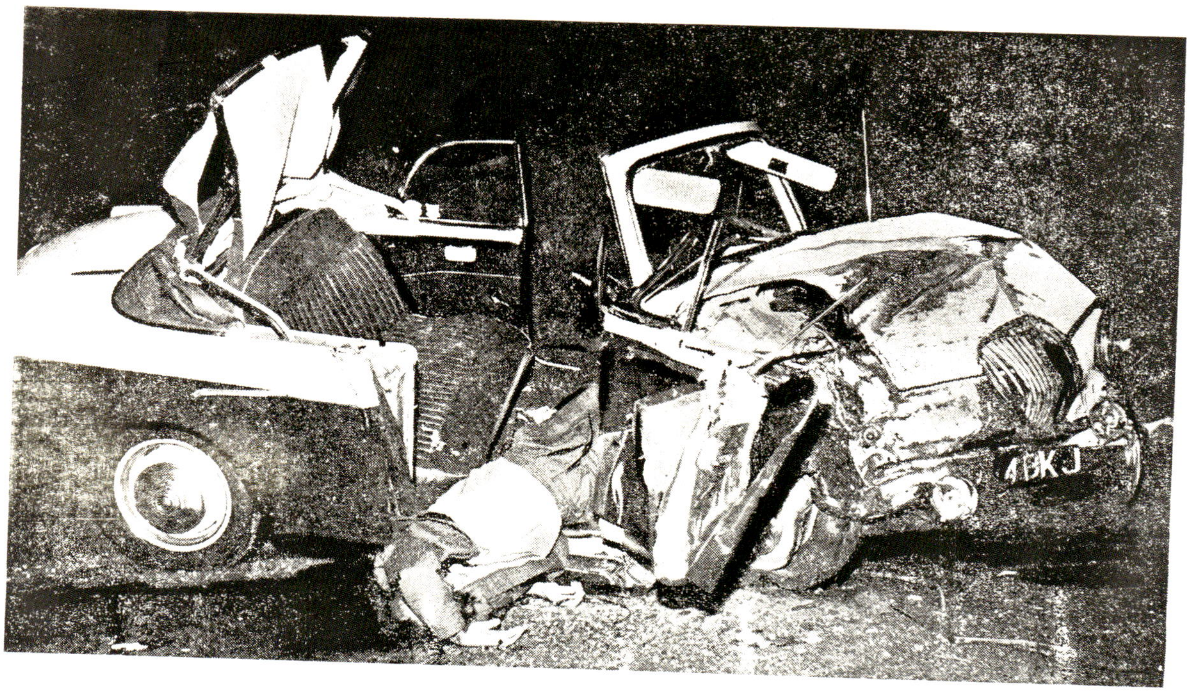

**Car Crash**, 1978. Screenprint, 30½ x 43 in.

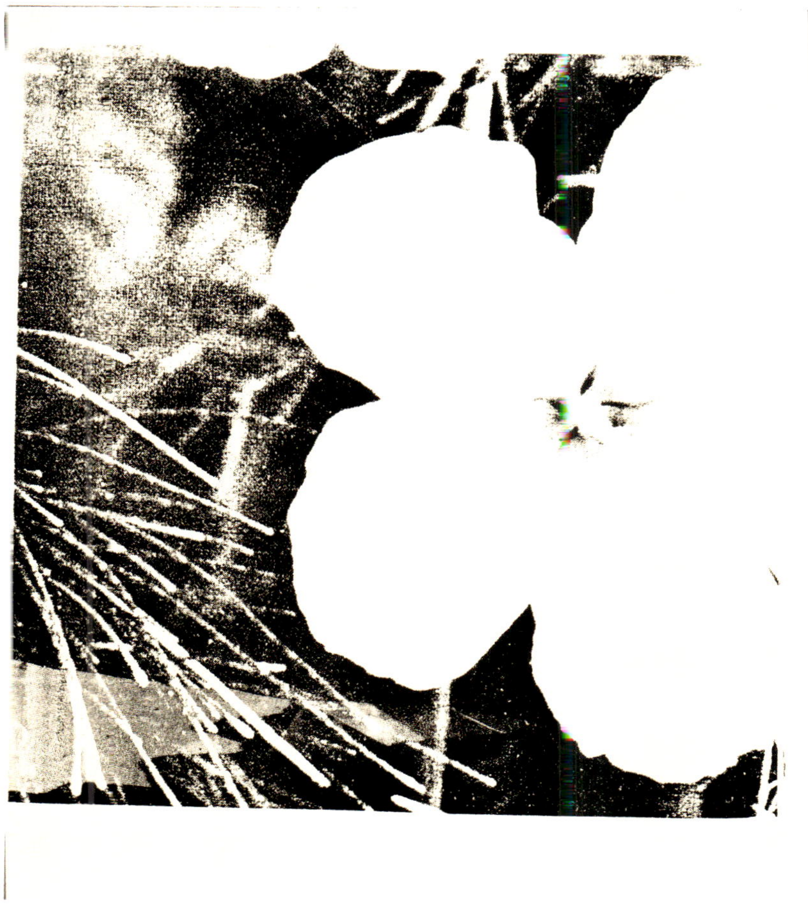

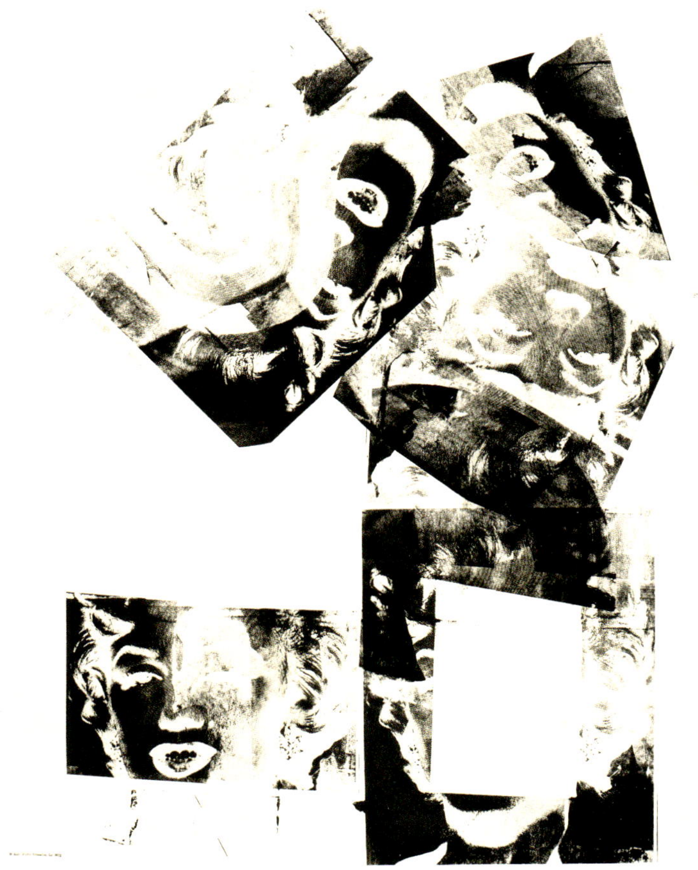

**Flower (Retrospective Series)**, 1978. Screenprint, 45 x 35 in.

**Marilyn Monroe (Marilyn) (Retrospective Series)**, 1978. Screenprint, 45 x 35 in.

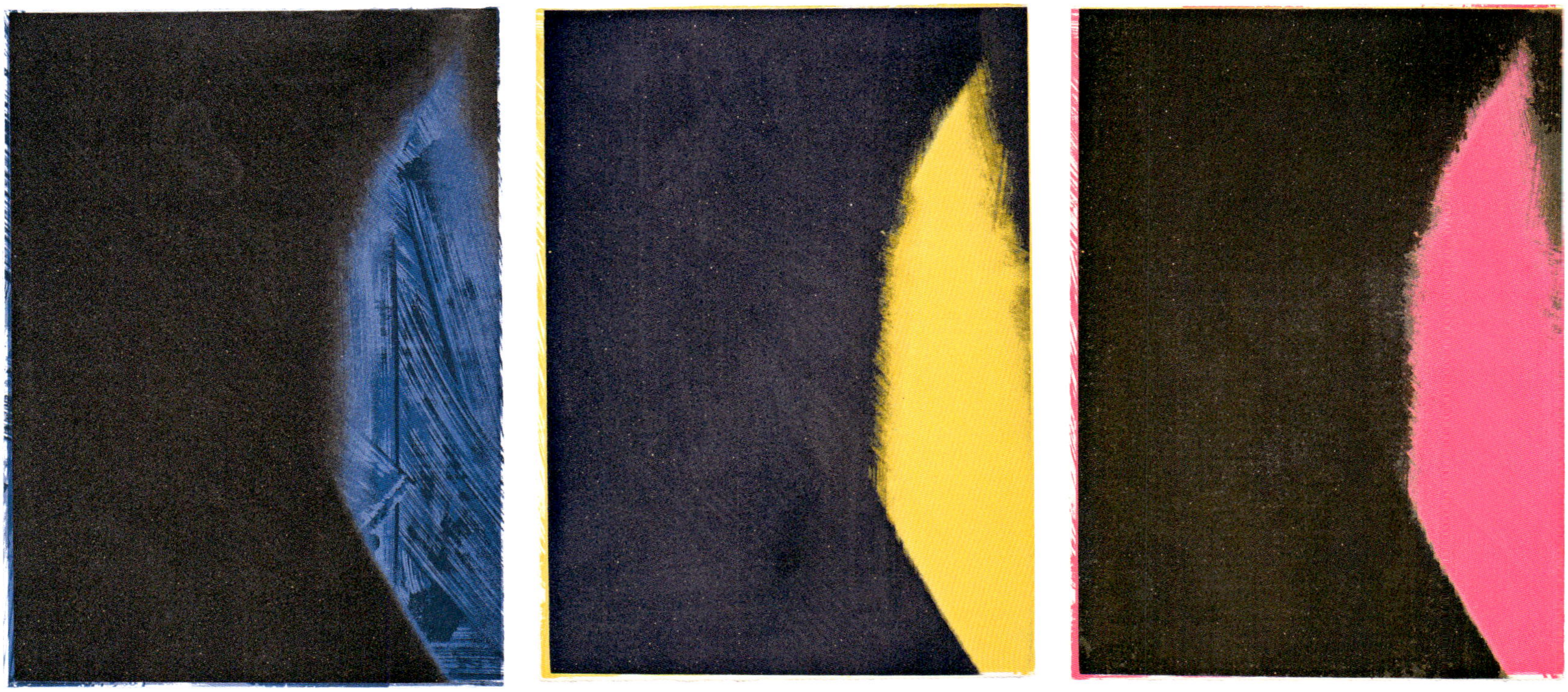

**Shadows I**, 1979. Screenprints with diamond dust, each 43 x 30½ in.

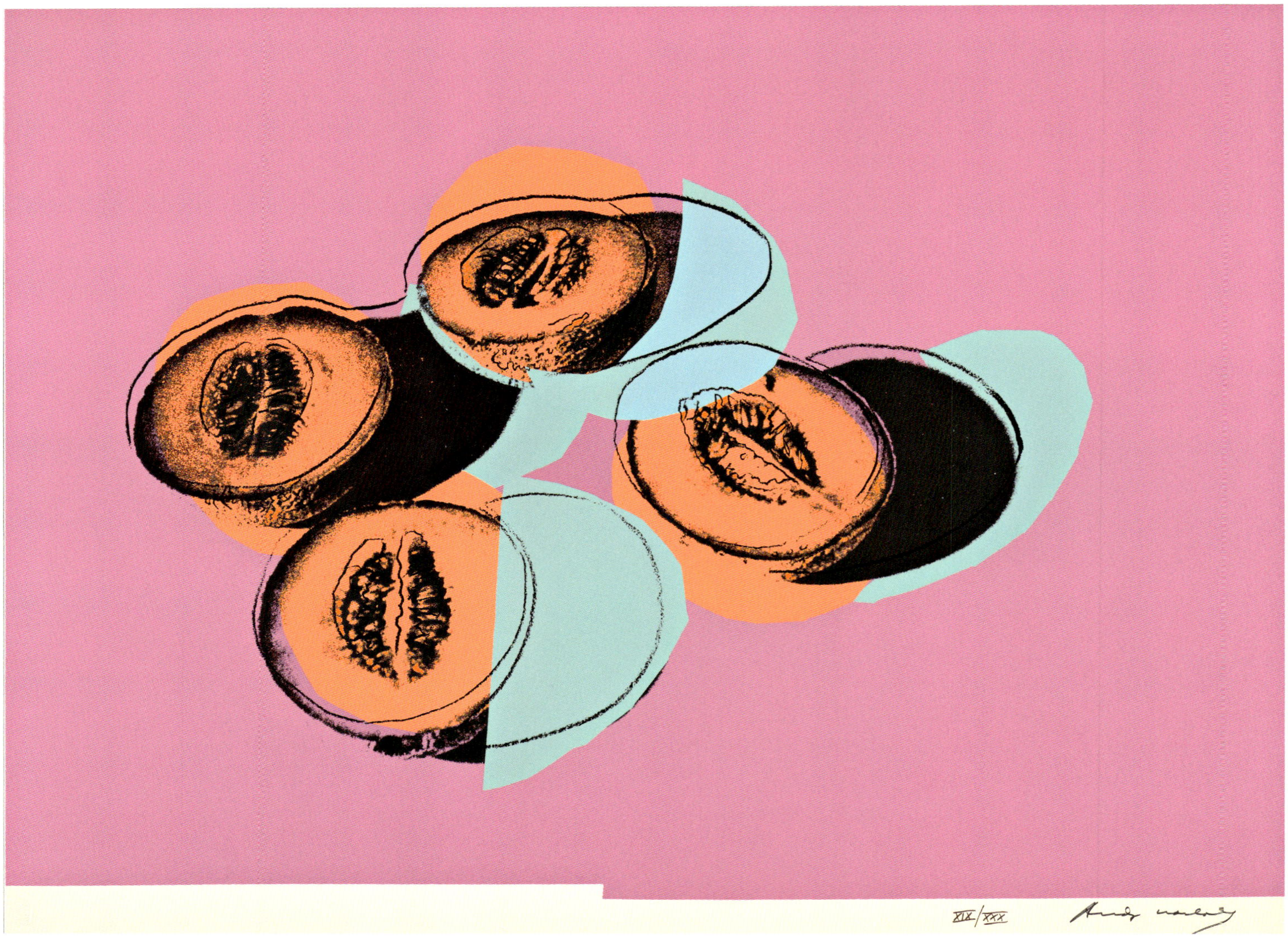

**Space Fruit: Still Lifes, Cantaloupes II**, 1979. Screenprint, 30 x 40 in.

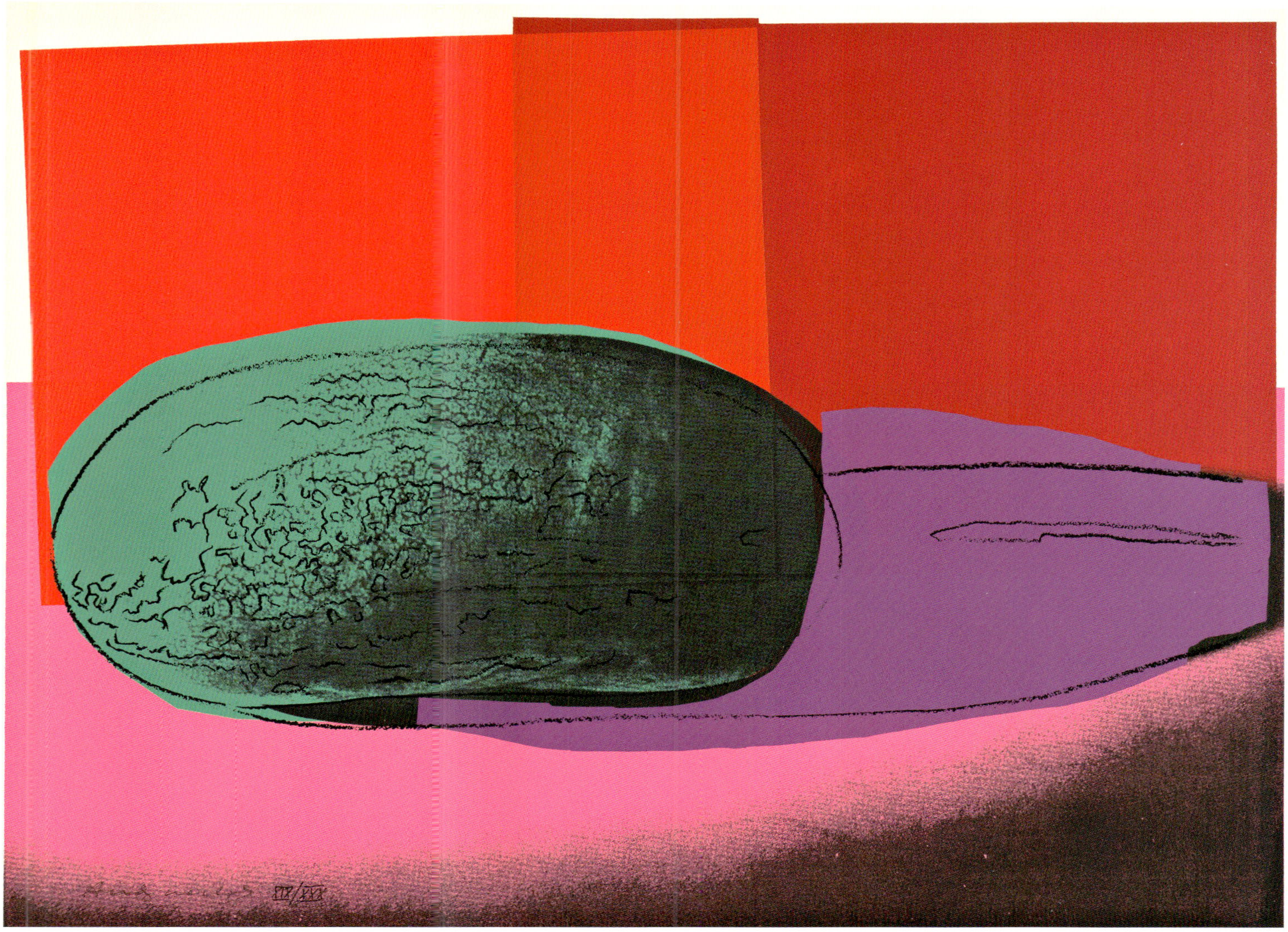

**Space Fruit: Still Lifes, Wctermelon**, 1979. Screenprint, 30 x 40 in.

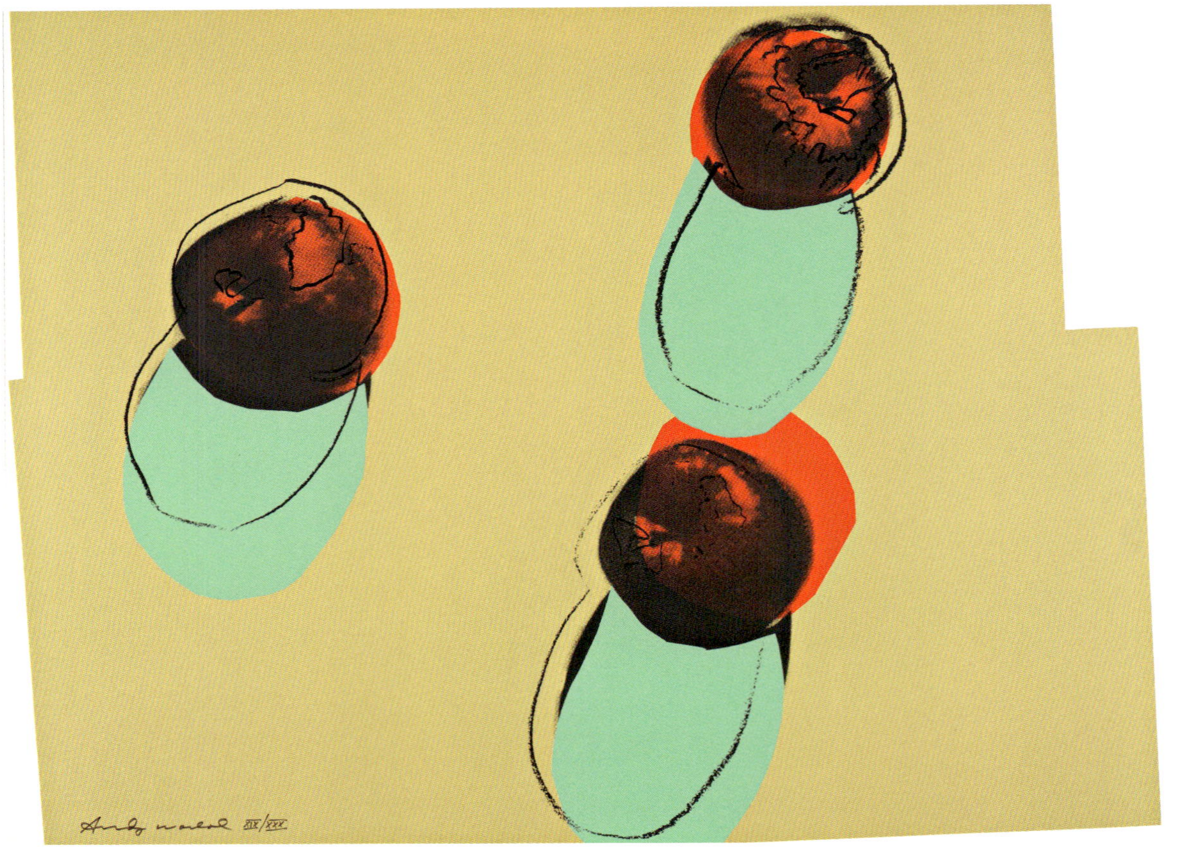

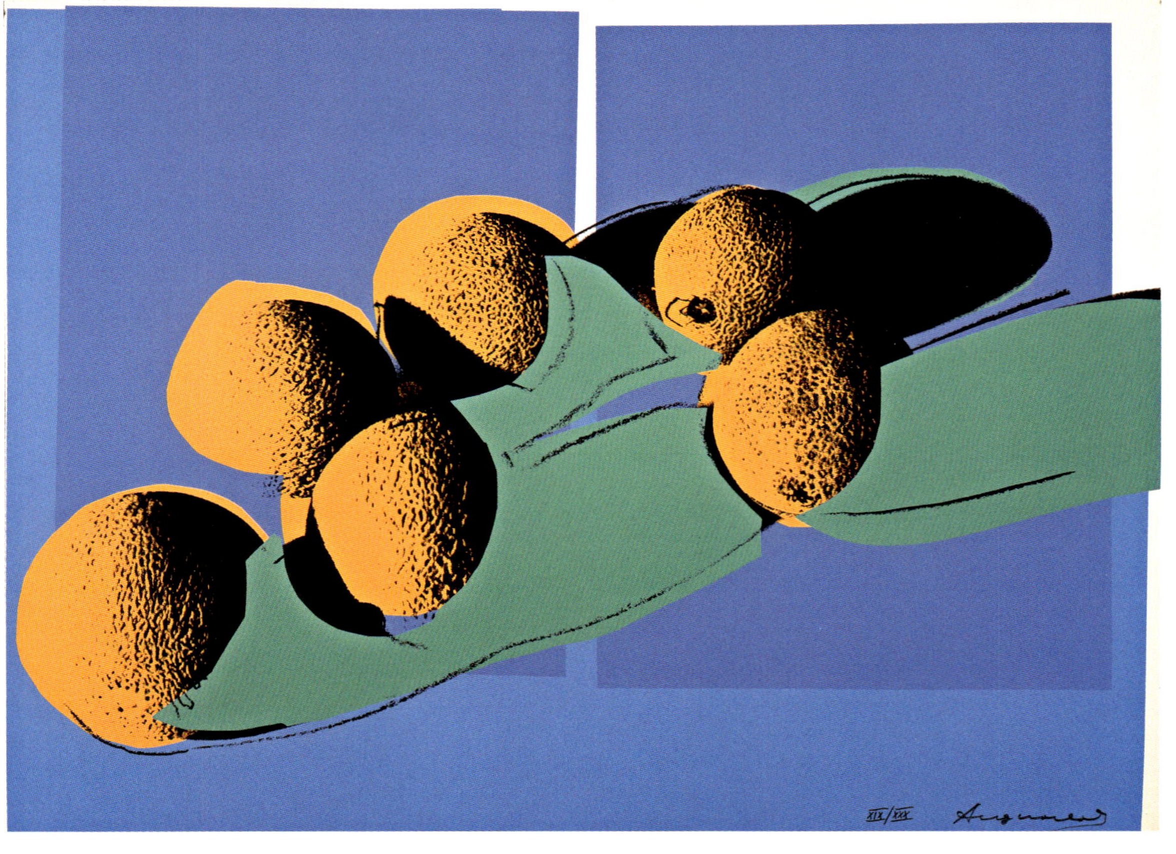

**Space Fruit: Still Lifes, Apples**,1979. Screenprint, 30 x 40 in.

**Space Fruit: Still Lifes, Cantaloupes I**,1979. Screenprint, 30 x 40 in.

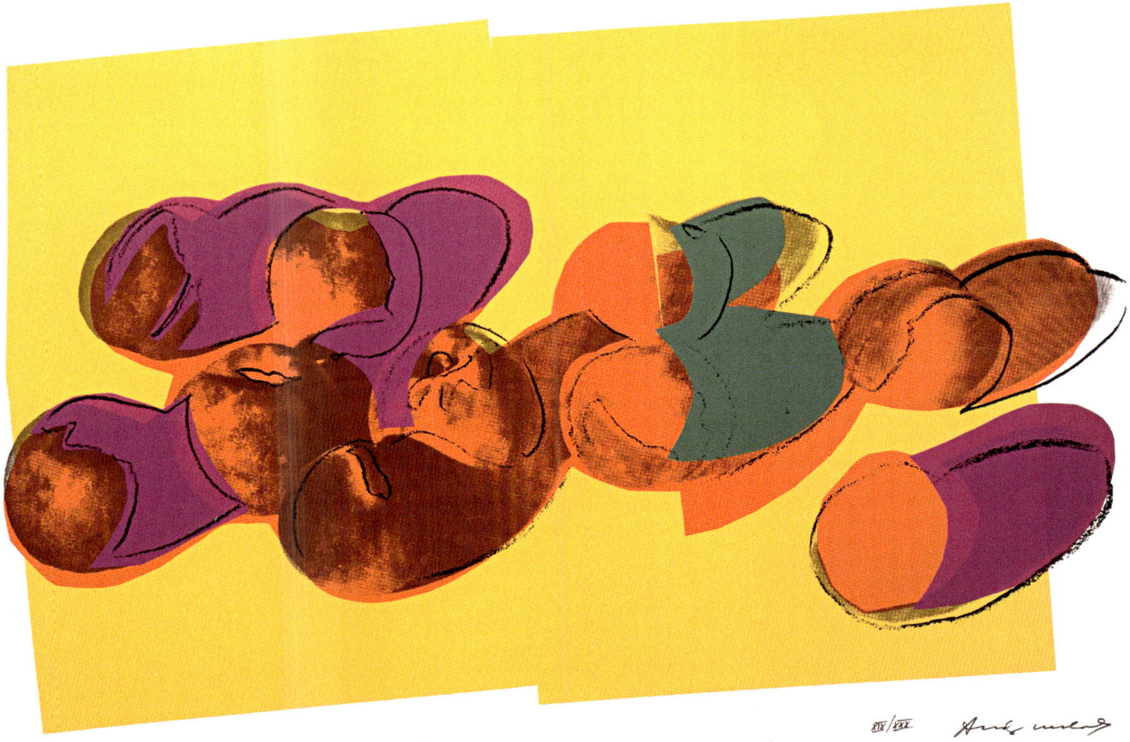

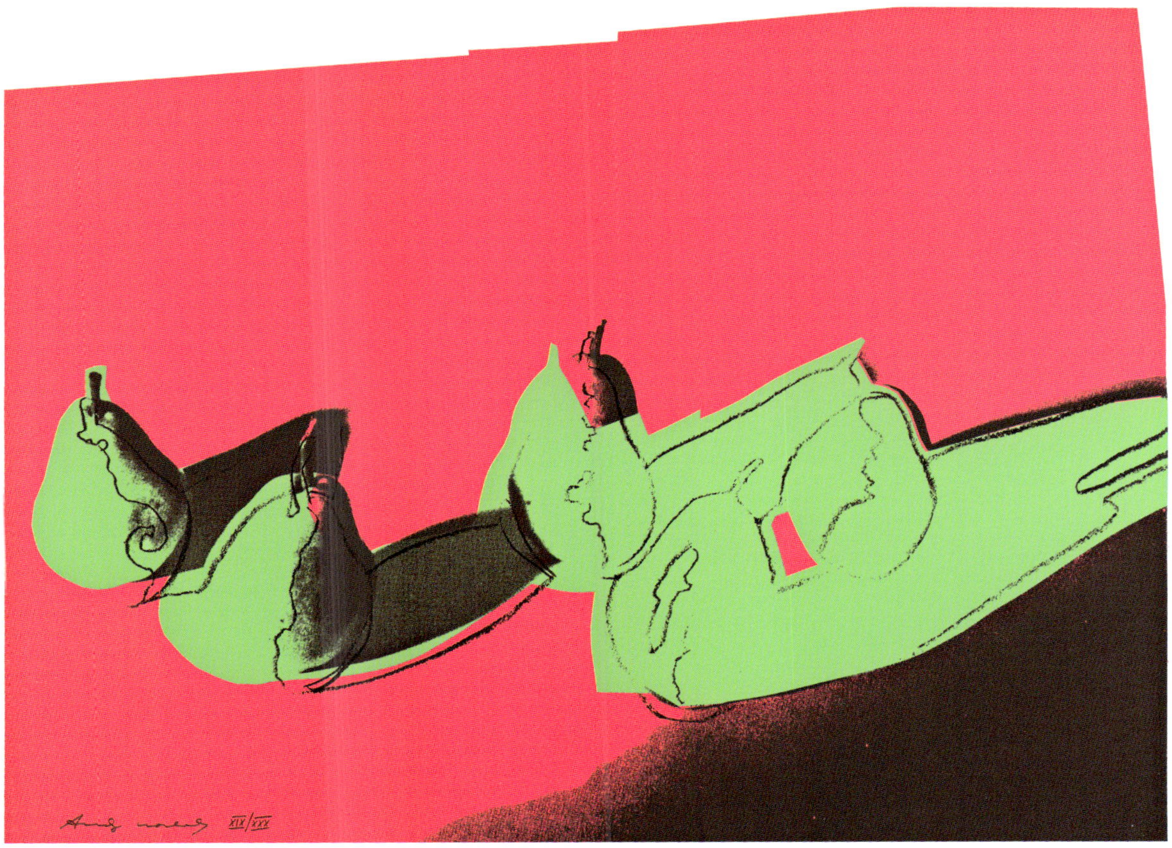

**Space Fruit: Still Lifes, Peaches**, 1979. Screenprint, 30 x 40 in.

**Space Fruit: Still Lifes, Pears**, 1979. Screenprint, 30 x 40 in.

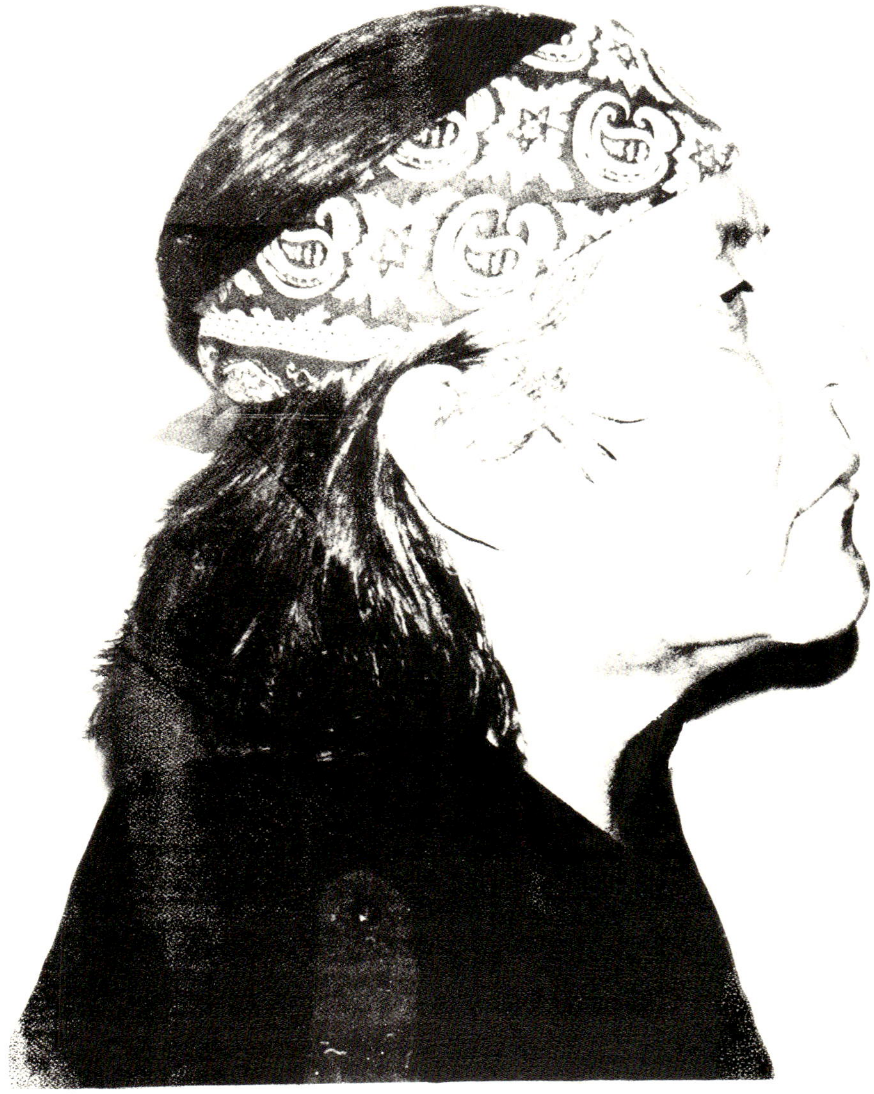

**R. C. Gorman**, 1979. Screenprint, 44½ x 41 in.

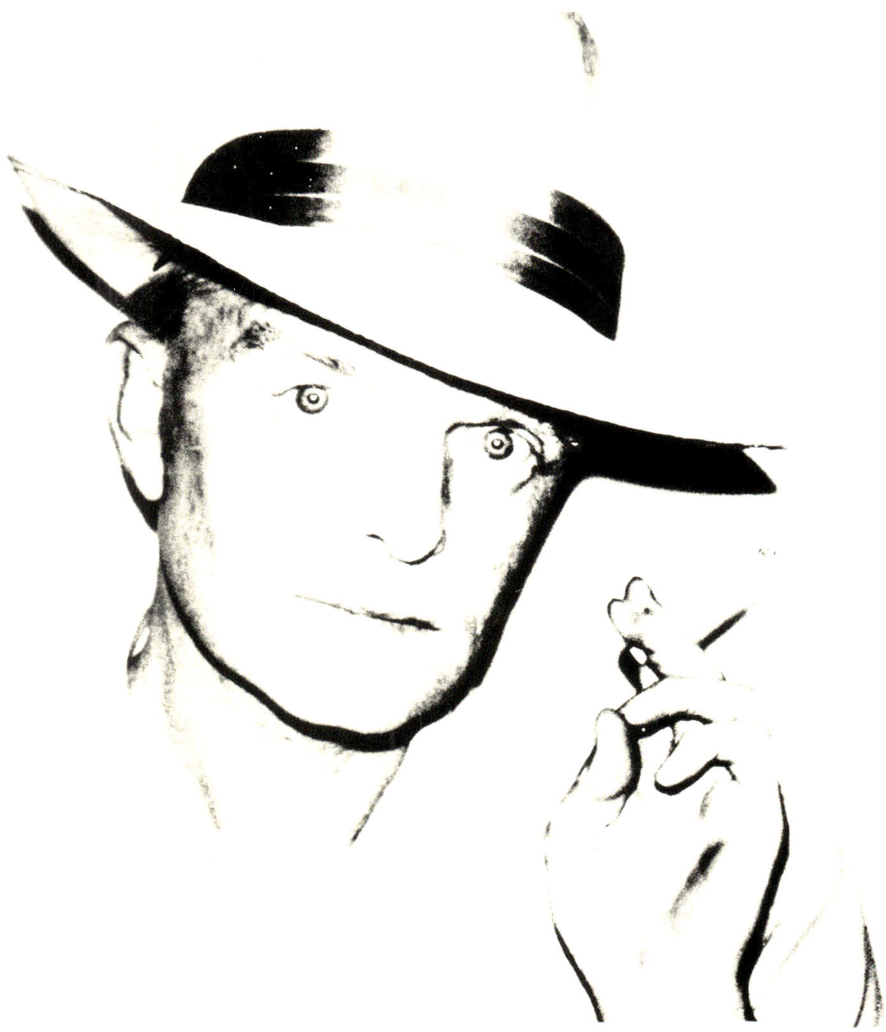

**Truman Capote**, 1979. Screenprint, 50⅛ x 41⅜ in.

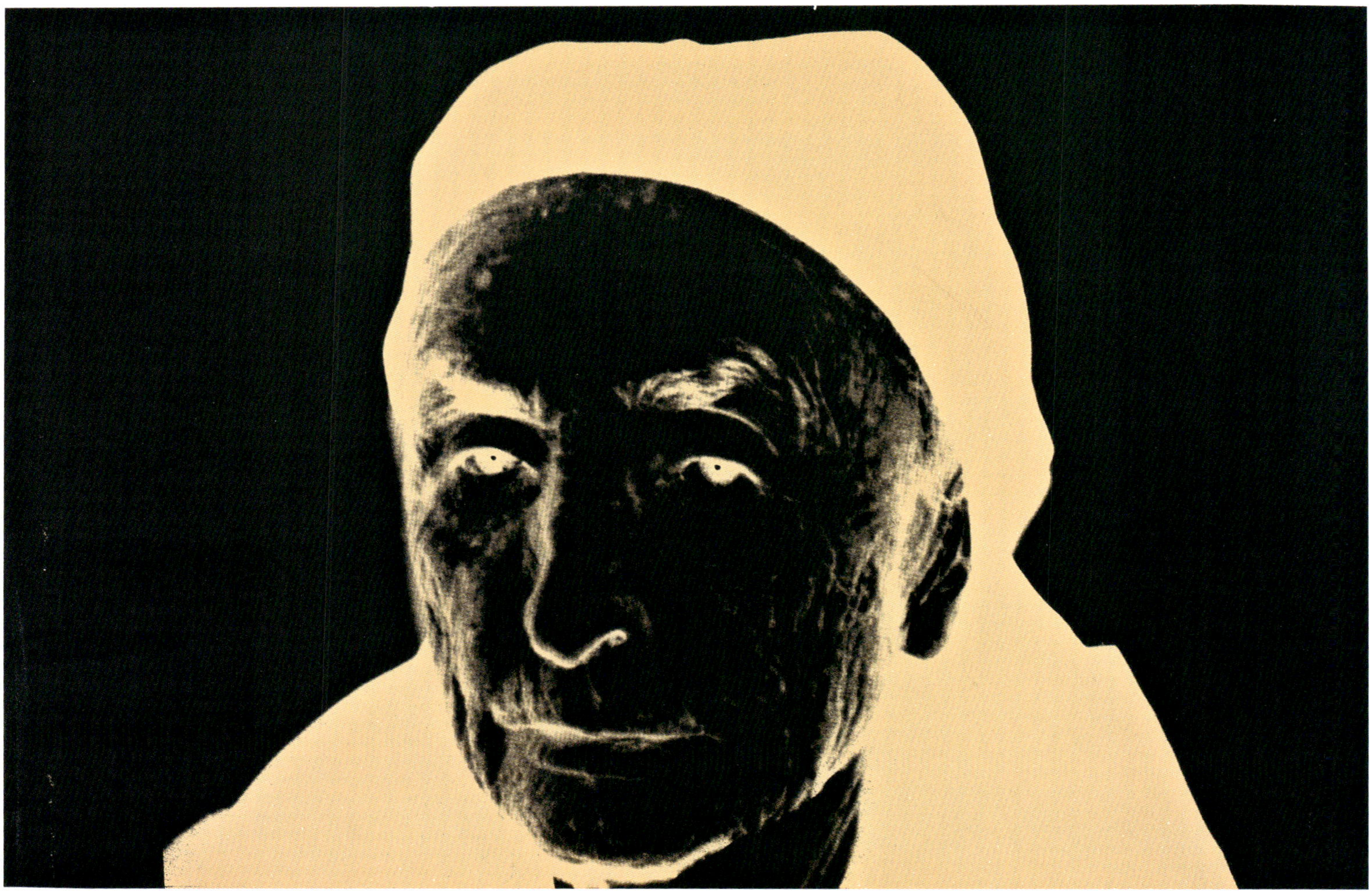

**Georgia O'Keeffe**, 1979. Screenprint with diamond dust, 40¼ x 59¾ in.

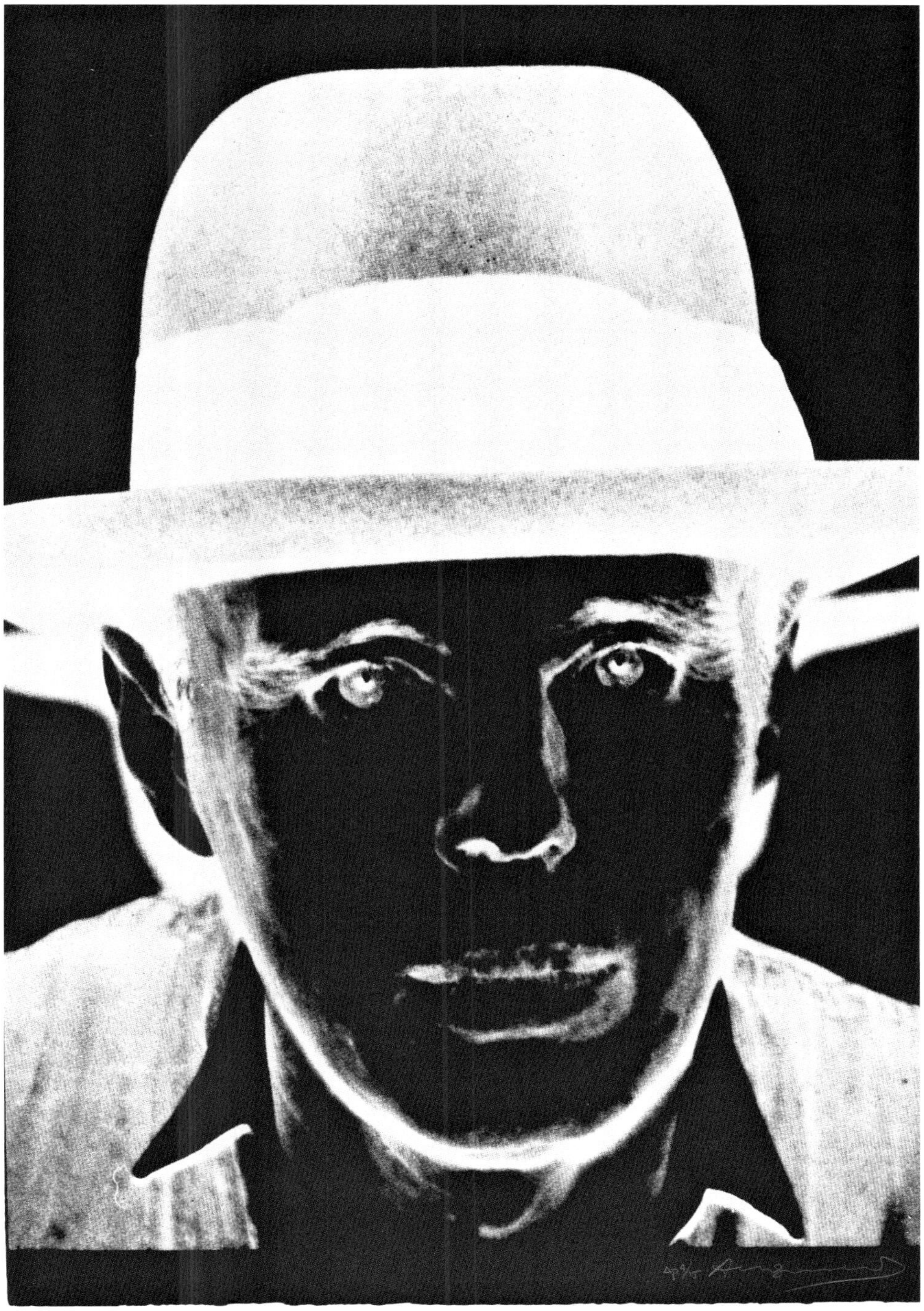

**Joseph Beuys**, 1980. Screenprint with diamond dust, 44 x 30 in.

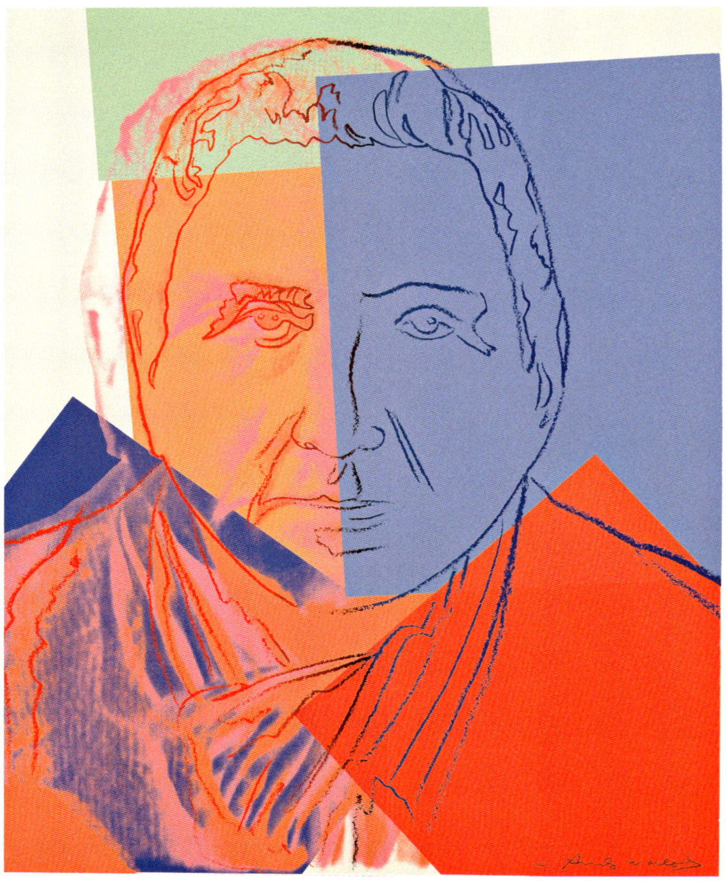

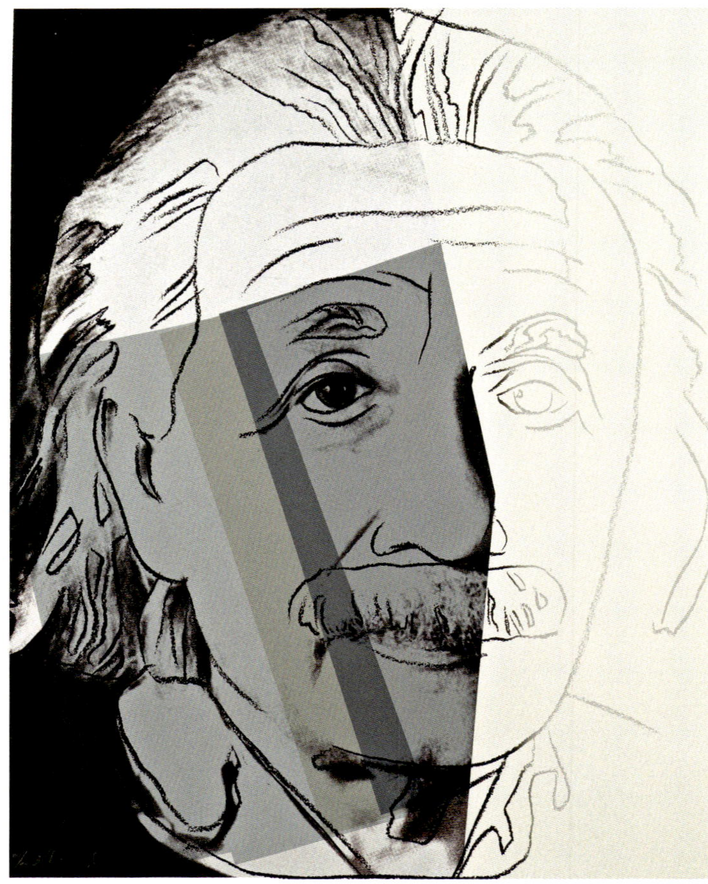

**Ten Portraits of Jews of the Twentieth Century: Gertrude Stein**, 1980. Screenprint, 40 x 32 in.
**Ten Portraits of Jews of the Twentieth Century: Albert Einstein**, 1980. Screenprint, 40 x 32 in.
**Ten Portraits of Jews of the Twentieth Century: Sarah Bernhardt**, 1980. Screenprint, 40 x 32 in.

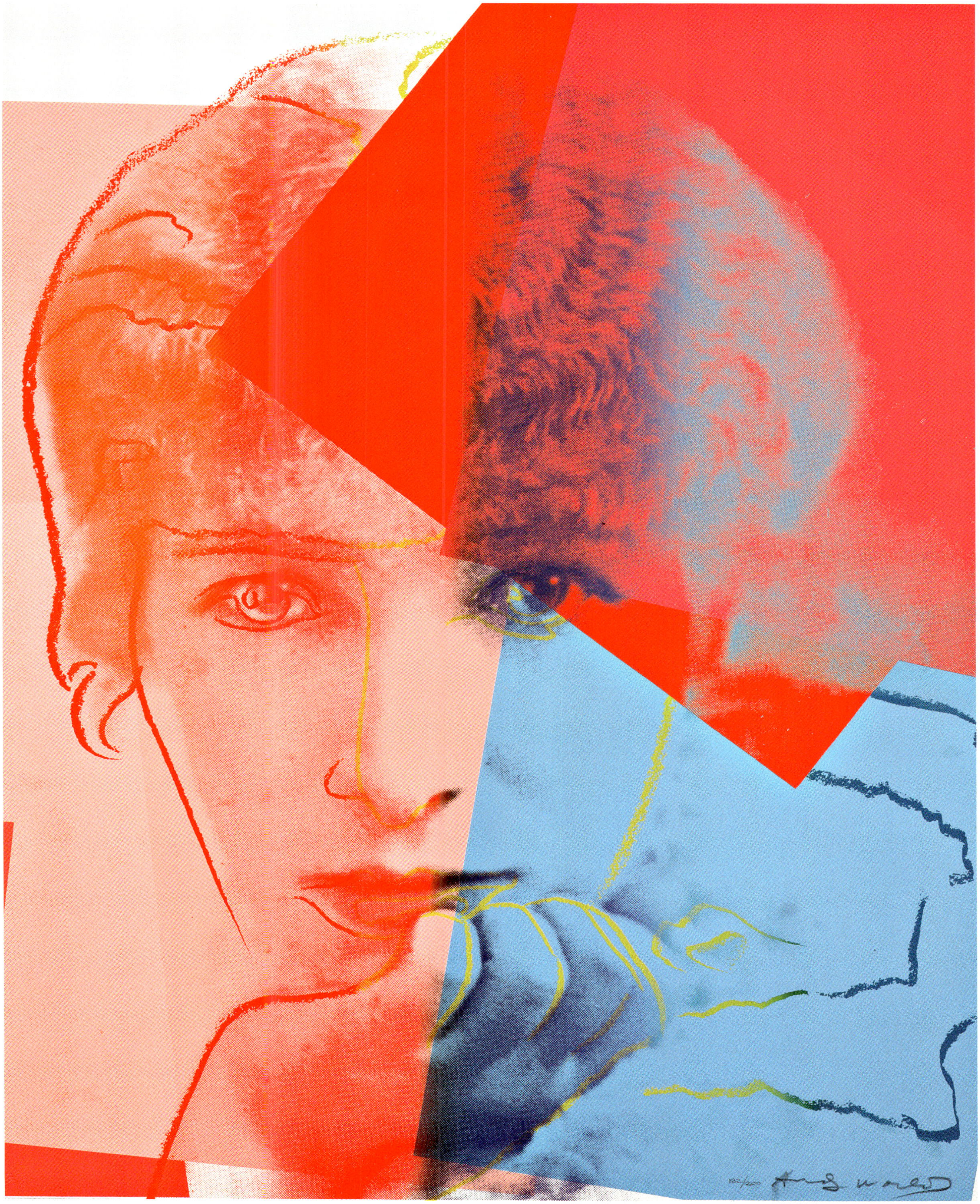

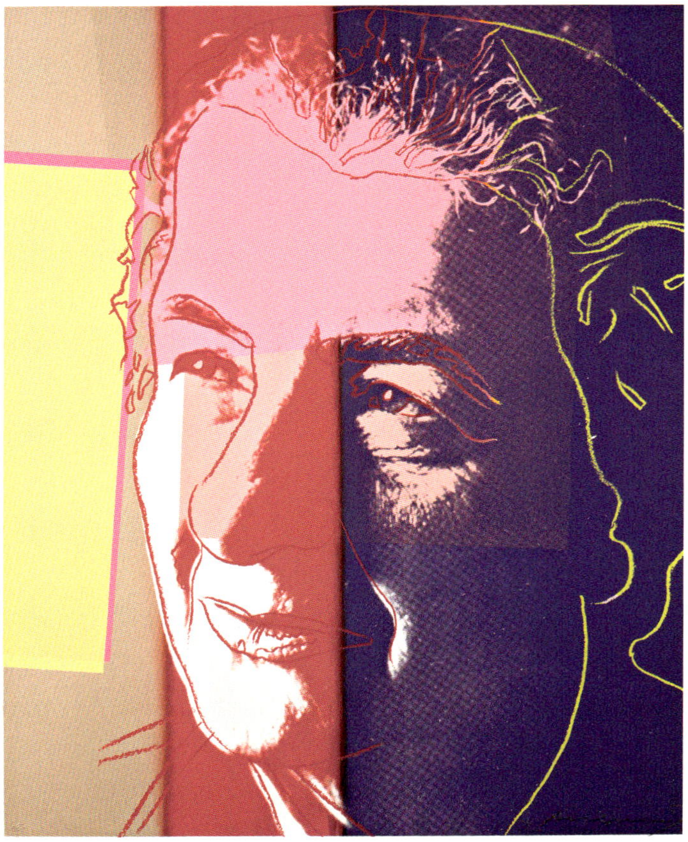

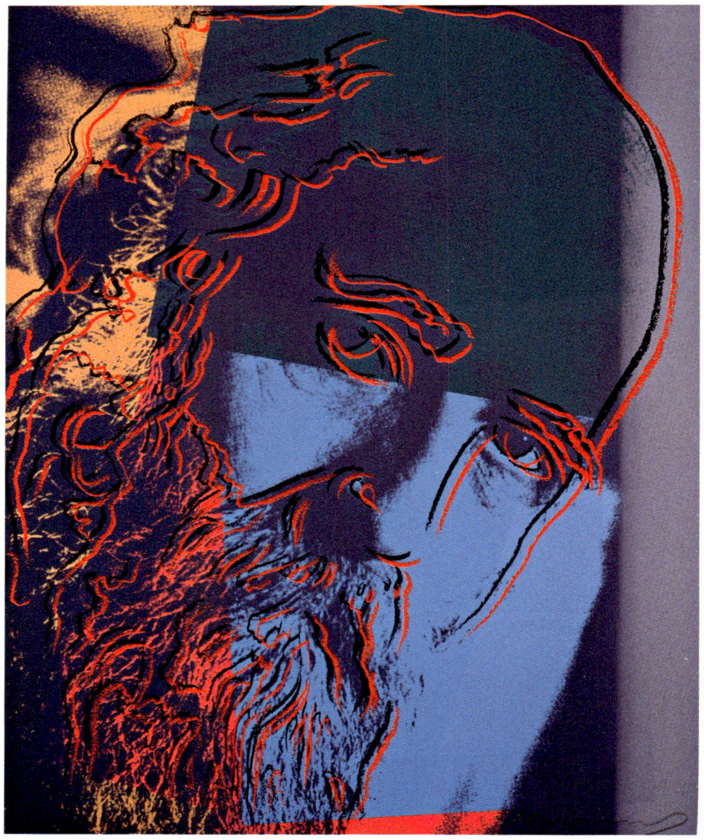

**Ten Portraits of Jews of the Twentieth Century: Golda Meir**, 1980. Screenprint, 40 x 32 in.

**Ten Portraits of Jews of the Twentieth Century: Martin Buber**, 1980. Screenprint, 40 x 32 in.

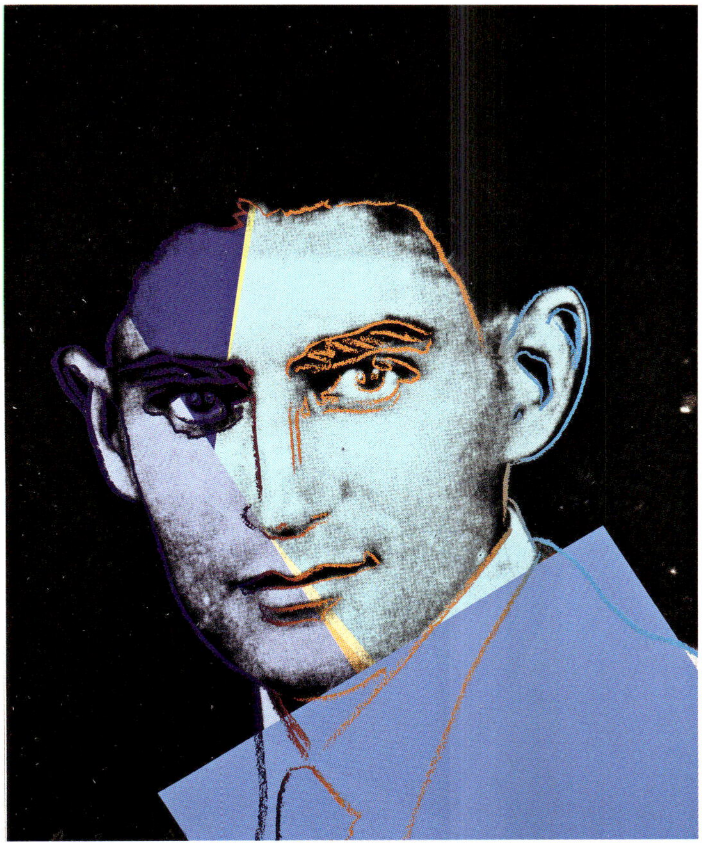

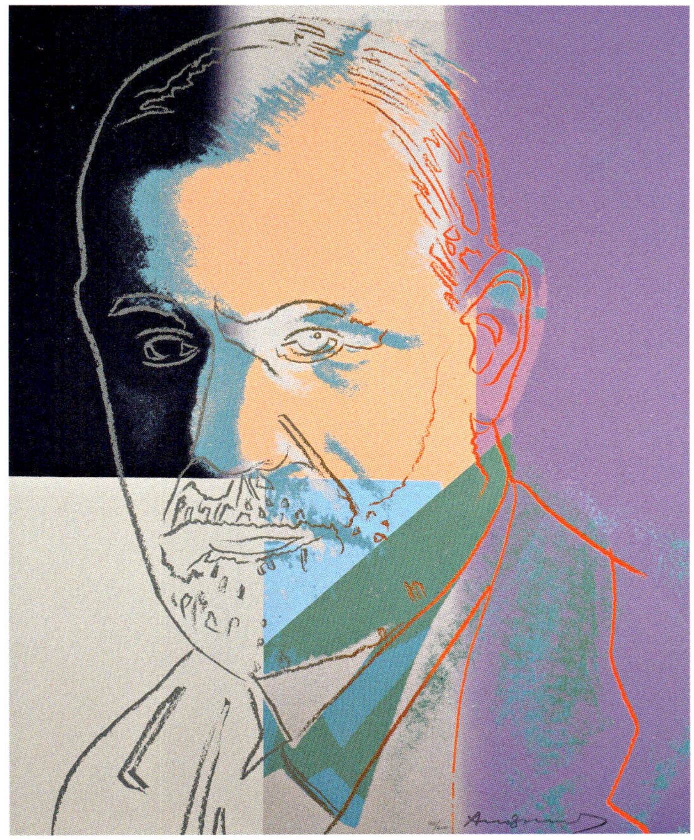

**Ten Portraits of Jews of the Twentieth Century: Franz Kafka**, 1980. Screenprint, 40 x 32 in.

**Ten Portraits of Jews of the Twentieth Century: Sigmund Freud**, 1980. Screenprint, 40 x 32 in.

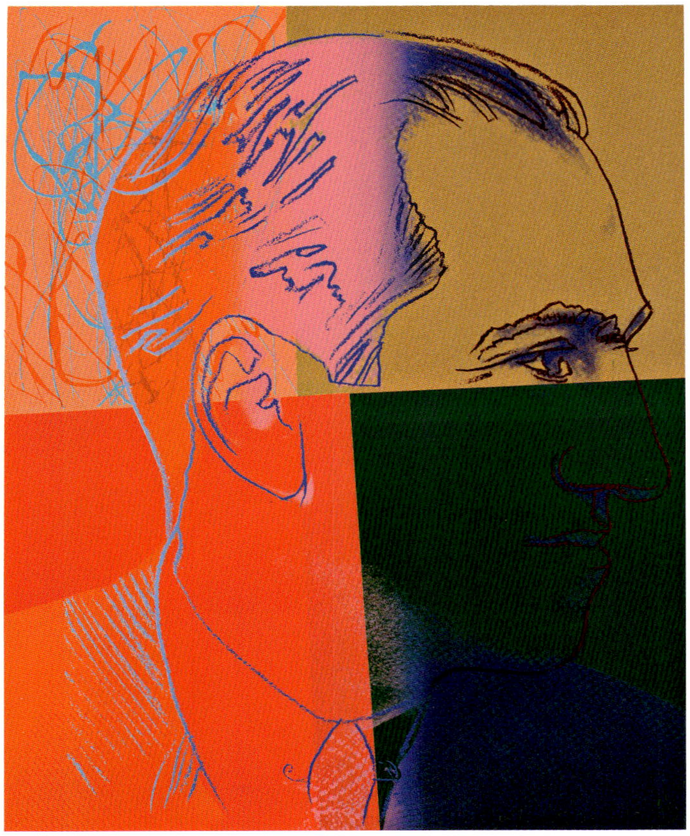

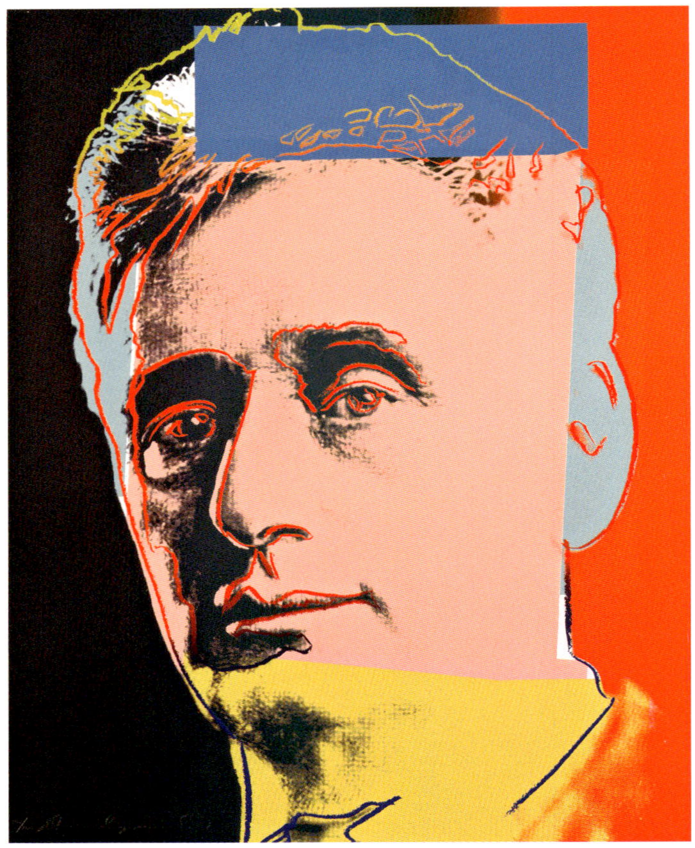

**Ten Portraits of Jews of the Twentieth Century: George Gershwin**, 1980. Screenprint, 40 x 32 in.
**Ten Portraits of Jews of the Twentieth Century: Louis Brandeis**, 1980. Screenprint, 40 x 32 in.
**Ten Portraits of Jews of the Twentieth Century: The Marx Brothers**, 1980. Screenprint, 40 x 32 in.

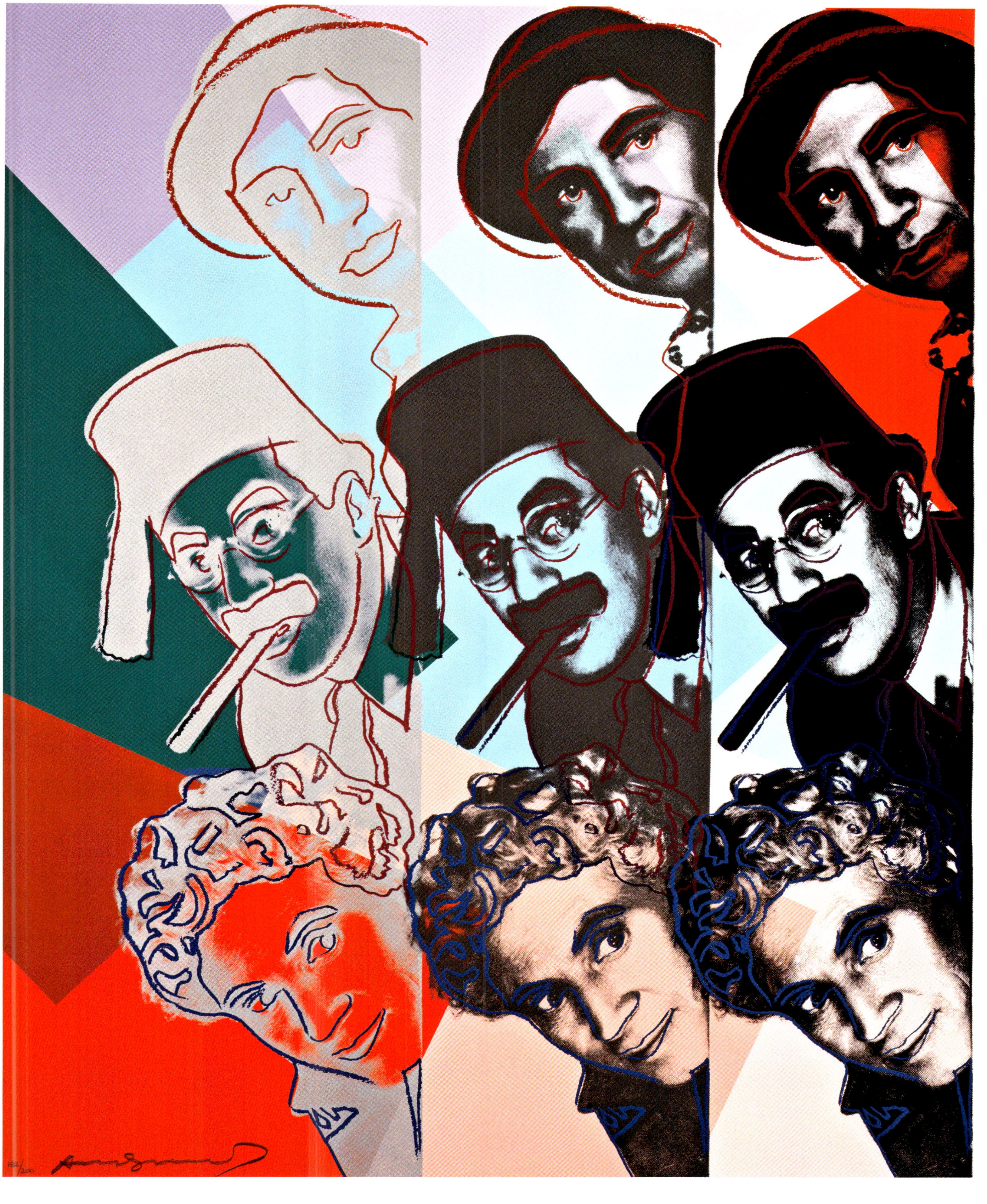

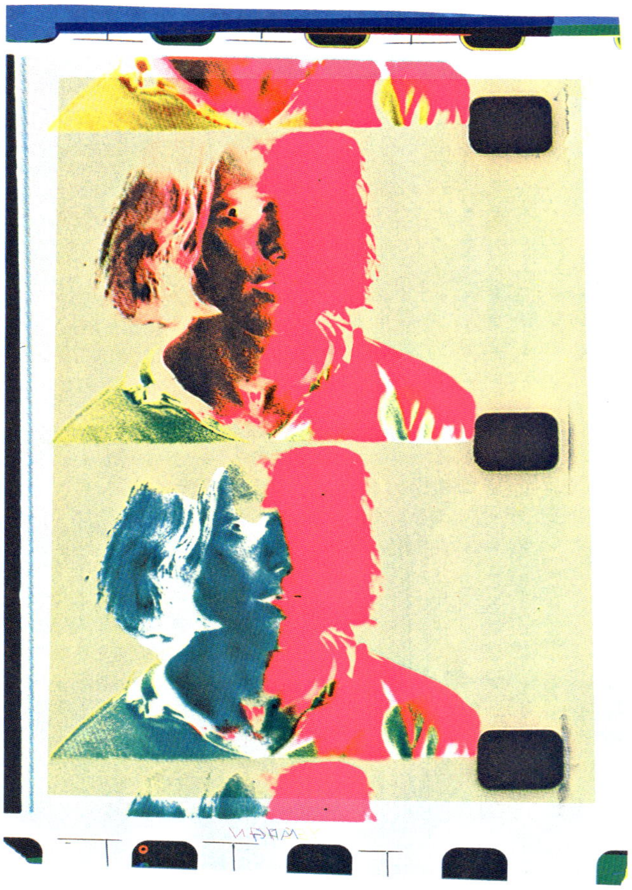

**Eric Emerson (Chelsea Girls)**, 1982. Screenprint, 30 x 22 in.

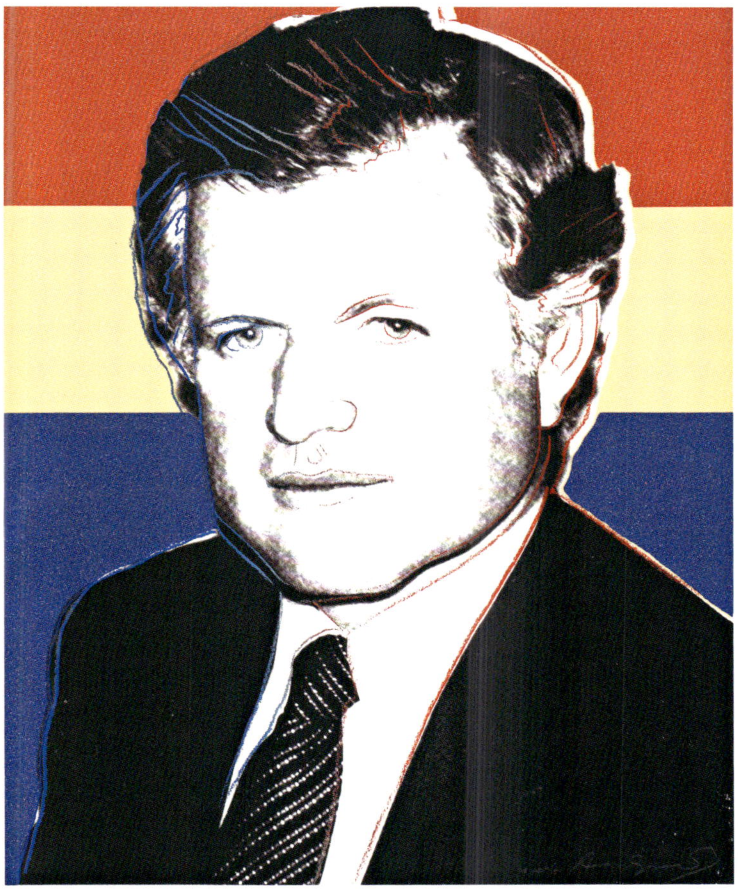

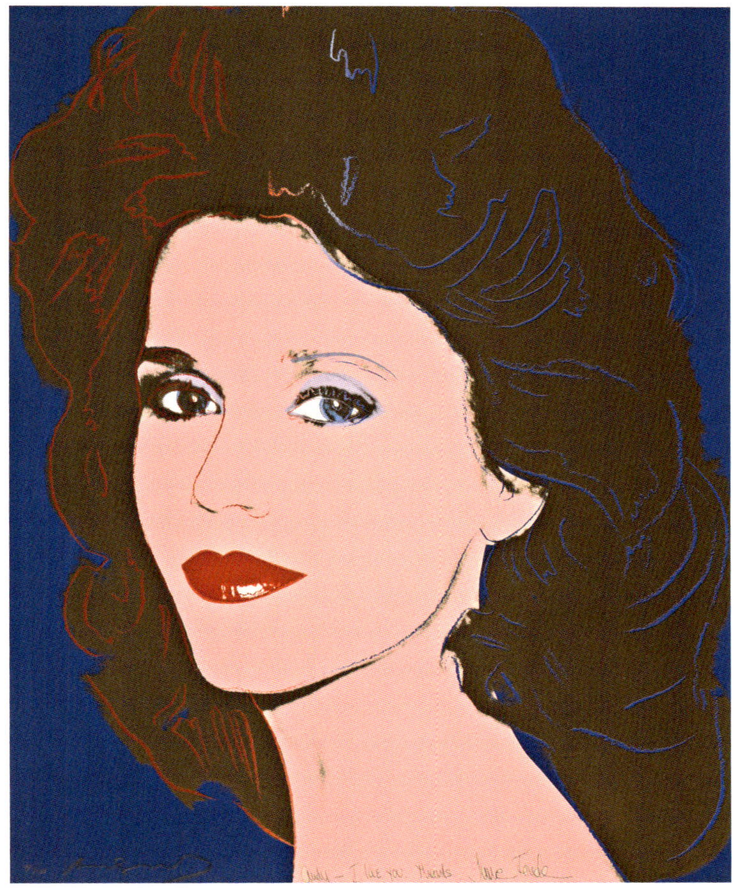

**Edward Kennedy (Deluxe Edition)**, 1980. Screenprint, 40 x 32 in.

**Jane Fonda**, 1982. Screenprint, 39½ x 31½ in.

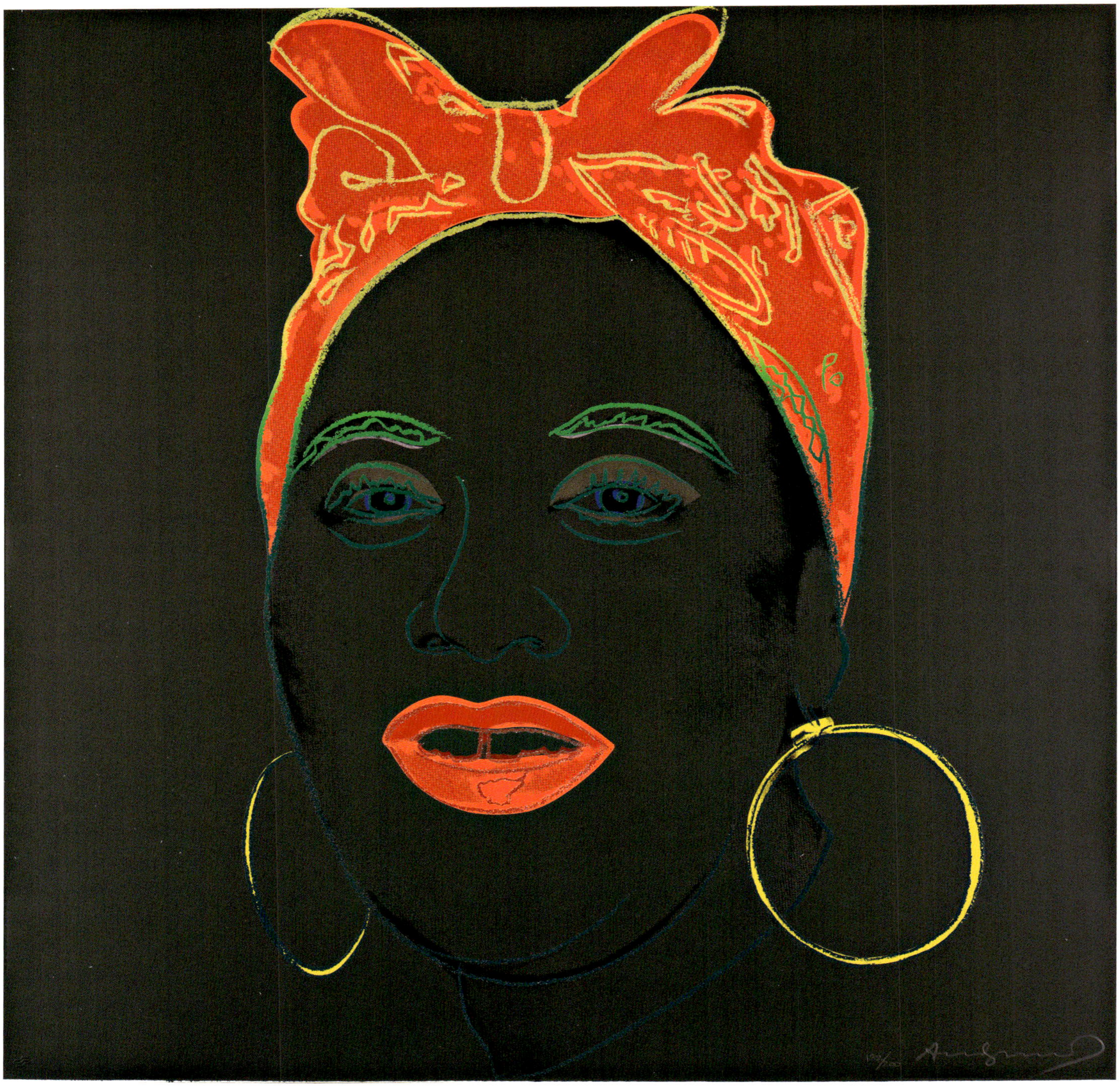

**Myths: Mammy**, 1981. Screenprint, 38 x 38 in.

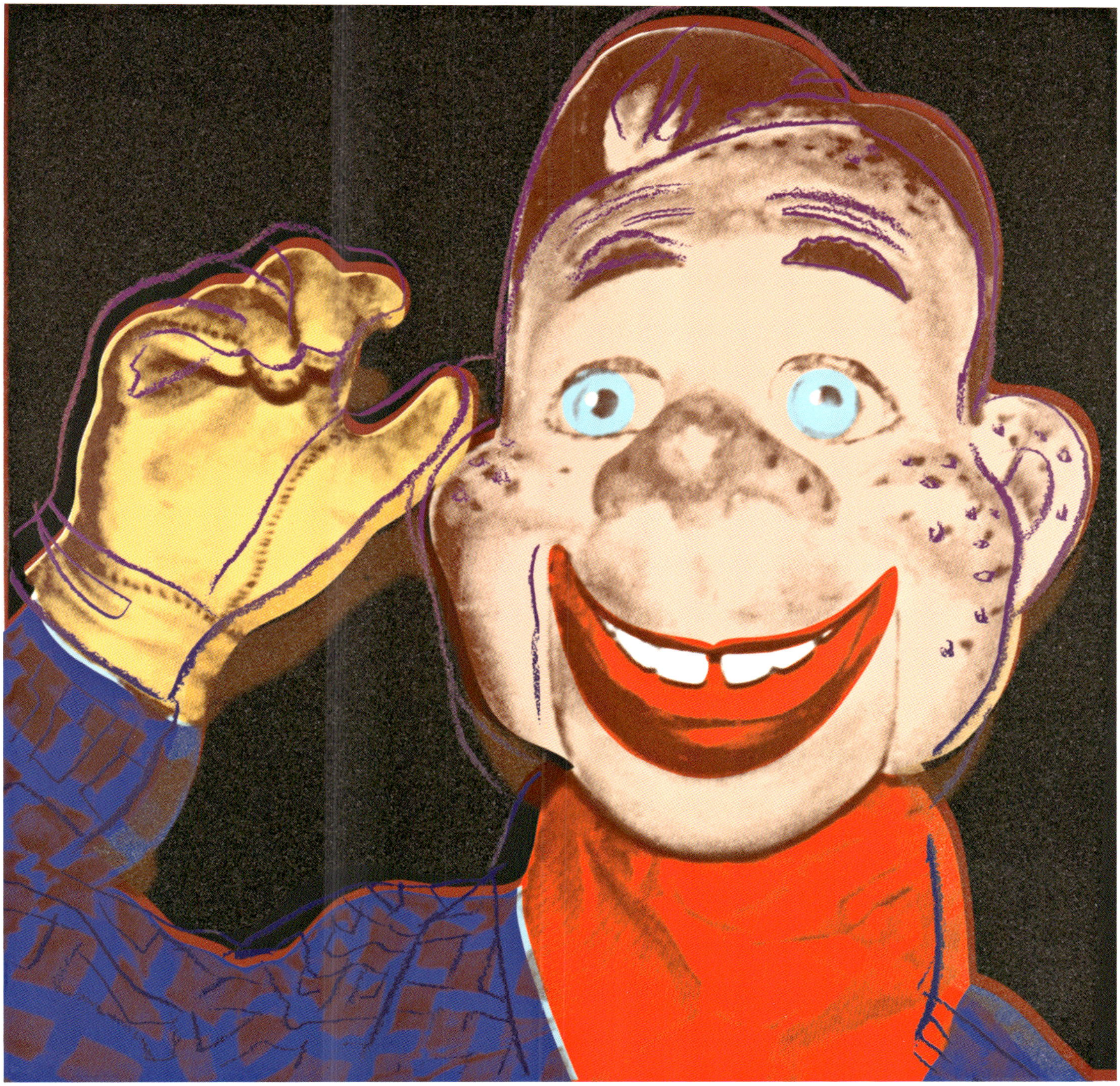

**Myths: Howdy Doody**, 1981. Screenprint with diamond dust, 38 x 38 in.

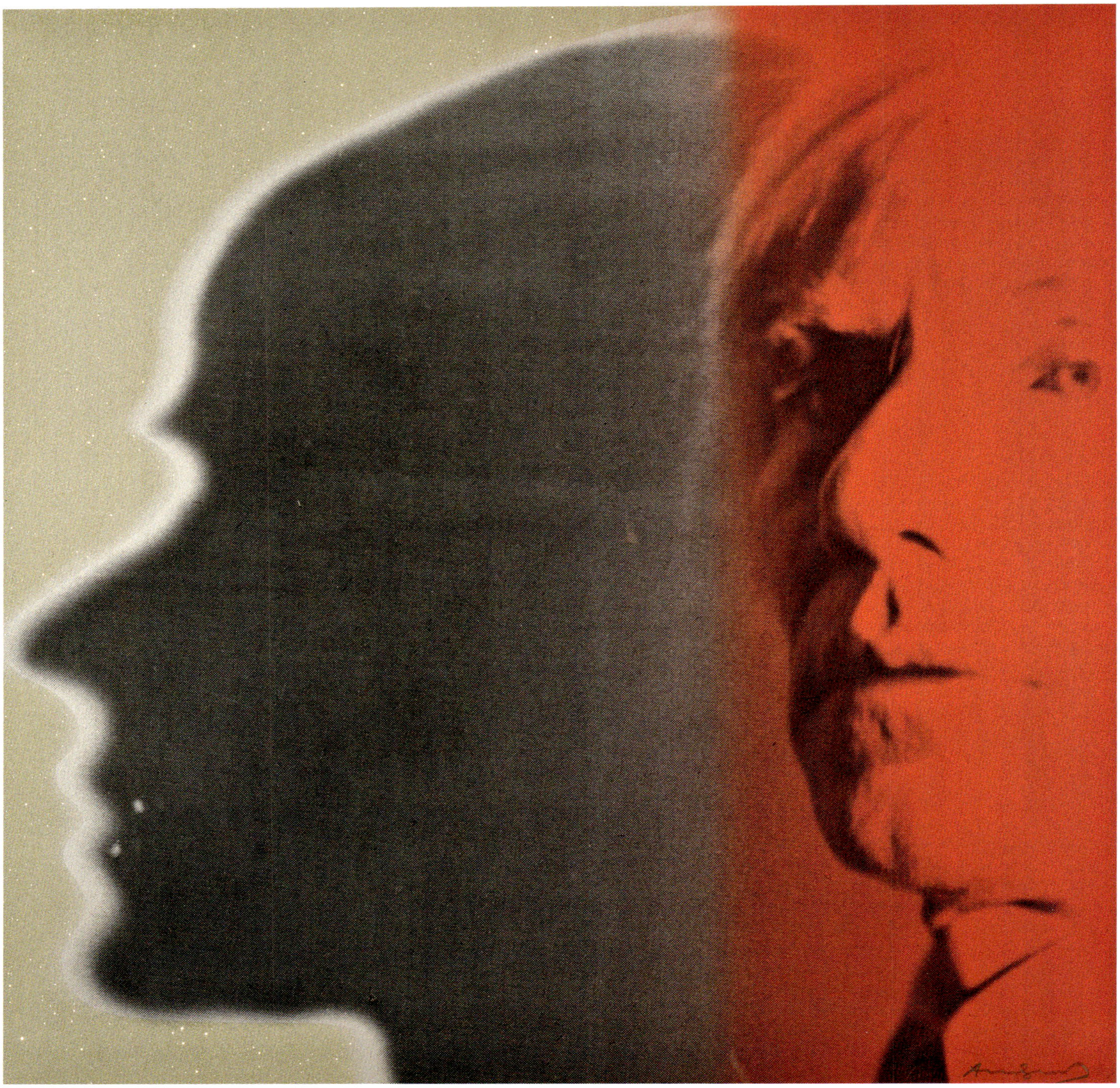

**Myths: The Shadow**, 1981. Screenprint, 38 x 38 in.

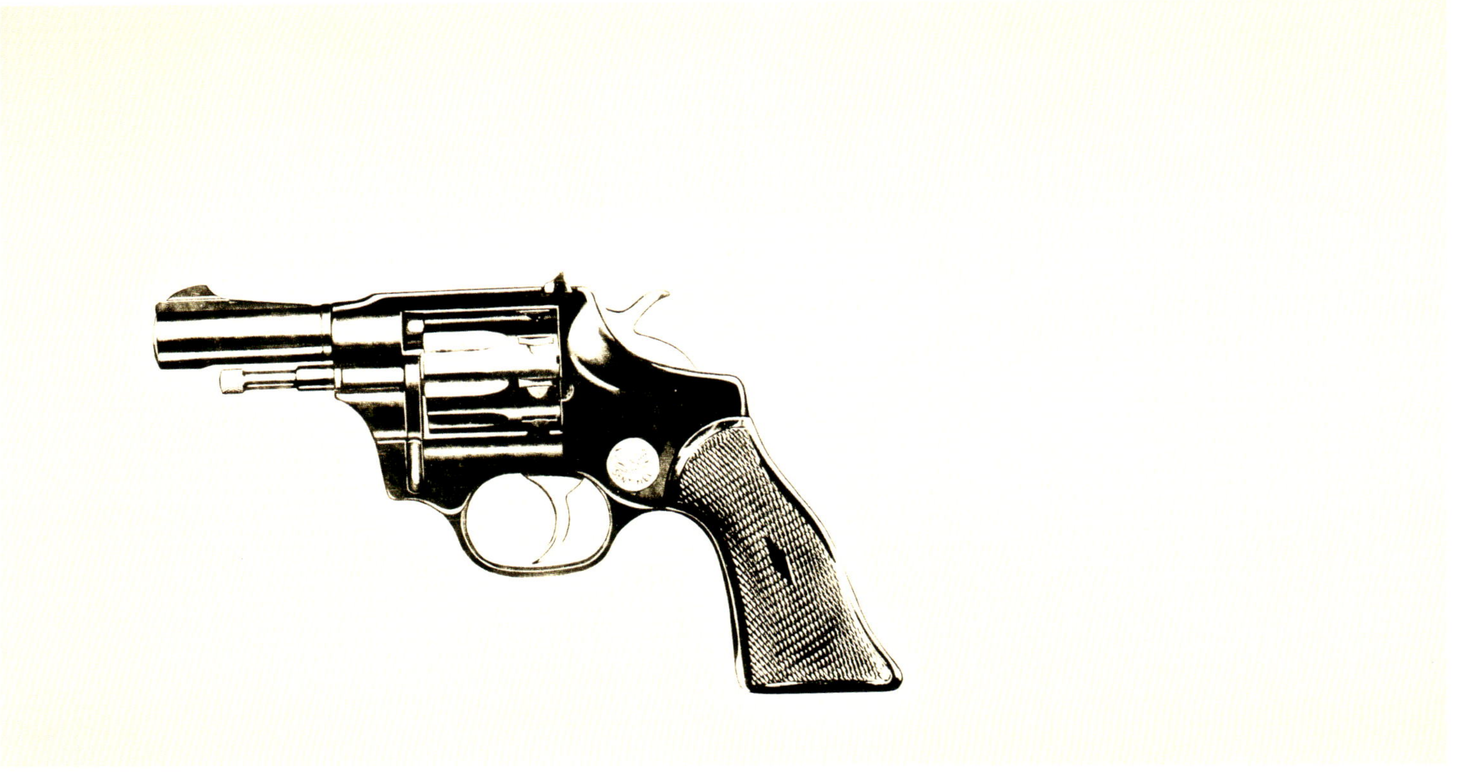

**Gun**, 1981. Screenprint, 22 x 39⅞ in.

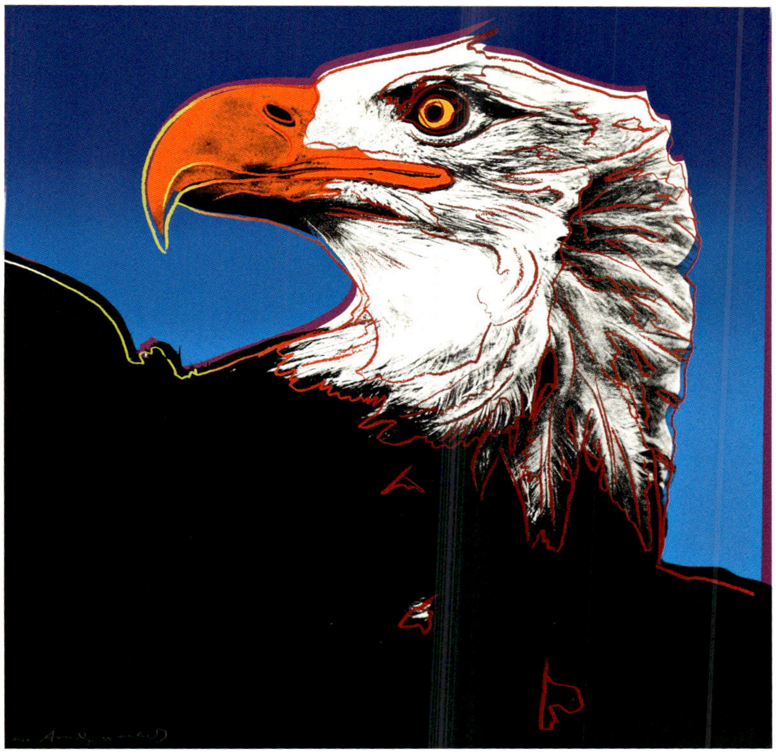

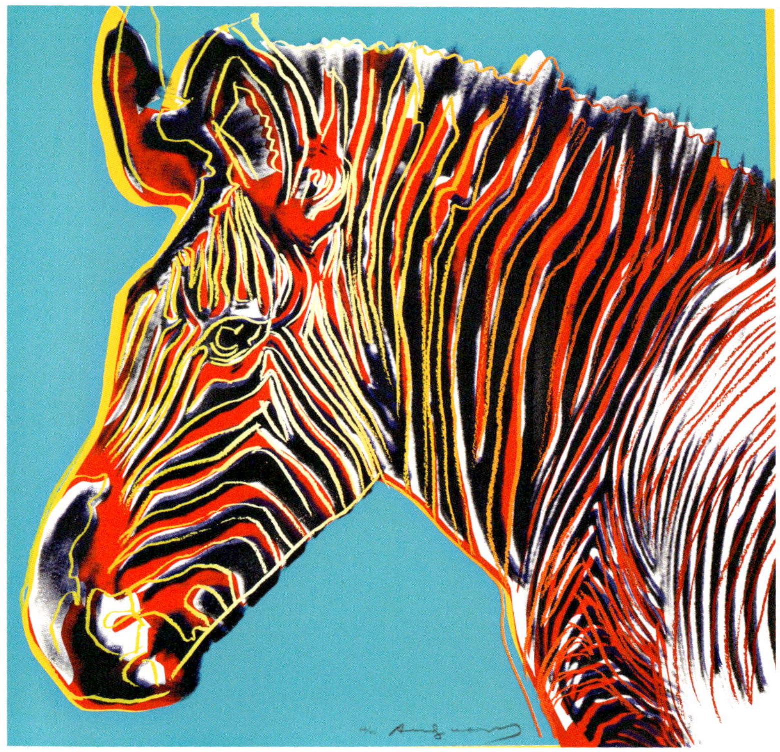

**Endangered Species: Bald Eagle**, 1983. Screenprint, 38 x 38 in.
**Endangered Species: Grevy's Zebra**, 1983. Screenprint, 38 x 38 in.
**Endangered Species: Orangutan**, 1983. Screenprint, 38 x 38 in.

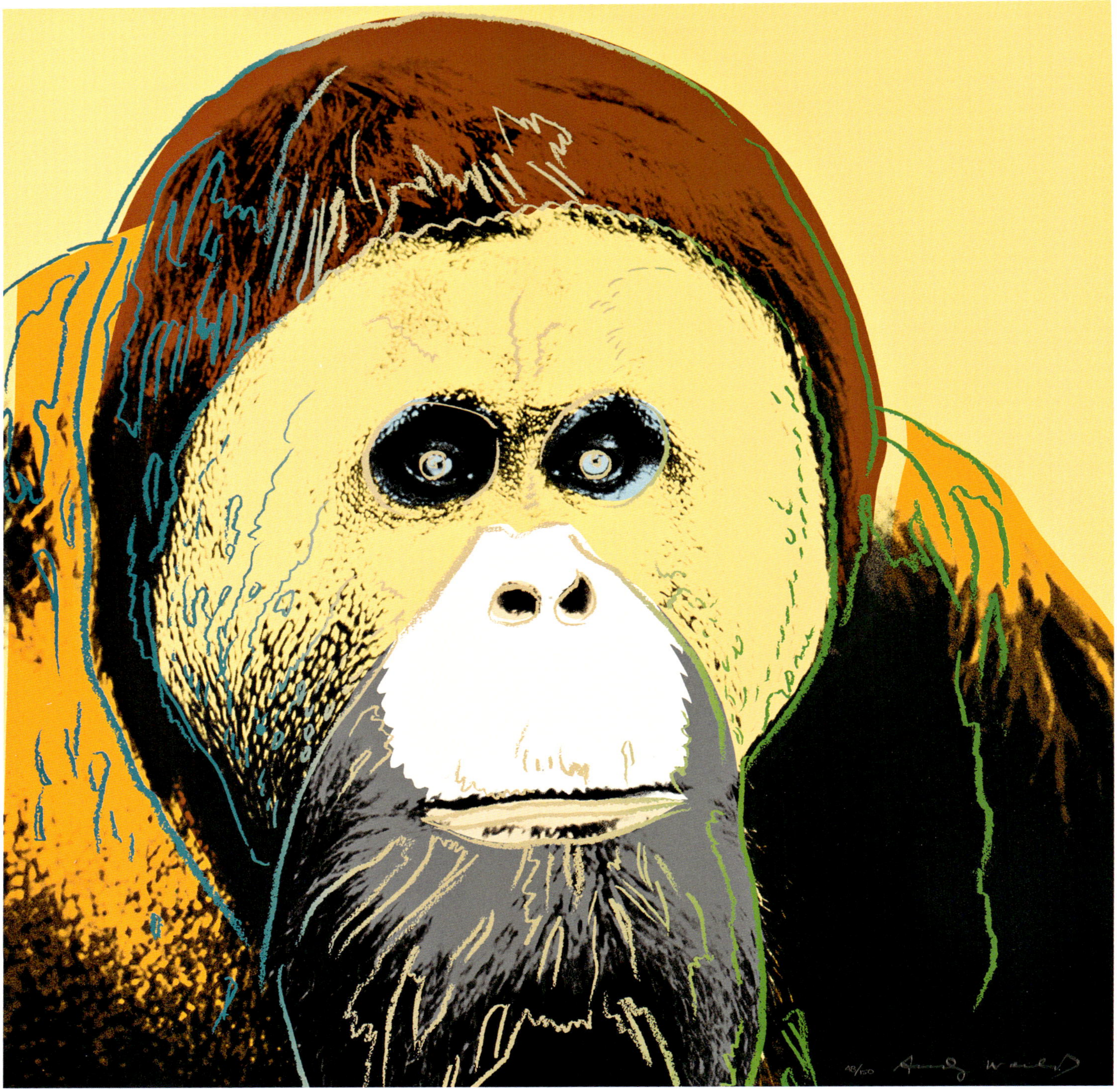

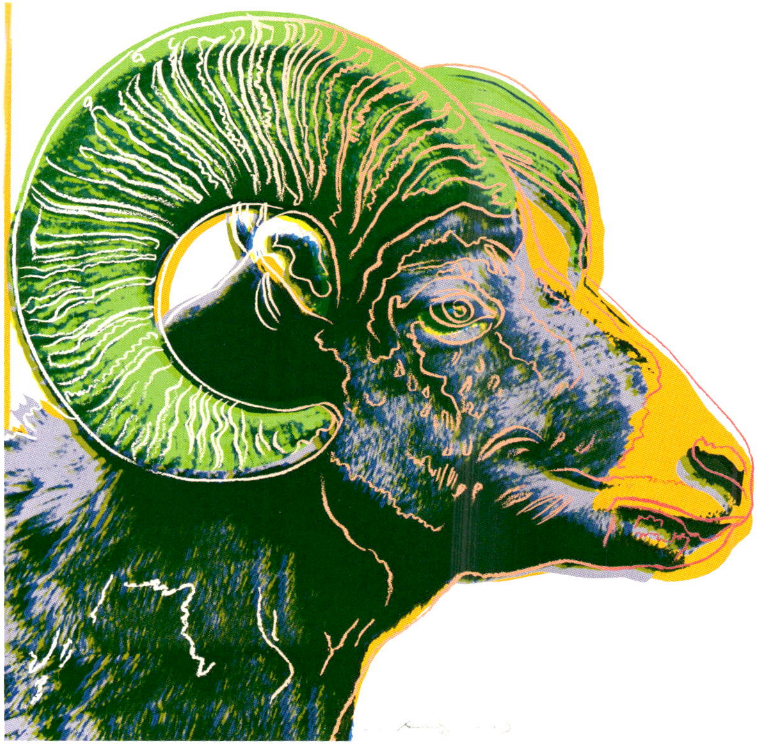

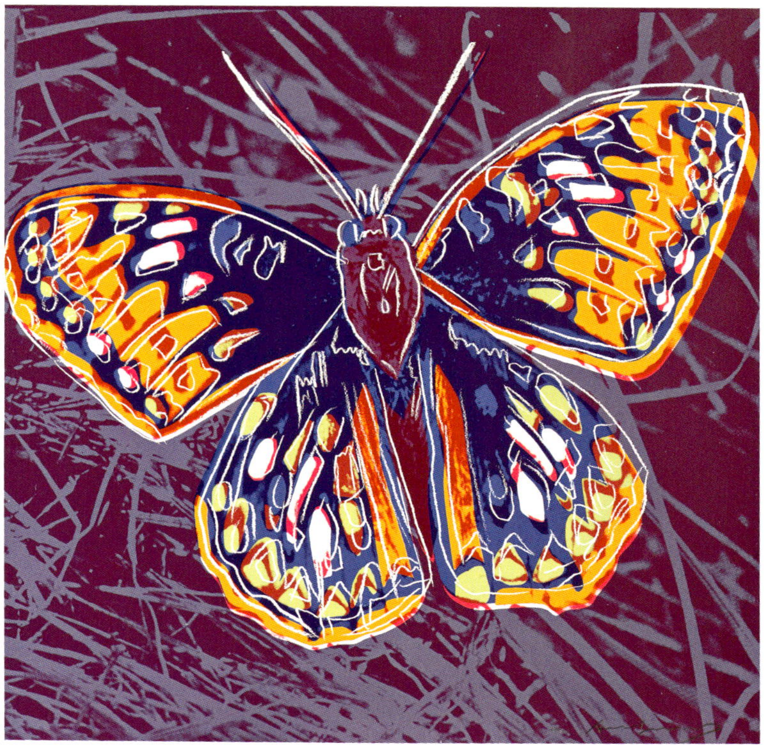

**Endangered Species: Bighorn Ram**, 1983. Screenprint, 38 x 38 in.

**Endangered Species: San Francisco Silverspot**, 1983. Screenprint, 38 x 38 in.

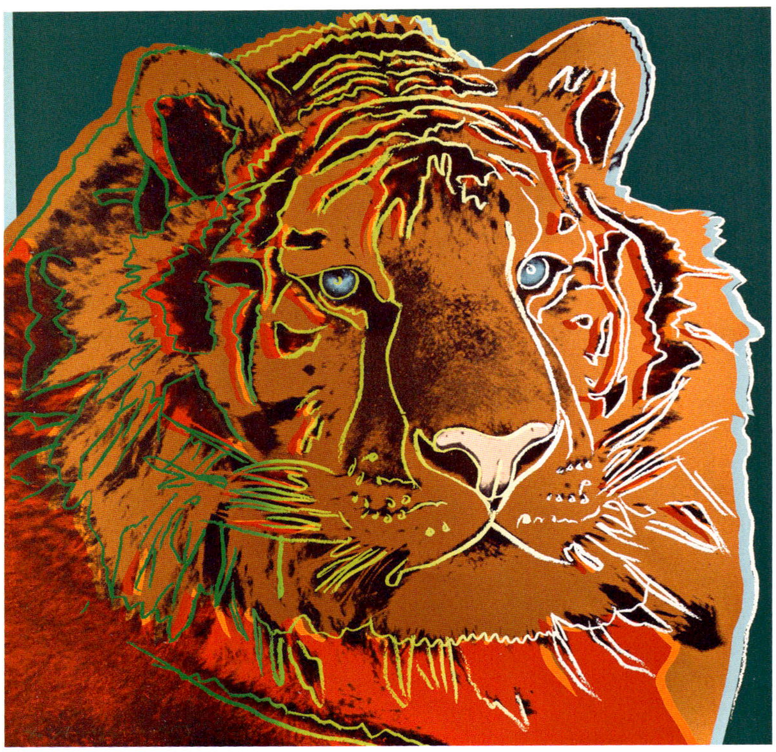

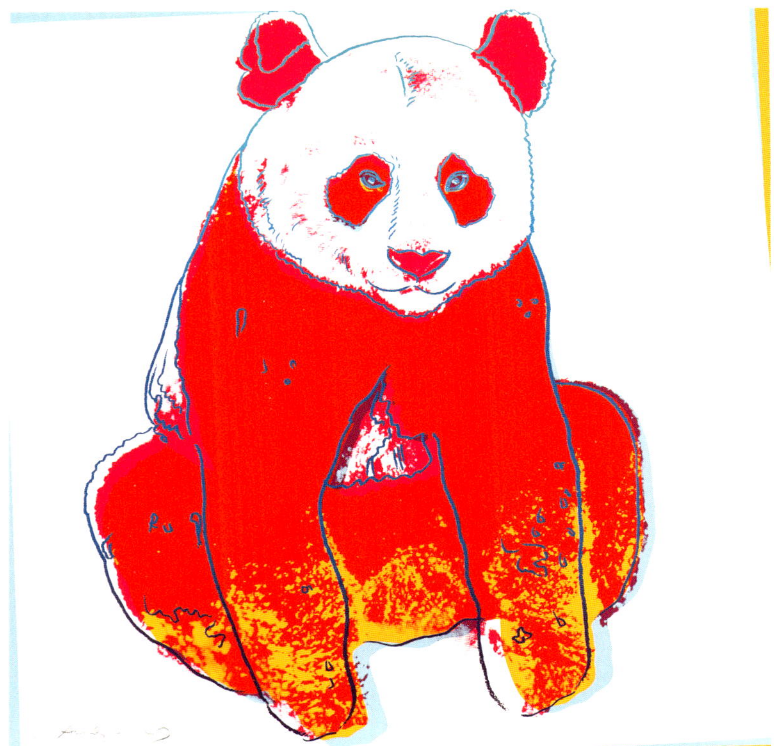

**Endangered Species: Siberian Tiger**, 1983. Screenprint, 38 x 38 in.
**Endangered Species: Giant Panda**, 1983. Screenprint, 38 x 38 in.

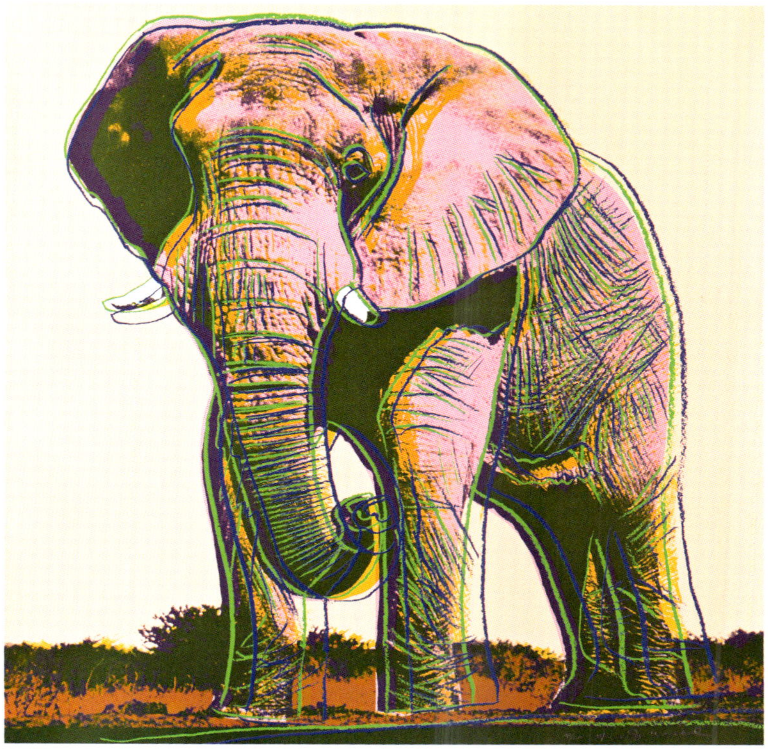

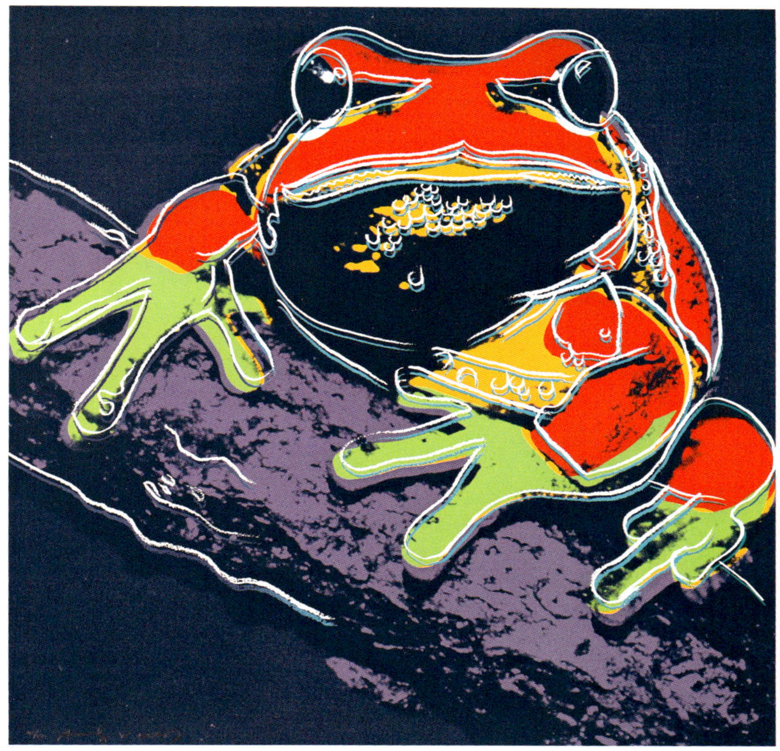

**Endangered Species: African Elephant**, 1983. Screenprint, 38 x 38 in.
**Endangered Species: Pine Barrens Tree Frog**, 1983. Screenprint, 38 x 38 in.
**Endangered Species: Black Rhinoceros**, 1983. Screenprint, 38 x 38 in.

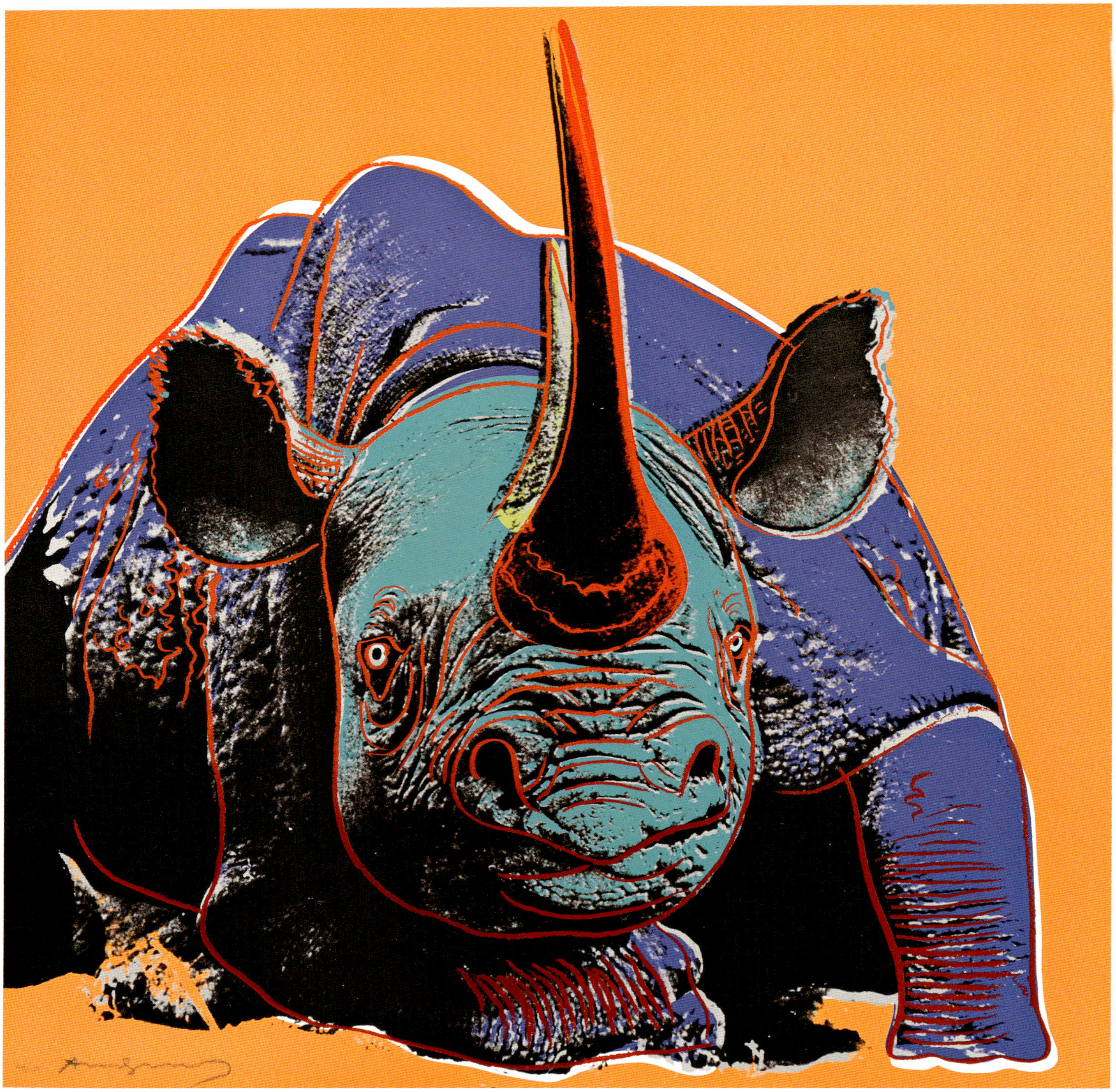

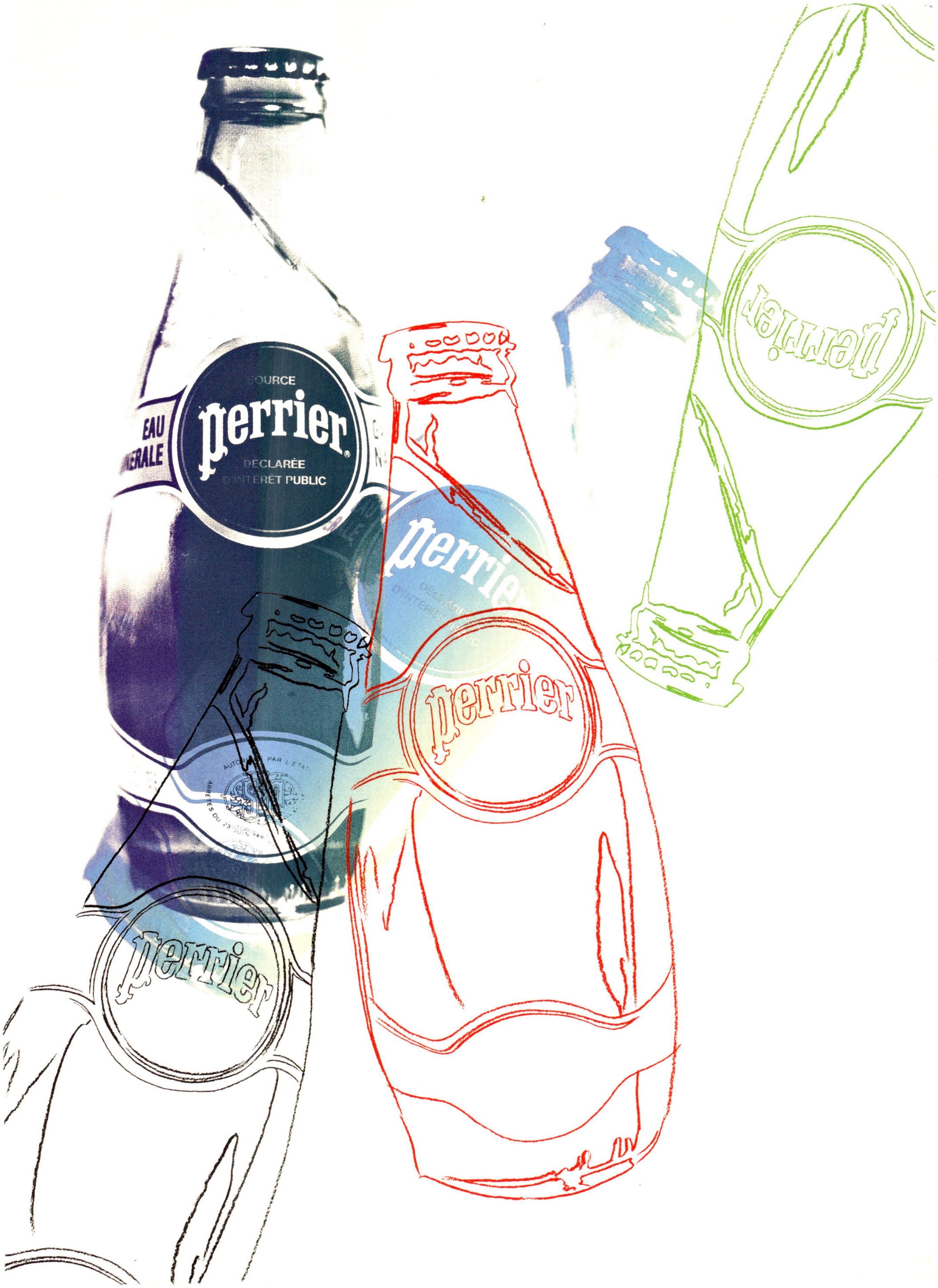
SOURCE
Perrier
DECLARÉE
D'INTERET PUBLIC
EAU
Perrier
Perrier
Perrier
Perrier

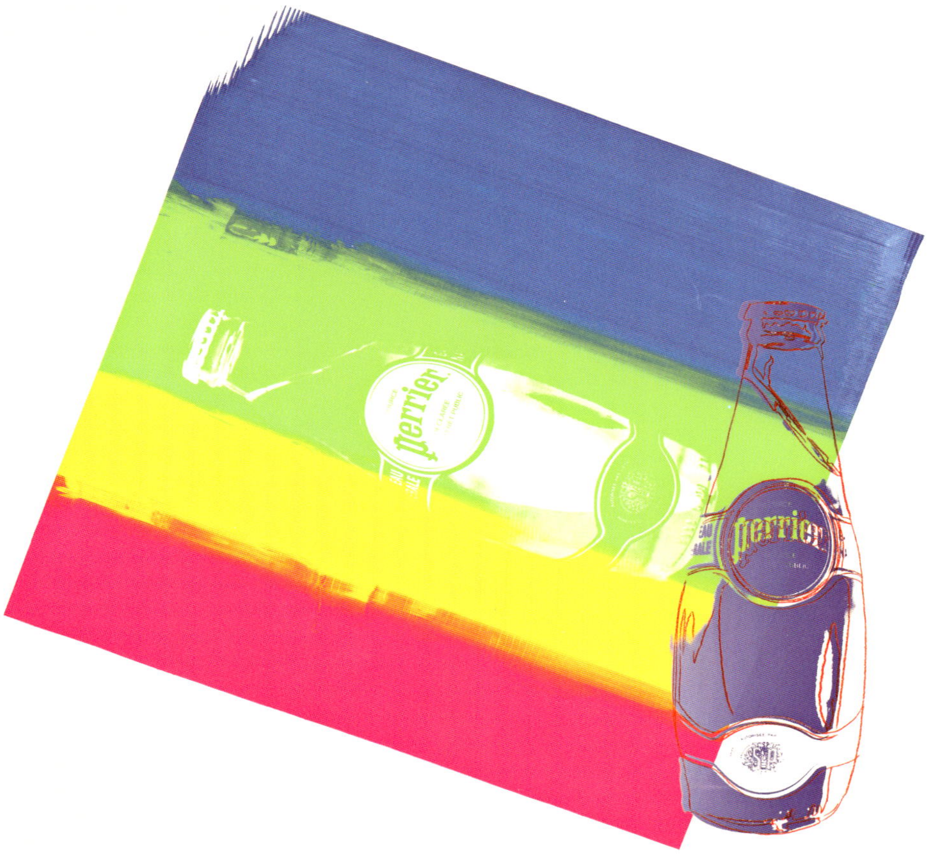


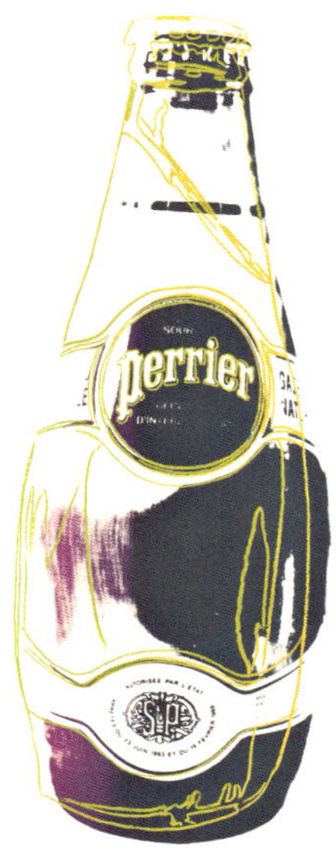


**Perrier**, 1983. Screenprint, 60 x 40⅛ in.

**Perrier**, 1983. Screenprint, 30½ x 43 in.

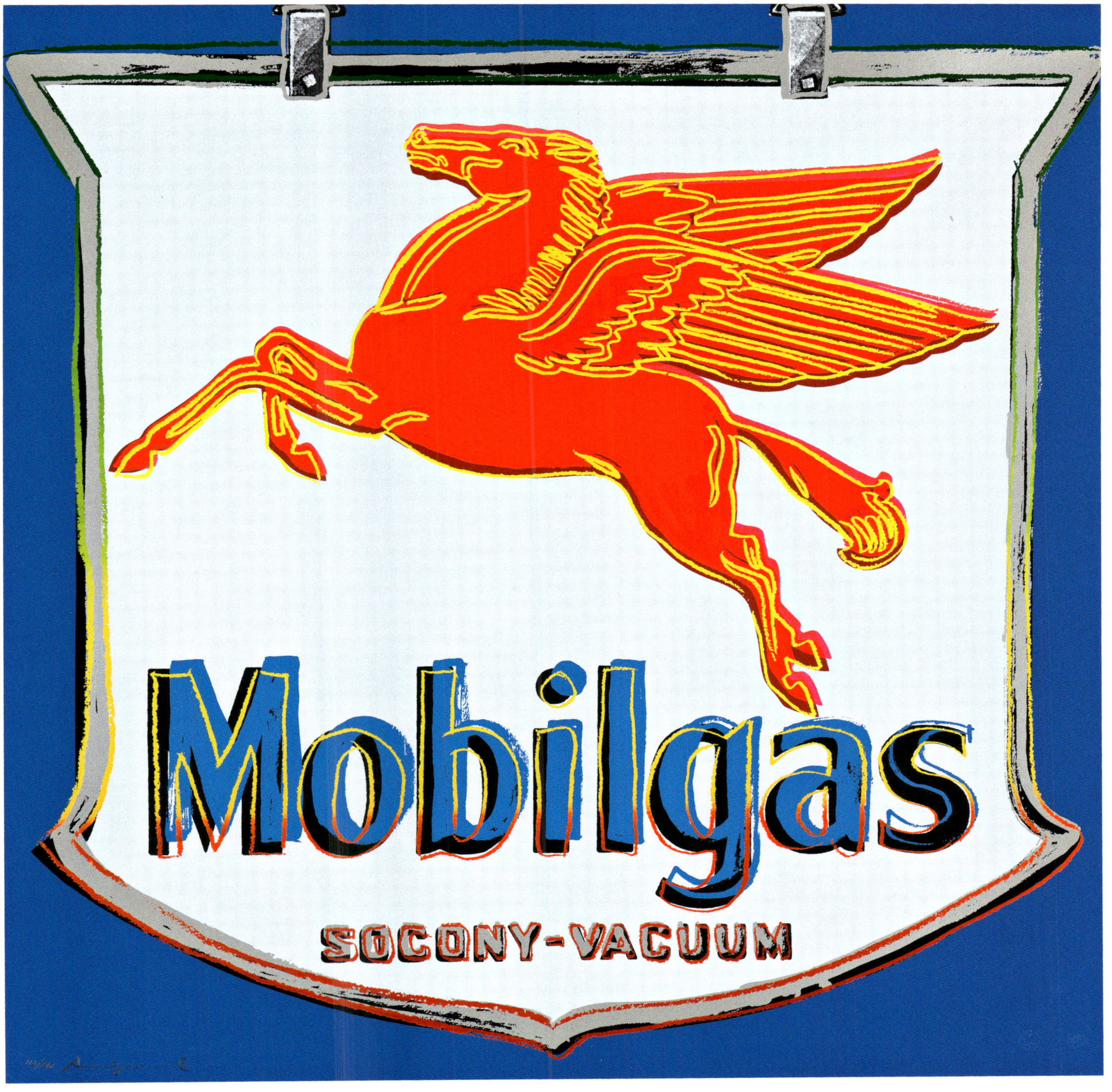


**Ads: Mobilgas**, 1985. Screenprint, 38 x 38 in.

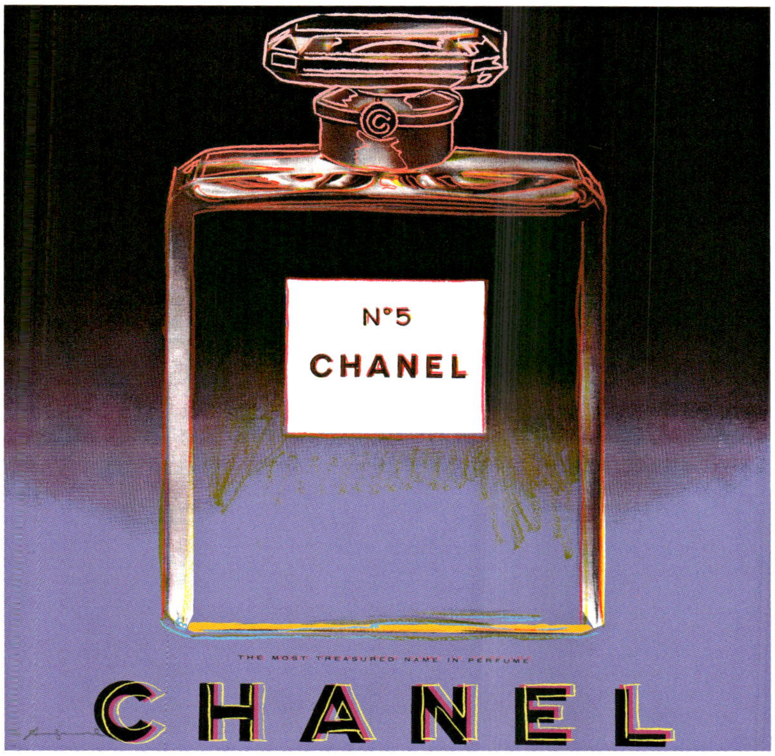


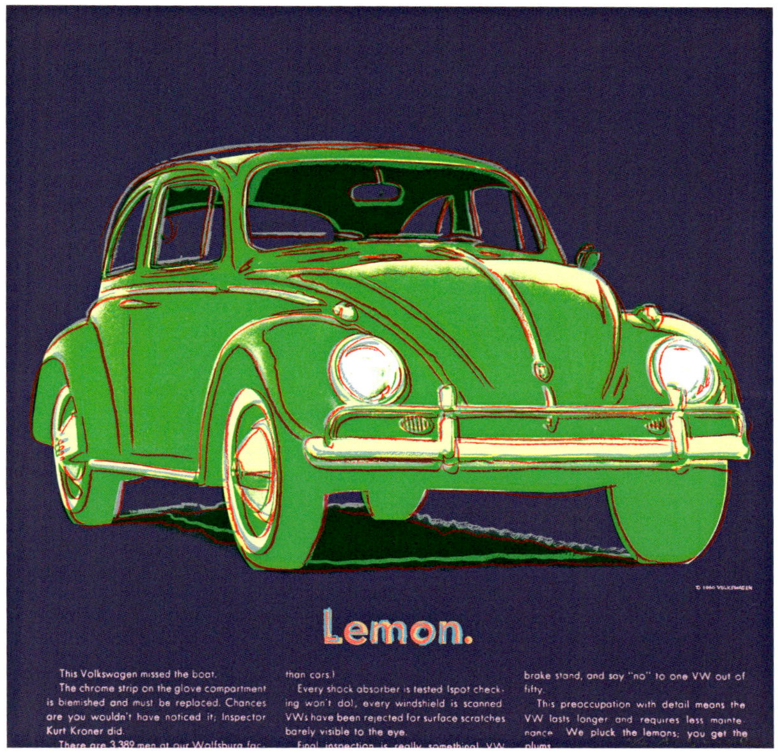


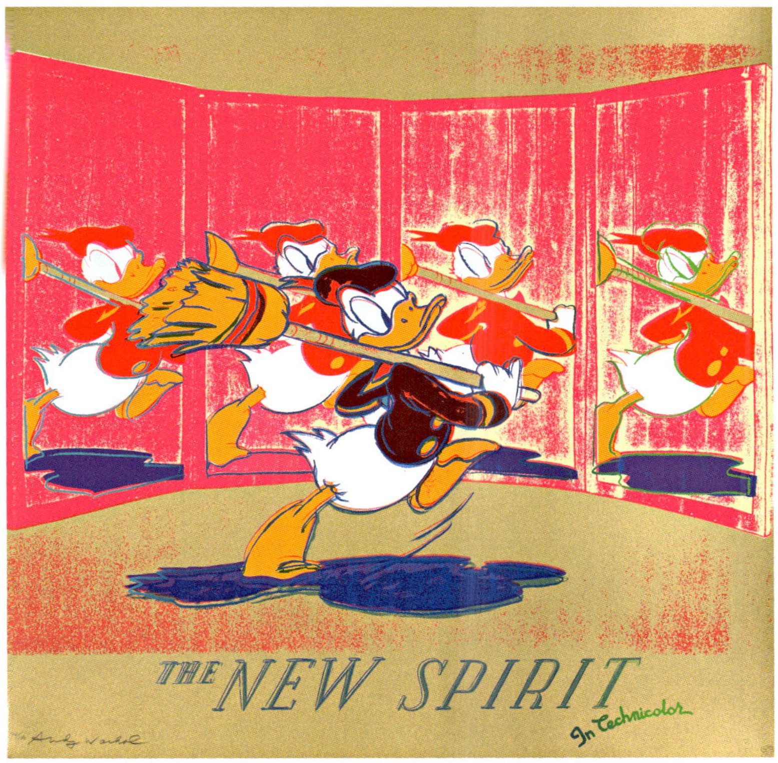


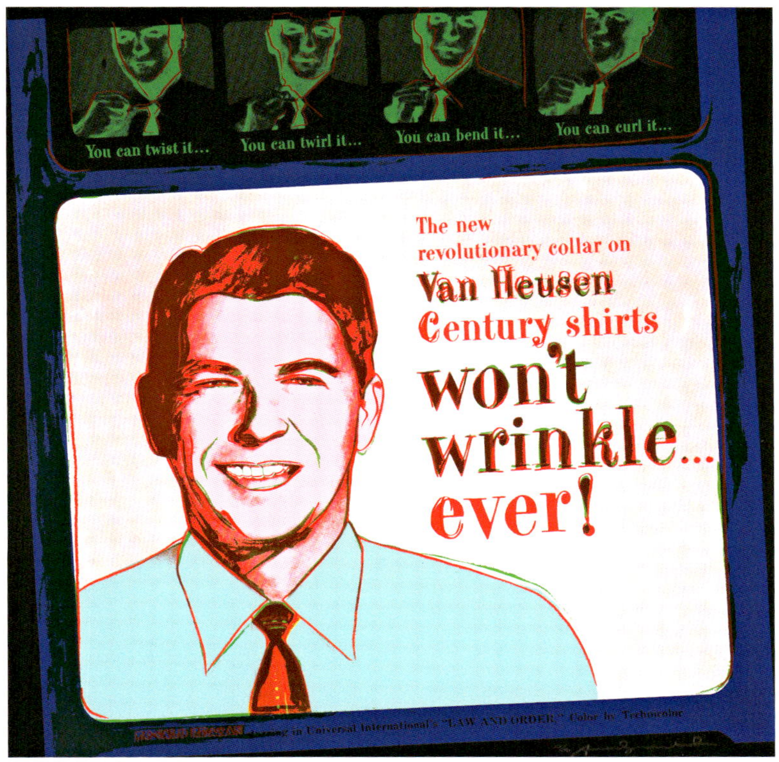


**Ads: Chanel**, 1985. Screenprint, 38 x 38 in.

**Ads: Volkswagen**, 1985. Screenprint, 38 x 38 in.

**Ads: The New Spirit (Donald Duck)**, 1985. Screenprint, 38 x 38 in.

**Ads: Van Heusen (Ronald Reagan)**, 1985. Screenprint, 38 x 38 in.

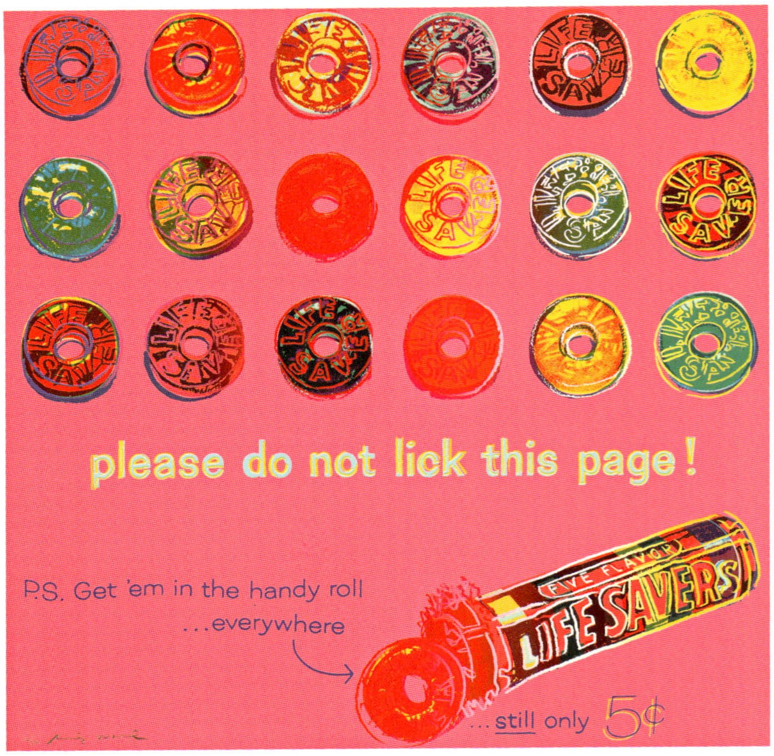


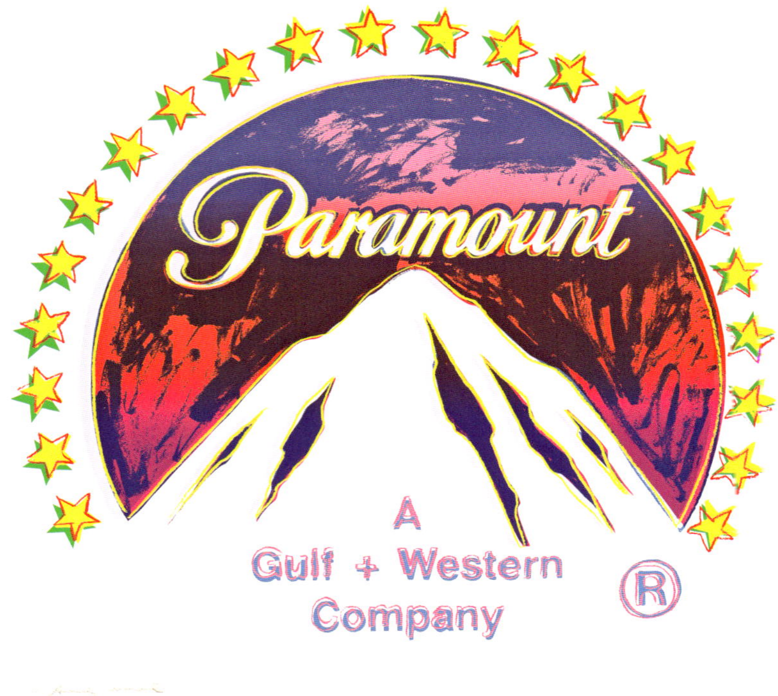


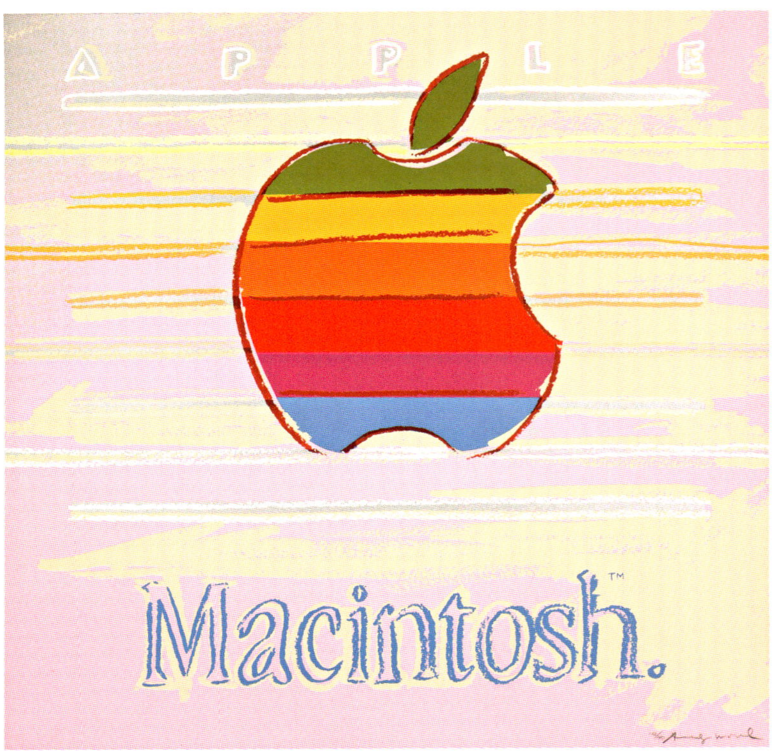


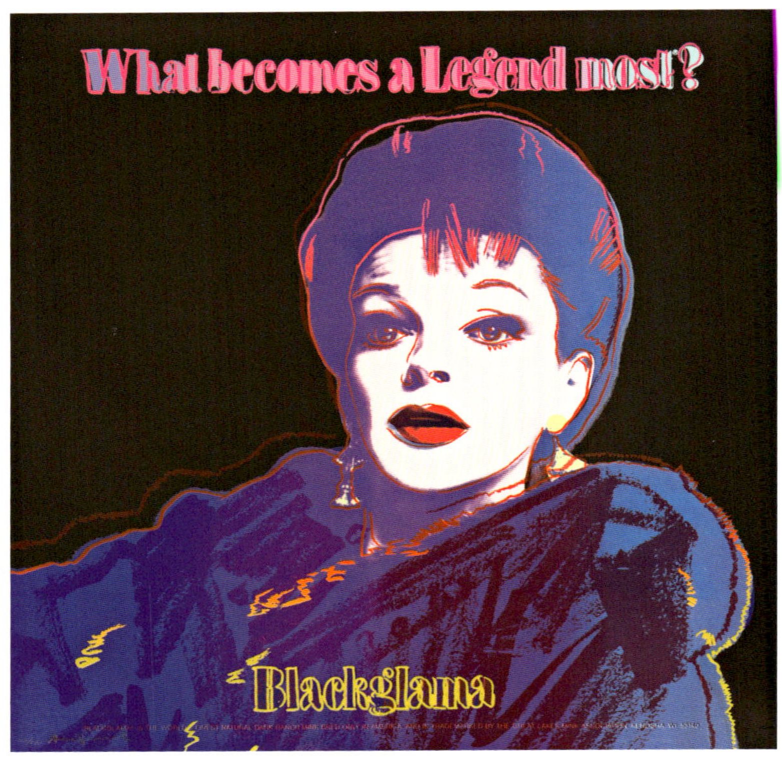


**Ads: Life Savers**, 1985. Screenprint, 38 x 38 in.

**Ads: Paramount**, 1985. Screenprint, 38 x 38 in.

**Ads: Apple**, 1985. Screenprint, 38 x 38 in.

**Ads: Blackglama (Judy Garland)**, 1985. Screenprint, 38 x 38 in.

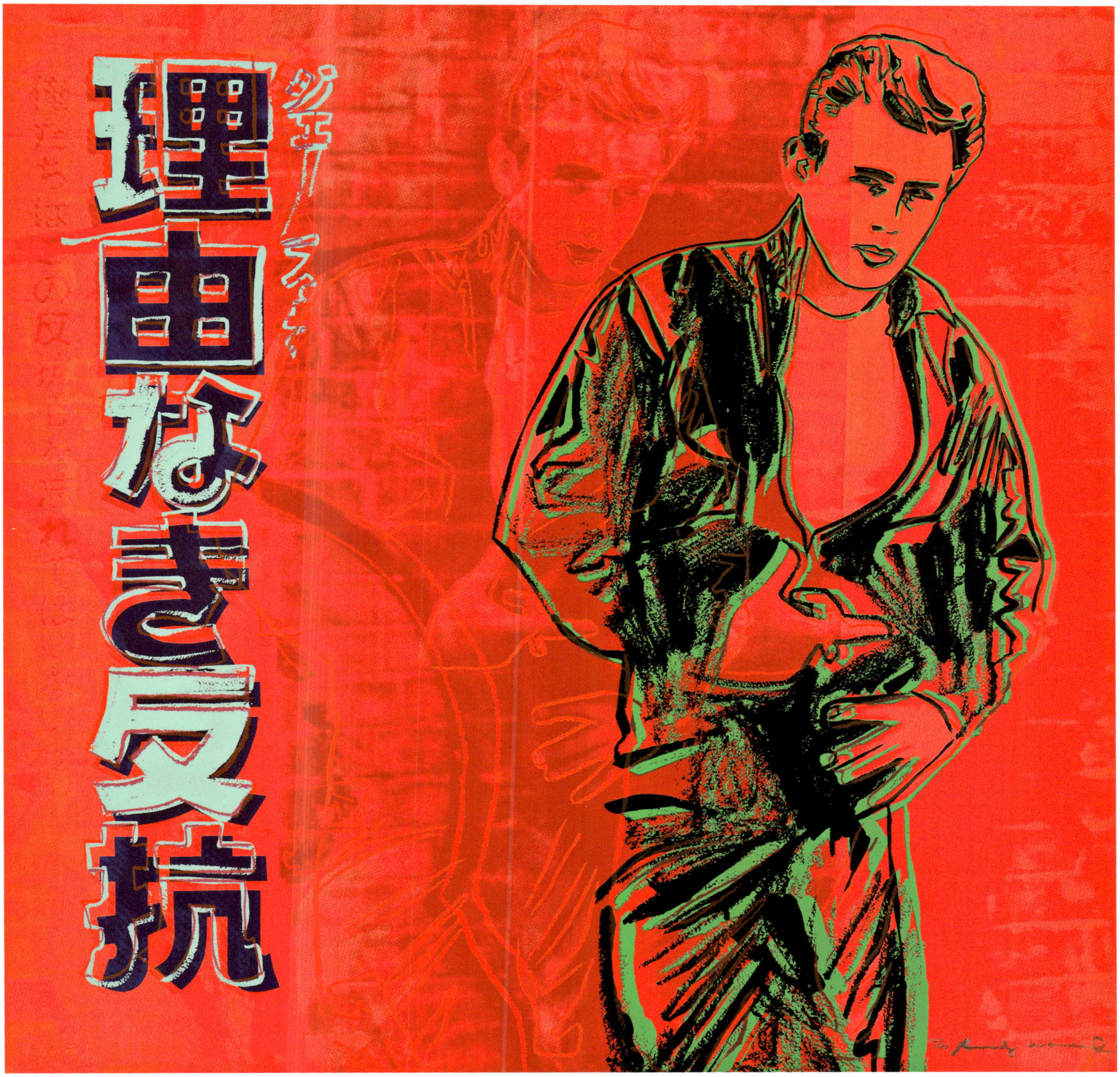


**Ads: Rebel Without a Cause (James Dean)**, 1985. Screenprint, 38 x 38 in.

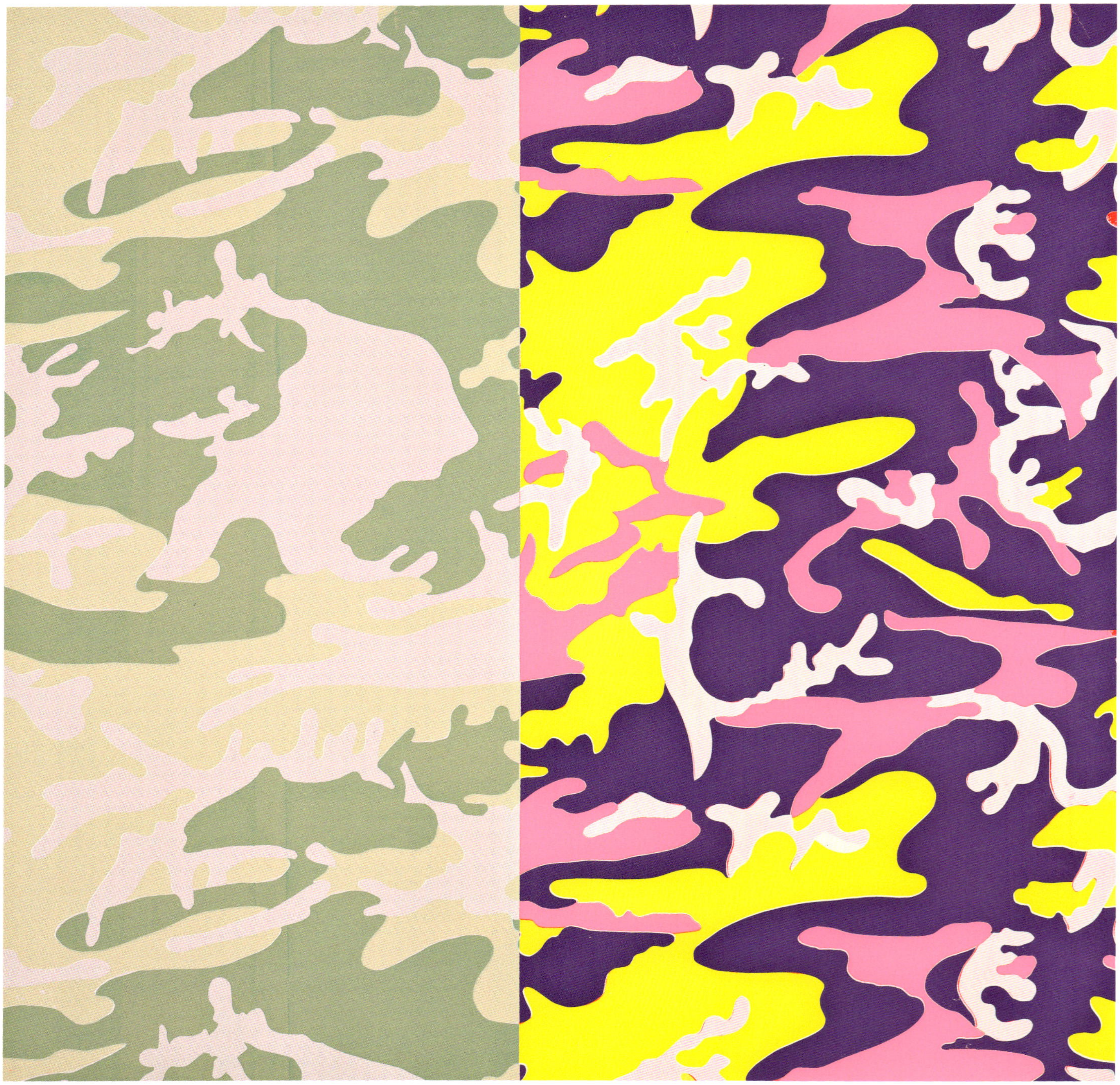

**Camouflage**, 1987. Screenprints, each 38 x 38 in.

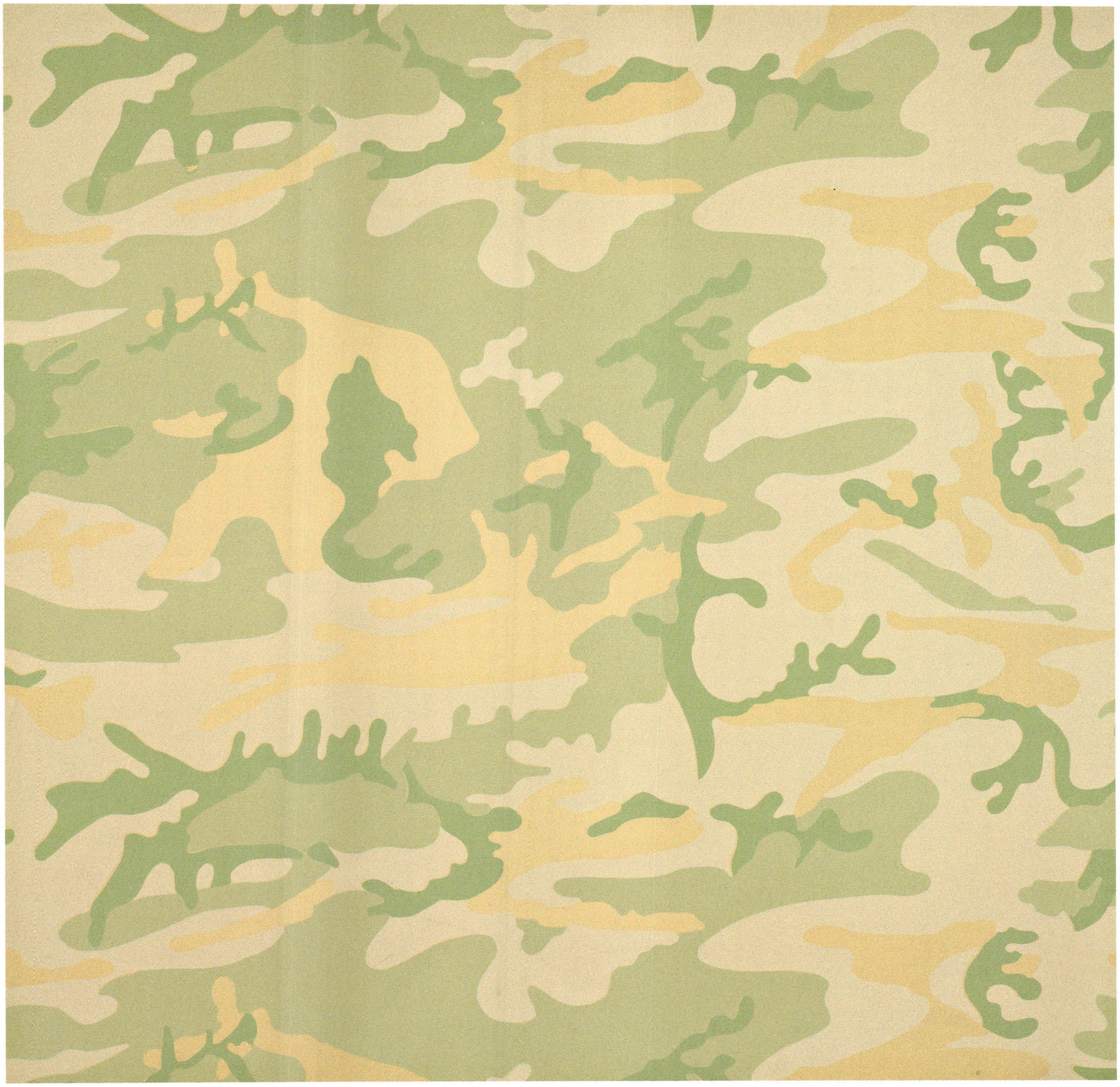

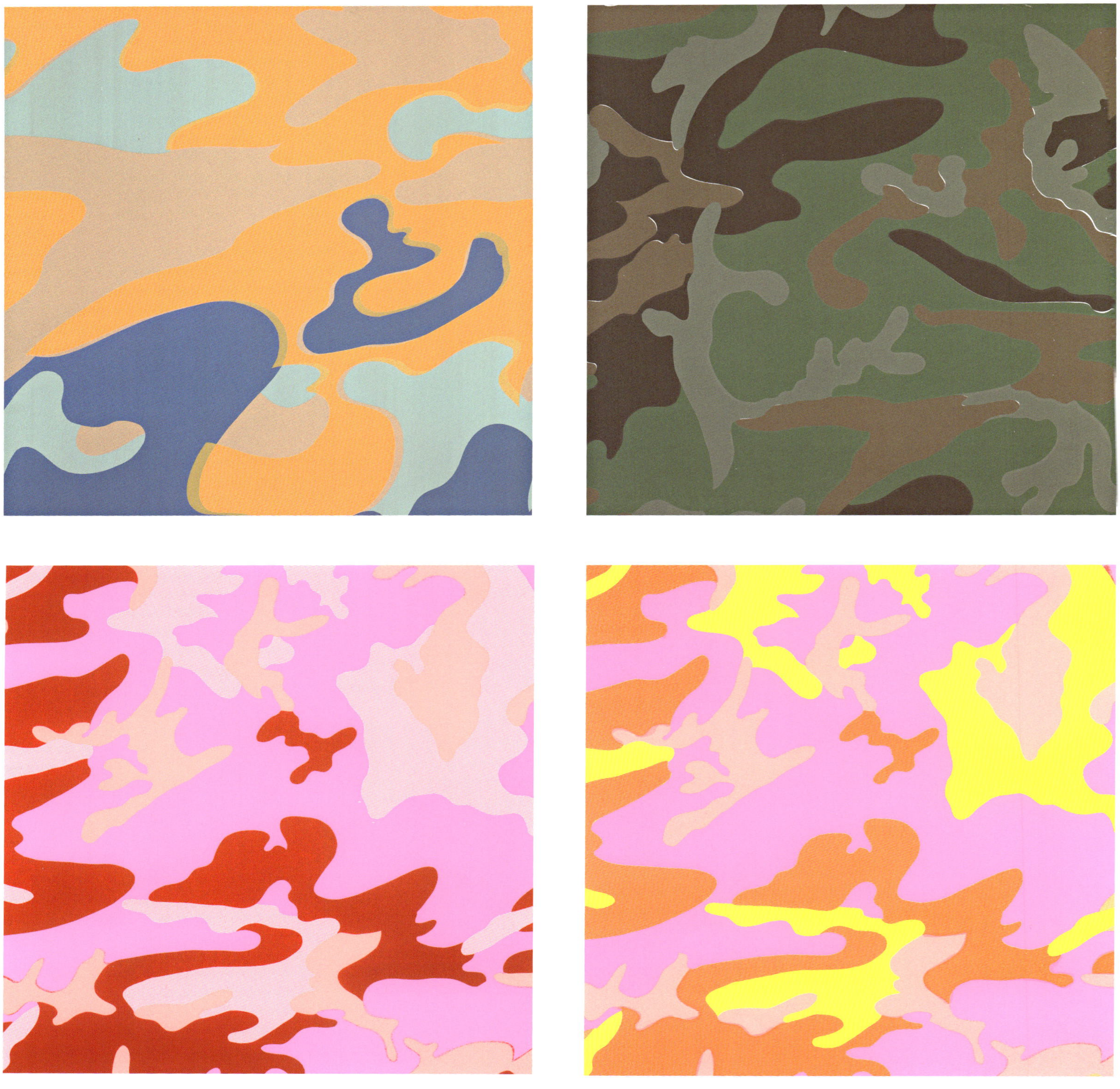

**Camouflage**, 1987. Screenprints, each 38 x 38 in.

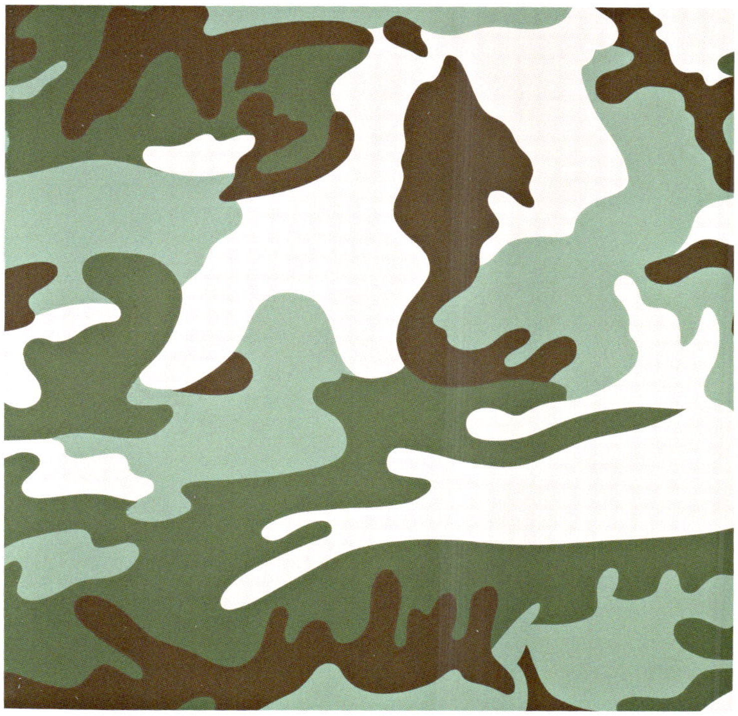
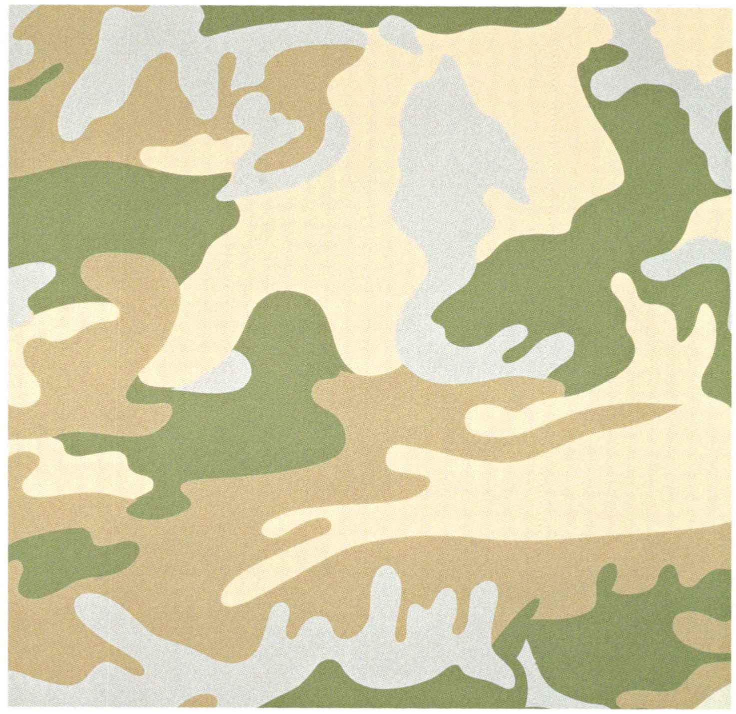
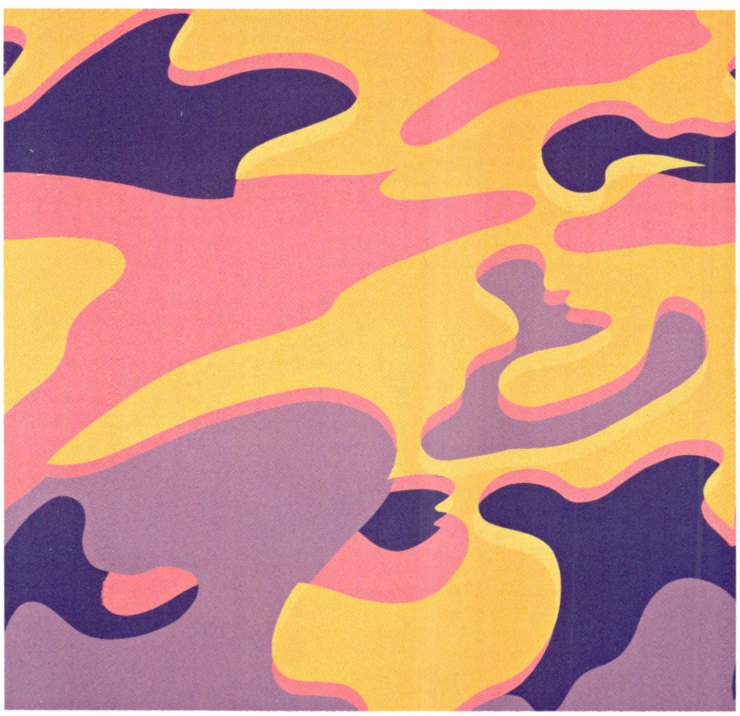
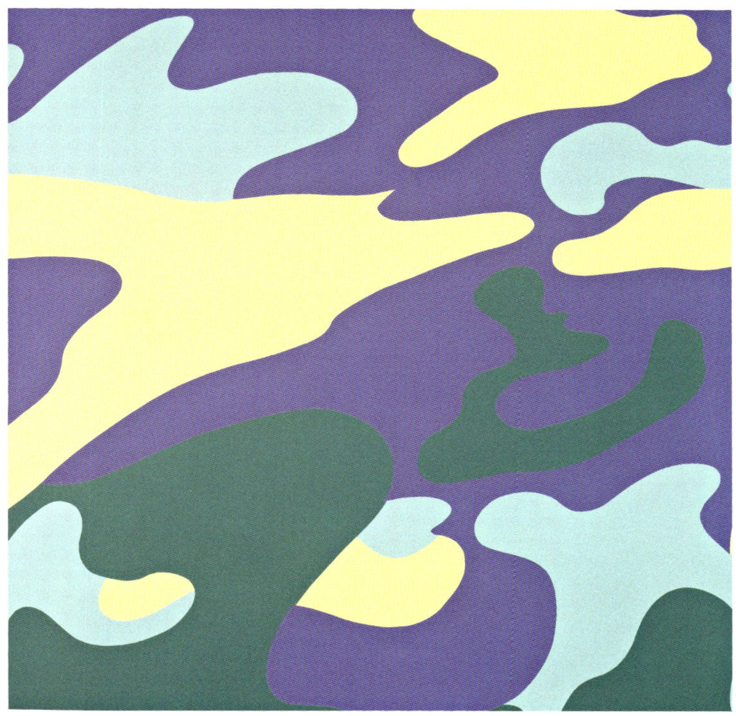

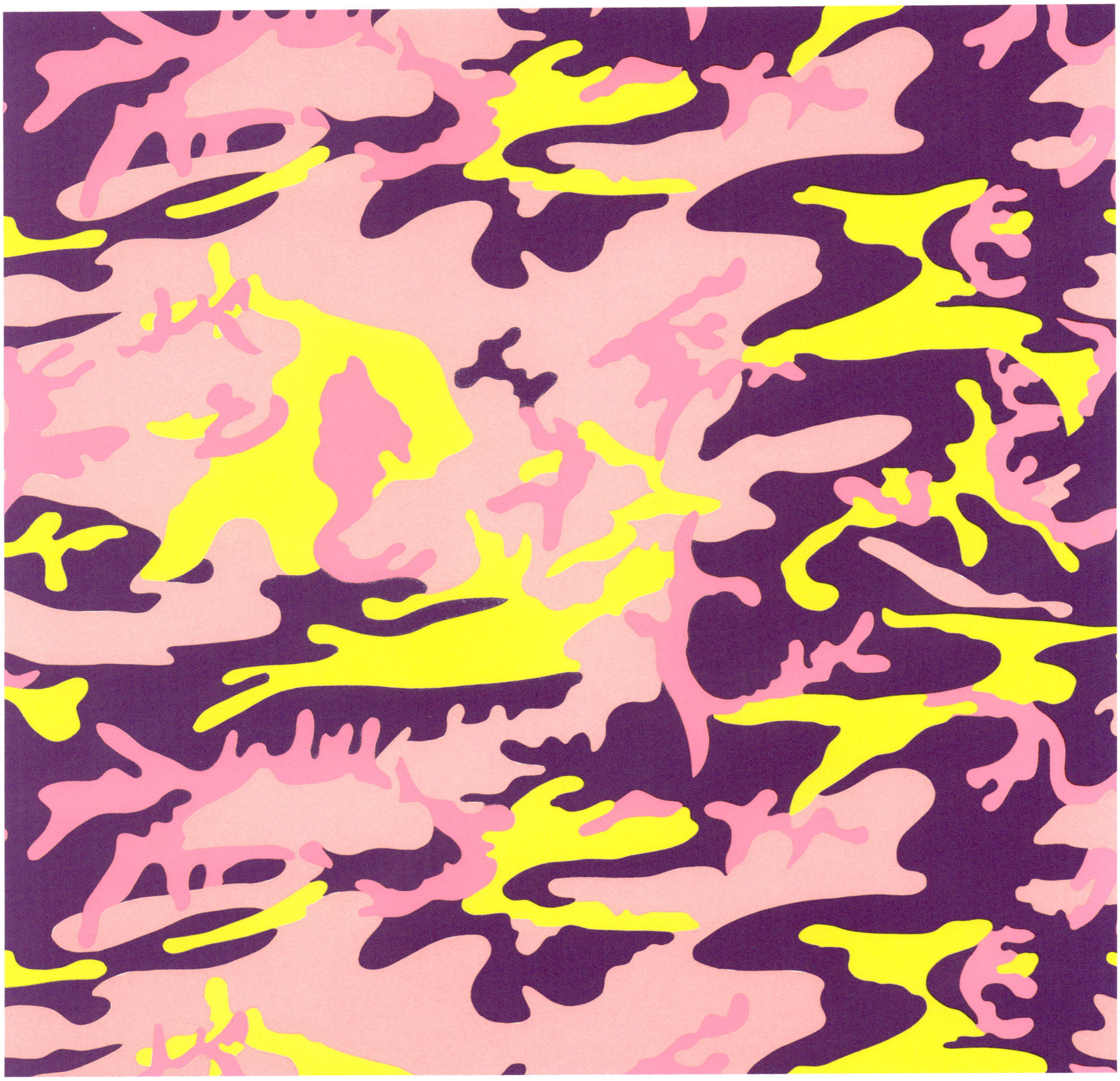

**Camouflage**, 1987. Screenprints, each 38 x 38 in.

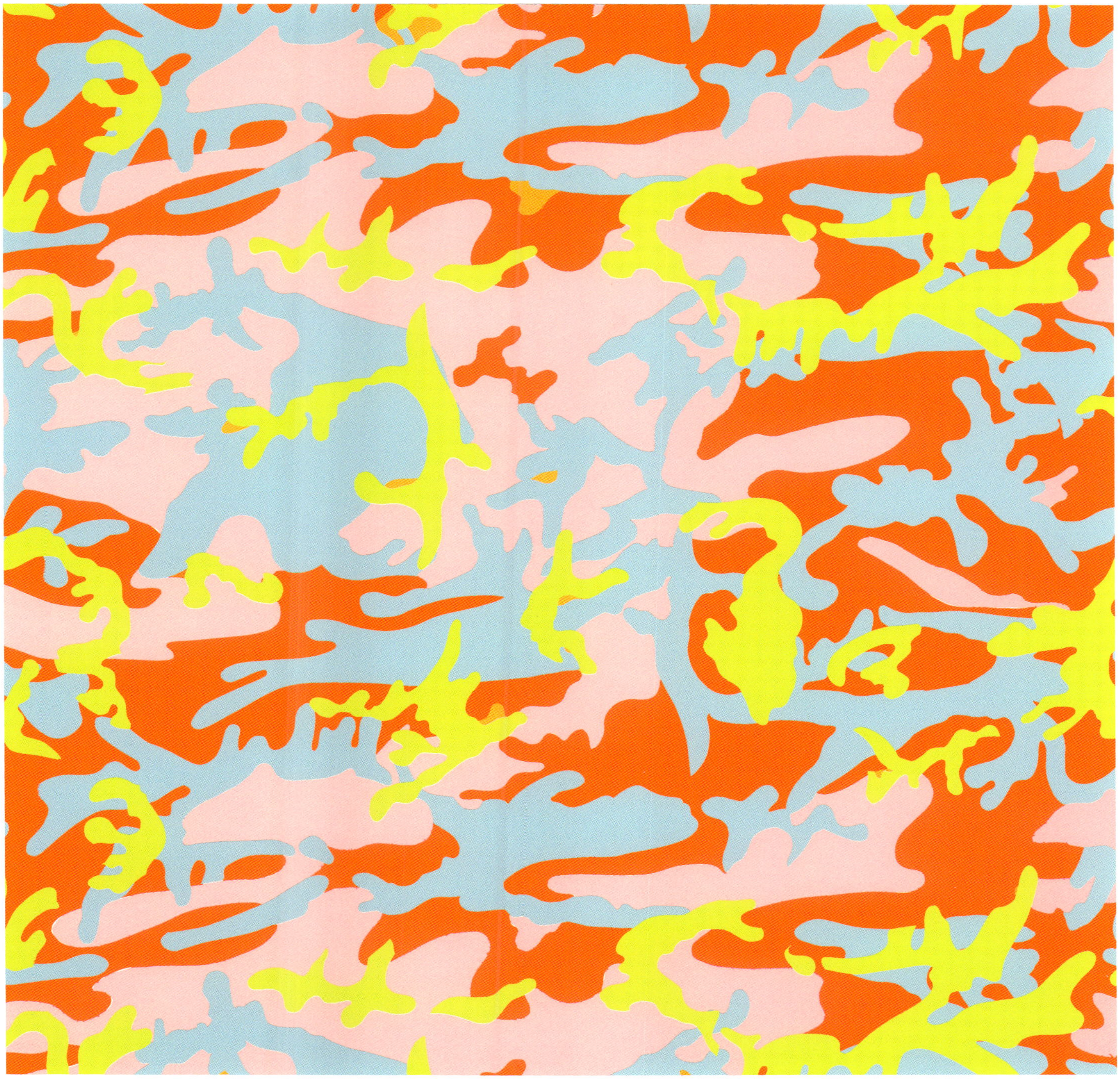

**Moonwalk**, 1987. Screenprint, 38 x 38 in.

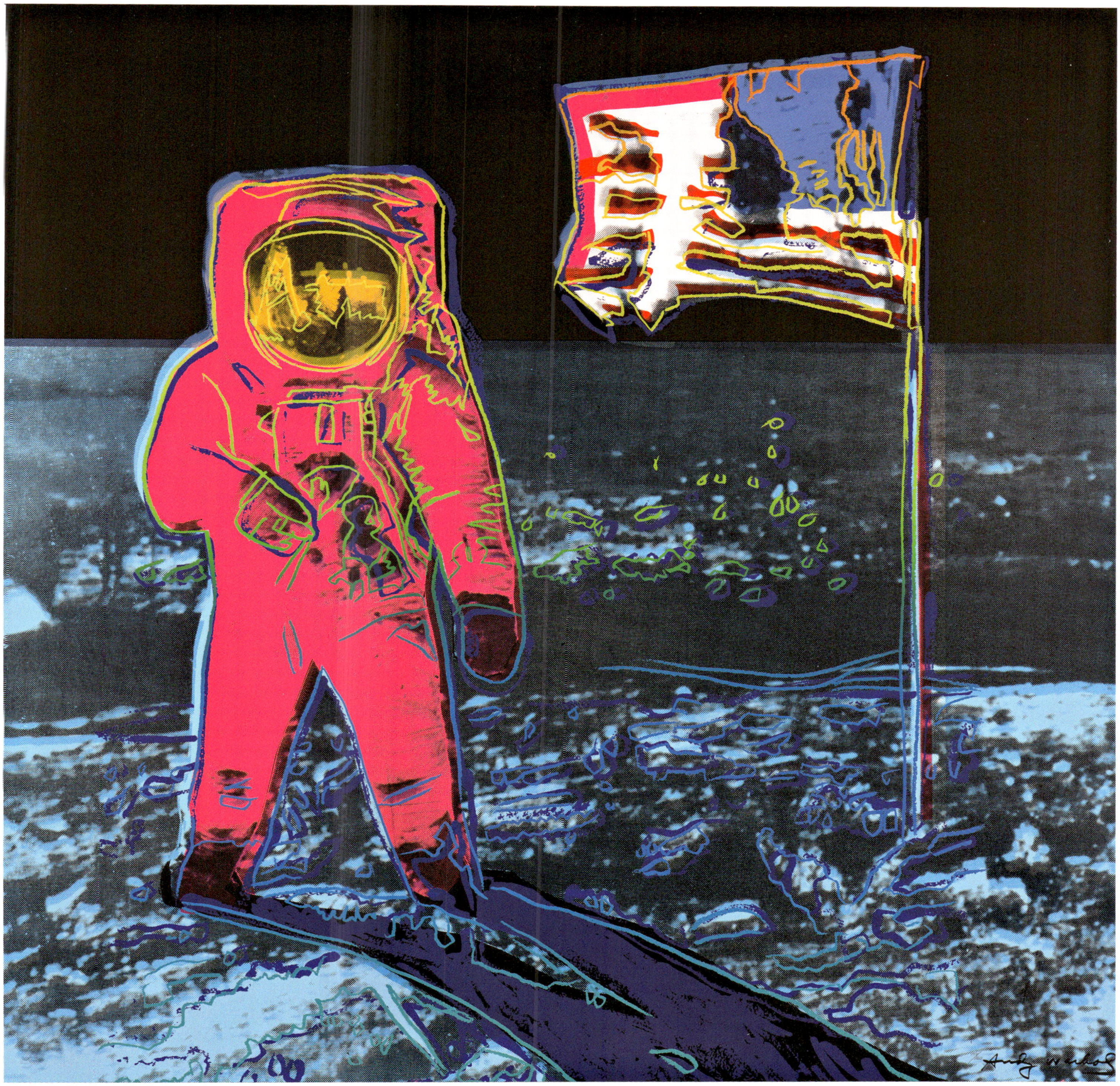

# Acknowledgments

The planning and work required to achieve a successful exhibition and publication are significant, and at the Portland Art Museum we are extremely fortunate to have dedicated staff members who ensure excellence. Special thanks for *Andy Warhol: Prints from the Collections of Jordan D. Schnitzer and His Family Foundation* go to Sara Krajewski, the Robert and Mercedes Eichholz Curator of Modern and Contemporary Art, who had the challenging task of winnowing a selection of works from the vast personal collections of Jordan D. Schnitzer. She shaped the exhibition's narrative with thoughtful curation and illuminated its themes with her insightful essays. Donald Urquhart, the director of collections and exhibitions at the Museum, played an essential role, from the initial conceptualization of the show to its design and installation. Assisting Don and Sara was Charles Campbell, curatorial associate for collections and exhibitions. With his invaluable organizational skills, he always helps bring big curatorial ideas into reality.

The Portland Art Museum is proud of our education and public programs that connect our audiences in unique and meaningful ways to our exhibitions. Overseeing this important area are Mike Murawski, director of education and public programs, and Stephanie Parrish, associate director of education and public programs. JS May, chief advancement officer, and Karie Burch, associate director of development, helped secure the essential resources for the exhibition. Laura Bartoff, director of communications, and Ian Gillingham, press and publications manager, partnered with the Museum's curatorial and educational teams early in the planning process to develop inventive promotional strategies.

Organizing an exhibition of the art of Andy Warhol is a challenging task, given its visual scope. We were fortunate to partner with the internationally recognized and Portland-based design firm ZIBA. Given the artist's notable legacy, ZIBA's designers were challenged to channel Warhol's thinking and sensitivities into the exhibition design. Their success was due to the efforts of Jonathan Irick and Malcom Lee. Implementing the ZIBA vision were the Museum's exceptional in-house designers and preparators. Special recognition is due to Michael Smith, art director, and Matthew Juniper, chief preparator.

This publication benefited greatly from the insightful essay by Richard H. Axsom, senior curator, Madison Museum of Contemporary Art; the catalogue design by Phil Kovacevich; and the editing of Carolyn Vaughan. Finally, assisting with every aspect of this project was Catherine Malone, collection manager for the Schnitzer collections for over thirteen years. Her knowledge, support, and committed leadership were essential to the realization of this substantial undertaking.

In addition to Jordan and the Harold & Arlene Schnitzer CARE Foundation, we would also like to acknowledge the support of the Standard, the James and Anne Crumpacker Family, ESCO Foundation, Sheryl Acheson/ Bonhams, Gail and Fred Jubitz, Ferguson Wellman, Laura S. Meier, Grace Serbu, Wells Fargo, Willamette Dental, and Thomas Lauderdale and his Pink Martini band, as well as the multitude of other major donors and contributors. On behalf of the Museum and the community, thank you.

**BRIAN FERRISO**

# Contributors

**RICHARD H. AXSOM**, senior curator at the Madison Museum of Contemporary Art, Wisconsin; former senior curator of prints and photographs at the Grand Rapids Art Museum; and professor emeritus of art history, University of Michigan has published extensively in the area of modern and contemporary prints. He prepared catalogues raisonnés for Frank Stella (1983, 2016), Ellsworth Kelly (1987, 2012), and Claes Oldenburg (1997), along with accompanying print retrospectives, and he contributed to the catalogue raisonné of Terry Winters's prints. He has also arranged retrospective exhibitions for the prints of Jasper Johns (2008) and Andy Warhol (2008). With coauthor David Platzker, he received the 1998 Charles Wittenborn Book Award for the Oldenburg book; his *Drawn from Nature: The Plant Lithographs of Ellsworth Kelly* earned the 2006 Book Award from the International Fine Print Dealers Association. Dr. Axsom is emeritus member of Print Council of America and currently sits on the editorial board of *Art in Print*.

**BRIAN FERRISO** is the Marilyn H. and Dr. Robert B. Pamplin Jr. Director and chief curator of the Portland Art Museum. Previously, he was executive director, president, and CEO of the Philbrook Museum of Art, Tulsa; acting director, deputy director, and senior director of curatorial affairs at the Milwaukee Art Museum; and assistant director of the David and Alfred Smart Museum of Art at the University of Chicago. In addition to overseeing numerous important exhibitions in Portland, Ferriso conceived of *Masterworks/Portland*, a series of single-work exhibitions; curated Raphael's *La Donna Velata* (2009), Thomas Moran's *Shoshone Falls on the Snake River* (2010), and Titian's *La Bella* (2011–12) and launched a series of highly successful design-focused exhibitions. He has published in a number of exhibition catalogues on nineteenth- and twentieth-century painting and architecture. He is currently president of the Association of Art Museum Directors and a trustee of the American Federation of Arts, and is the recipient of the 2012 Excellency Award from the Foundation for Italian Art and Culture. Additionally, Ferriso is a practicing artist, who studied with Frank Mason of the Art Students League in New York City.

**SARA KRAJEWSKI** is the Robert and Mercedes Eichholz Curator of Modern and Contemporary Art at the Portland Art Museum. Arriving in Portland in 2015, she relaunched the Miller Meigs Series of Contemporary Art Exhibitions with *Josh Kline: Freedom*, a project at the intersection of technology, politics, and activism, and organized the current Andy Warhol print retrospective. From 2012 to 2015, she was the director of INOVA (Institute of Visual Arts) at the University of Wisconsin–Milwaukee, where she curated an array of interdisciplinary exhibitions and performances. She was curator at the Henry Art Gallery, Seattle, from 2004 to 2012, focusing on solo artist projects and group exhibitions exploring photography's impact on visual culture. Krajewski is the recipient of a 2012 Curatorial Fellowship from the Andy Warhol Foundation for the Visual Arts for research into emerging transdisciplinary artistic practices. She has also held curatorial positions at the Madison Museum of Contemporary Art and the Harvard Art Museums.

**JORDAN D. SCHNITZER** is president of his family's real estate investment company, Harsch Investment Properties, located in Portland, Oregon, with offices in six Western states. He is known for his philanthropy as well as for having served on numerous art, cultural, and social service boards and commissions. For more than twenty-five years, he has been widely known for establishing programs to exhibit prints and multiples at regional universities and nationally prominent art museums. Works are loaned from the Jordan D. Schnitzer Collection and the Jordan Schnitzer Family Foundation Collection, whose combined holdings exceed 9,500 prints by regional, national, and internationally recognized artists, including in-depth holdings of some of the most important modern and contemporary artists. He has organized more than a hundred exhibitions, which have traveled to seventy-five museums, including traveling exhibitions of the prints of Andy Warhol, Ellsworth Kelly, Roy Lichtenstein, and John Baldessari. For more information see www.jordanschnitzer.org.

Published by the Jordan Schnitzer Family Foundation in conjunction with the exhibition *Andy Warhol: Prints from the Collections of Jordan D. Schnitzer and His Family Foundation,* Portland Art Museum, Oregon, October 8, 2016–January 1, 2017.



Designed by Phil Kovacevich
Edited by Carolyn Vaughan
Proofread by Carrie Wicks

Printed in Italy by Contitipocolor, SPA

All measurements are in inches. Height precedes width.

Front cover: *Sunset,* 1972. Screenprint, 34 x 34 in.

Back cover: *Campbell's Soup I,* 1968. Screenprint, 35 x 23 in.

Endpapers: *Cow 1966,* 1966, screenprint on paper, six panels, each 28 x 46 in.

Frontispiece: *Self-Portrait,* 1977. Screenprint, 45 x 35 in.

Page 4: *Andy Warhol tracing Campbell's Soup silkscreen, The Factory, NYC, circa 1965*
Photograph © Estate of Nat Finkelstein

Page 11: *Andy Warhol silkscreening in process (with Gerard Malanga), The Factory, NYC, circa 1965*
Photograph © Estate of Nat Finkelstein

Page 12: *Andy Warhol and Cows,* © Fred W. McDarrah/Getty Images

Page 50: *Andy Warhol, New York,* 1966 © Herve Gloaguen/Getty Images

Page 63: From TIME, April 12, 1954 © 1954 Time Inc.. All rights reserved. Used by permission and protected by the Copyright Laws of the United States. The printing, copying, redistribution, or retransmission of this Content without express written permission is prohibited.

ISBN 978-0-692-76447-3
Library of Congress Control Number: 2016950821



Distributed by D.A.P.
Distributed Art Publishers
155 Sixth Avenue
2nd Floor
New York, NY 10013
artbook.com

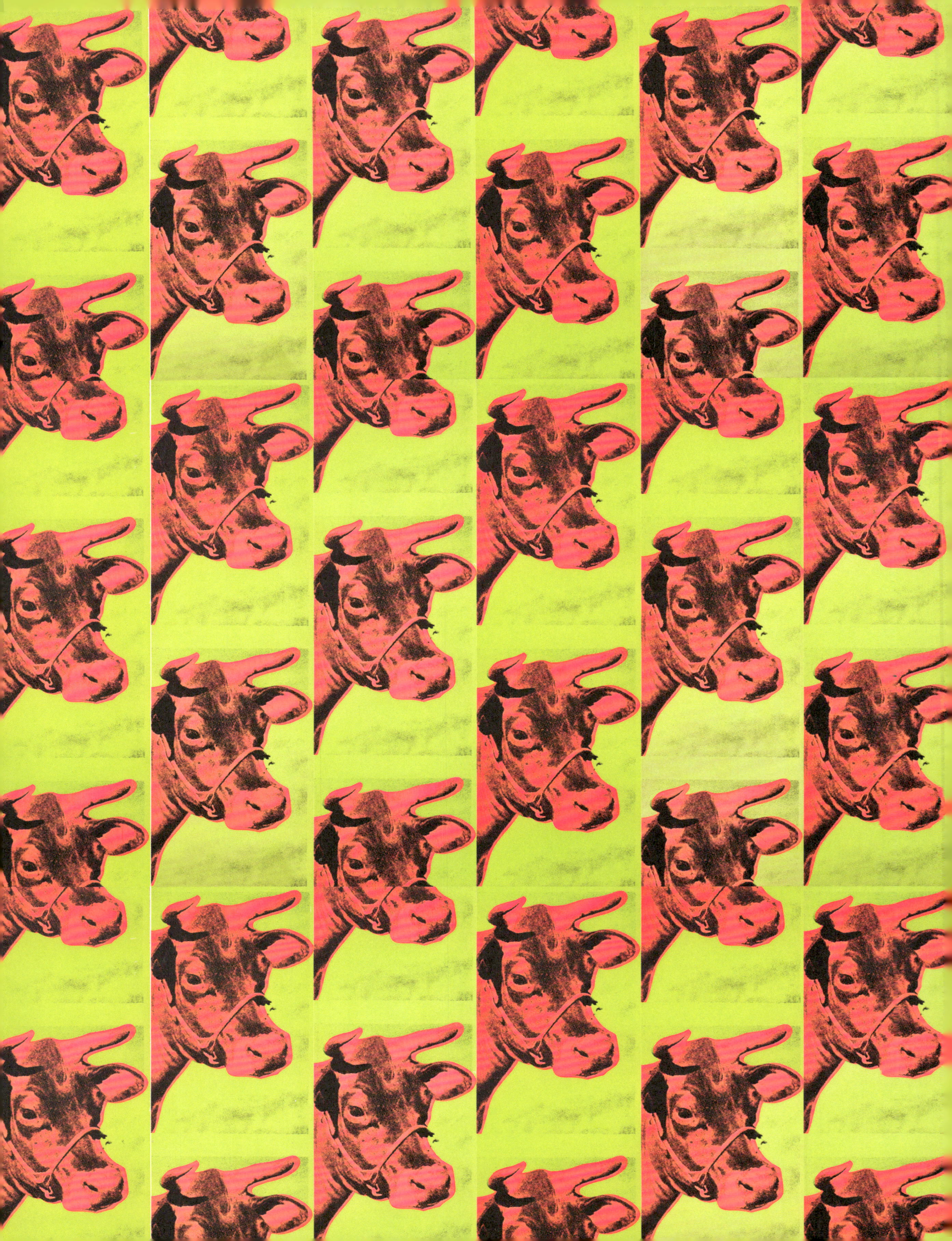